Artful

an adaptation of the novel by Peter David

D1242630

NOVEL BY:
Peter David

ADAPTED BY:
Nicole D'Andria

ARTWORK BY:
Laura Neubert

COLORS BY:
Laur Rea
& Laura Neubert (issue 2)

BACKGROUND ASSISTANCE BY:
Sarah Benkin (issue 4)
& Mia Goodwin (issue 5)

LETTERS:
Justin Birch

Bryan Seaton: Publisher/ CEO • Shawn Gabborin: Editor In Chief
Jason Martin: Publisher-Danger Zone • Nicole D'Andria: Marketing Director/Editor
Jim Dietz: Social Media Manager • Danielle Davison: Executive Administrator
Chad Cicconi: Chimney Sweep • Shawn Pryor: President of Creator Relations

PETER DAVID'S ARTFUL TPB. July 2017. Copyright Peter David and Action Lab Entertainment, Inc. 2017. Published by Action Lab Comics. All rights reserved.
All characters are fictional. Any likeness to anyone living or dead is purely coincidental. No part of this publication may be reproduced or transmitted without
permission, except for small excerpts for review purposes. Printed in Canada. First printing.

Author's Preface

REINTRODUCES US TO THE ACCLAIMED MR. JACK DAWKINS, KNOWN TO SUNDRY AS THE ARTFUL DODGER, AND LAMENTS THE INATTENTION PAID HIM AS COMPARED TO MORE SIMPERING EXAMPLES OF THE DAY

It has been an inordinate amount of time since Jack Dawkins was left in the dire straits as described by his previous biographer, the acclaimed Mr. Dickens who, for all the right and proper praise heaped on him, nevertheless seemed to have his priorities ever so slightly out of whack in his previous visitation with Mr. Dawkins, described and referred to by various and sundry as the Artful Dodger, or Dodger, or the Artful, depending upon your familiarity with, and respect for, the personage in question.

This is a rather shocking lapse in an otherwise laudable writing career that spanned two score of years in the first half of the nineteenth century. Mr. Dickens, a.k.a. Boz, received an understandable amount of acclaim for a career that included a variety of tomes of uplifting tales typically detailing the lives of people facing overwhelming odds in a society that seemed bound and determined to destroy them and, more often than not, ended up having their spirits crushed right before their lives were ruthlessly snatched from whatever was left from their battered and broken bodies. The sort of tales, in short, that could only prompt the reader to rejoice in whatever minor travails afflicted their own meager existences since, whatever it was they were facing, it paled to insignificance in comparison to the relentless onslaught of misery and mayhem visited upon many of Mr. Dickens' cast of orphans, thieves, hapless fools and misanthropes.

Standing upon the shoulders of many of these, however, remains Dodger, the renowned snatcher of handkerchiefs, purses, snuff boxes and the like.

Why Mr. Dickens, in his biography of that particular moment captured in time, preferred to focus on the adventures of the orphan parish child, Oliver Twist, remains a matter of speculation and mystery to all subsequent scribes of those long-departed times: of a London nearly two centuries gone, back when it was a pox-infested, grimy, depressing, fog-bound, class-favoring, sprawling, noxious, odorous, and overall distasteful place to live and breathe and sicken and die, as opposed to modern times wherein the pox has been largely attended to, so that's progress of a sort.

This is not to be uncharitable to Master Twist, who knew little enough charity in the first decade or so of his young life. Nor do we wish to detract from the eventual happy turn that his fortunes took. Nevertheless, the more unkind observer (which we would like to think that we are not, but our actions would lead us to believe we are) would have to make note of the fact that Master Twist spent an ungodly amount of his page time weeping for some reason or other. Whatever circumstance confronted him, his default reaction was to burst into tears, which makes him seem to us—not intended to disparage the fairer sex, but still—a bit womanish. This famed orphan of the storm tended to bob about as helplessly as a cork (embracing the cliché in order to maintain the metaphor) until matters happened to, through no effort of his own, land him upon safe and welcoming shores.

Contrast him to the Artful who, when last Mr. Dickens graced us with his presence, was seen standing in the dock of a London courthouse, having been pinched for snatching a silver snuff box out of the pocket of some pompous individual who no doubt needed it far less than the Artful. Indeed, it should be noted that so formidable an individual was Dodger that the circumstances of his being apprehended by the authorities was not even witnessed by the reader of Master Twist's "adventures." Instead they were described in tragic detail by Master Charley Bates or, as he was frequently referred to equally tragically, Master Bates. Faced with a pompous judge, standing there figuratively but not literally naked and exposed, the Artful Dodger disdained to defend himself or his actions, loudly declared that this was not the shop for justice, and that his lawyer would certainly attend to the scoundrels inconveniencing the Artful directly if he were not currently breakfasting with the Vice President of the House of Commons. It was a performance of sheerest bravado that would have made lesser men leap to their feet and applaud, as opposed to greater men who merely scowled and declared that the formidable Artful was to be transported forthwith to the untamed and thoroughly criminal continent of Australia. Imagine, if you will, Oliver Twist in the same predicament. There is little doubt that his defense would have been to fall to his knees, sobbing and lamenting his lot in life, a performance that would unquestionably have united lesser and greater men to shunt the little whiner off the continent and into the Atlantic as expeditiously as possible, conceivably without benefit of boat.

Indeed, if pictures are worth a thousand words (and admittedly we have already consumed nearly nine hundred of them) then one not need think beyond the classic renderings of the two gentlemen in question. Conjure Oliver Twist to your mind and you will doubtless envision him looking upward in a pathetic, supplicating manner, holding up his empty bowl of gruel and uttering the immortal words, "Please, sir, I want some more." Hardly an anthem of defiant, brazen challenge to authority. Master Twist's defenders will point to this moment as a transformative one in which the young hero asks for more because he can stomach no further dismissive treatment. Untrue. He asked for seconds because he lost a draw of a short straw, taken as a consequence of an older bully boy in the workhouse demanding that someone bring him a second helping lest the starved older boy wind up consuming his bunkmate, and the boys took this threat seriously. (Although even we, skeptics of Master Twist's rightful place in the pantheon of heroes, will indeed applaud politely for his subsequent assault on a noxious older lad who spoke disparagingly of Oliver's mother. Then again, there are lines that even the most simpering of boys will not see crossed.)

So there is the classic image of young Oliver in your mind's eye: a failed beggar with an empty bowl. Now set next to it your mental picture of the Artful Dodger, described by Mister Dickens thusly:

"He was a snub-nosed, flat-browed, common-faced boy enough, and as dirty a juvenile as one would wish to see; but he had about him all the airs and manners of a man. He was short of his age with rather bow-legs and little, sharp, ugly eyes. His hat was stuck on the top of his head so lightly, that it threatened to fall off every moment, and should have done so, very often, if the wearer had not had a knack of every now and then giving his head a sudden twitch, which brought it back to its old place again. He wore a man's coat, which reached nearly to his heels. He had turned the cuffs back, halfway up his arm, to get his hands out of the sleeves: apparently with the ultimate view of thrusting them into the pockets of his corduroy trousers; for there he kept them. He was, altogether, as roystering and swaggering a young gentleman as ever stood four feet six, or something less, in his bluchers."

Two questions immediately come to mind. The first, of course, are the definitions of "roystering" and "bluchers." The former means "blustering" and the latter are half boots, typically of leather, so that puzzler is easily attended to.

Of greater curiosity is: why did the adventures of such a memorably described, thoroughly engaging, and far more captivatingly visualized young man, always pictured with a cocky smile and upraised, mocking eyebrow rather than tears of pathos trickling down his face, play second fiddle in the great orchestra of fiction to the simpering Master Twist?

We are moved to conclude that a full and accurate description of Dodger's history, from his earliest days to his subsequent escapades, would have necessitated the detailing of the Artful's association with the unseemly creatures known as vampyres. It is our speculation that Mr. Dickens, despite his having taken up the unsavory profession of writer, nevertheless considered himself a gentleman, and there were some aspects of life that gentlemen simply did not wish to address. For that matter, it was entirely possible that he did not wish to alarm the citizenry of London and its surroundings with the knowledge that vampyres lurked within their midst. It was tragic enough for the average citizen to know that bloodsucking monsters known as tax collectors already existed; to be informed that there were inhuman bloodsuckers stalking the night as well, desiring to sink their fangs elsewhere other than their bank accounts, might simply have been too much for people to bear. It was one thing for Mr. Dickens to be able to acknowledge the existence of the supernatural, as he did in *A Christmas Carol*, for that could easily be seen as a fairy tale rather than the exacting biographical study that it was. (Indeed, had Scrooge possessed the Artful's contacts and resources and used those to avail himself of the services of an exorcist, then the tale might well have concluded very differently.) But *Oliver Twist* was far too much of a genuine slice of life to allow the unlife to intrude, at least substantively.

Which is not to say that the original story does not hint of the existence of vampyres. Any conscientious reading of the text will make it plain. We will provide two examples for any who may doubt us, both of which will be particularly germane to the tale you are about to pursue.

First, it should be noted that in order to spare private citizens embarrassment, whether deserved or not, and very likely legal actions against himself for libel and slander, whether deserved or not, Mr. Dickens tended to assign whimsical and entirely descriptive fictitious names to his cast. So renowned for this was he that to describe a name as "Dickensian" is to say that it is aptly ironic. In other words, there is a truth to it that may well be obscure to the owner but evident to observers.

Consider, then, young Oliver's antagonist in Chapter XI of the original volume: a formidable, powerful, and utterly cruel police magistrate with the name of Mr. Fang. Let us dwell upon that name and evoke it yet again: Mr. Fang, who slunk through merely the one chapter of Mr. Dickens' tale, but will be allowed to assume the full measure of his villainy in this recounting.

It staggers credulity to think that the name is a random happenstance. With a name like Mr. Fang, what else *could* the magistrate be *but* a vampyre? His subsequent dealings with Jack Dawkins, the Artful Dodger, who—as we will see in these pages—becomes inadvertently drawn into the web of Mr. Fang's plots through an act of consideration while momentarily forgetting that no good deed goes unpunished, could not be ignored if one is to give a fair and accurate recounting of Dodger's activities.

And then there is the matter of Fagin, routinely referred to as "the Jew" back in the day when the mere act of not being a Christian was to make one suspect, if not an outright potential criminal. These, of course, are far more enlightened times, when it is only acceptable to believe that not being a Christian is likely to mean one is a criminal only if one is a Muslim, and therefore we shall refer to Fagin merely by his surname.

This would be the selfsame Fagin who prefers to hide within the shadows and never faces the harsh light of day.

This would be the selfsame Fagin who is shown preparing food from time to time, but never consuming it.

The selfsame Fagin who sits in a commons house and, while others are drinking, is reading a magazine.

The selfsame Fagin who, when handed a glass of wine by the evil, but decidedly human, Bill Sikes, is described as putting it to his lips, drinks not from it, and then claims he has had sufficient to quench his thirst.

Consider the name itself: A simple rearrangement of two letters provides "I Fang," delineating a distinct connection to the other gentleman named Fang already extant in the book.

His clothing, all in black. A hat, broad brimmed to keep the damaging rays of the sun at bay, should he be unlucky enough to be dragged from the confines of his hidey holes, as indeed happened in the course of the original novel.

And his physical description: *"And as, absorbed in thought, he bit back his long black nails, he disclosed among his toothless gums a few such fangs as should have been a dog's or rats."*

Damning evidence? Superficial at best? Many men, not to mention boys, were transported or hung on far less substantive testimony than that. There were many courts in London where the above would be more than sufficient to see Fagin with a wooden stake driven through his heart, presuming the officers of the court believed in such things. Unless, of course, magistrate Mr. Fang were overseeing the proceedings, in which case he would pooh-pooh the entire notion of vampyres as being the province of madmen and fools, which naturally would be self-serving.

How these matters will intersect, how Dodger wound up encountering his true destiny as a challenger to creatures seen and unseen will be the subject of the following tale. We know that these are disturbing subjects, and only hope that Mr. Dickens and his heirs and descendants, not to mention his long-departed shade who may well be dwelling nearby and reading this narrative over your shoulder and shaking his head and muttering, "The Dickens, you say," and urging his long-desiccated body to spin in its grave, will not take too much offense in the unsavory, but no less true matters, being brought into the sort of light that it typically loathes.

- Peter David

CHAPTER ONE

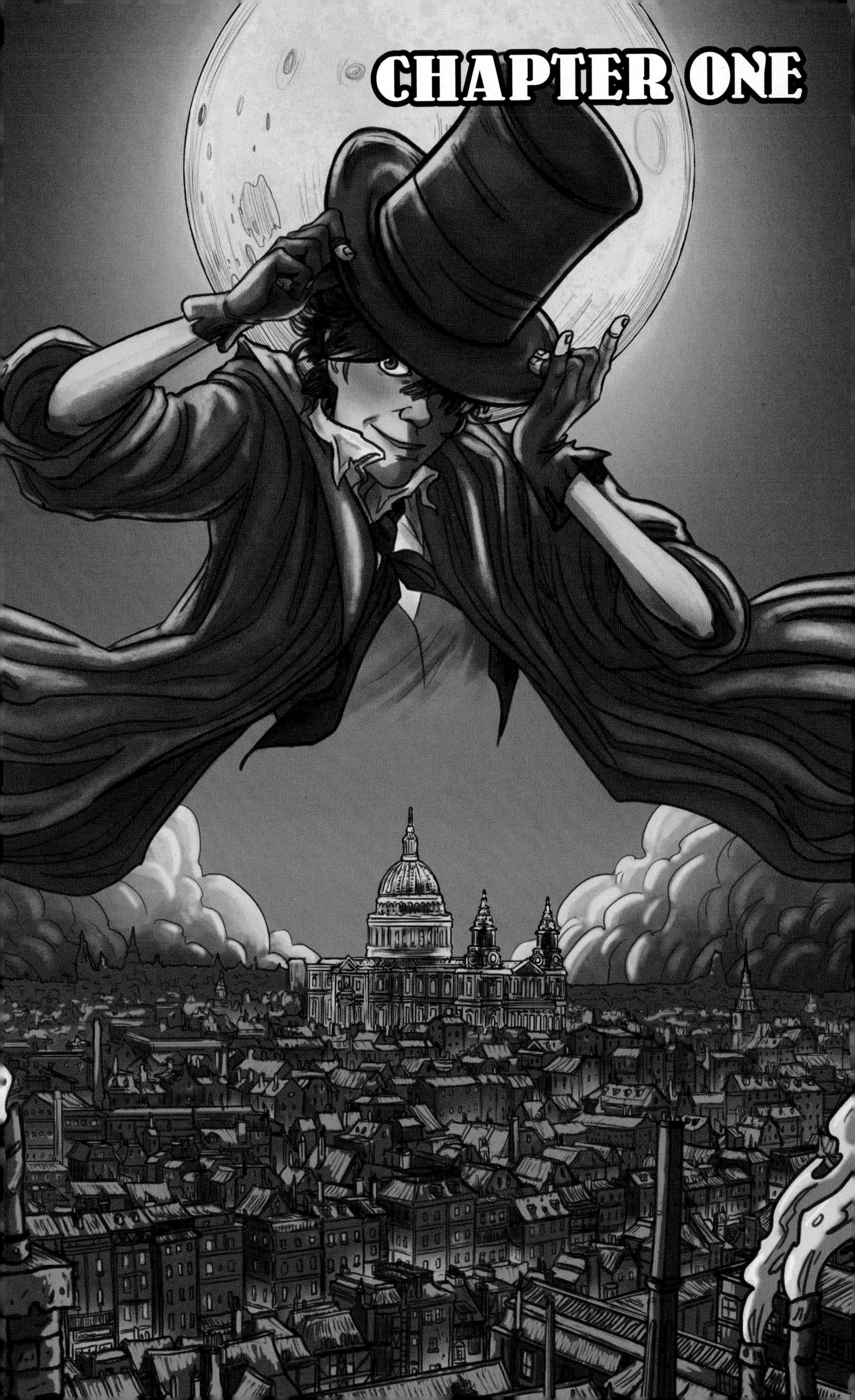

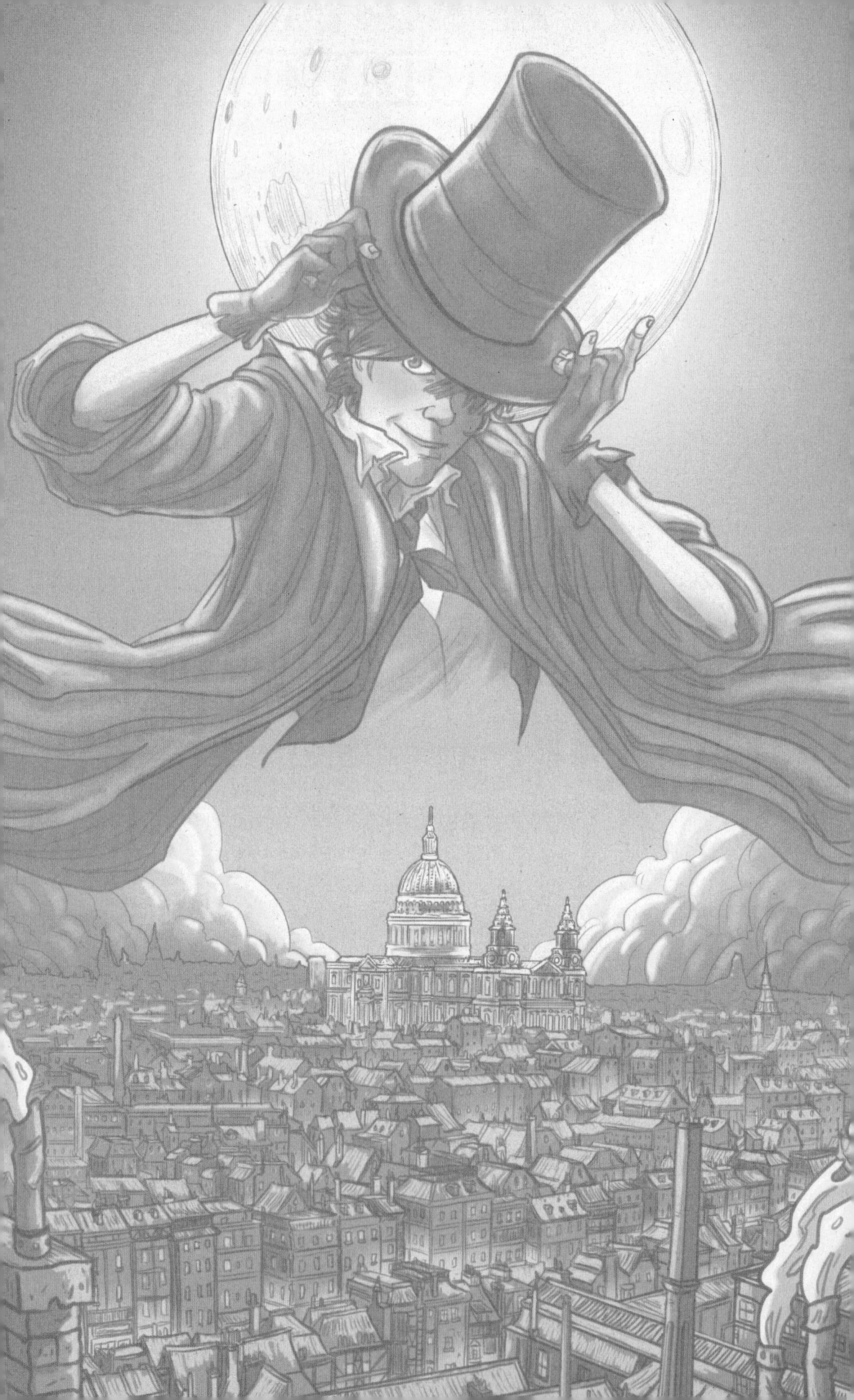

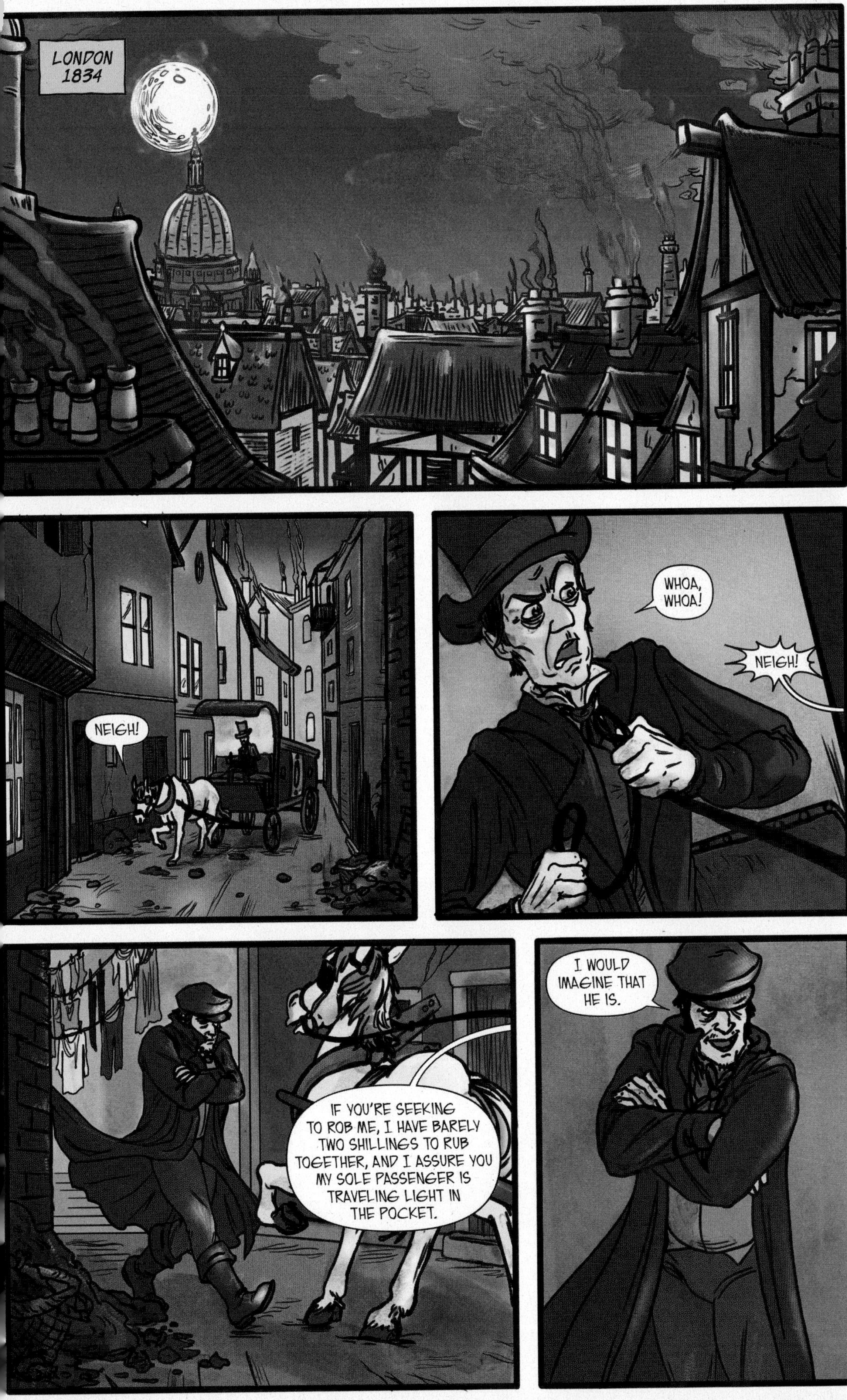
LONDON 1834
NEIGH!
WHOA, WHOA!
NEIGH!
IF YOU'RE SEEKING TO ROB ME, I HAVE BARELY TWO SHILLINGS TO RUB TOGETHER, AND I ASSURE YOU MY SOLE PASSENGER IS TRAVELING LIGHT IN THE POCKET.
I WOULD IMAGINE THAT HE IS.

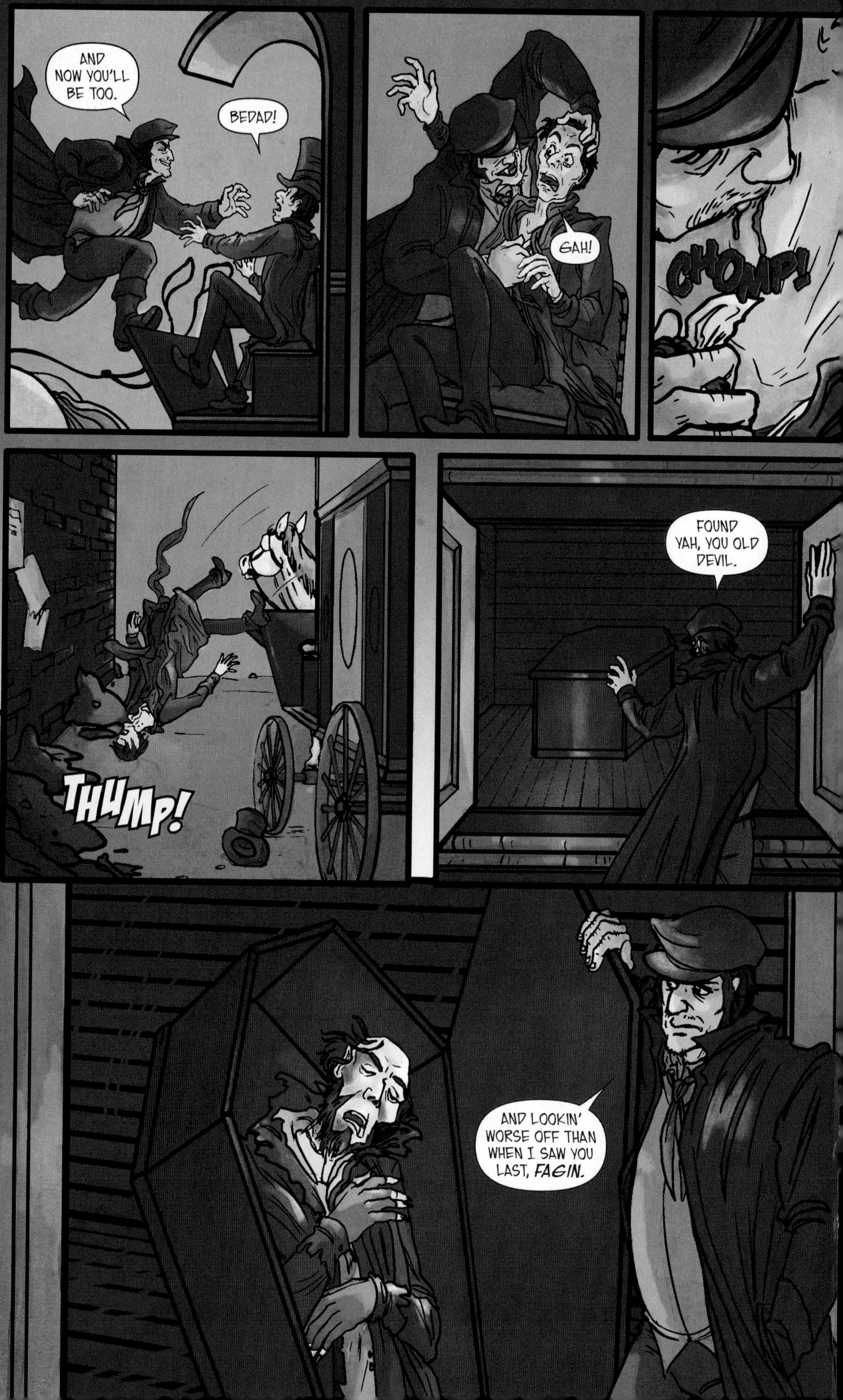
AND NOW YOU'LL BE TOO.
BEDAD!
GAH!
CHOMP!
THUMP!
FOUND YAH, YOU OLD DEVIL.
AND LOOKIN' WORSE OFF THAN WHEN I SAW YOU LAST, FAGIN.

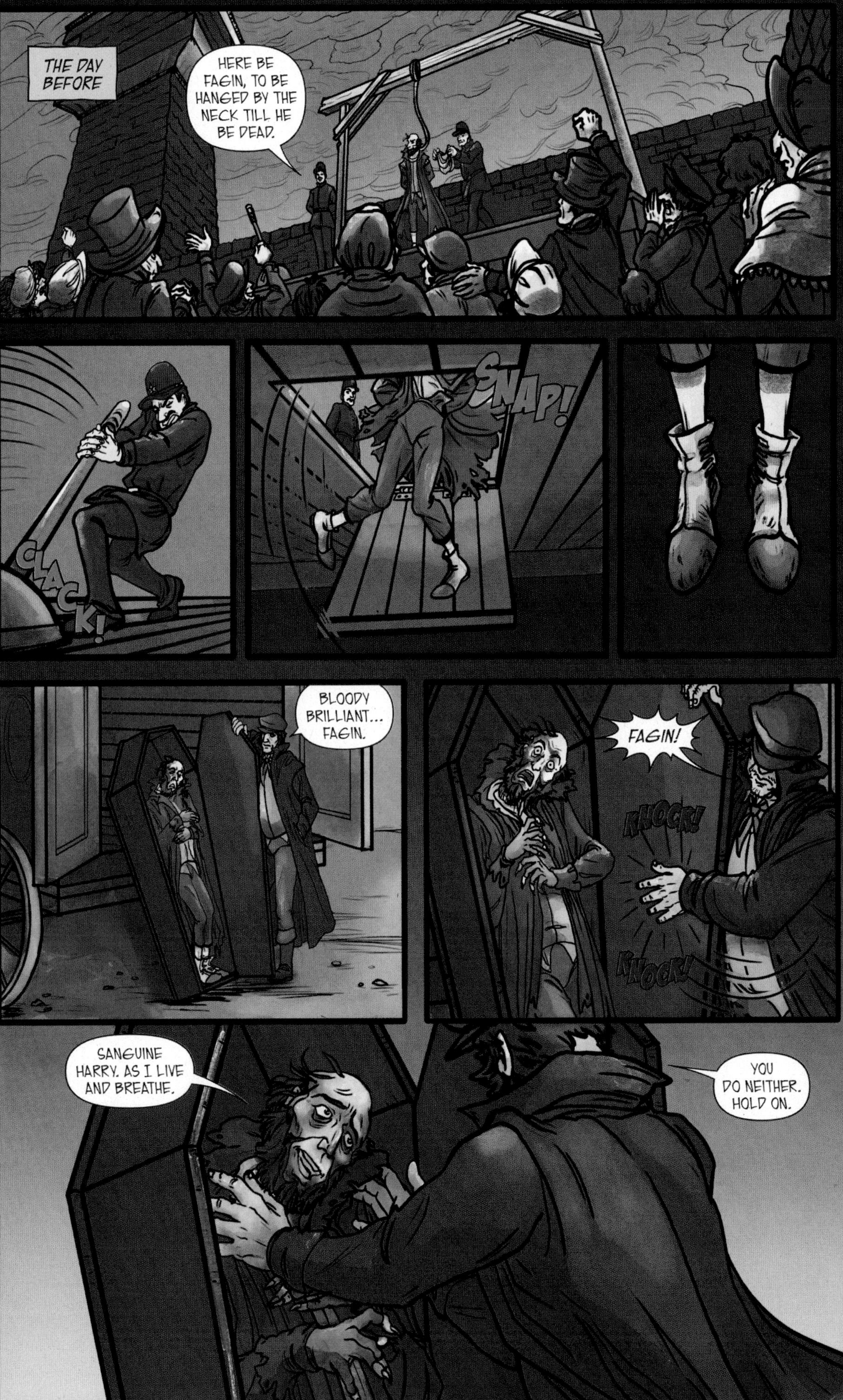
THE DAY BEFORE
HERE BE FAGIN, TO BE HANGED BY THE NECK TILL HE BE DEAD.
CLACK!
SNAP!
BLOODY BRILLIANT... FAGIN.
FAGIN!
KNOCK!
KNOCK!
SANGUINE HARRY. AS I LIVE AND BREATHE.
YOU DO NEITHER. HOLD ON.

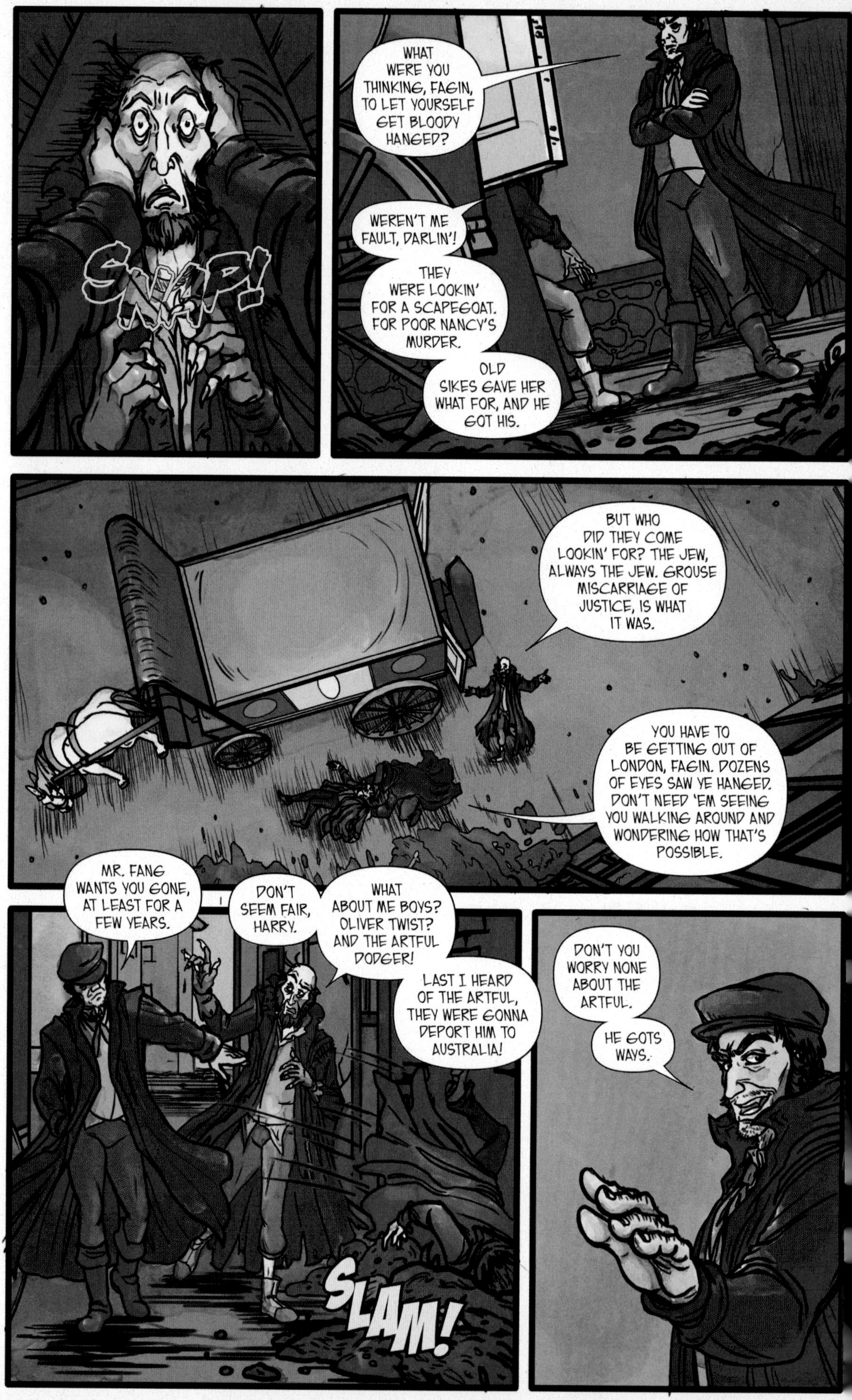
SNAP!
WHAT WERE YOU THINKING, FAGIN, TO LET YOURSELF GET BLOODY HANGED?
WEREN'T ME FAULT, DARLIN'!
THEY WERE LOOKIN' FOR A SCAPEGOAT. FOR POOR NANCY'S MURDER.
OLD SIKES GAVE HER WHAT FOR, AND HE GOT HIS.
BUT WHO DID THEY COME LOOKIN' FOR? THE JEW, ALWAYS THE JEW. GROUSE MISCARRIAGE OF JUSTICE, IS WHAT IT WAS.
YOU HAVE TO BE GETTING OUT OF LONDON, FAGIN. DOZENS OF EYES SAW YE HANGED. DON'T NEED 'EM SEEING YOU WALKING AROUND AND WONDERING HOW THAT'S POSSIBLE.
MR. FANG WANTS YOU GONE, AT LEAST FOR A FEW YEARS.
DON'T SEEM FAIR, HARRY.
WHAT ABOUT ME BOYS? OLIVER TWIST? AND THE ARTFUL DODGER!
LAST I HEARD OF THE ARTFUL, THEY WERE GONNA DEPORT HIM TO AUSTRALIA!
SLAM!
DON'T YOU WORRY NONE ABOUT THE ARTFUL.
HE GOTS WAYS.

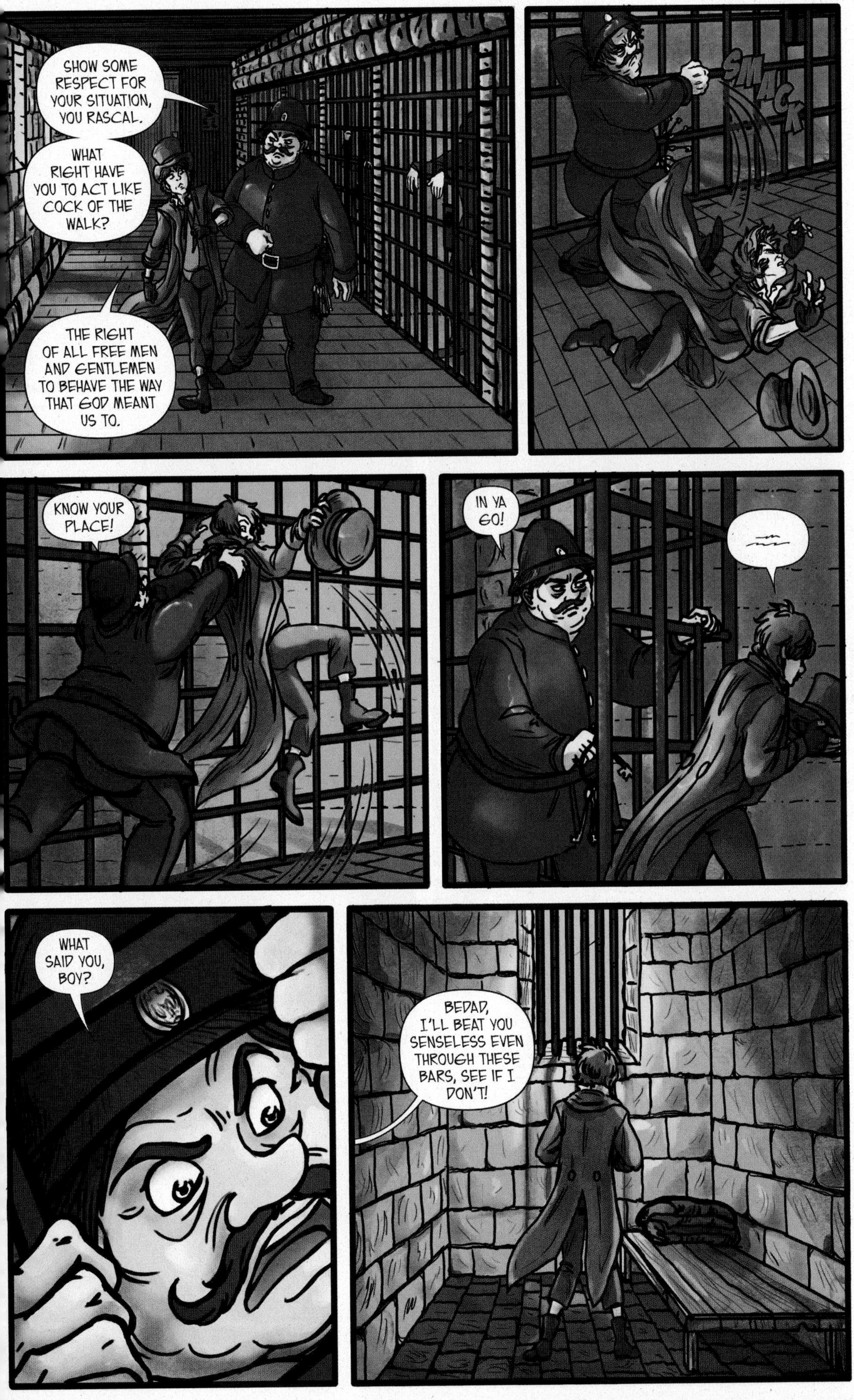
SHOW SOME RESPECT FOR YOUR SITUATION, YOU RASCAL.
WHAT RIGHT HAVE YOU TO ACT LIKE COCK OF THE WALK?
THE RIGHT OF ALL FREE MEN AND GENTLEMEN TO BEHAVE THE WAY THAT GOD MEANT US TO.
SMACK
KNOW YOUR PLACE!
IN YA GO!
WHAT SAID YOU, BOY?
BEDAD, I'LL BEAT YOU SENSELESS EVEN THROUGH THESE BARS, SEE IF I DON'T!

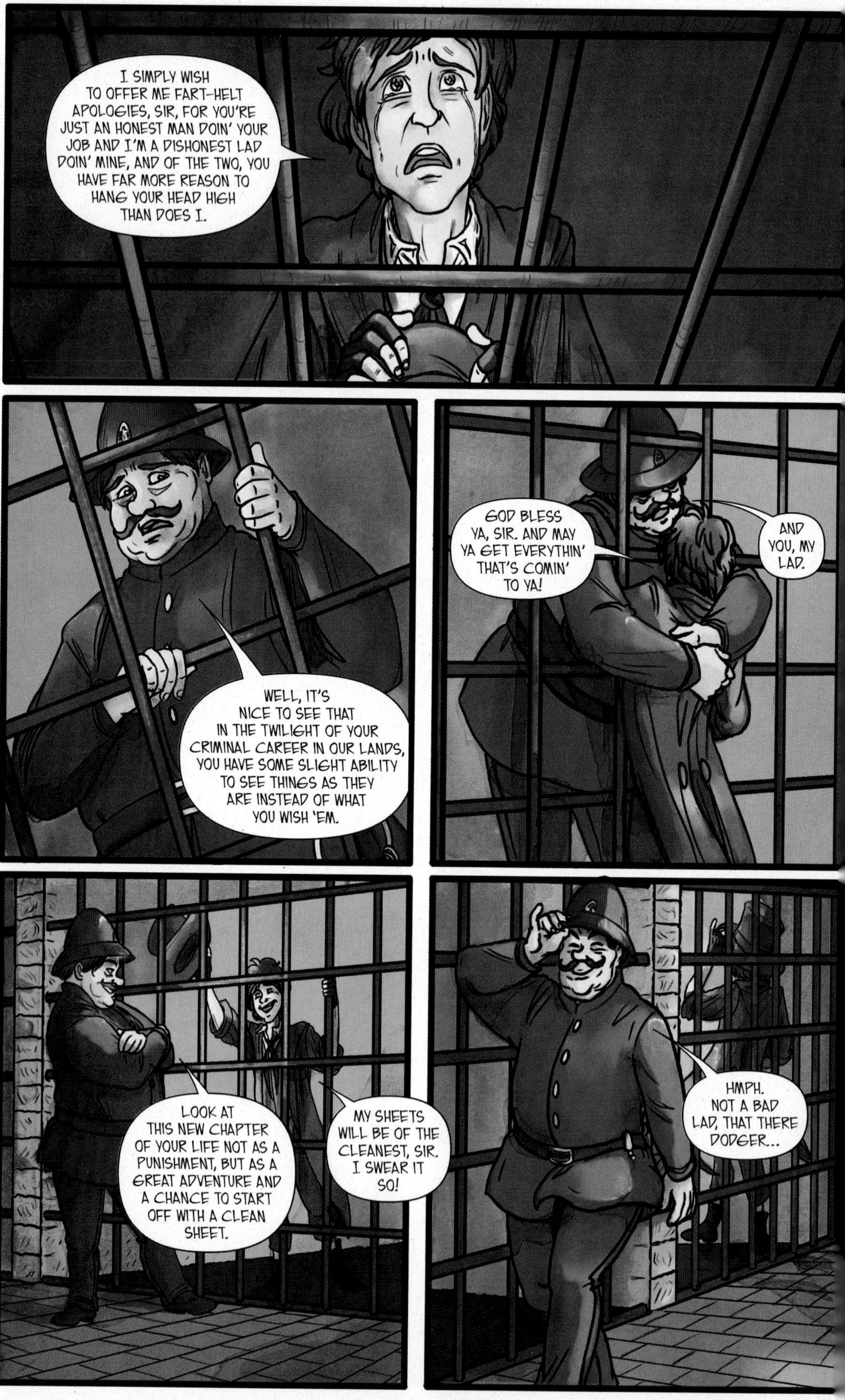
I SIMPLY WISH TO OFFER ME FART-HELT APOLOGIES, SIR, FOR YOU'RE JUST AN HONEST MAN DOIN' YOUR JOB AND I'M A DISHONEST LAD DOIN' MINE, AND OF THE TWO, YOU HAVE FAR MORE REASON TO HANG YOUR HEAD HIGH THAN DOES I.
WELL, IT'S NICE TO SEE THAT IN THE TWILIGHT OF YOUR CRIMINAL CAREER IN OUR LANDS, YOU HAVE SOME SLIGHT ABILITY TO SEE THINGS AS THEY ARE INSTEAD OF WHAT YOU WISH 'EM.
GOD BLESS YA, SIR. AND MAY YA GET EVERYTHIN' THAT'S COMIN' TO YA!
AND YOU, MY LAD.
LOOK AT THIS NEW CHAPTER OF YOUR LIFE NOT AS A PUNISHMENT, BUT AS A GREAT ADVENTURE AND A CHANCE TO START OFF WITH A CLEAN SHEET.
MY SHEETS WILL BE OF THE CLEANEST, SIR. I SWEAR IT SO!
HMPH. NOT A BAD LAD, THAT THERE DODGER...

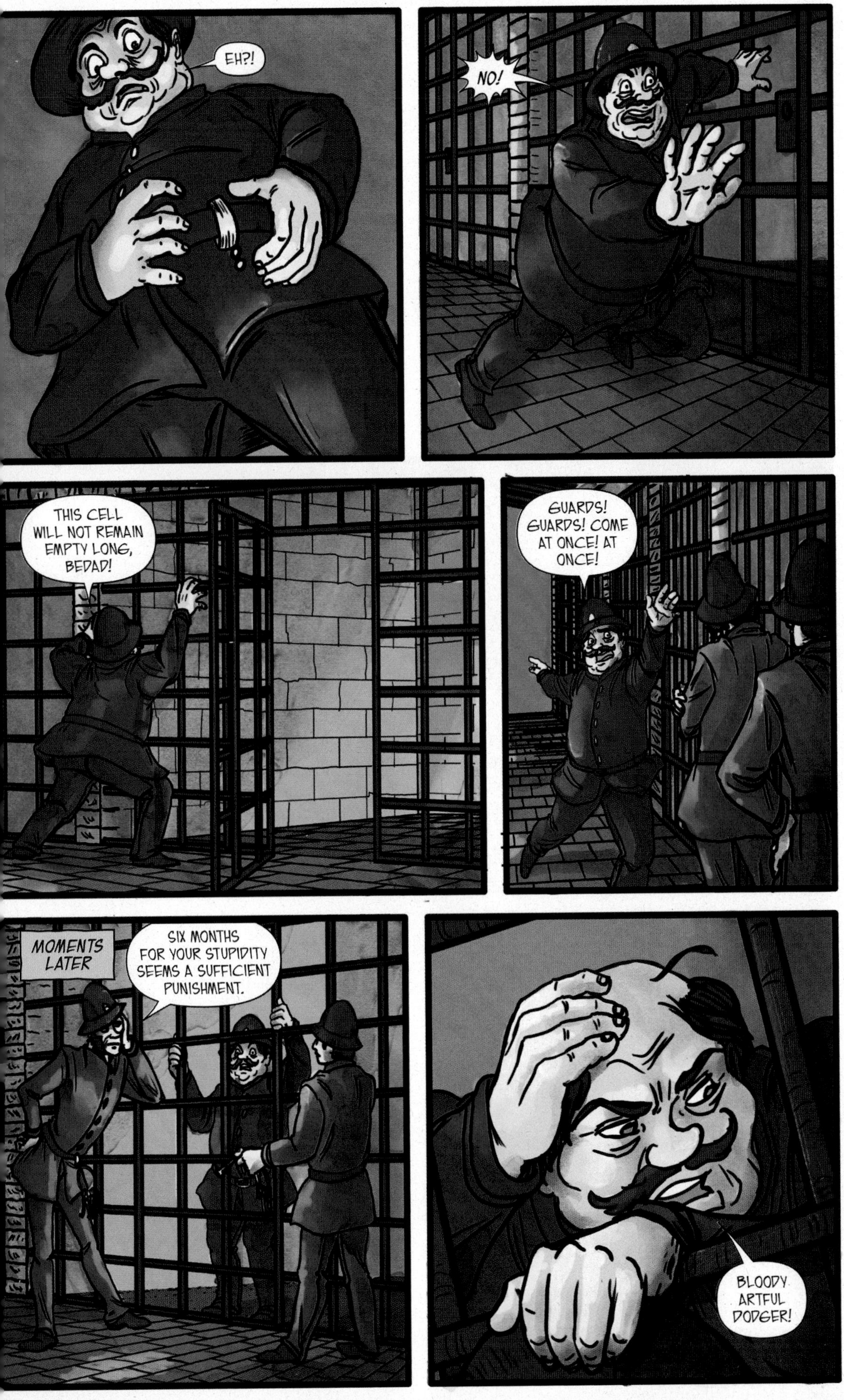
EH?!
NO!
THIS CELL WILL NOT REMAIN EMPTY LONG, BEDAD!
GUARDS! GUARDS! COME AT ONCE! AT ONCE!
MOMENTS LATER
SIX MONTHS FOR YOUR STUPIDITY SEEMS A SUFFICIENT PUNISHMENT.
BLOODY ARTFUL DODGER!

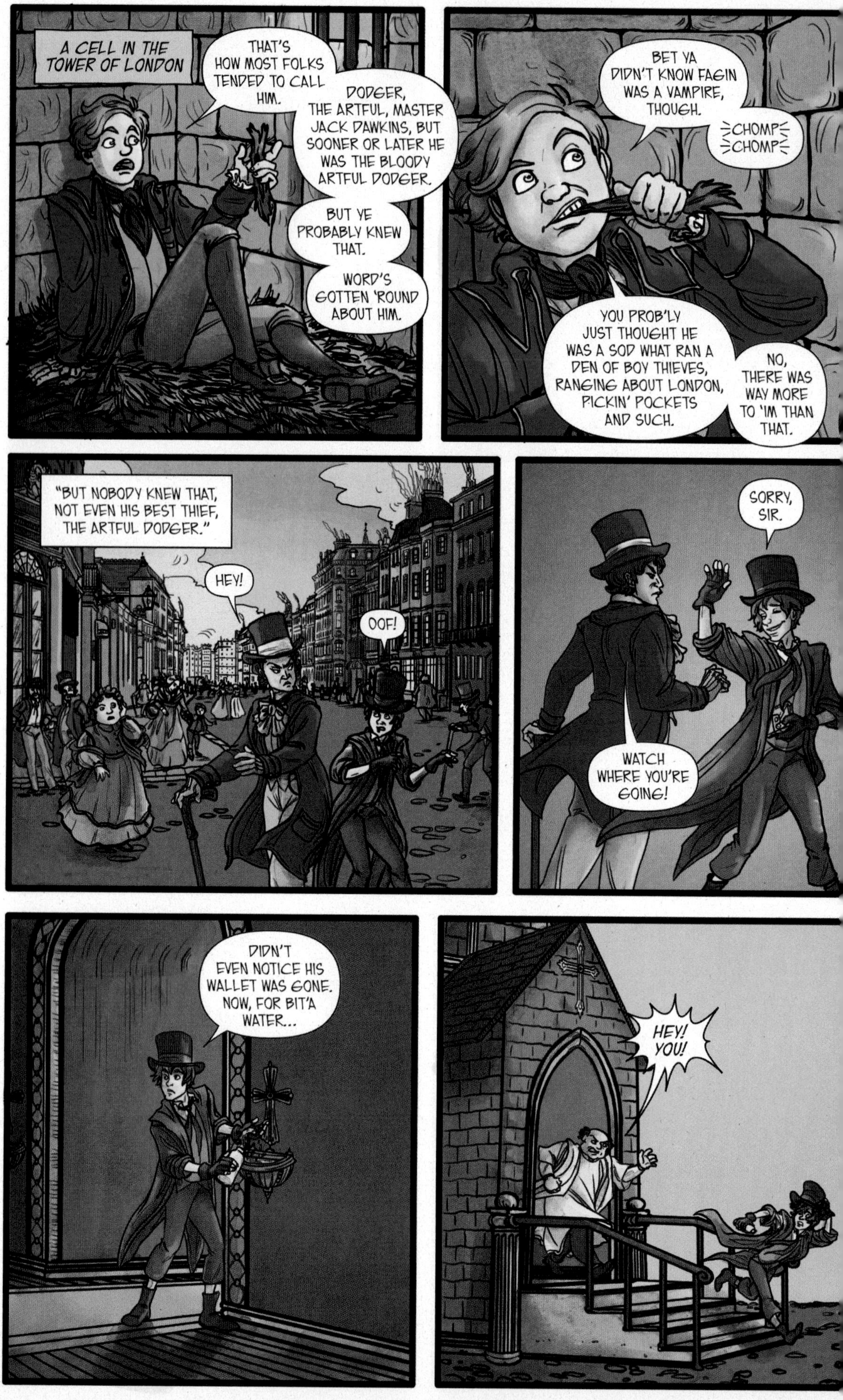
A CELL IN THE TOWER OF LONDON
THAT'S HOW MOST FOLKS TENDED TO CALL HIM.
DODGER, THE ARTFUL, MASTER JACK DAWKINS, BUT SOONER OR LATER HE WAS THE BLOODY ARTFUL DODGER.
BUT YE PROBABLY KNEW THAT.
WORD'S GOTTEN 'ROUND ABOUT HIM.
BET YA DIDN'T KNOW FAGIN WAS A VAMPIRE, THOUGH.
CHOMP
CHOMP
YOU PROB'LY JUST THOUGHT HE WAS A SOD WHAT RAN A DEN OF BOY THIEVES, RANGING ABOUT LONDON, PICKIN' POCKETS AND SUCH.
NO, THERE WAS WAY MORE TO 'IM THAN THAT.
"BUT NOBODY KNEW THAT, NOT EVEN HIS BEST THIEF, THE ARTFUL DODGER."
HEY!
OOF!
SORRY, SIR.
WATCH WHERE YOU'RE GOING!
DIDN'T EVEN NOTICE HIS WALLET WAS GONE. NOW, FOR BIT'A WATER...
HEY! YOU!

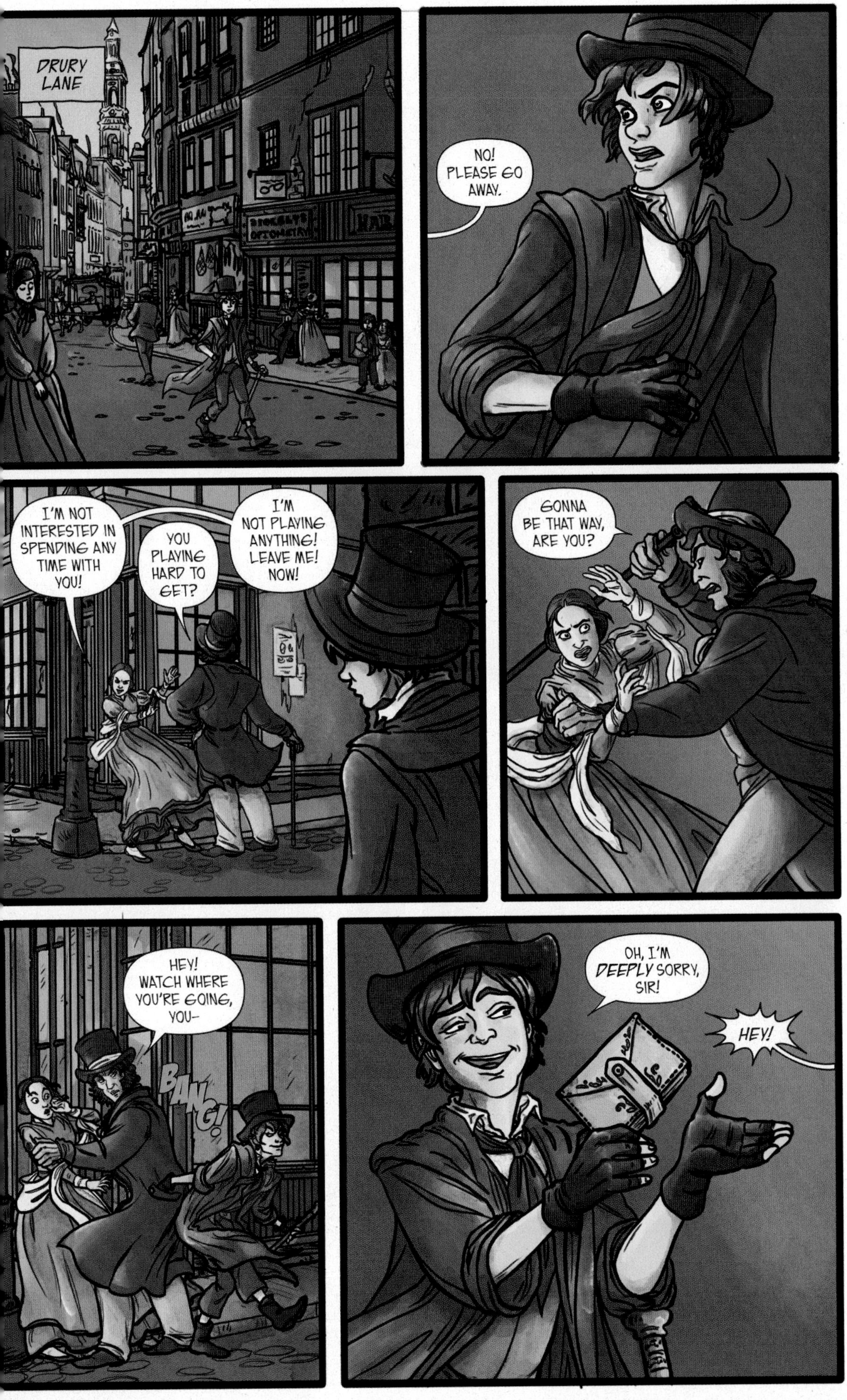
DRURY LANE
NO! PLEASE GO AWAY.
I'M NOT INTERESTED IN SPENDING ANY TIME WITH YOU!
YOU PLAYING HARD TO GET?
I'M NOT PLAYING ANYTHING! LEAVE ME! NOW!
GONNA BE THAT WAY, ARE YOU?
HEY! WATCH WHERE YOU'RE GOING, YOU-
BANG!
OH, I'M DEEPLY SORRY, SIR!
HEY!

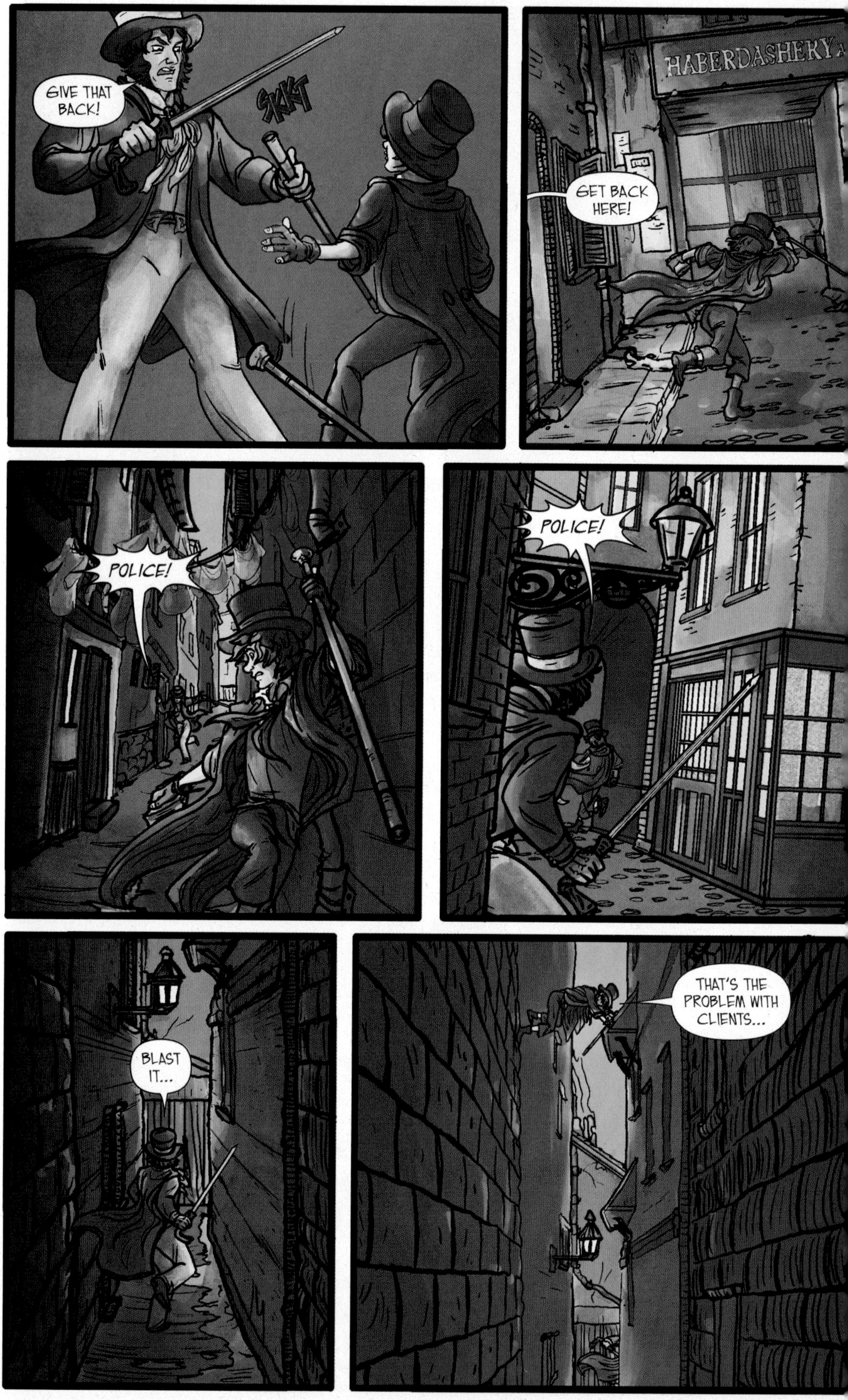
GIVE THAT BACK!
SKKT
HABERDASHERY
GET BACK HERE!
POLICE!
POLICE!
BLAST IT...
THAT'S THE PROBLEM WITH CLIENTS...

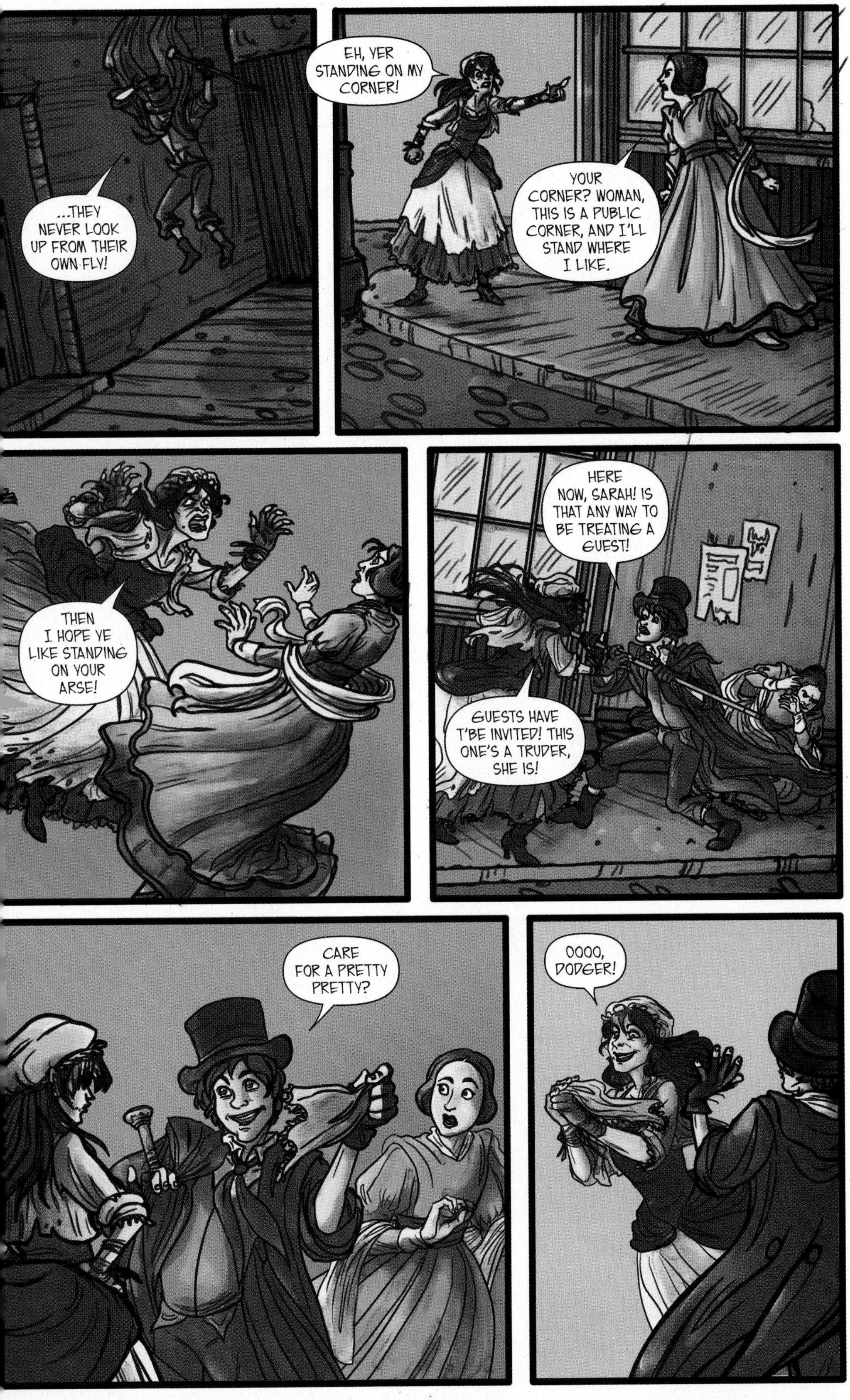
...THEY NEVER LOOK UP FROM THEIR OWN FLY!
EH, YER STANDING ON MY CORNER!
YOUR CORNER? WOMAN, THIS IS A PUBLIC CORNER, AND I'LL STAND WHERE I LIKE.
THEN I HOPE YE LIKE STANDING ON YOUR ARSE!
HERE NOW, SARAH! IS THAT ANY WAY TO BE TREATING A GUEST!
GUESTS HAVE T'BE INVITED! THIS ONE'S A TRUDER, SHE IS!
CARE FOR A PRETTY PRETTY?
OOOO, DODGER!

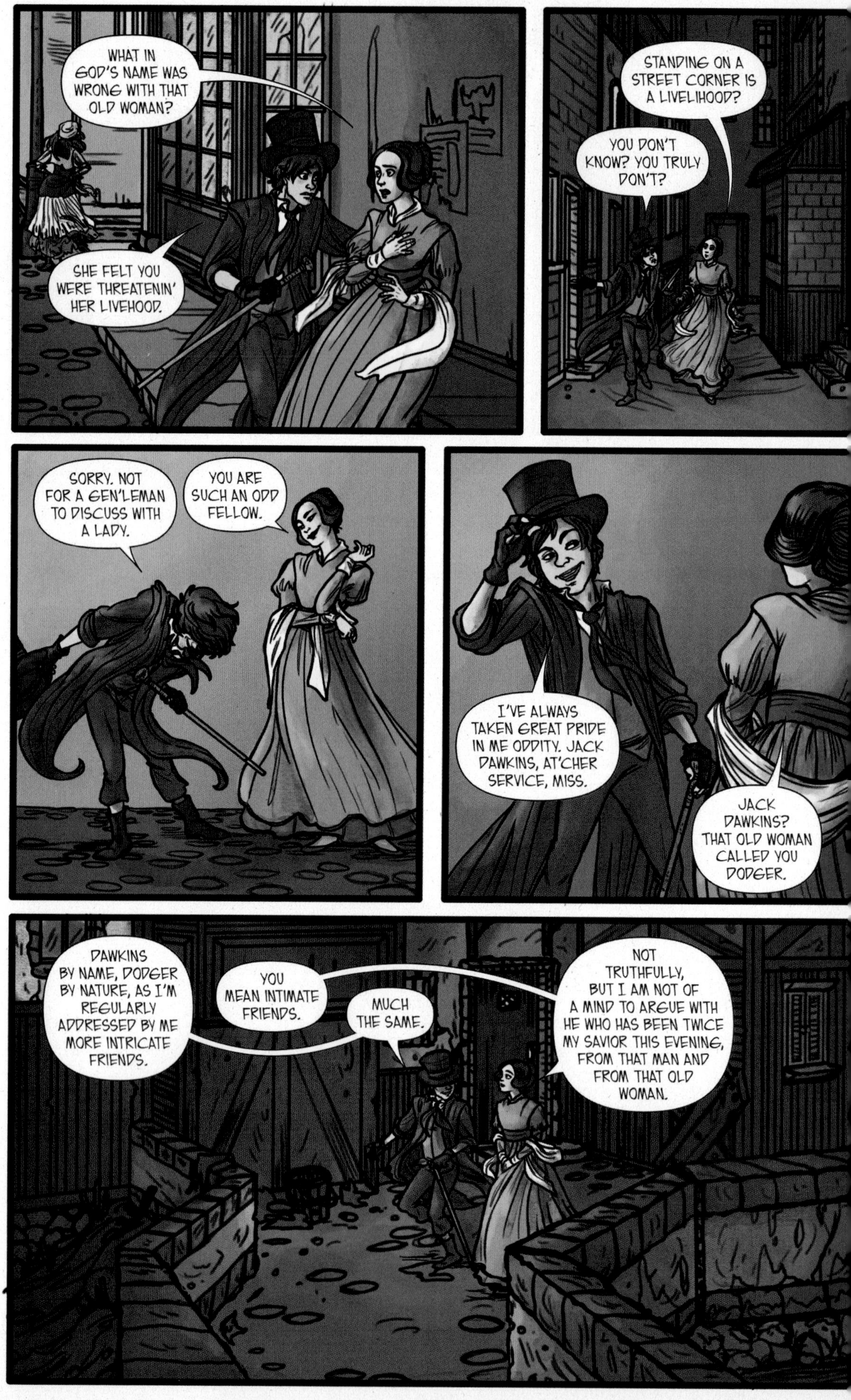
WHAT IN GOD'S NAME WAS WRONG WITH THAT OLD WOMAN?
SHE FELT YOU WERE THREATENIN' HER LIVEHOOD.
STANDING ON A STREET CORNER IS A LIVELIHOOD?
YOU DON'T KNOW? YOU TRULY DON'T?
SORRY. NOT FOR A GEN'LEMAN TO DISCUSS WITH A LADY.
YOU ARE SUCH AN ODD FELLOW.
I'VE ALWAYS TAKEN GREAT PRIDE IN ME ODDITY. JACK DAWKINS, AT'CHER SERVICE, MISS.
JACK DAWKINS? THAT OLD WOMAN CALLED YOU DODGER.
DAWKINS BY NAME, DODGER BY NATURE, AS I'M REGULARLY ADDRESSED BY ME MORE INTRICATE FRIENDS.
YOU MEAN INTIMATE FRIENDS.
MUCH THE SAME.
NOT TRUTHFULLY, BUT I AM NOT OF A MIND TO ARGUE WITH HE WHO HAS BEEN TWICE MY SAVIOR THIS EVENING, FROM THAT MAN AND FROM THAT OLD WOMAN.

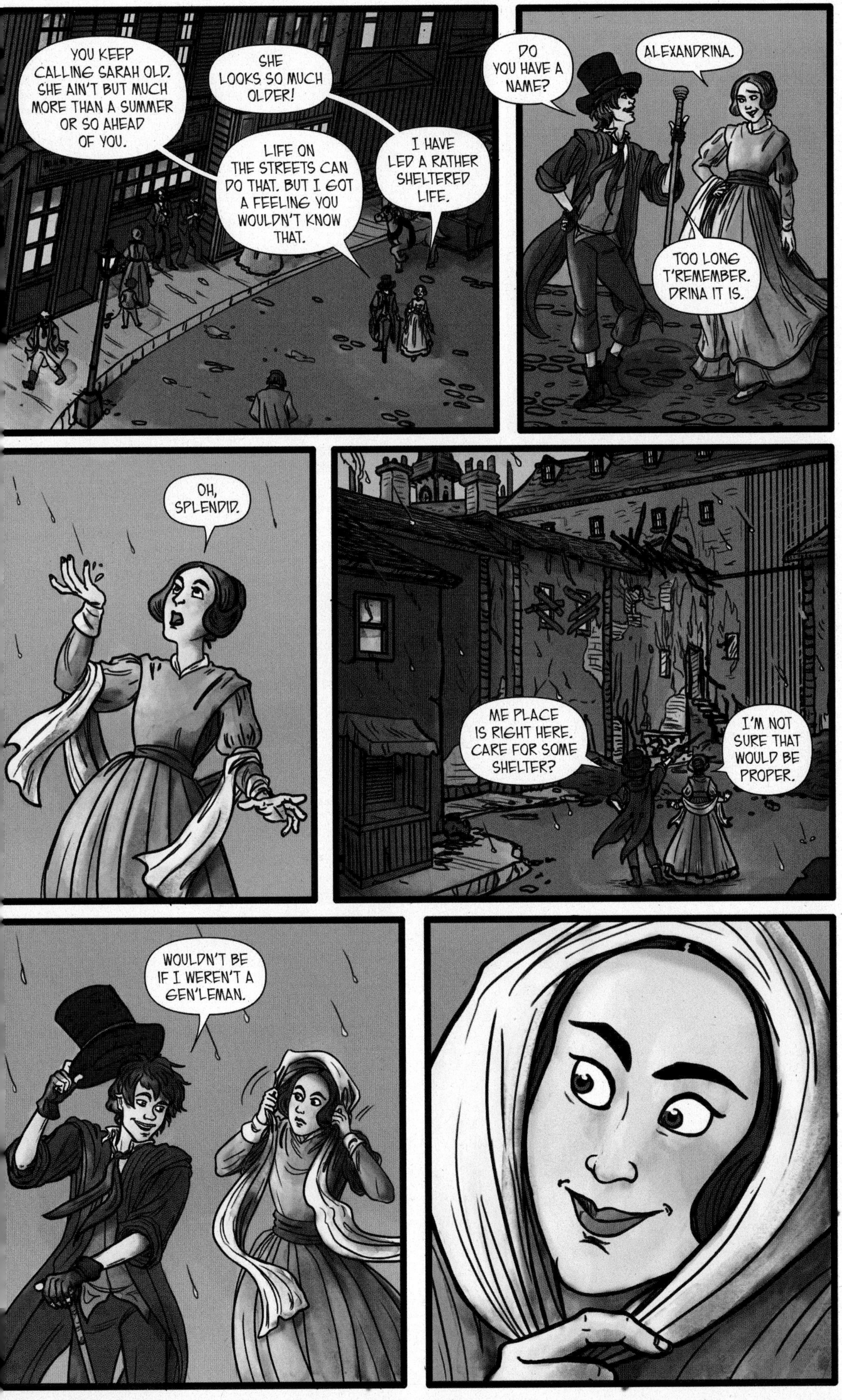
YOU KEEP CALLING SARAH OLD. SHE AIN'T BUT MUCH MORE THAN A SUMMER OR SO AHEAD OF YOU.
SHE LOOKS SO MUCH OLDER!
LIFE ON THE STREETS CAN DO THAT. BUT I GOT A FEELING YOU WOULDN'T KNOW THAT.
I HAVE LED A RATHER SHELTERED LIFE.
DO YOU HAVE A NAME?
ALEXANDRINA.
TOO LONG T'REMEMBER. DRINA IT IS.
OH, SPLENDID.
ME PLACE IS RIGHT HERE. CARE FOR SOME SHELTER?
I'M NOT SURE THAT WOULD BE PROPER.
WOULDN'T BE IF I WEREN'T A GEN'LEMAN.

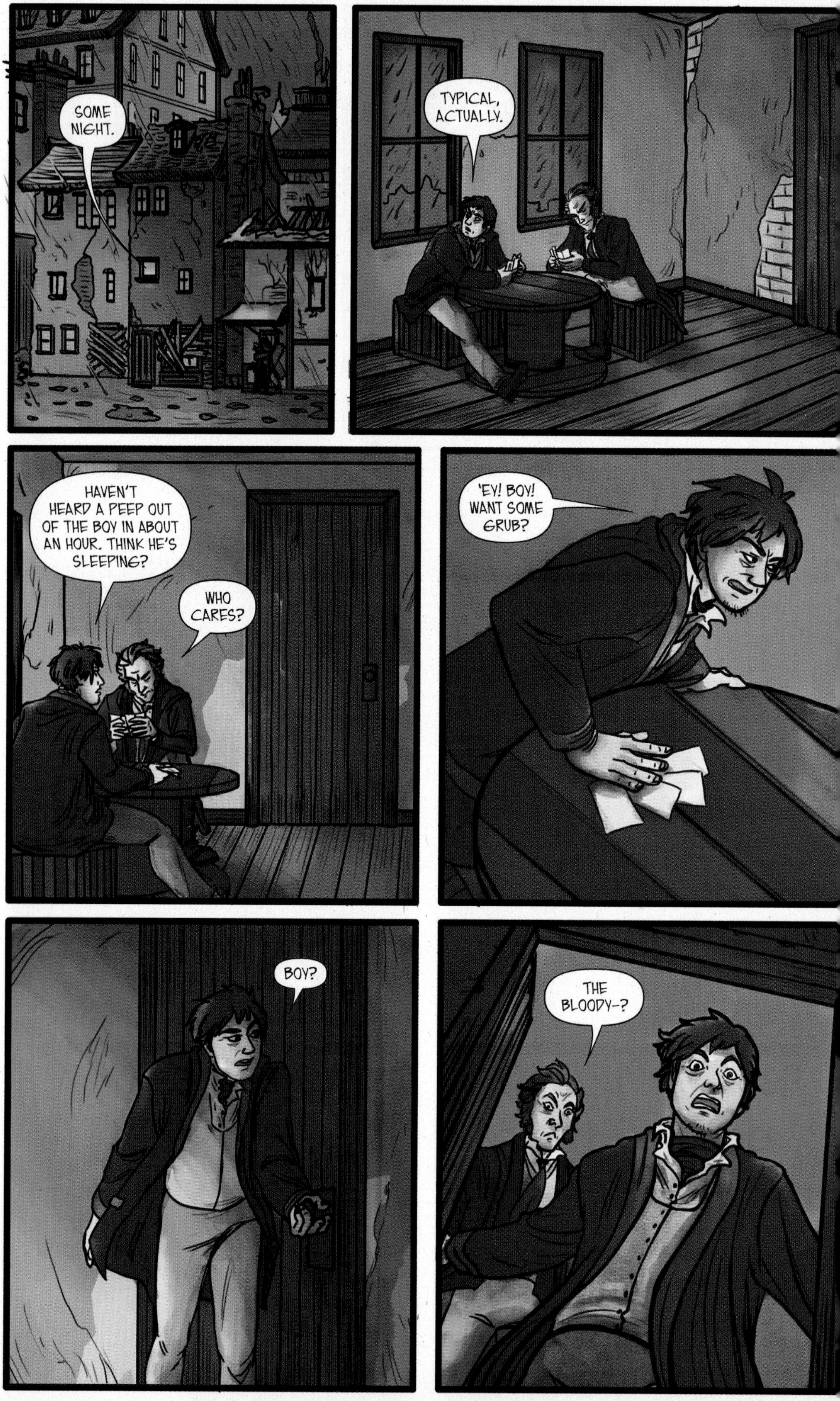
SOME NIGHT.
TYPICAL, ACTUALLY.
HAVEN'T HEARD A PEEP OUT OF THE BOY IN ABOUT AN HOUR. THINK HE'S SLEEPING?
WHO CARES?
'EY! BOY! WANT SOME GRUB?
BOY?
THE BLOODY-?

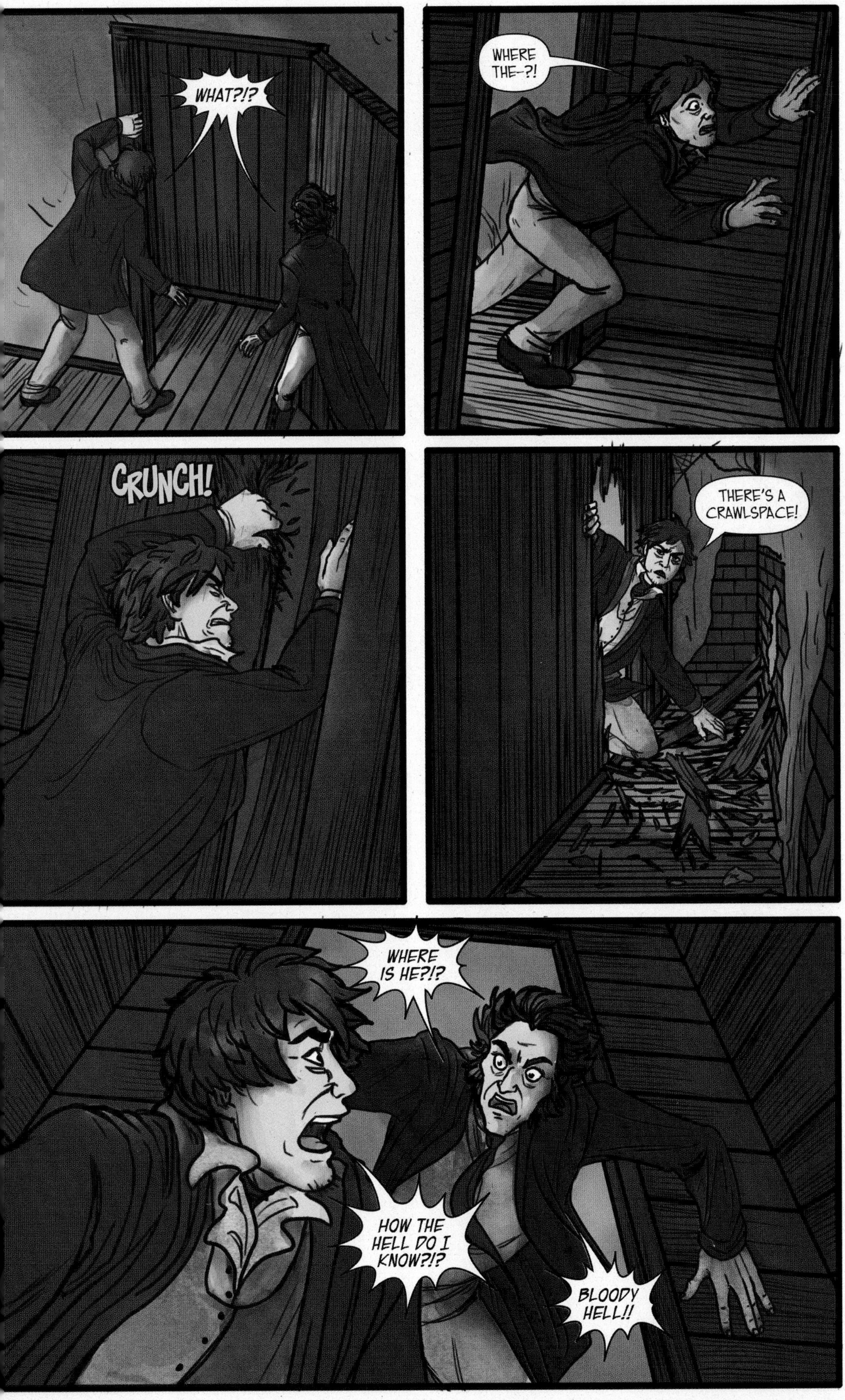

WHAT?!?
WHERE THE--?!
CRUNCH!
THERE'S A CRAWLSPACE!
WHERE IS HE?!?
HOW THE HELL DO I KNOW?!?
BLOODY HELL!!

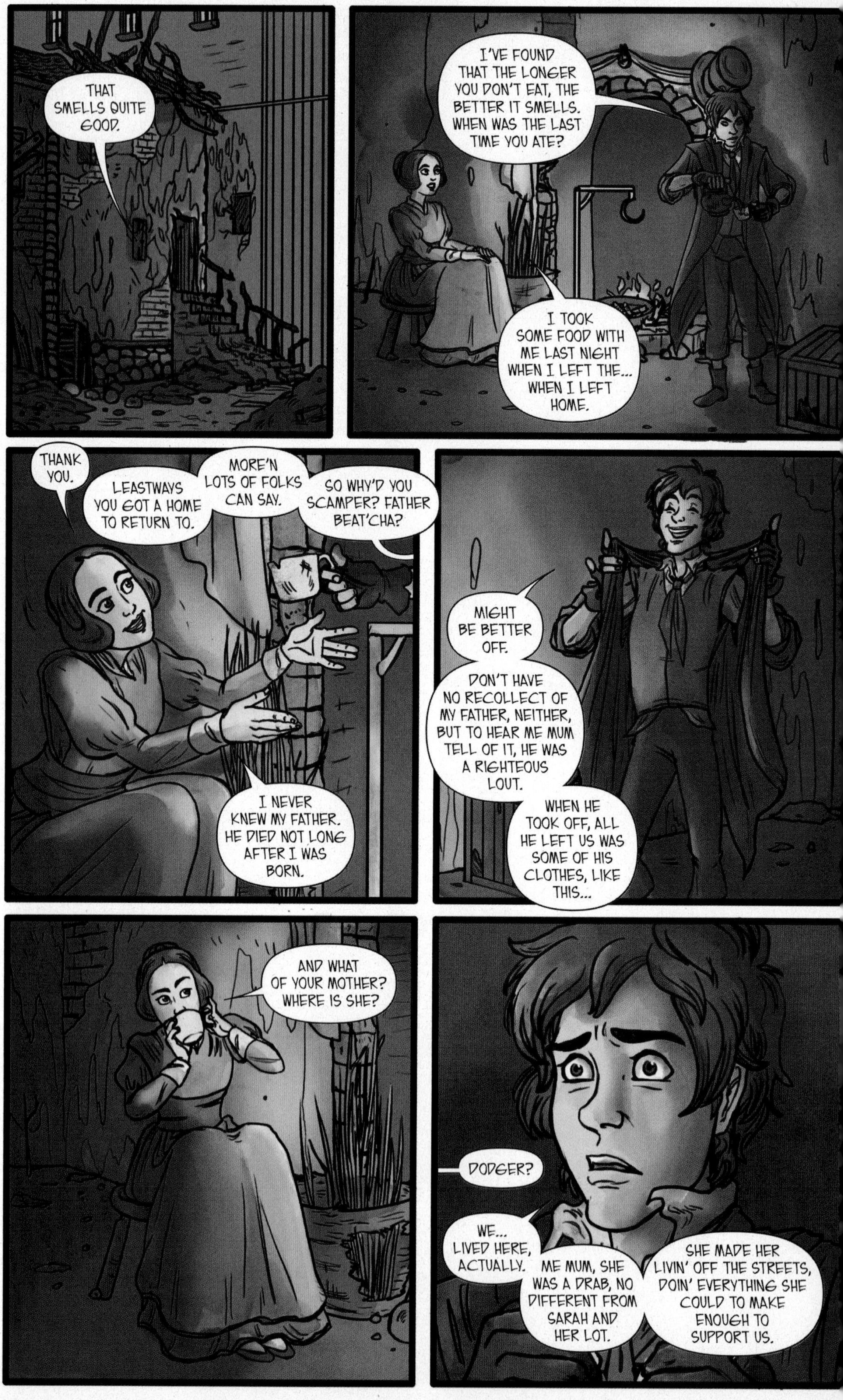
THAT SMELLS QUITE GOOD.
I'VE FOUND THAT THE LONGER YOU DON'T EAT, THE BETTER IT SMELLS. WHEN WAS THE LAST TIME YOU ATE?
I TOOK SOME FOOD WITH ME LAST NIGHT WHEN I LEFT THE... WHEN I LEFT HOME.
THANK YOU.
LEASTWAYS YOU GOT A HOME TO RETURN TO.
MORE'N LOTS OF FOLKS CAN SAY.
SO WHY'D YOU SCAMPER? FATHER BEAT'CHA?
I NEVER KNEW MY FATHER. HE DIED NOT LONG AFTER I WAS BORN.
MIGHT BE BETTER OFF.
DON'T HAVE NO RECOLLECT OF MY FATHER, NEITHER, BUT TO HEAR ME MUM TELL OF IT, HE WAS A RIGHTEOUS LOUT.
WHEN HE TOOK OFF, ALL HE LEFT US WAS SOME OF HIS CLOTHES, LIKE THIS...
AND WHAT OF YOUR MOTHER? WHERE IS SHE?
DODGER?
WE... LIVED HERE, ACTUALLY.
ME MUM, SHE WAS A DRAB, NO DIFFERENT FROM SARAH AND HER LOT.
SHE MADE HER LIVIN' OFF THE STREETS, DOIN' EVERYTHING SHE COULD TO MAKE ENOUGH TO SUPPORT US.

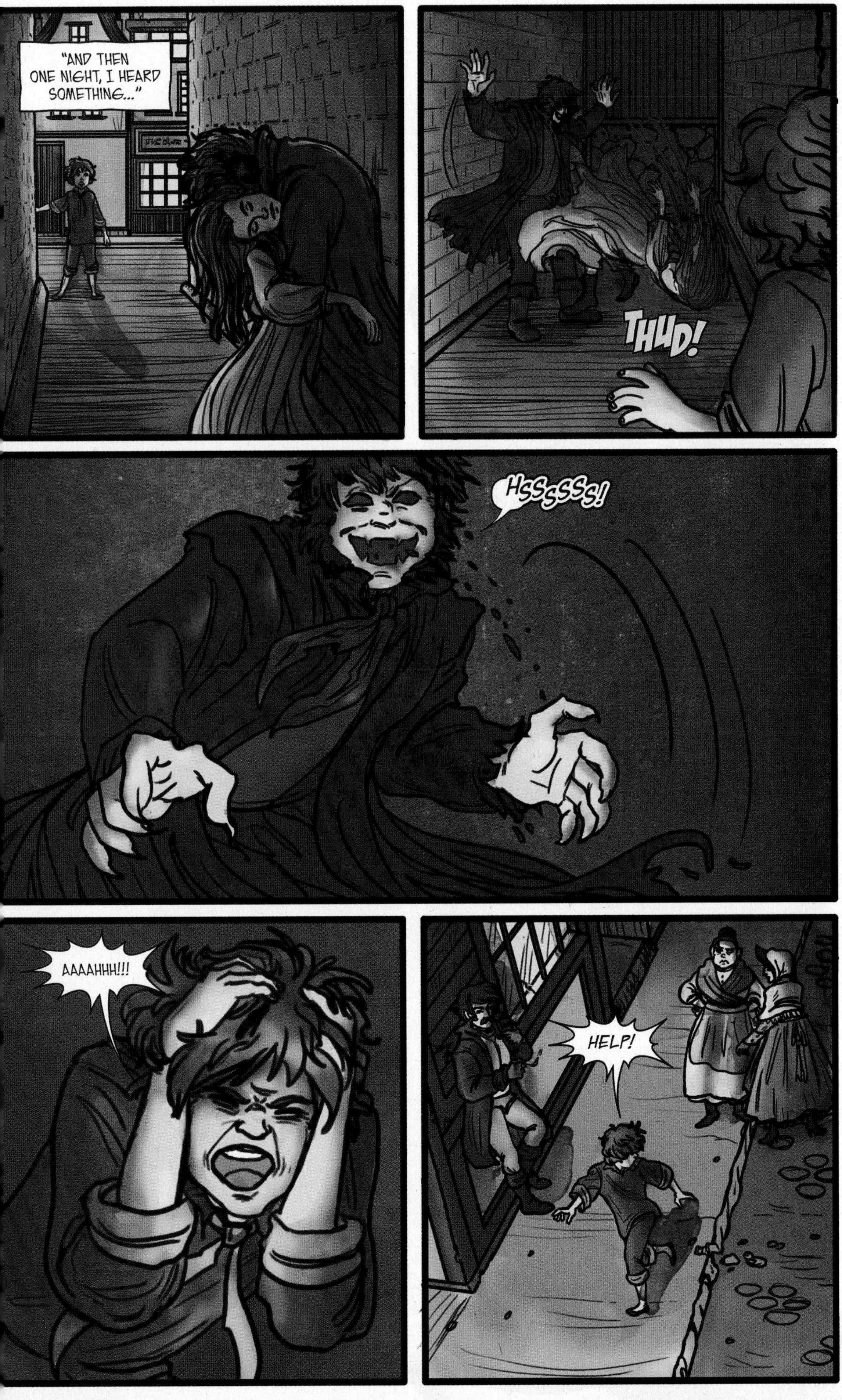

"AND THEN ONE NIGHT, I HEARD SOMETHING..."
THUD!
HSSSSSS!
AAAAHHH!!!
HELP!

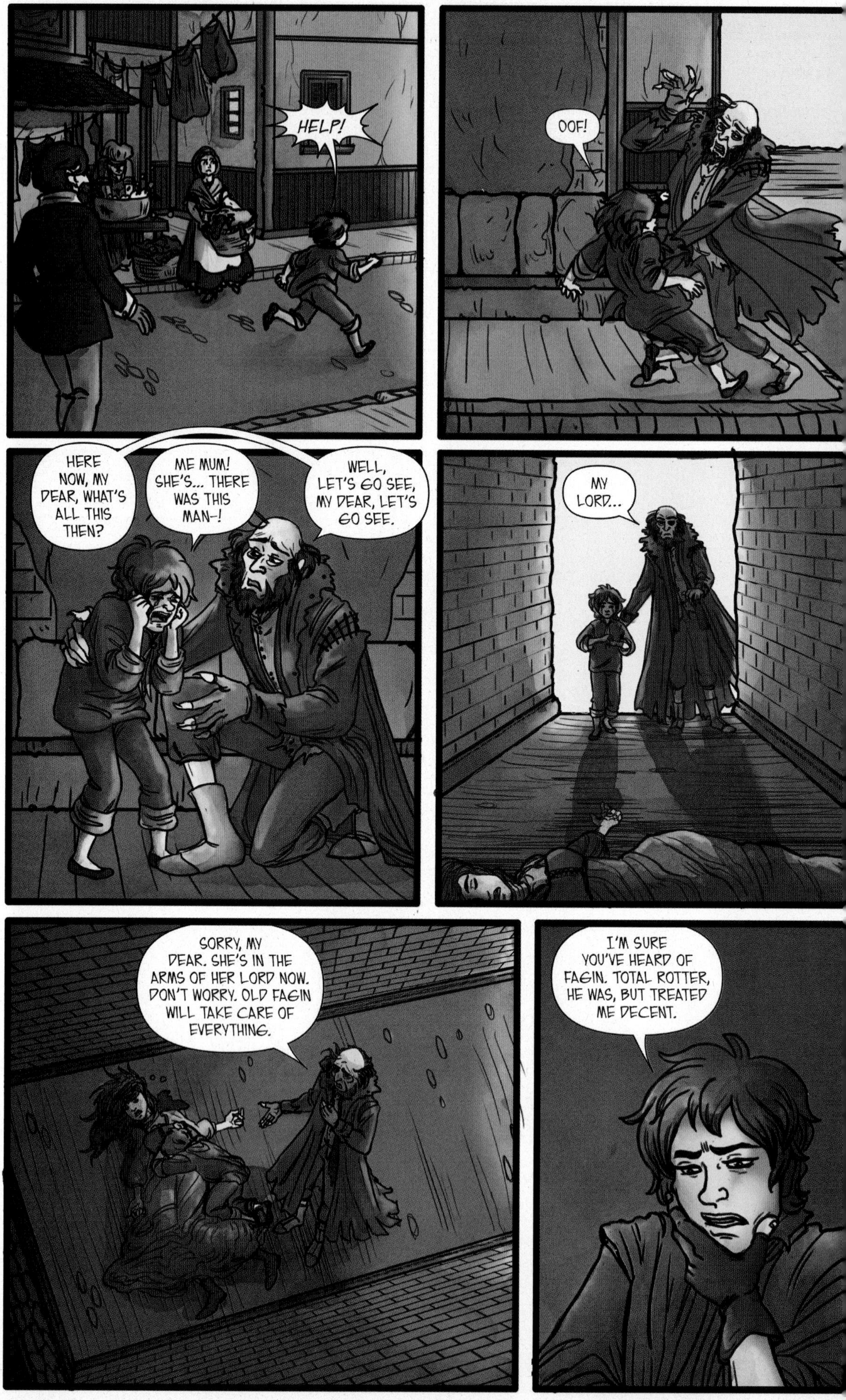
HELP!
OOF!
HERE NOW, MY DEAR, WHAT'S ALL THIS THEN?
ME MUM! SHE'S... THERE WAS THIS MAN-!
WELL, LET'S GO SEE, MY DEAR, LET'S GO SEE.
MY LORD...
SORRY, MY DEAR. SHE'S IN THE ARMS OF HER LORD NOW. DON'T WORRY. OLD FAGIN WILL TAKE CARE OF EVERYTHING.
I'M SURE YOU'VE HEARD OF FAGIN. TOTAL ROTTER, HE WAS, BUT TREATED ME DECENT.

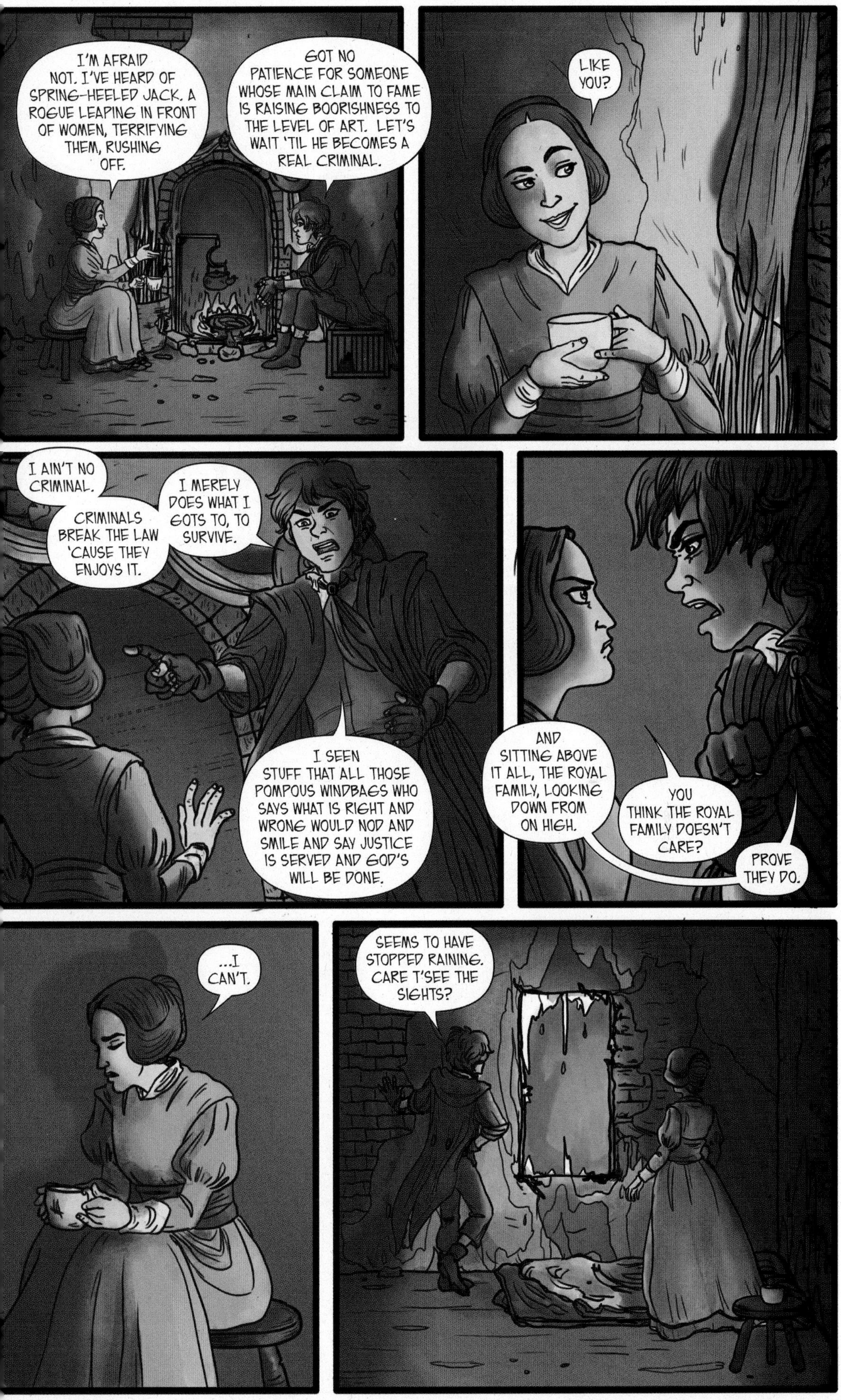
I'M AFRAID NOT. I'VE HEARD OF SPRING-HEELED JACK. A ROGUE LEAPING IN FRONT OF WOMEN, TERRIFYING THEM, RUSHING OFF.
GOT NO PATIENCE FOR SOMEONE WHOSE MAIN CLAIM TO FAME IS RAISING BOORISHNESS TO THE LEVEL OF ART. LET'S WAIT 'TIL HE BECOMES A REAL CRIMINAL.
LIKE YOU?
I AIN'T NO CRIMINAL.
CRIMINALS BREAK THE LAW 'CAUSE THEY ENJOYS IT.
I MERELY DOES WHAT I GOTS TO, TO SURVIVE.
I SEEN STUFF THAT ALL THOSE POMPOUS WINDBAGS WHO SAYS WHAT IS RIGHT AND WRONG WOULD NOD AND SMILE AND SAY JUSTICE IS SERVED AND GOD'S WILL BE DONE.
AND SITTING ABOVE IT ALL, THE ROYAL FAMILY, LOOKING DOWN FROM ON HIGH.
YOU THINK THE ROYAL FAMILY DOESN'T CARE?
PROVE THEY DO.
...I CAN'T.
SEEMS TO HAVE STOPPED RAINING. CARE T'SEE THE SIGHTS?

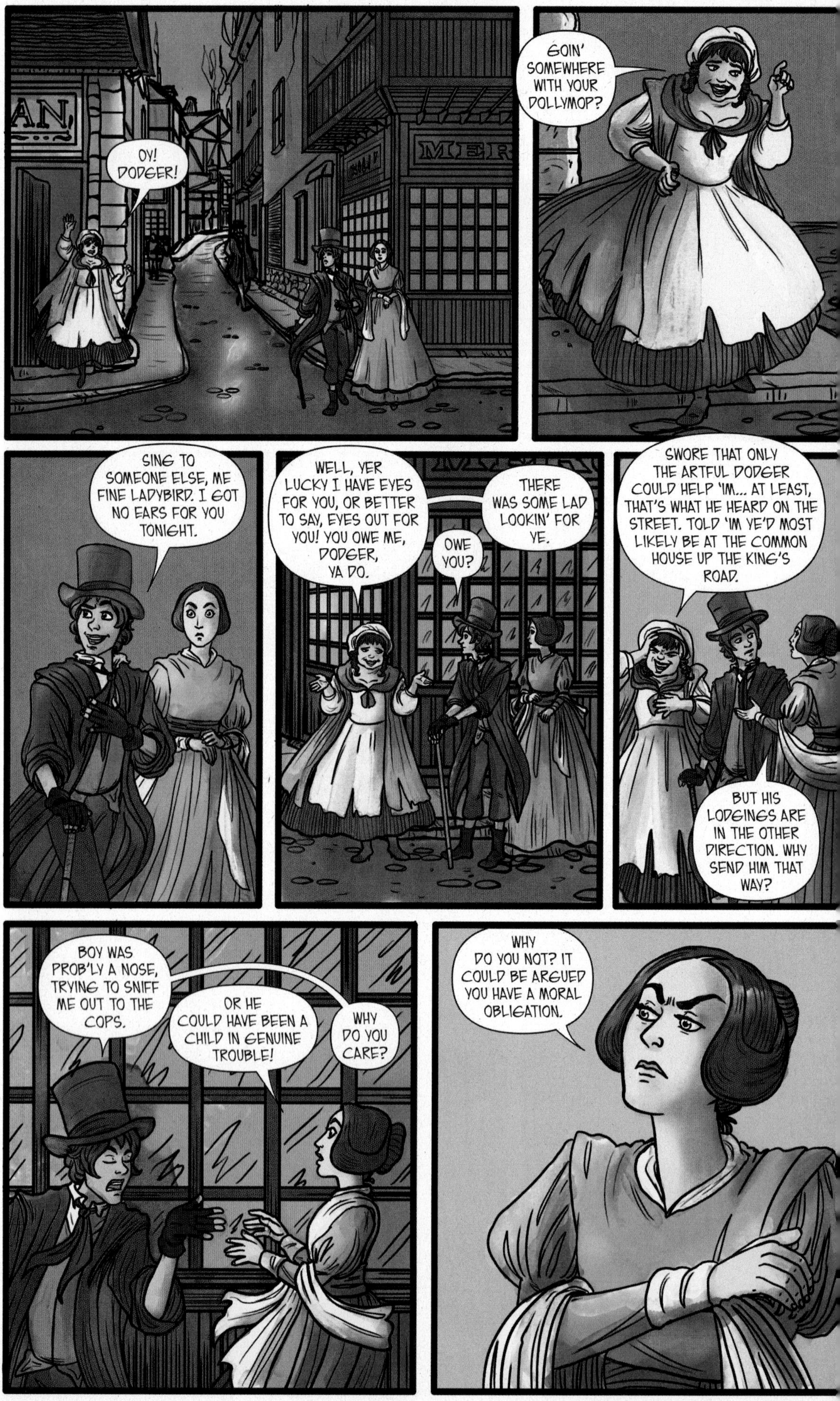
OY! DODGER!
GOIN' SOMEWHERE WITH YOUR DOLLYMOP?
SING TO SOMEONE ELSE, ME FINE LADYBIRD. I GOT NO EARS FOR YOU TONIGHT.
WELL, YER LUCKY I HAVE EYES FOR YOU, OR BETTER TO SAY, EYES OUT FOR YOU! YOU OWE ME, DODGER, YA DO.
OWE YOU?
THERE WAS SOME LAD LOOKIN' FOR YE.
SWORE THAT ONLY THE ARTFUL DODGER COULD HELP 'IM... AT LEAST, THAT'S WHAT HE HEARD ON THE STREET. TOLD 'IM YE'D MOST LIKELY BE AT THE COMMON HOUSE UP THE KING'S ROAD.
BUT HIS LODGINGS ARE IN THE OTHER DIRECTION. WHY SEND HIM THAT WAY?
BOY WAS PROB'LY A NOSE, TRYING TO SNIFF ME OUT TO THE COPS.
OR HE COULD HAVE BEEN A CHILD IN GENUINE TROUBLE!
WHY DO YOU CARE?
WHY DO YOU NOT? IT COULD BE ARGUED YOU HAVE A MORAL OBLIGATION.

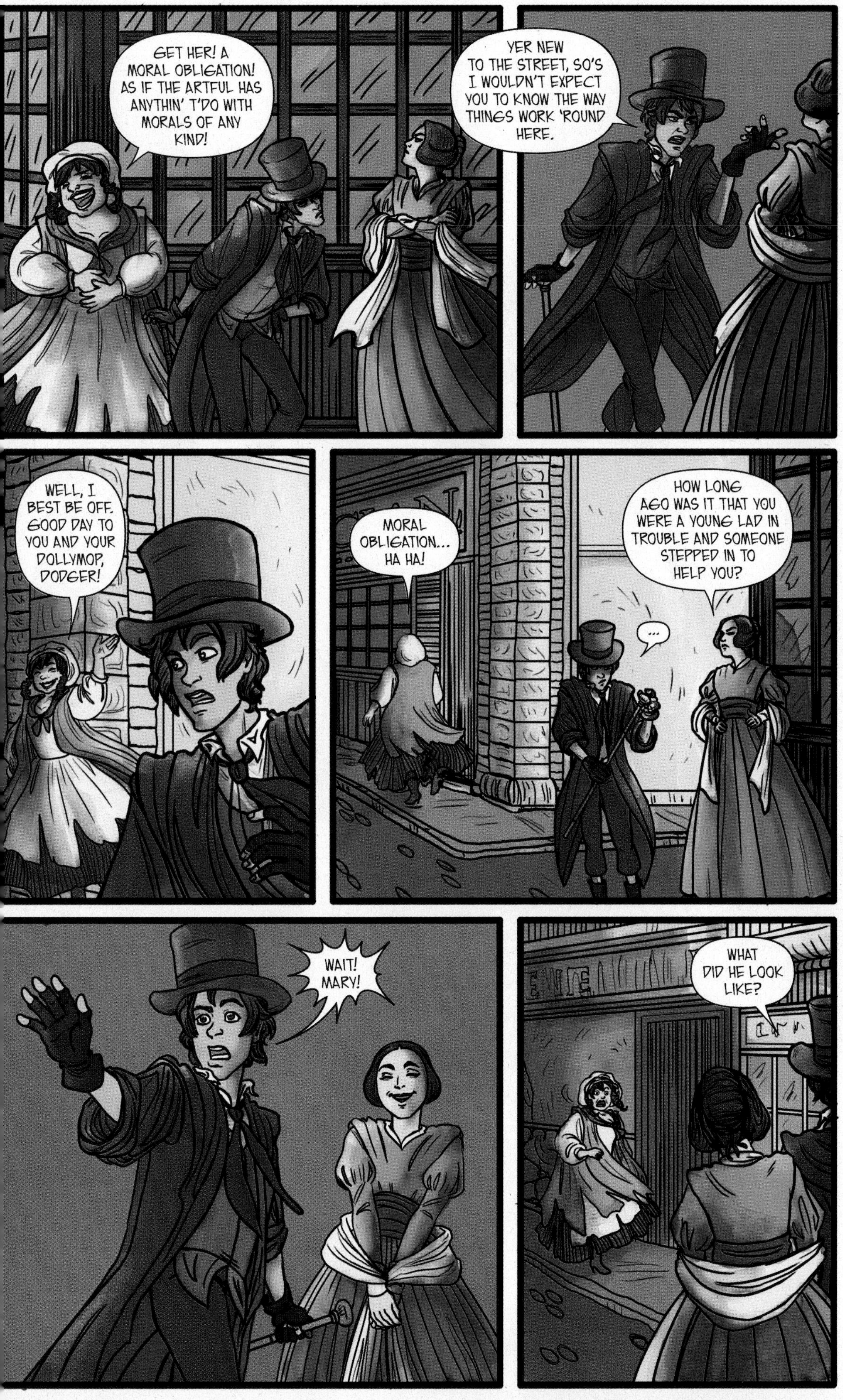
GET HER! A MORAL OBLIGATION! AS IF THE ARTFUL HAS ANYTHIN' T'DO WITH MORALS OF ANY KIND!
YER NEW TO THE STREET, SO'S I WOULDN'T EXPECT YOU TO KNOW THE WAY THINGS WORK 'ROUND HERE.
WELL, I BEST BE OFF. GOOD DAY TO YOU AND YOUR DOLLYMOP, DODGER!
MORAL OBLIGATION... HA HA!
...
HOW LONG AGO WAS IT THAT YOU WERE A YOUNG LAD IN TROUBLE AND SOMEONE STEPPED IN TO HELP YOU?
WAIT! MARY!
WHAT DID HE LOOK LIKE?

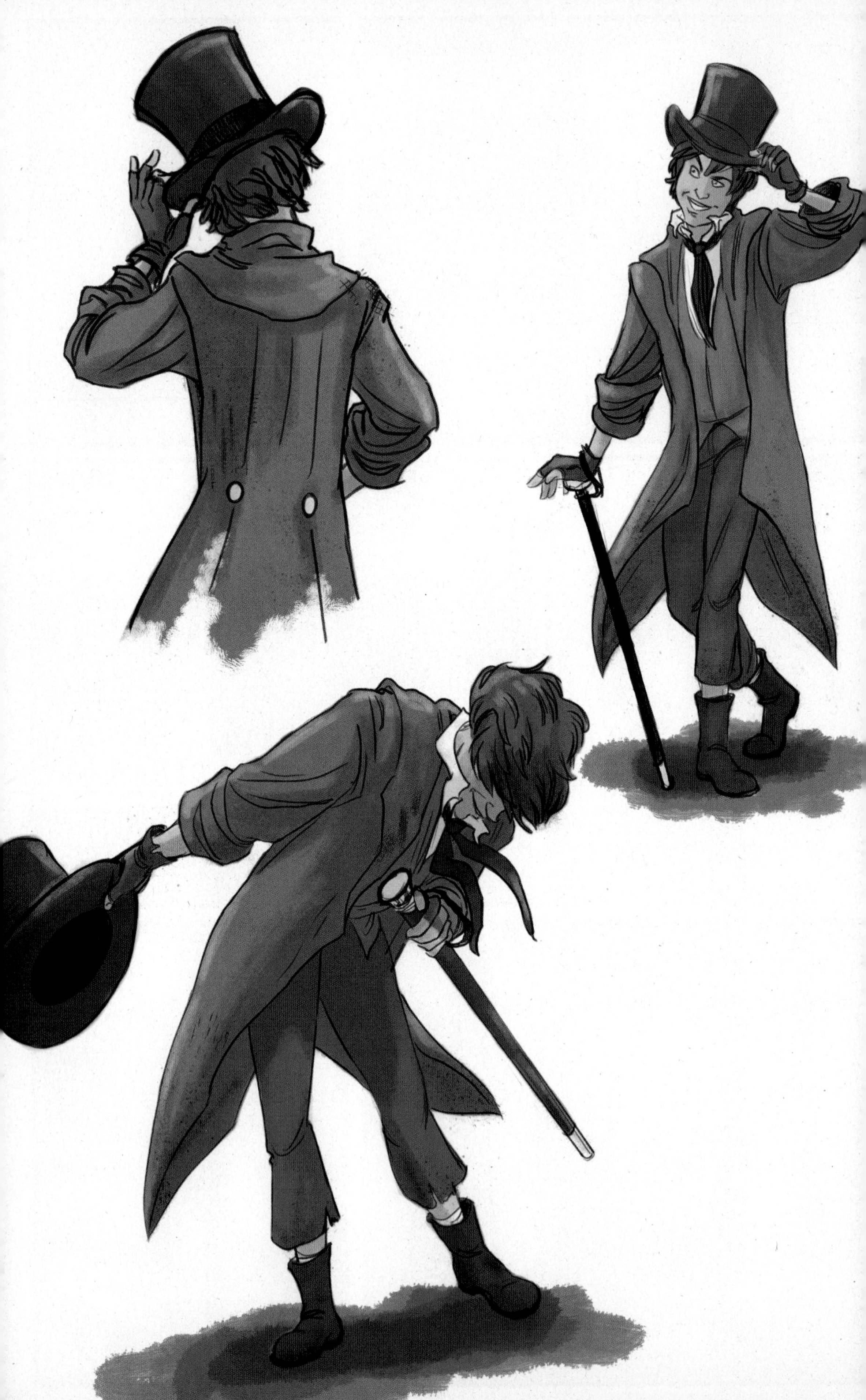

CHAPTER TWO

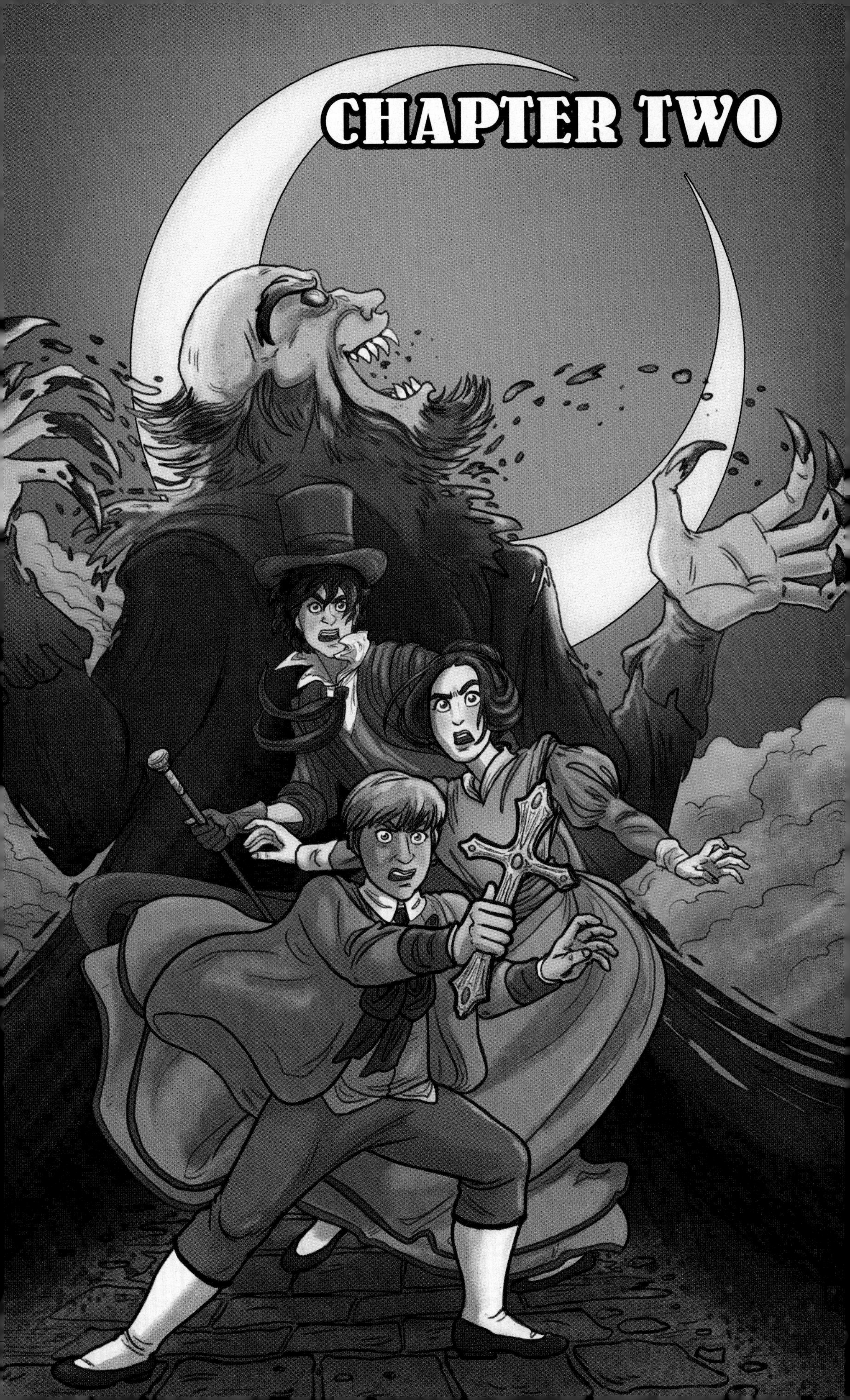

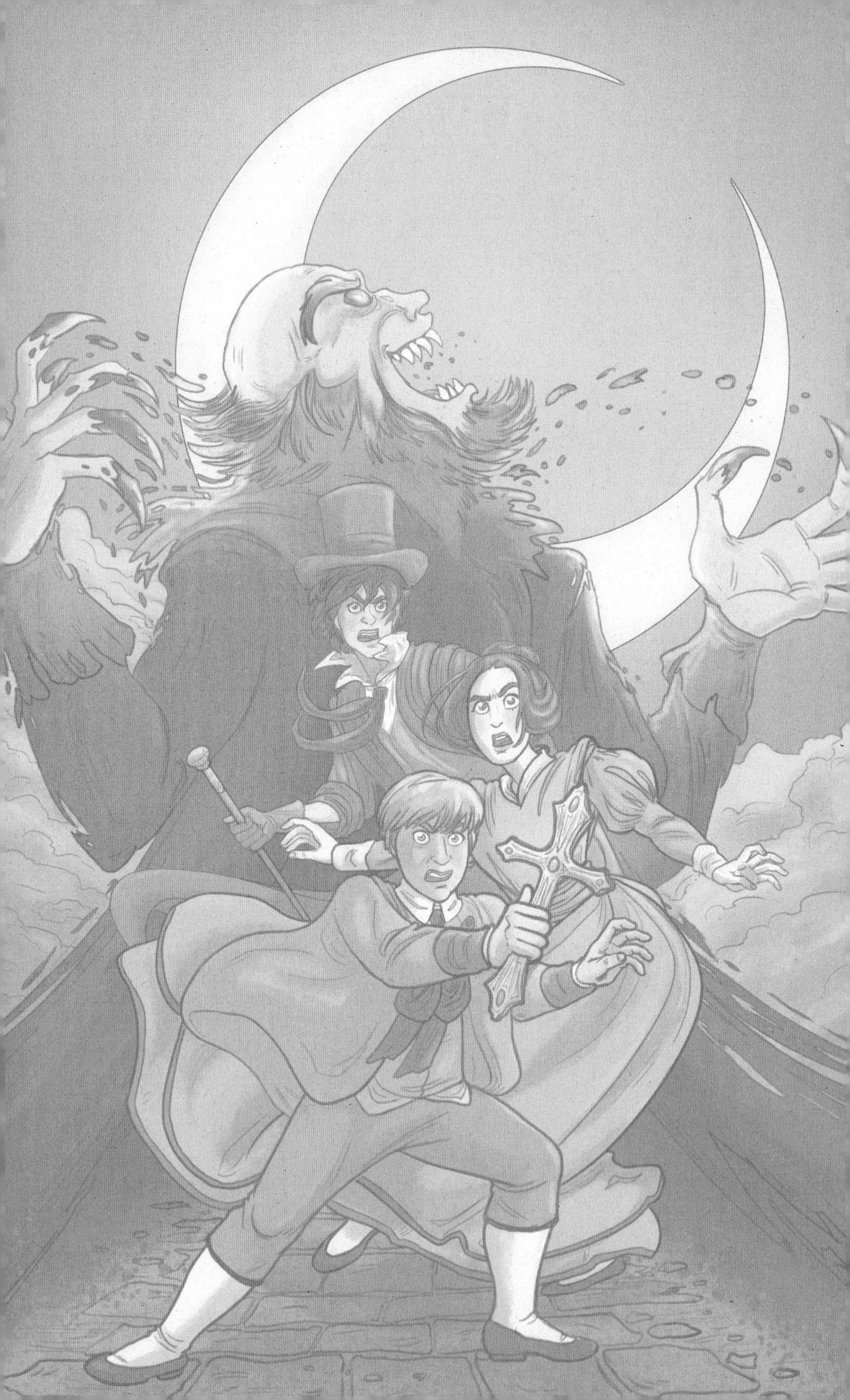

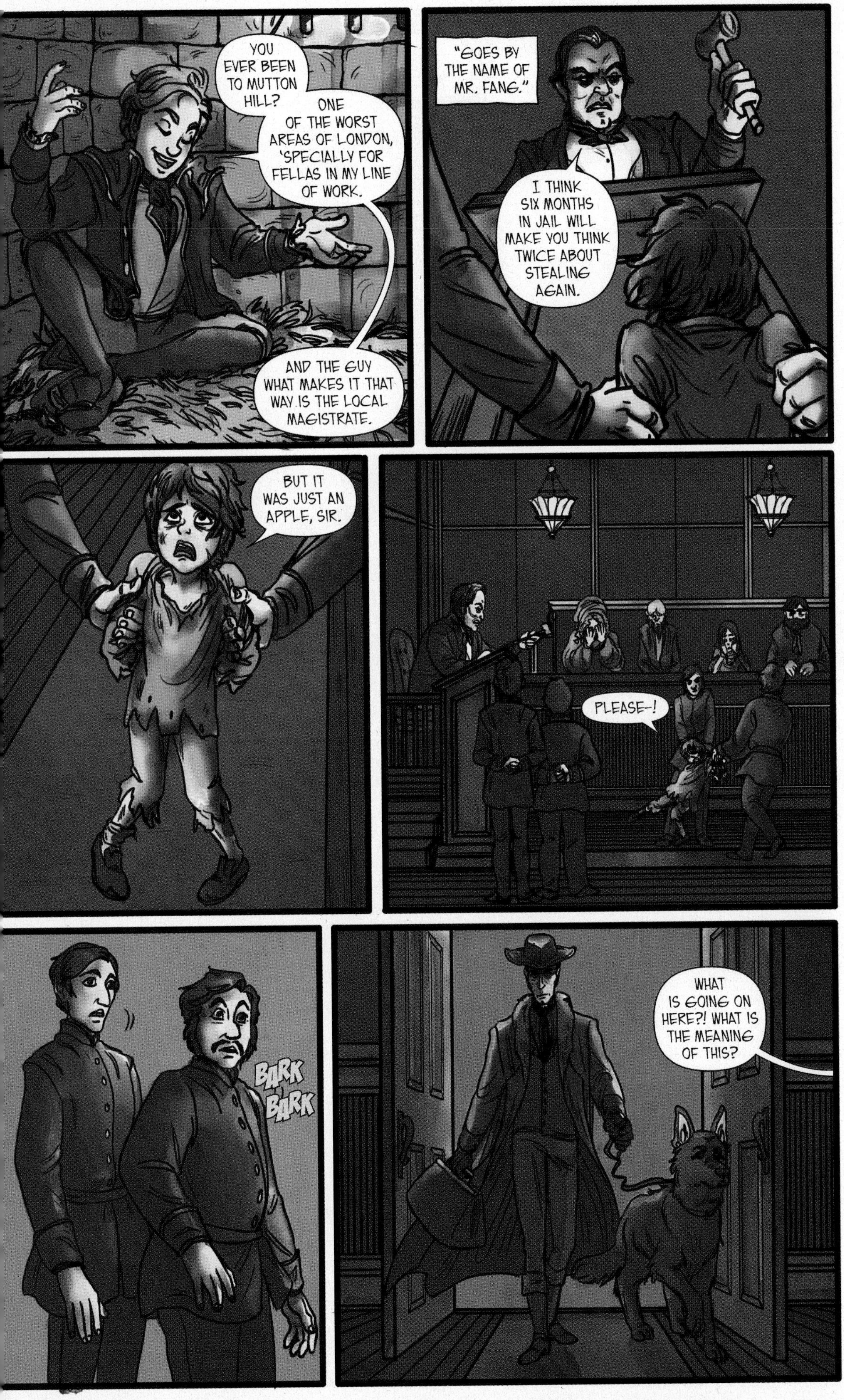
YOU EVER BEEN TO MUTTON HILL?
ONE OF THE WORST AREAS OF LONDON, 'SPECIALLY FOR FELLAS IN MY LINE OF WORK.
AND THE GUY WHAT MAKES IT THAT WAY IS THE LOCAL MAGISTRATE.
"GOES BY THE NAME OF MR. FANG."
I THINK SIX MONTHS IN JAIL WILL MAKE YOU THINK TWICE ABOUT STEALING AGAIN.
BUT IT WAS JUST AN APPLE, SIR.
PLEASE--!
BARK BARK
WHAT IS GOING ON HERE?! WHAT IS THE MEANING OF THIS?

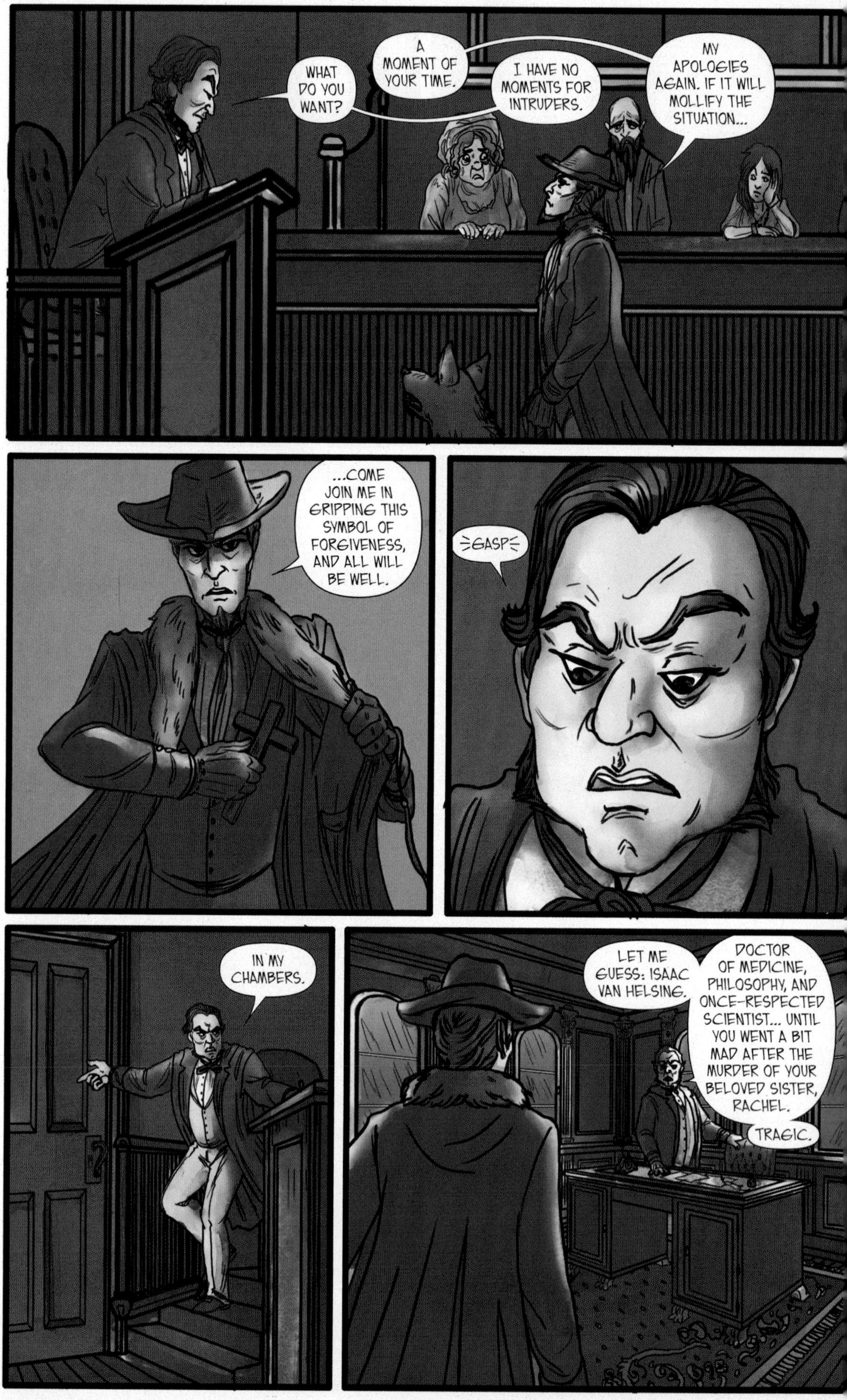
WHAT DO YOU WANT?
A MOMENT OF YOUR TIME.
I HAVE NO MOMENTS FOR INTRUDERS.
MY APOLOGIES AGAIN. IF IT WILL MOLLIFY THE SITUATION...
...COME JOIN ME IN GRIPPING THIS SYMBOL OF FORGIVENESS, AND ALL WILL BE WELL.
GASP
IN MY CHAMBERS.
LET ME GUESS: ISAAC VAN HELSING.
DOCTOR OF MEDICINE, PHILOSOPHY, AND ONCE-RESPECTED SCIENTIST... UNTIL YOU WENT A BIT MAD AFTER THE MURDER OF YOUR BELOVED SISTER, RACHEL.
TRAGIC.

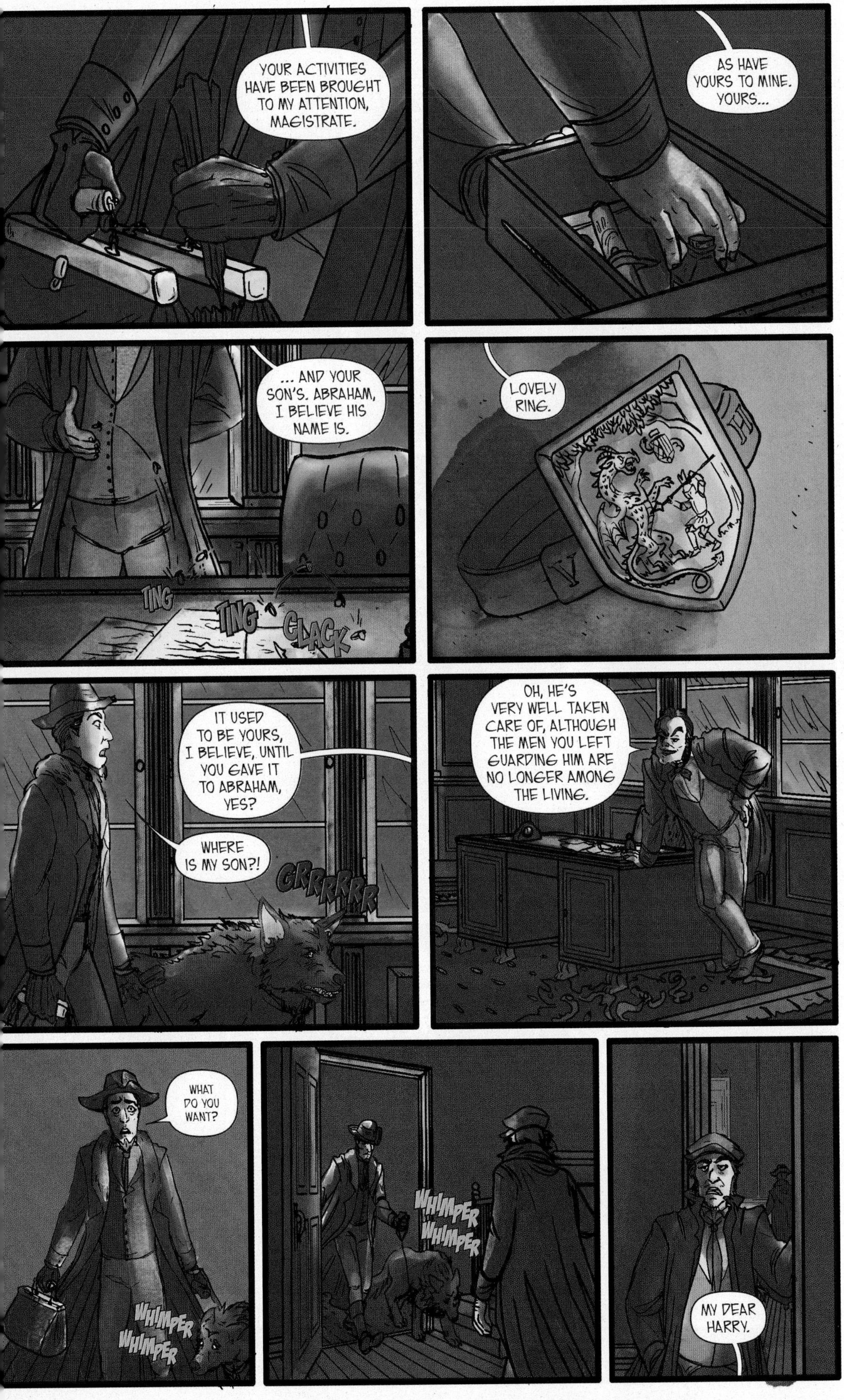
YOUR ACTIVITIES HAVE BEEN BROUGHT TO MY ATTENTION, MAGISTRATE.
AS HAVE YOURS TO MINE. YOURS...
... AND YOUR SON'S. ABRAHAM, I BELIEVE HIS NAME IS.
TING
TING
CLACK
LOVELY RING.
IT USED TO BE YOURS, I BELIEVE, UNTIL YOU GAVE IT TO ABRAHAM, YES?
WHERE IS MY SON?!
GRRRRRR
OH, HE'S VERY WELL TAKEN CARE OF, ALTHOUGH THE MEN YOU LEFT GUARDING HIM ARE NO LONGER AMONG THE LIVING.
WHAT DO YOU WANT?
WHIMPER
WHIMPER
WHIMPER
WHIMPER
MY DEAR HARRY.

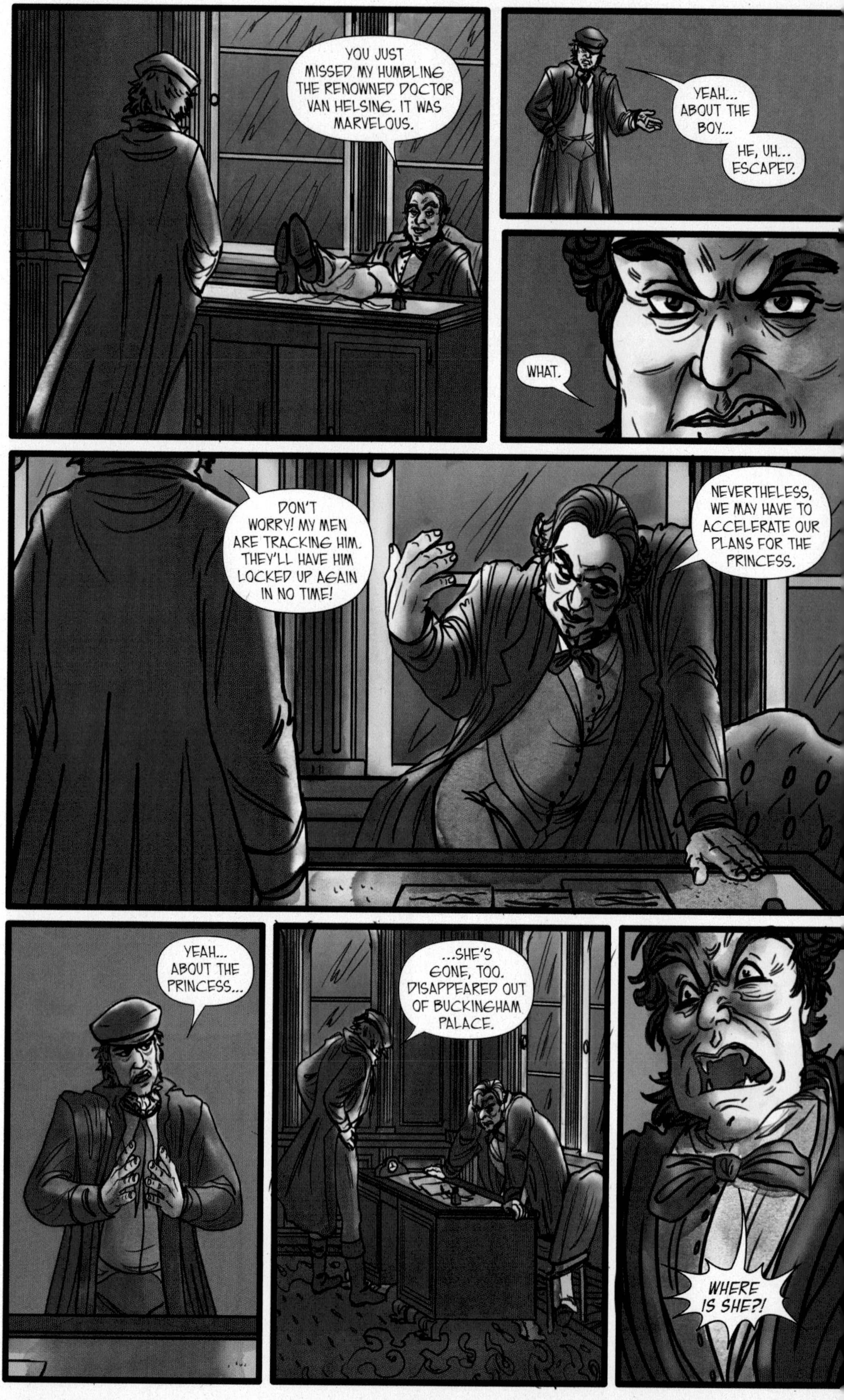
YOU JUST MISSED MY HUMBLING THE RENOWNED DOCTOR VAN HELSING. IT WAS MARVELOUS.
YEAH... ABOUT THE BOY...
HE, UH... ESCAPED.
WHAT.
DON'T WORRY! MY MEN ARE TRACKING HIM. THEY'LL HAVE HIM LOCKED UP AGAIN IN NO TIME!
NEVERTHELESS, WE MAY HAVE TO ACCELERATE OUR PLANS FOR THE PRINCESS.
YEAH... ABOUT THE PRINCESS...
...SHE'S GONE, TOO. DISAPPEARED OUT OF BUCKINGHAM PALACE.
WHERE IS SHE?!

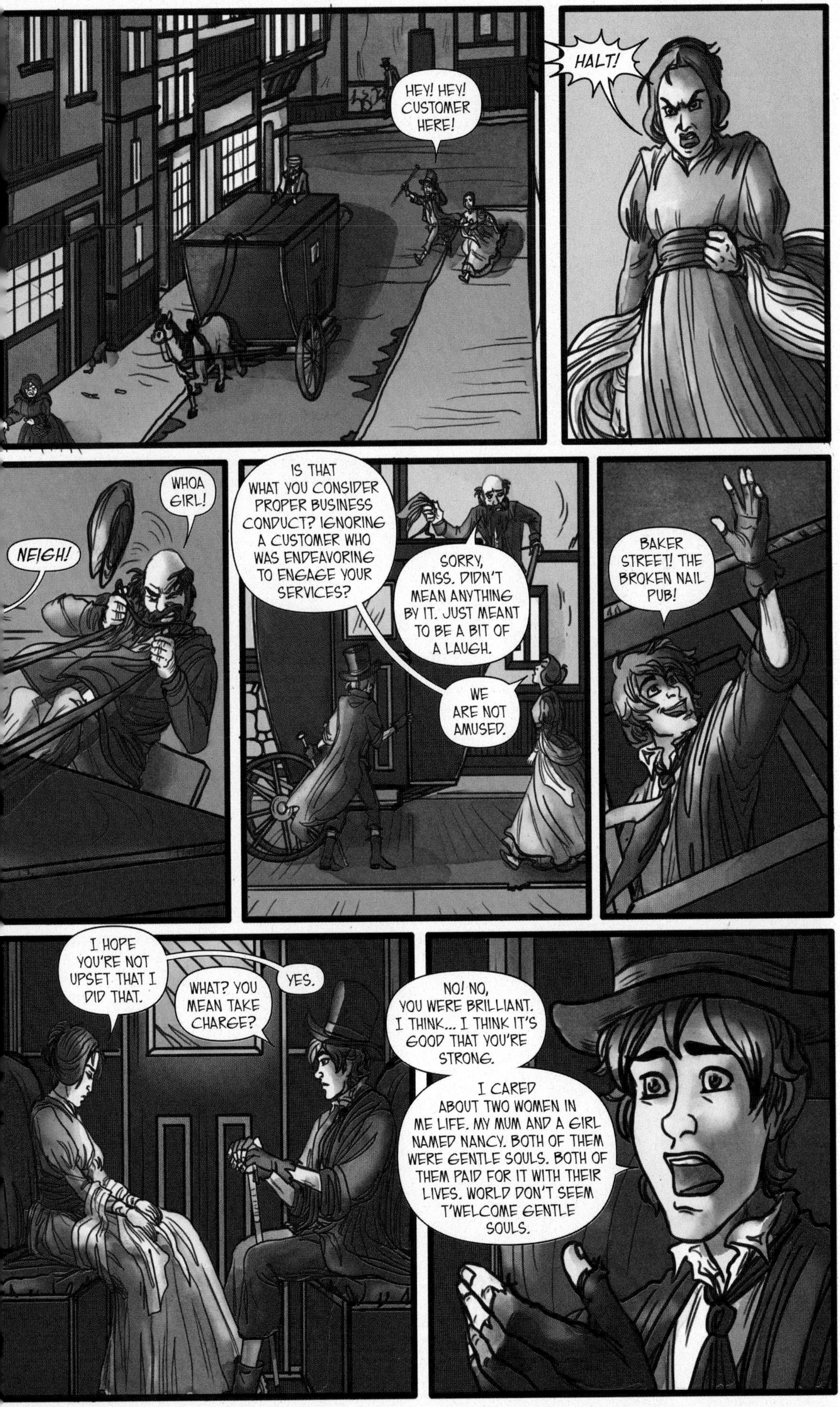
HEY! HEY! CUSTOMER HERE!
HALT!
WHOA GIRL!
NEIGH!
IS THAT WHAT YOU CONSIDER PROPER BUSINESS CONDUCT? IGNORING A CUSTOMER WHO WAS ENDEAVORING TO ENGAGE YOUR SERVICES?
SORRY, MISS. DIDN'T MEAN ANYTHING BY IT. JUST MEANT TO BE A BIT OF A LAUGH.
WE ARE NOT AMUSED.
BAKER STREET! THE BROKEN NAIL PUB!
I HOPE YOU'RE NOT UPSET THAT I DID THAT.
WHAT? YOU MEAN TAKE CHARGE?
YES.
NO! NO, YOU WERE BRILLIANT. I THINK... I THINK IT'S GOOD THAT YOU'RE STRONG.
I CARED ABOUT TWO WOMEN IN ME LIFE. MY MUM AND A GIRL NAMED NANCY. BOTH OF THEM WERE GENTLE SOULS. BOTH OF THEM PAID FOR IT WITH THEIR LIVES. WORLD DON'T SEEM T'WELCOME GENTLE SOULS.

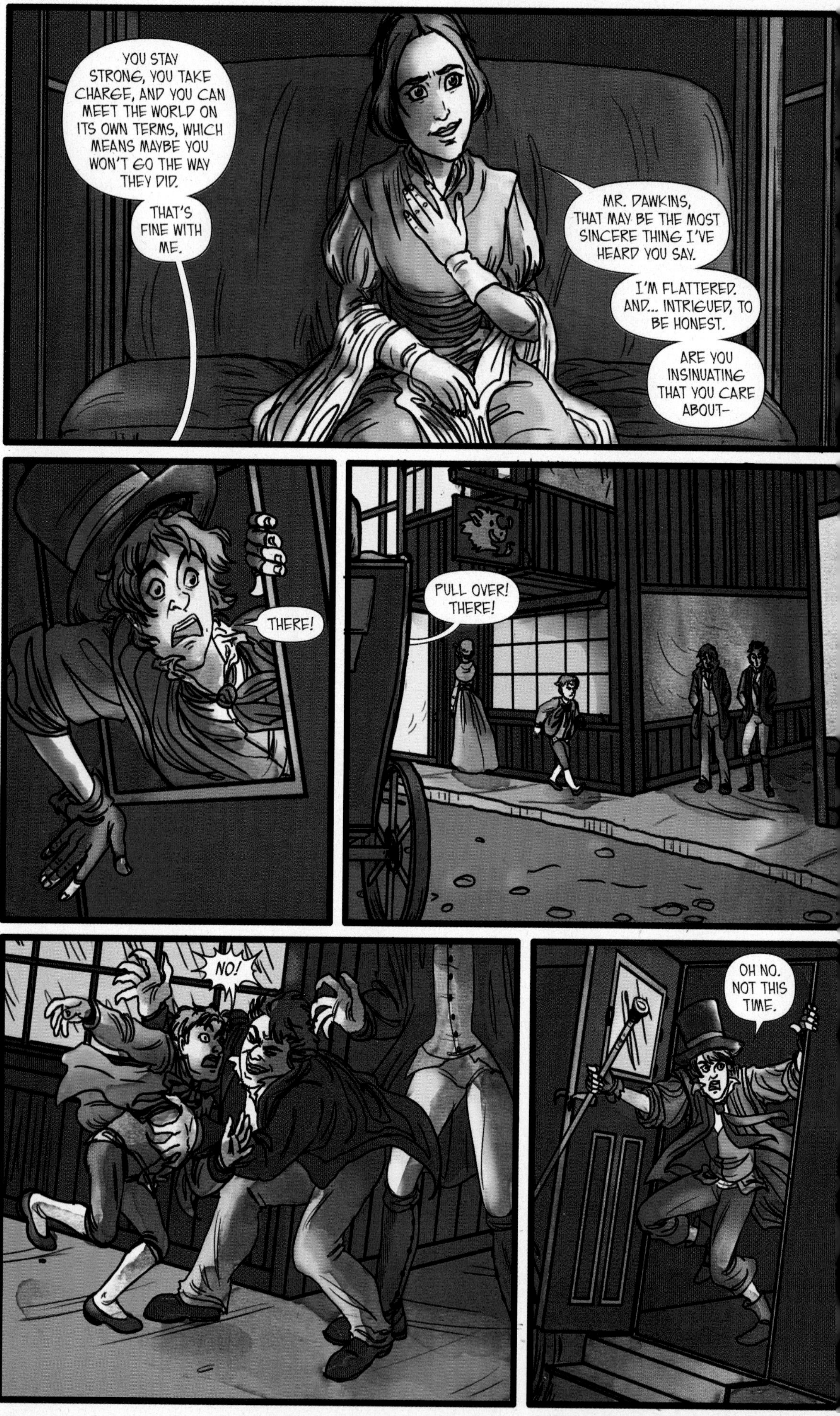
YOU STAY STRONG, YOU TAKE CHARGE, AND YOU CAN MEET THE WORLD ON ITS OWN TERMS, WHICH MEANS MAYBE YOU WON'T GO THE WAY THEY DID.
THAT'S FINE WITH ME.
MR. DAWKINS, THAT MAY BE THE MOST SINCERE THING I'VE HEARD YOU SAY.
I'M FLATTERED. AND... INTRIGUED, TO BE HONEST.
ARE YOU INSINUATING THAT YOU CARE ABOUT-
THERE!
PULL OVER! THERE!
NO!
OH NO. NOT THIS TIME.

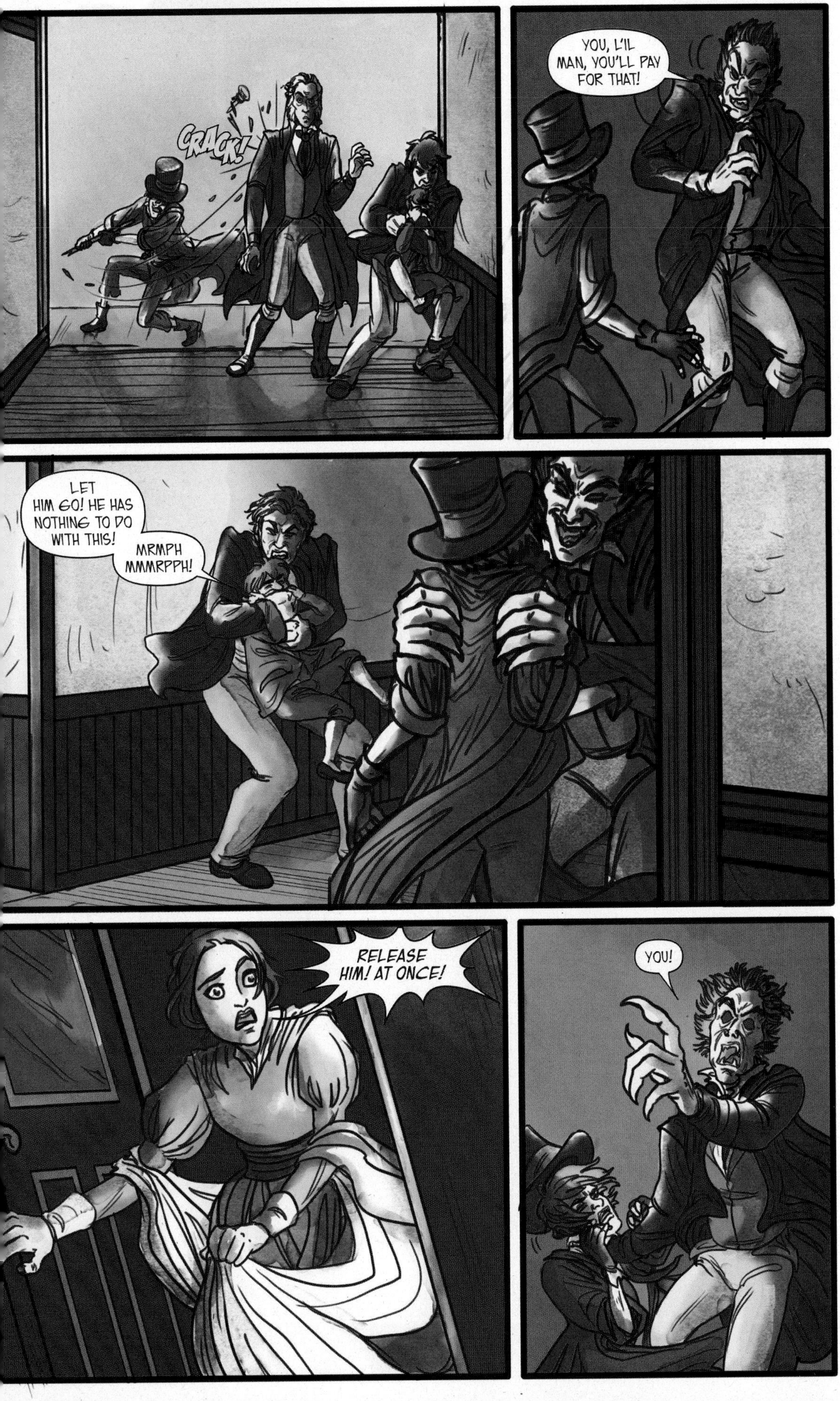
CRACK!
YOU, L'IL MAN, YOU'LL PAY FOR THAT!
LET HIM GO! HE HAS NOTHING TO DO WITH THIS!
MRMPH MMMRPPH!
RELEASE HIM! AT ONCE!
YOU!

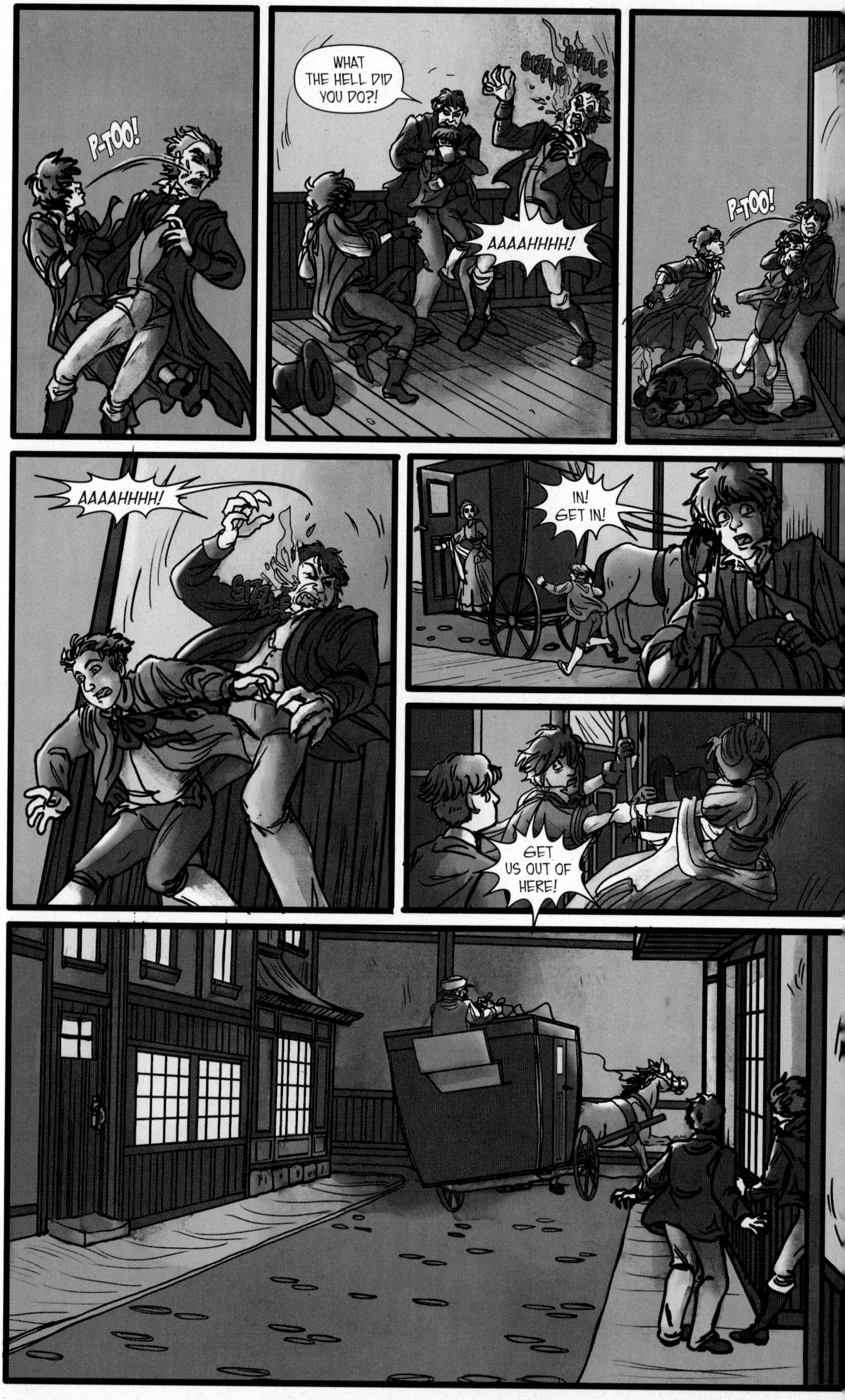
P-TOO!
WHAT THE HELL DID YOU DO?!
SIZZLE SIZZLE
AAAAHHHH!
P-TOO!
AAAAHHHH!
SIZZLE
IN! GET IN!
GET US OUT OF HERE!

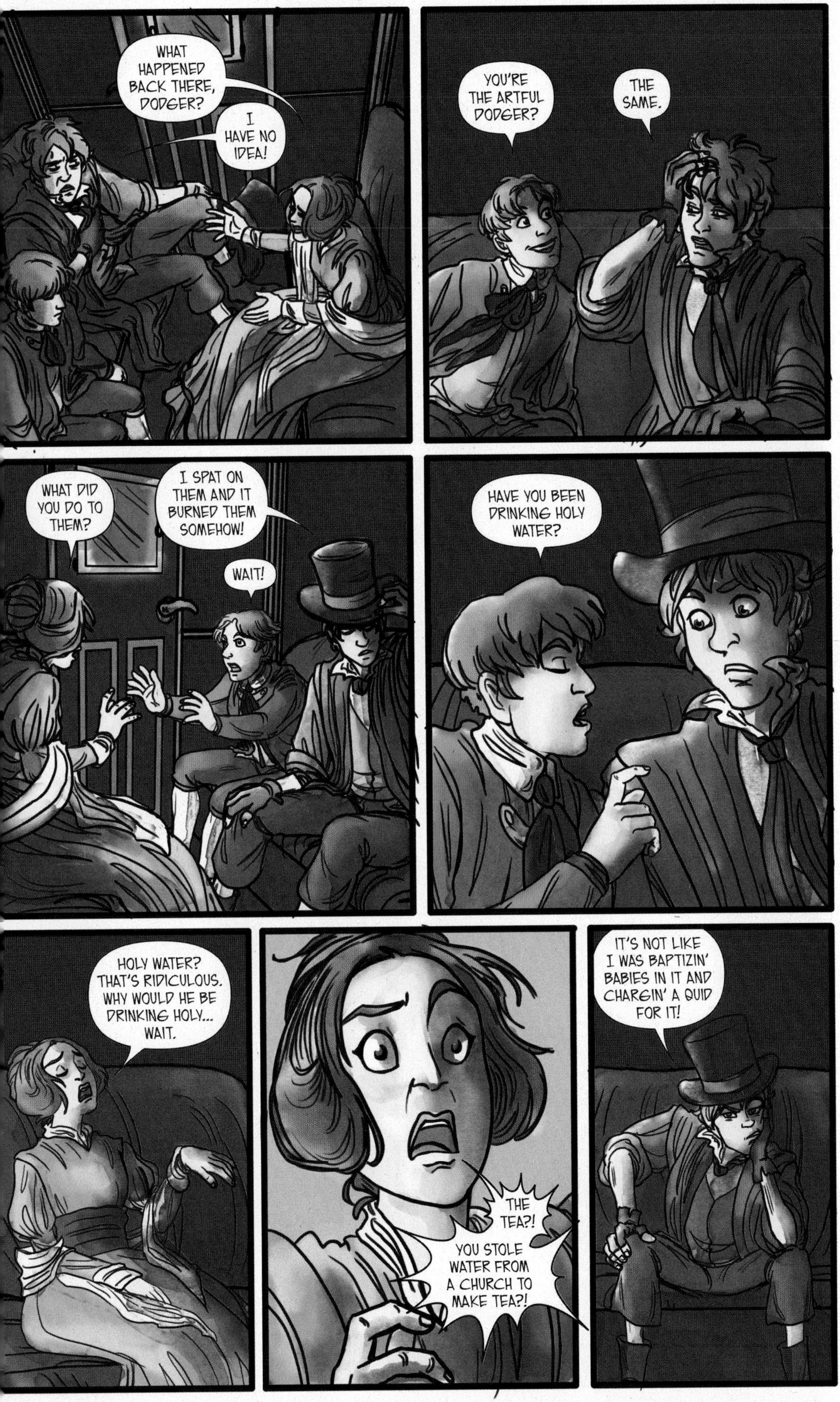
WHAT HAPPENED BACK THERE, DODGER?
I HAVE NO IDEA!
YOU'RE THE ARTFUL DODGER?
THE SAME.
WHAT DID YOU DO TO THEM?
I SPAT ON THEM AND IT BURNED THEM SOMEHOW!
WAIT!
HAVE YOU BEEN DRINKING HOLY WATER?
HOLY WATER? THAT'S RIDICULOUS. WHY WOULD HE BE DRINKING HOLY... WAIT.
THE TEA?!
YOU STOLE WATER FROM A CHURCH TO MAKE TEA?!
IT'S NOT LIKE I WAS BAPTIZIN' BABIES IN IT AND CHARGIN' A QUID FOR IT!

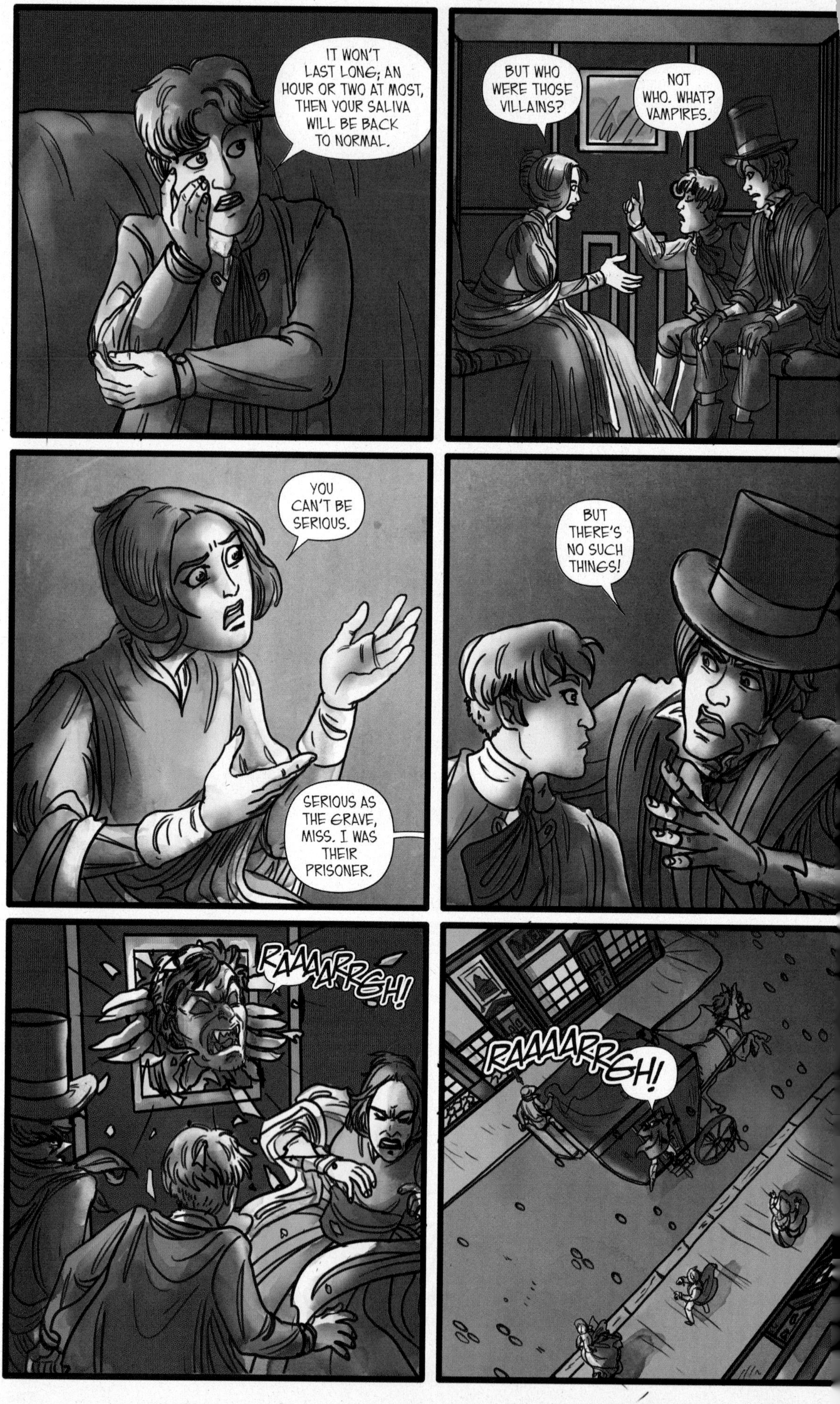
IT WON'T LAST LONG; AN HOUR OR TWO AT MOST, THEN YOUR SALIVA WILL BE BACK TO NORMAL.
BUT WHO WERE THOSE VILLAINS?
NOT WHO. WHAT? VAMPIRES.
YOU CAN'T BE SERIOUS.
SERIOUS AS THE GRAVE, MISS. I WAS THEIR PRISONER.
BUT THERE'S NO SUCH THINGS!
RAAAARRGH!
RAAAARRGH!

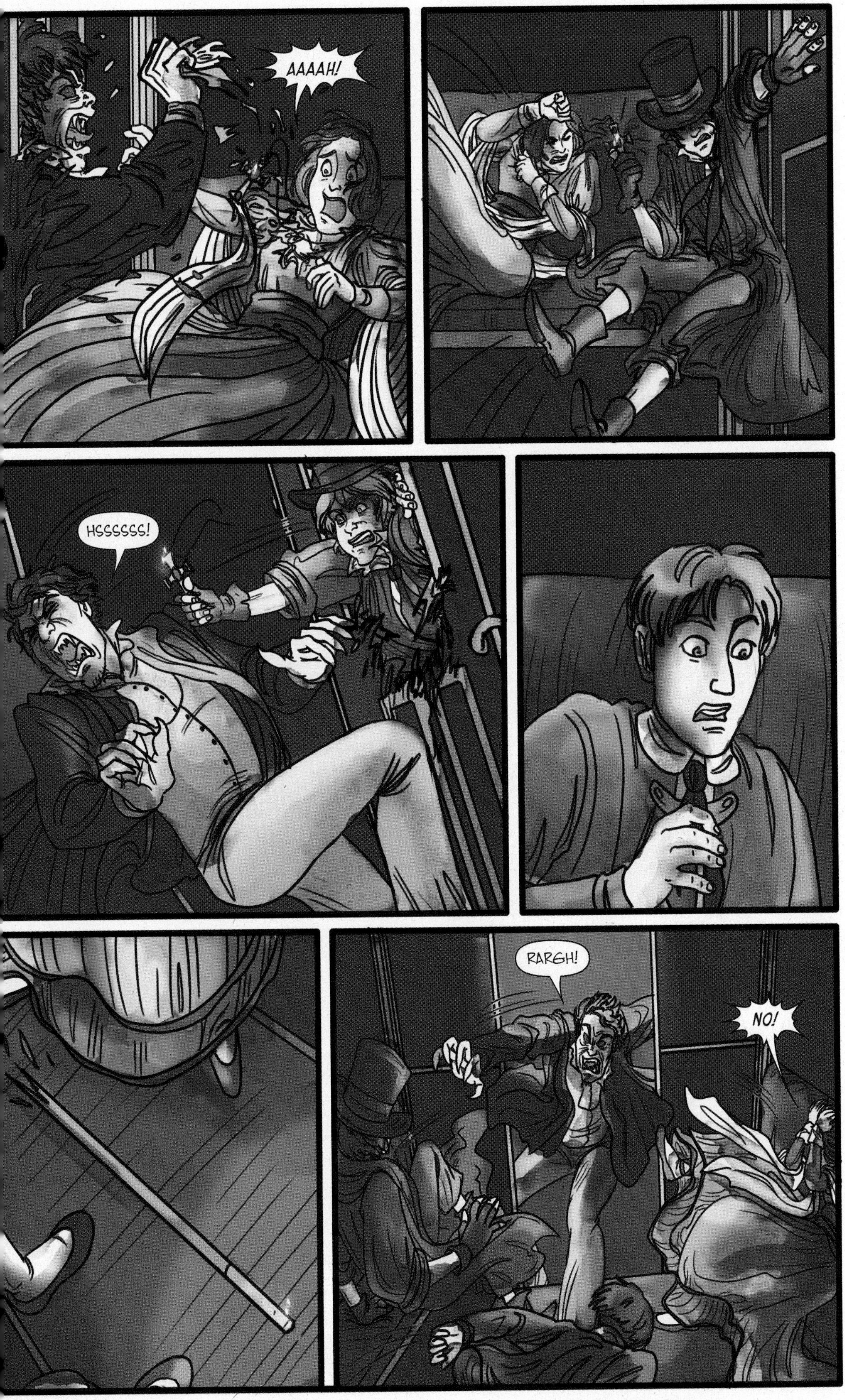
AAAAH!
HSSSSSS!
RARGH!
NO!

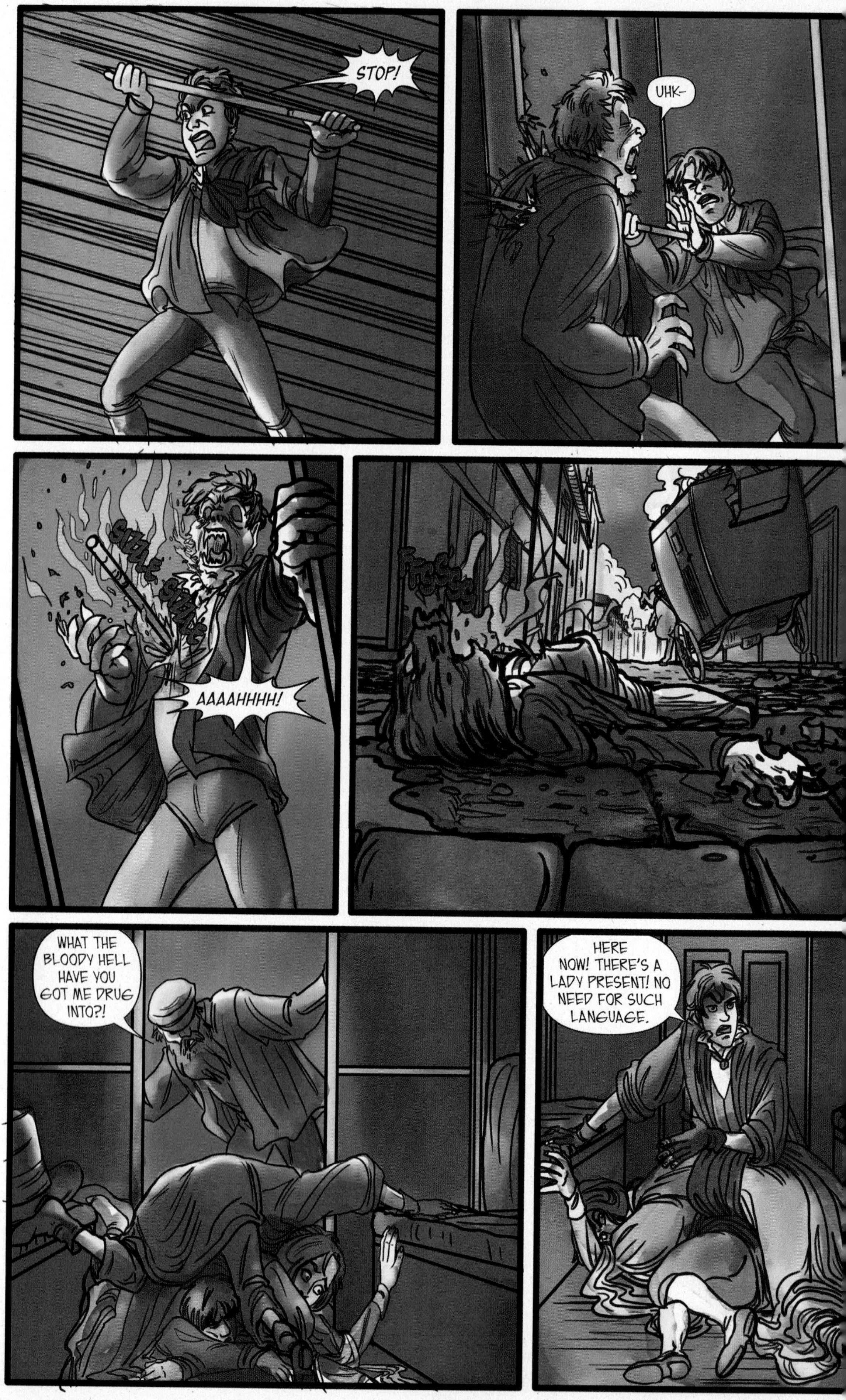
STOP!
UHK-
SIZZLE SIZZLE
AAAAHHHH!
WHAT THE BLOODY HELL HAVE YOU GOT ME DRUG INTO?!
HERE NOW! THERE'S A LADY PRESENT! NO NEED FOR SUCH LANGUAGE.

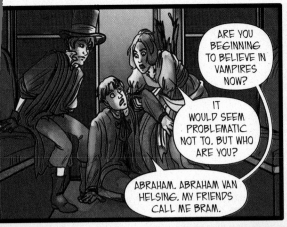

ARE YOU BEGINNING TO BELIEVE IN VAMPIRES NOW?

IT WOULD SEEM PROBLEMATIC NOT TO. BUT WHO ARE YOU?

ABRAHAM. ABRAHAM VAN HELSING. MY FRIENDS CALL ME BRAM.

LOOK, YOU LOT! EITHER GIVE ME A DESTINATION SO I CAN BE QUIT OF YOU, OR GET THE HELL OUT OF MY CAB!

WE NEED TO GO TO THE POLICE, OR THE MAGISTRATES...

NO. WE CAN'T TRUST ANYONE IN AUTHORITY. THAT'S WHAT MY FATHER SAID.

LET'S GO TO YOUR FATHER, THEN.

I'VE NO IDEA WHERE HE IS.

ALL RIGHT, ALL RIGHT... I KNOW A PLACE!

I WOUND UP THERE ONCE, YEARS AGO.

THE WOMEN TOOK CARE OF ME.

THE WOMEN?

NUNS. IT'S AN ABBEY. IT'LL BE PERFECT!

WE NEED TO GO TO PURFLEET.

IN ESSEX?

YEAH.

ARE YOU SURE IT'LL BE SAFE?

ABSOLUTELY.

IF THERE'S ONE PLACE THAT WILL HAVE NOTHIN' TO DO WITH VAMPIRES OR ANY MATTER OF MONSTERS, IT'S CARFAX ABBEY.

NOT AS SAFE AS YE'D THINK, LAD.

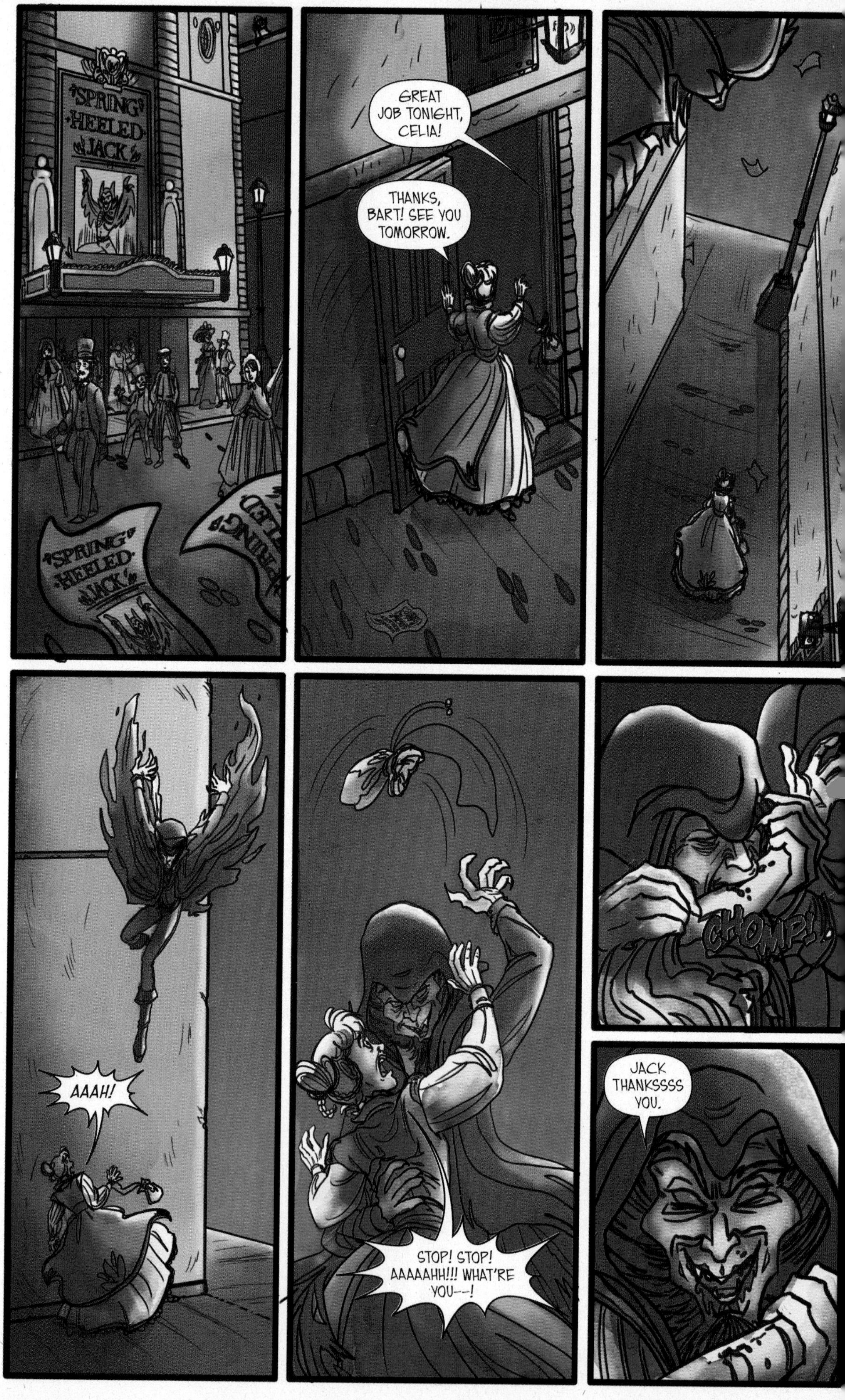
SPRING HEELED JACK
GREAT JOB TONIGHT, CELIA!
THANKS, BART! SEE YOU TOMORROW.
AAAH!
STOP! STOP! AAAAAHH!!! WHAT'RE YOU--!
CHOMP!
JACK THANKSSSS YOU.

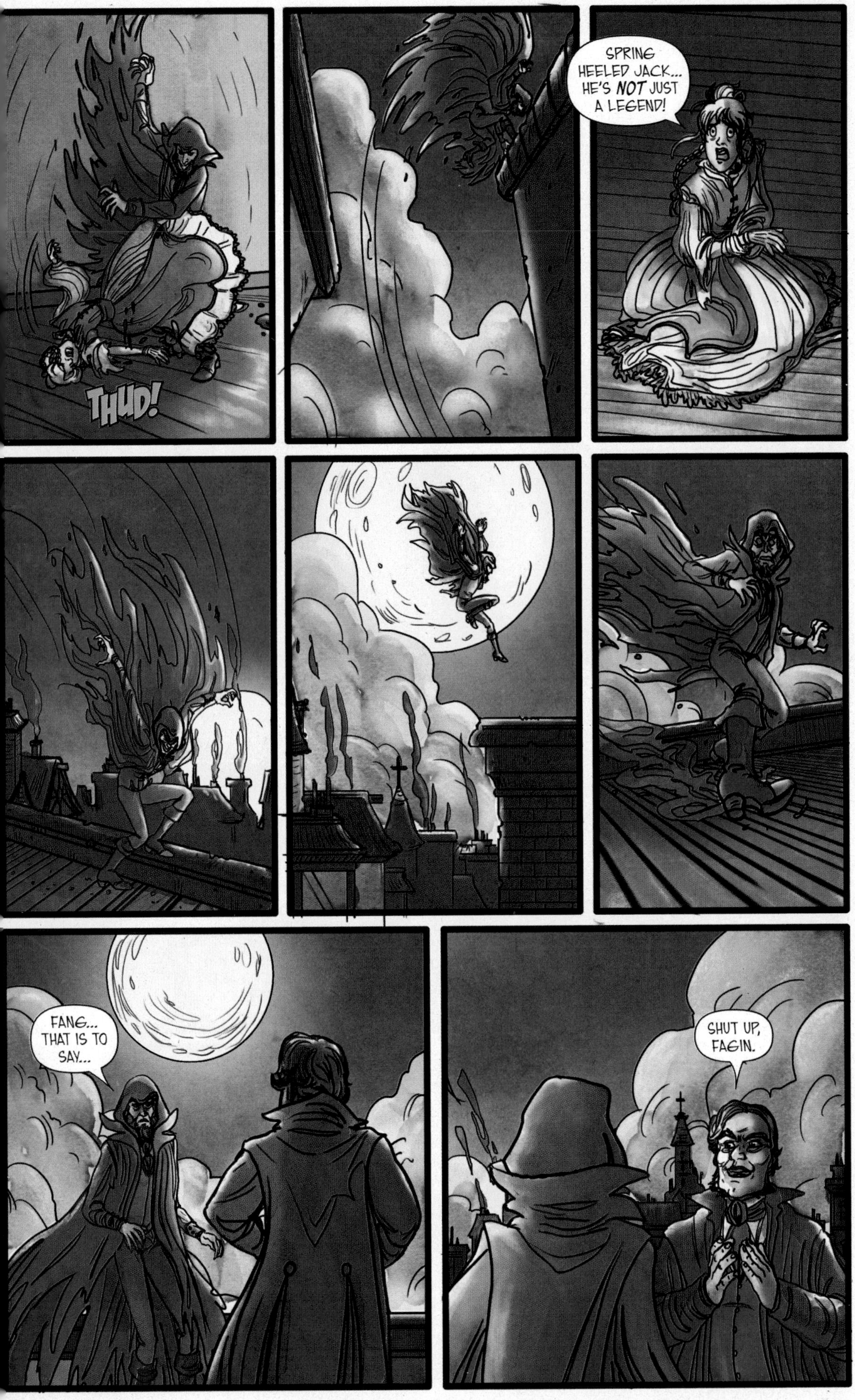
THUD!
SPRING HEELED JACK... HE'S NOT JUST A LEGEND!
FANG... THAT IS TO SAY...
SHUT UP, FAGIN.

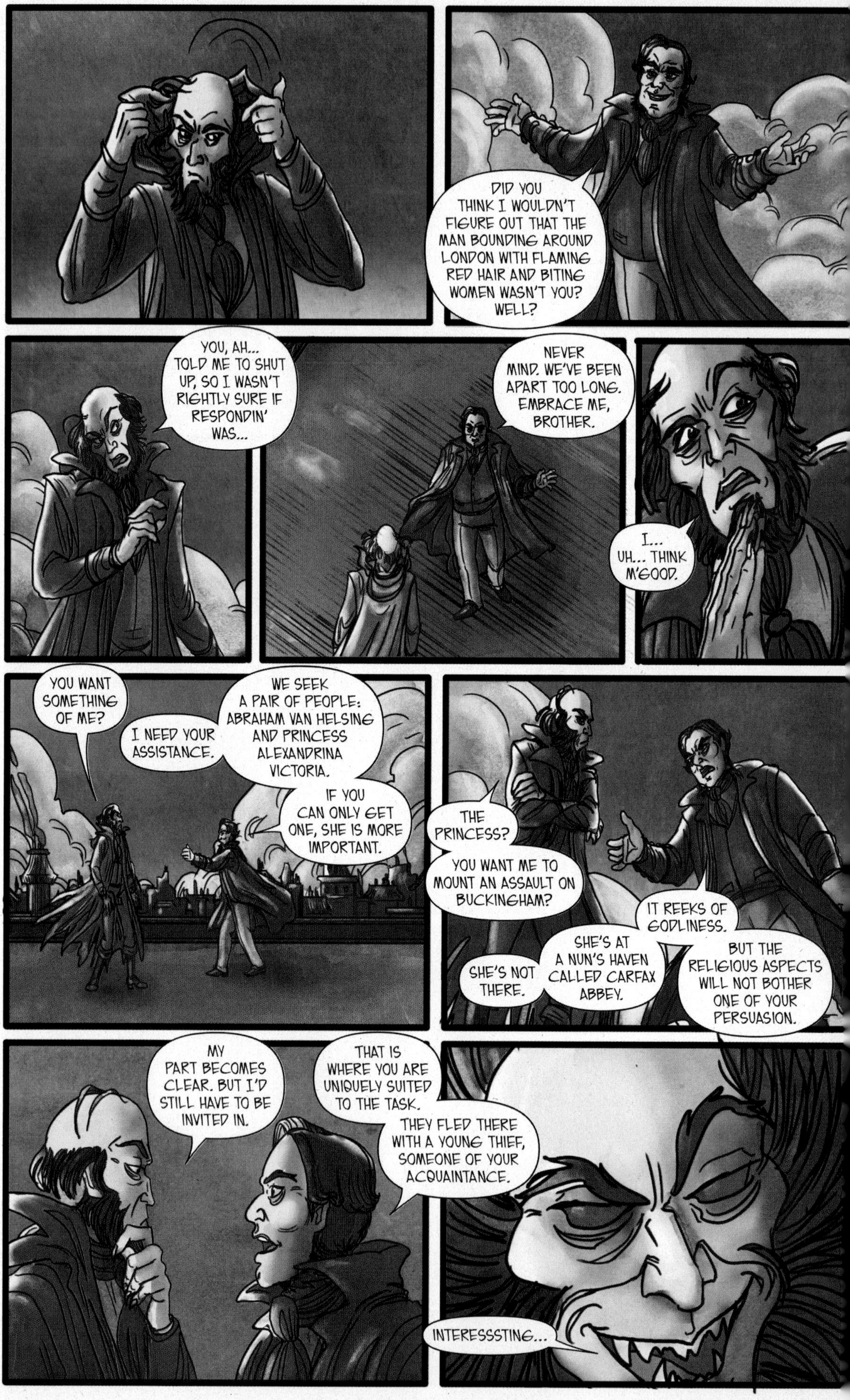
DID YOU THINK I WOULDN'T FIGURE OUT THAT THE MAN BOUNDING AROUND LONDON WITH FLAMING RED HAIR AND BITING WOMEN WASN'T YOU? WELL?
YOU, AH... TOLD ME TO SHUT UP, SO I WASN'T RIGHTLY SURE IF RESPONDIN' WAS...
NEVER MIND. WE'VE BEEN APART TOO LONG. EMBRACE ME, BROTHER.
I... UH... THINK M'GOOD.
YOU WANT SOMETHING OF ME?
I NEED YOUR ASSISTANCE.
WE SEEK A PAIR OF PEOPLE: ABRAHAM VAN HELSING AND PRINCESS ALEXANDRINA VICTORIA.
IF YOU CAN ONLY GET ONE, SHE IS MORE IMPORTANT.
THE PRINCESS?
YOU WANT ME TO MOUNT AN ASSAULT ON BUCKINGHAM?
IT REEKS OF GODLINESS.
SHE'S NOT THERE.
SHE'S AT A NUN'S HAVEN CALLED CARFAX ABBEY.
BUT THE RELIGIOUS ASPECTS WILL NOT BOTHER ONE OF YOUR PERSUASION.
MY PART BECOMES CLEAR. BUT I'D STILL HAVE TO BE INVITED IN.
THAT IS WHERE YOU ARE UNIQUELY SUITED TO THE TASK.
THEY FLED THERE WITH A YOUNG THIEF, SOMEONE OF YOUR ACQUAINTANCE.
INTERESSSTING...

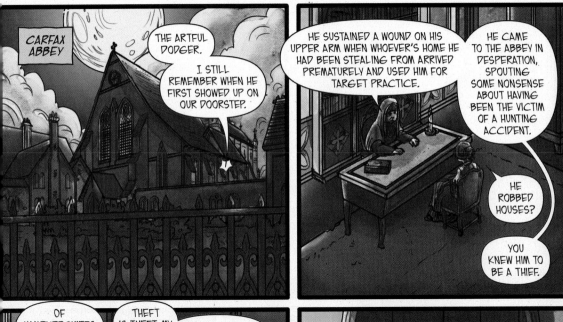

CARFAX ABBEY

THE ARTFUL DODGER.

I STILL REMEMBER WHEN HE FIRST SHOWED UP ON OUR DOORSTEP.

HE SUSTAINED A WOUND ON HIS UPPER ARM WHEN WHOEVER'S HOME HE HAD BEEN STEALING FROM ARRIVED PREMATURELY AND USED HIM FOR TARGET PRACTICE.

HE CAME TO THE ABBEY IN DESPERATION, SPOUTING SOME NONSENSE ABOUT HAVING BEEN THE VICTIM OF A HUNTING ACCIDENT.

HE ROBBED HOUSES?

YOU KNEW HIM TO BE A THIEF.

OF HANDKERCHIEFS AND SUCH. A PICKPOCKET...

THEFT IS THEFT, MY DEAR. UNACCEPTABLE BEHAVIOR KNOWS NO DEGREES.

NOW HE SHOWS UP HERE WITH A YOUNG BOY SPOUTING MONSTER TALES AND YOU...

YOU DO NOT BELIEVE ME?

THAT YOU'RE THE PRINCESS ALEXANDRINA VICTORIA? WOULD YOU?

DO YOU KNOW WHAT THIS IS?

THE ROYAL SEAL OF ENGLAND.

I NEED PAPER AND PEN, AND WAX TO SEAL THE LETTER WITH.

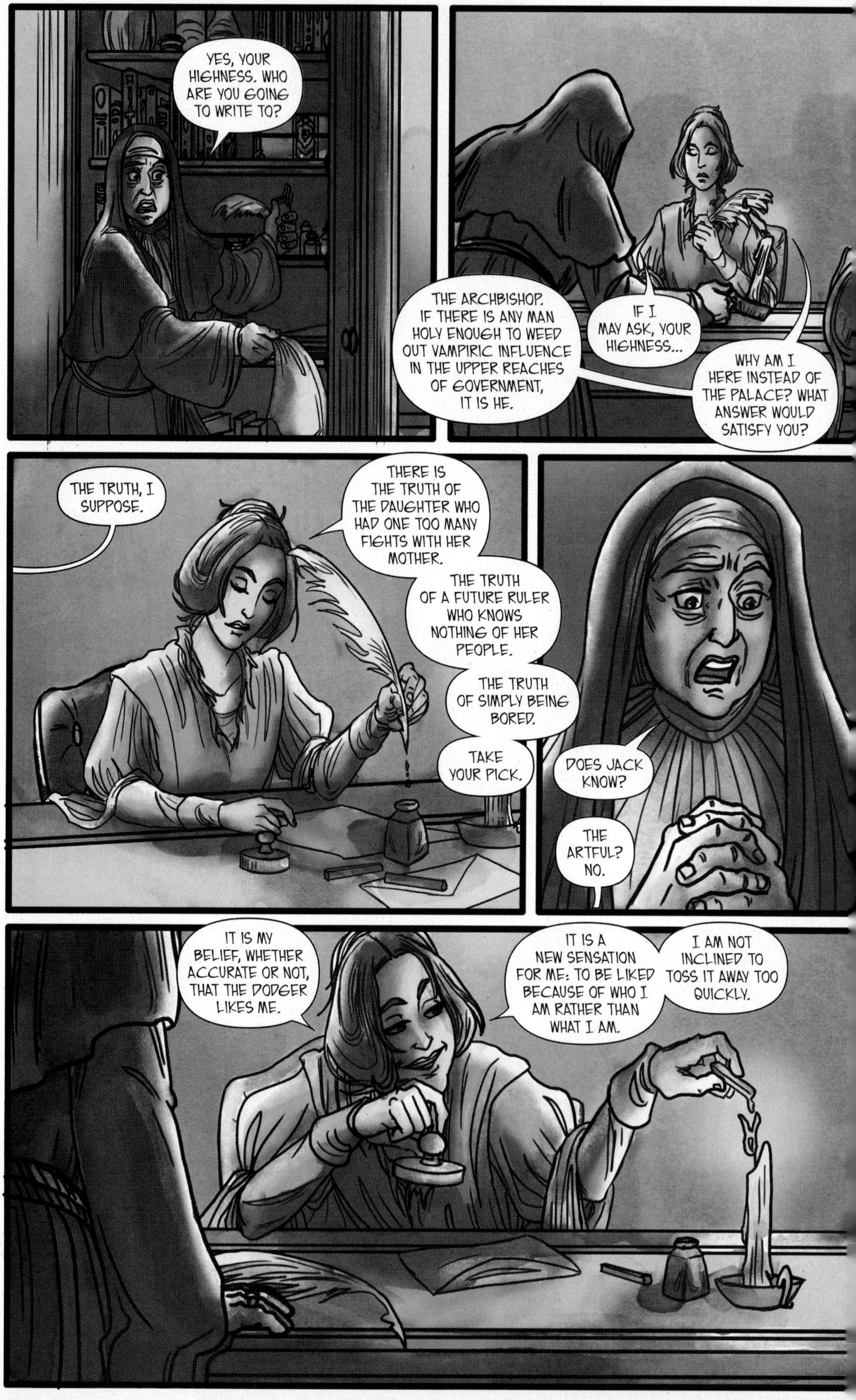
YES, YOUR HIGHNESS. WHO ARE YOU GOING TO WRITE TO?
THE ARCHBISHOP. IF THERE IS ANY MAN HOLY ENOUGH TO WEED OUT VAMPIRIC INFLUENCE IN THE UPPER REACHES OF GOVERNMENT, IT IS HE.
IF I MAY ASK, YOUR HIGHNESS...
WHY AM I HERE INSTEAD OF THE PALACE? WHAT ANSWER WOULD SATISFY YOU?
THE TRUTH, I SUPPOSE.
THERE IS THE TRUTH OF THE DAUGHTER WHO HAD ONE TOO MANY FIGHTS WITH HER MOTHER.
THE TRUTH OF A FUTURE RULER WHO KNOWS NOTHING OF HER PEOPLE.
THE TRUTH OF SIMPLY BEING BORED.
TAKE YOUR PICK.
DOES JACK KNOW?
THE ARTFUL? NO.
IT IS MY BELIEF, WHETHER ACCURATE OR NOT, THAT THE DODGER LIKES ME.
IT IS A NEW SENSATION FOR ME: TO BE LIKED BECAUSE OF WHO I AM RATHER THAN WHAT I AM.
I AM NOT INCLINED TO TOSS IT AWAY TOO QUICKLY.

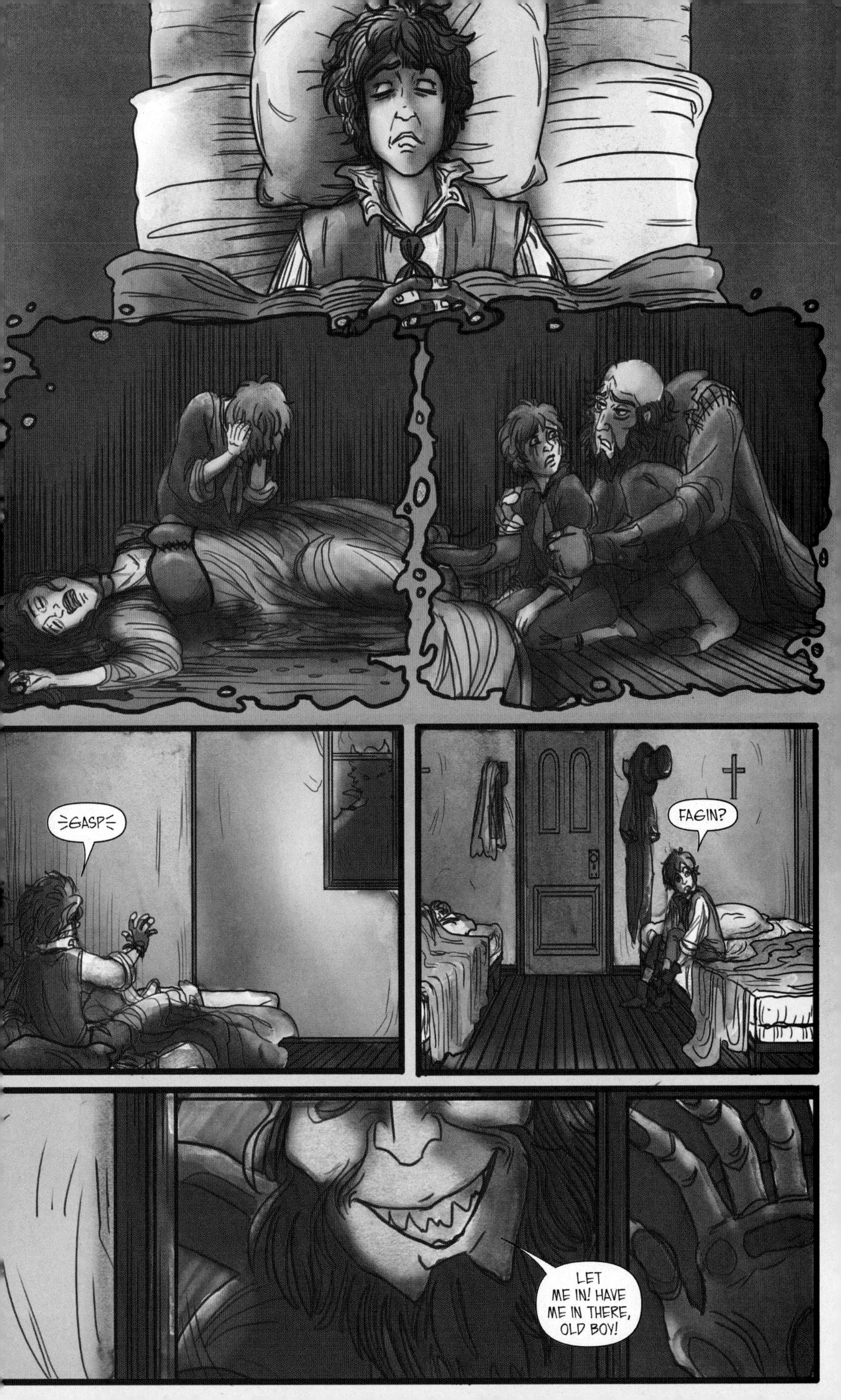
GASP
FAGIN?
LET ME IN! HAVE ME IN THERE, OLD BOY!

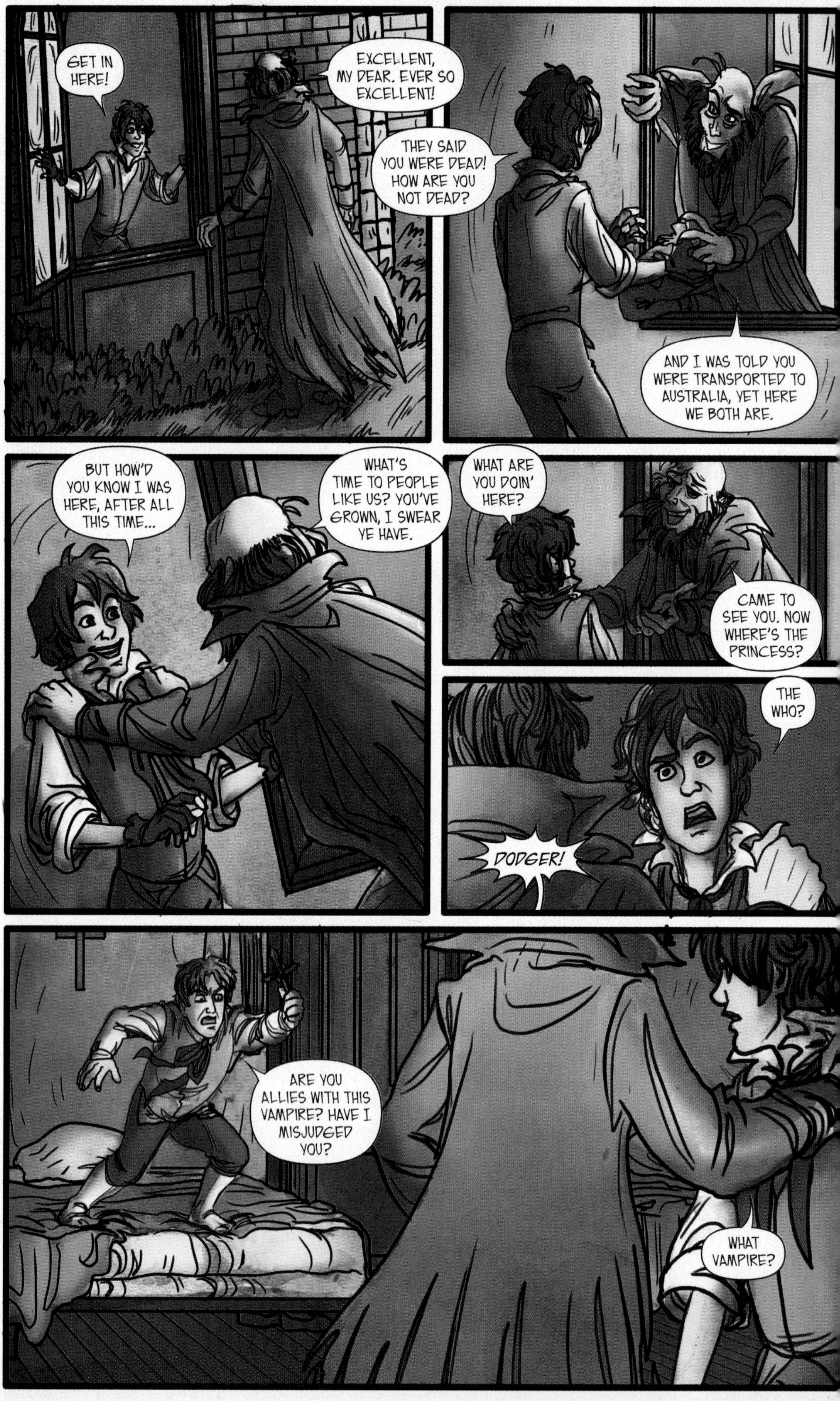
GET IN HERE!
EXCELLENT, MY DEAR. EVER SO EXCELLENT!
THEY SAID YOU WERE DEAD! HOW ARE YOU NOT DEAD?
AND I WAS TOLD YOU WERE TRANSPORTED TO AUSTRALIA, YET HERE WE BOTH ARE.
BUT HOW'D YOU KNOW I WAS HERE, AFTER ALL THIS TIME...
WHAT'S TIME TO PEOPLE LIKE US? YOU'VE GROWN, I SWEAR YE HAVE.
WHAT ARE YOU DOIN' HERE?
CAME TO SEE YOU. NOW WHERE'S THE PRINCESS?
THE WHO?
DODGER!
ARE YOU ALLIES WITH THIS VAMPIRE? HAVE I MISJUDGED YOU?
WHAT VAMPIRE?

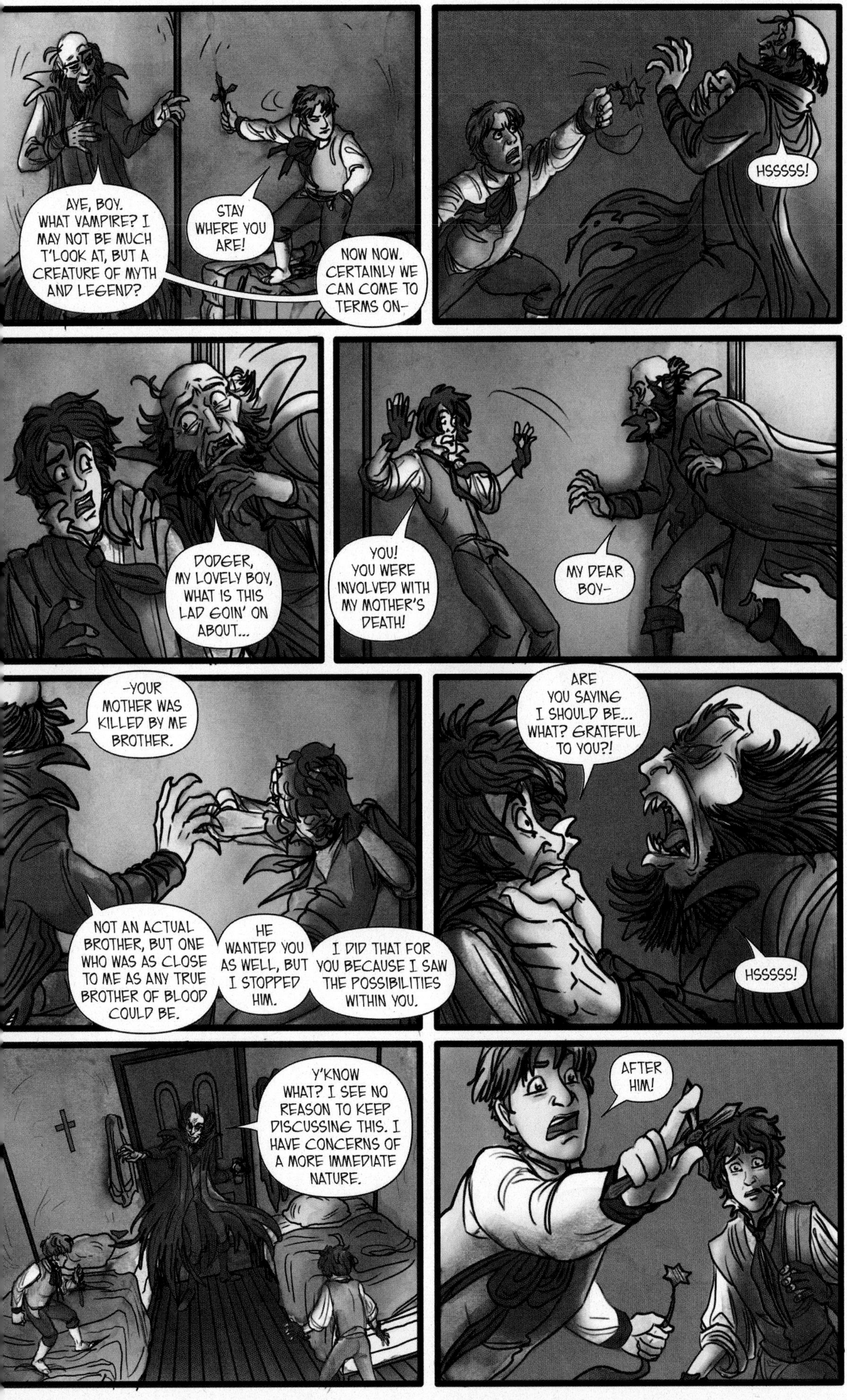
AYE, BOY. WHAT VAMPIRE? I MAY NOT BE MUCH T'LOOK AT, BUT A CREATURE OF MYTH AND LEGEND?
STAY WHERE YOU ARE!
NOW NOW. CERTAINLY WE CAN COME TO TERMS ON–
HSSSSS!
DODGER, MY LOVELY BOY, WHAT IS THIS LAD GOIN' ON ABOUT...
YOU! YOU WERE INVOLVED WITH MY MOTHER'S DEATH!
MY DEAR BOY–
–YOUR MOTHER WAS KILLED BY ME BROTHER.
NOT AN ACTUAL BROTHER, BUT ONE WHO WAS AS CLOSE TO ME AS ANY TRUE BROTHER OF BLOOD COULD BE.
HE WANTED YOU AS WELL, BUT I STOPPED HIM.
I DID THAT FOR YOU BECAUSE I SAW THE POSSIBILITIES WITHIN YOU.
ARE YOU SAYING I SHOULD BE... WHAT? GRATEFUL TO YOU?!
HSSSSS!
Y'KNOW WHAT? I SEE NO REASON TO KEEP DISCUSSING THIS. I HAVE CONCERNS OF A MORE IMMEDIATE NATURE.
AFTER HIM!

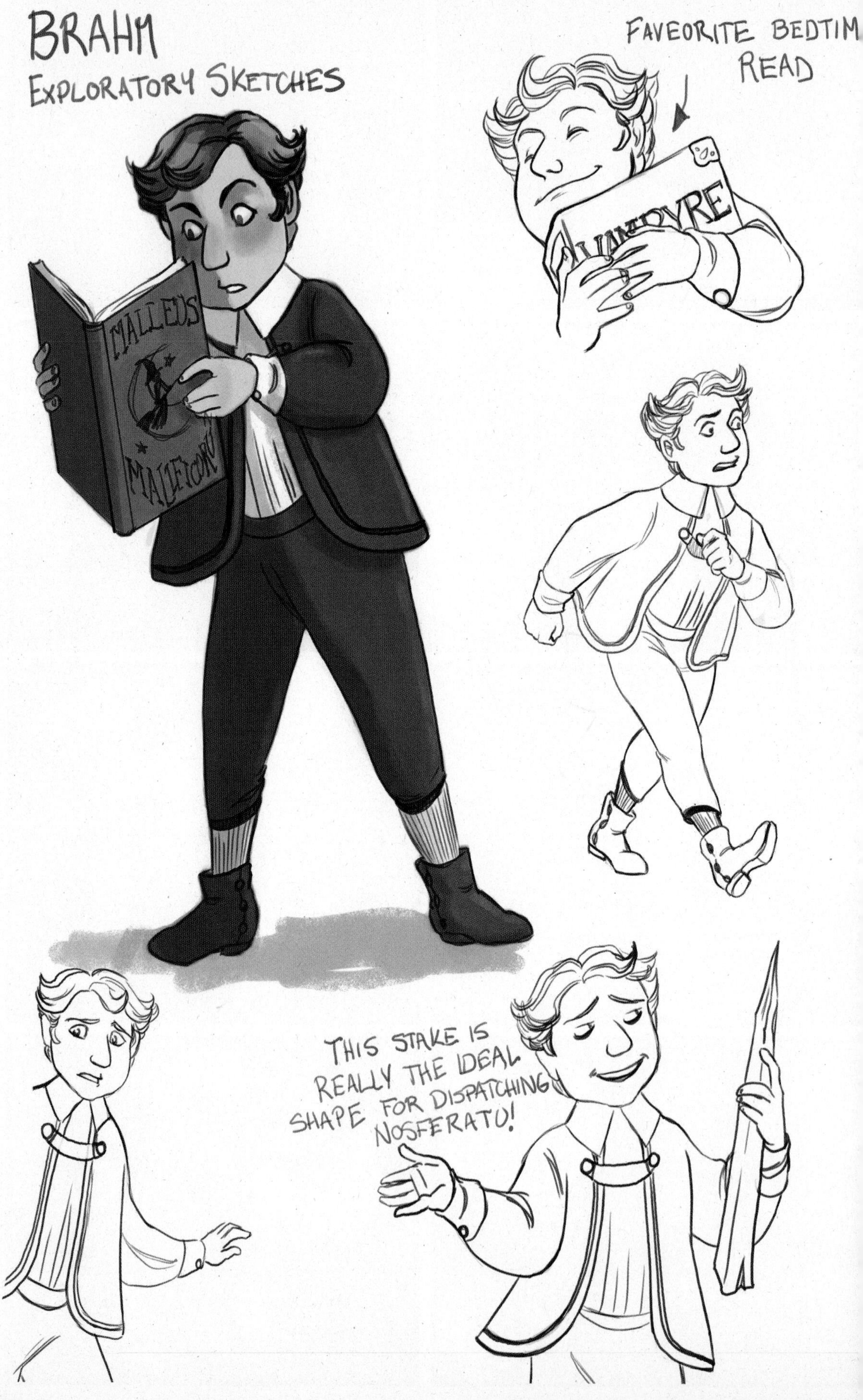
BRAHM
EXPLORATORY SKETCHES
FAVEORITE BEDTIM
READ
MALLEUS
THIS STAKE IS REALLY THE IDEAL SHAPE FOR DISPATCHING NOSFERATU!

CHAPTER THREE

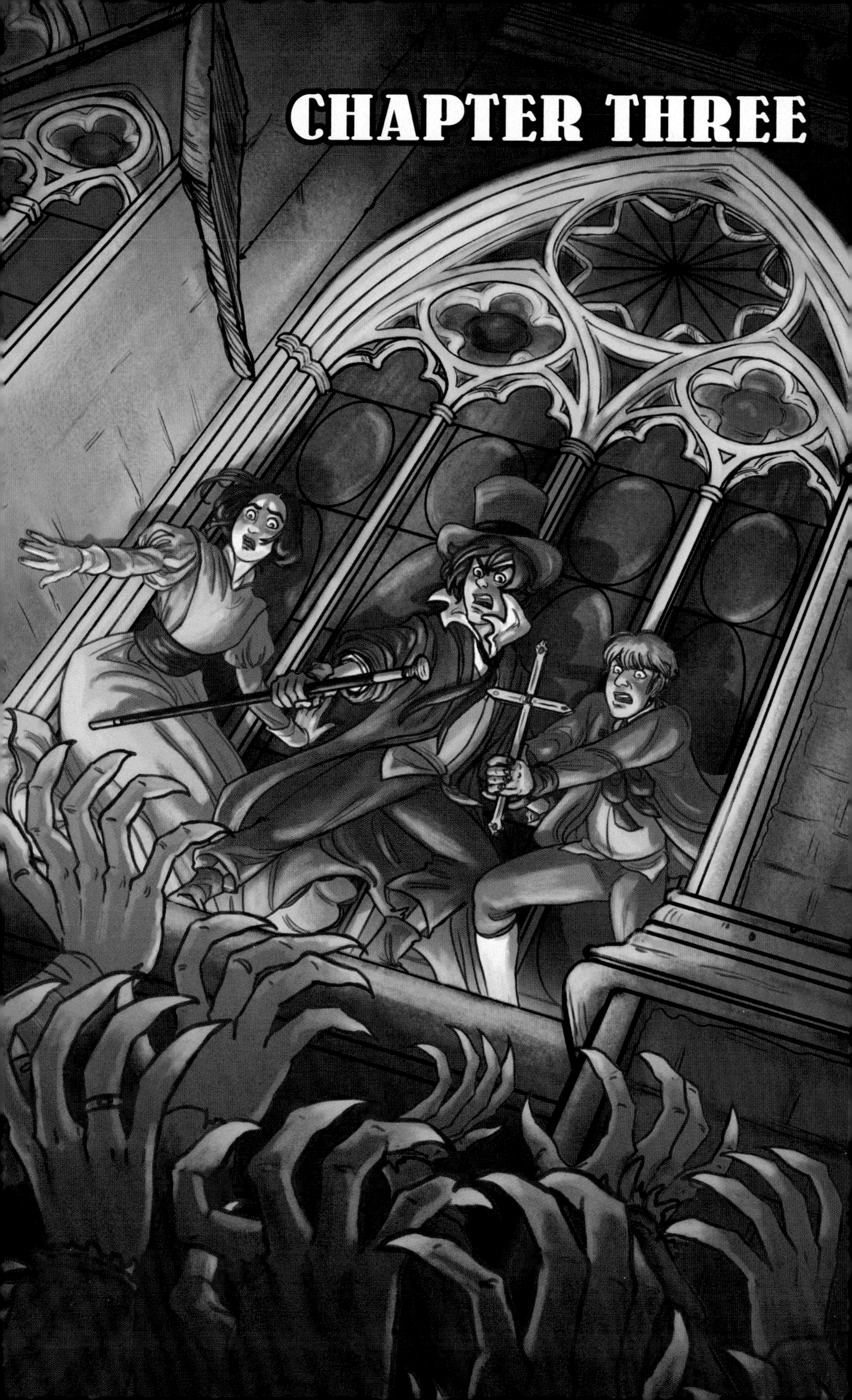

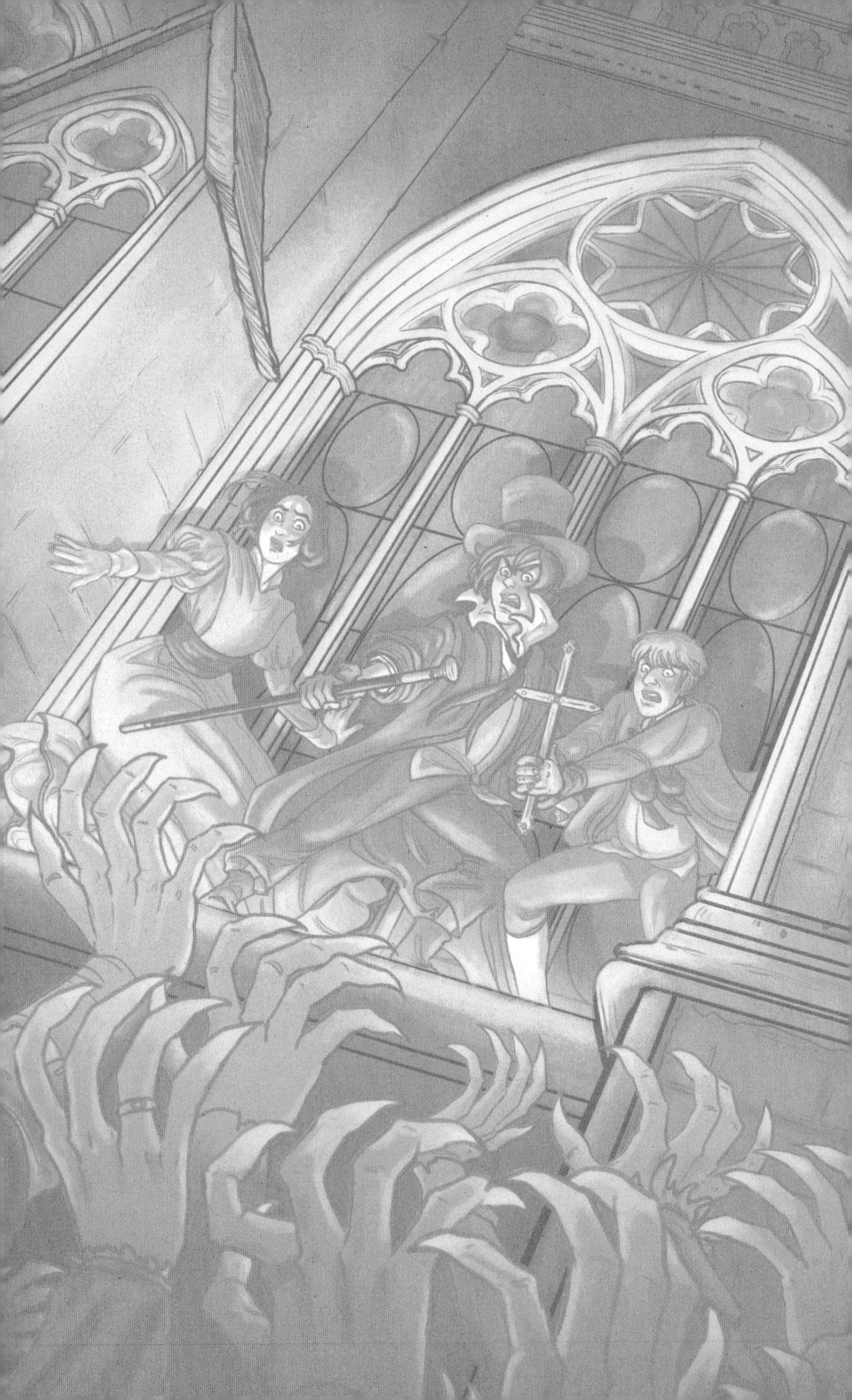

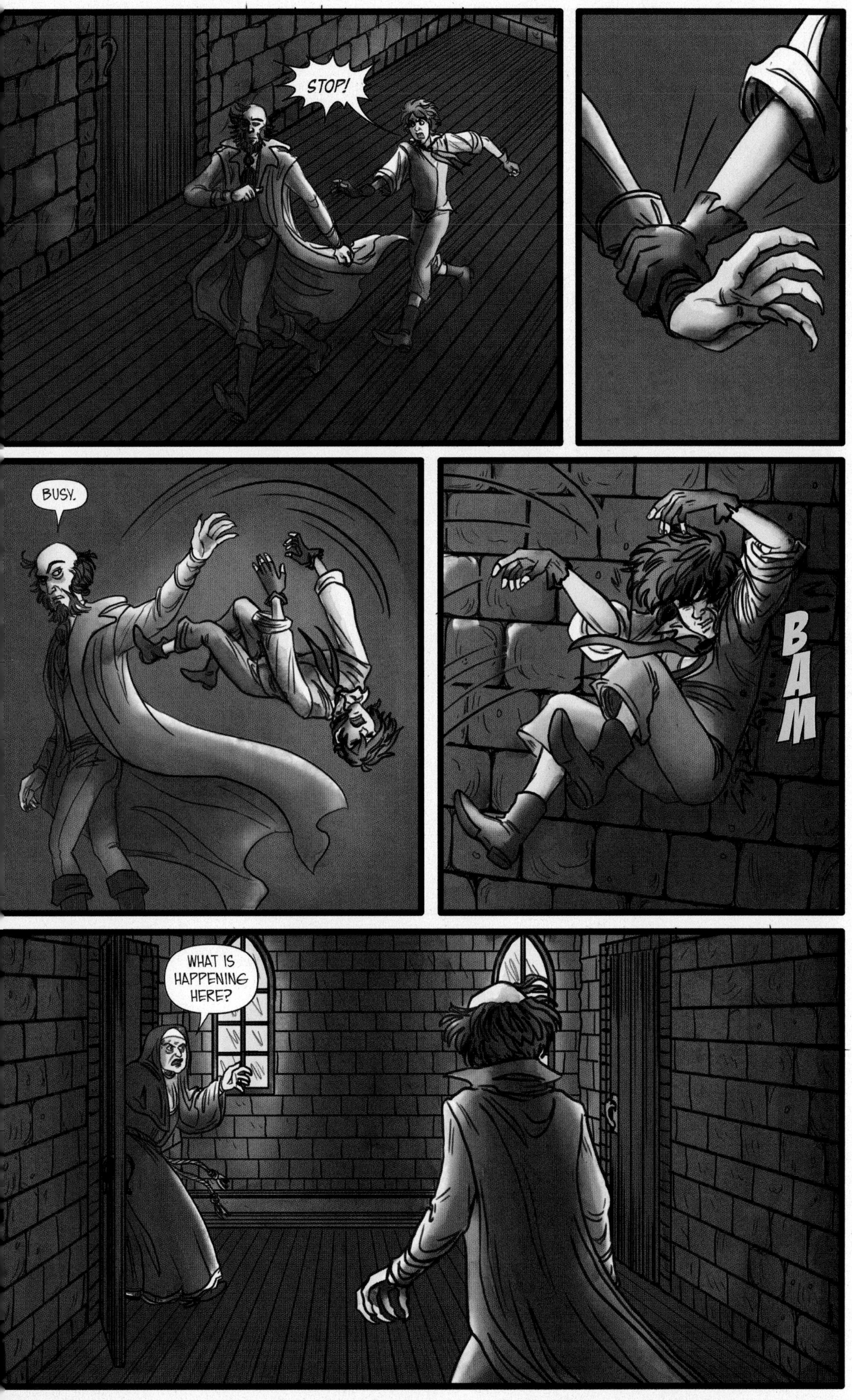
STOP!
BUSY.
BAM
WHAT IS HAPPENING HERE?

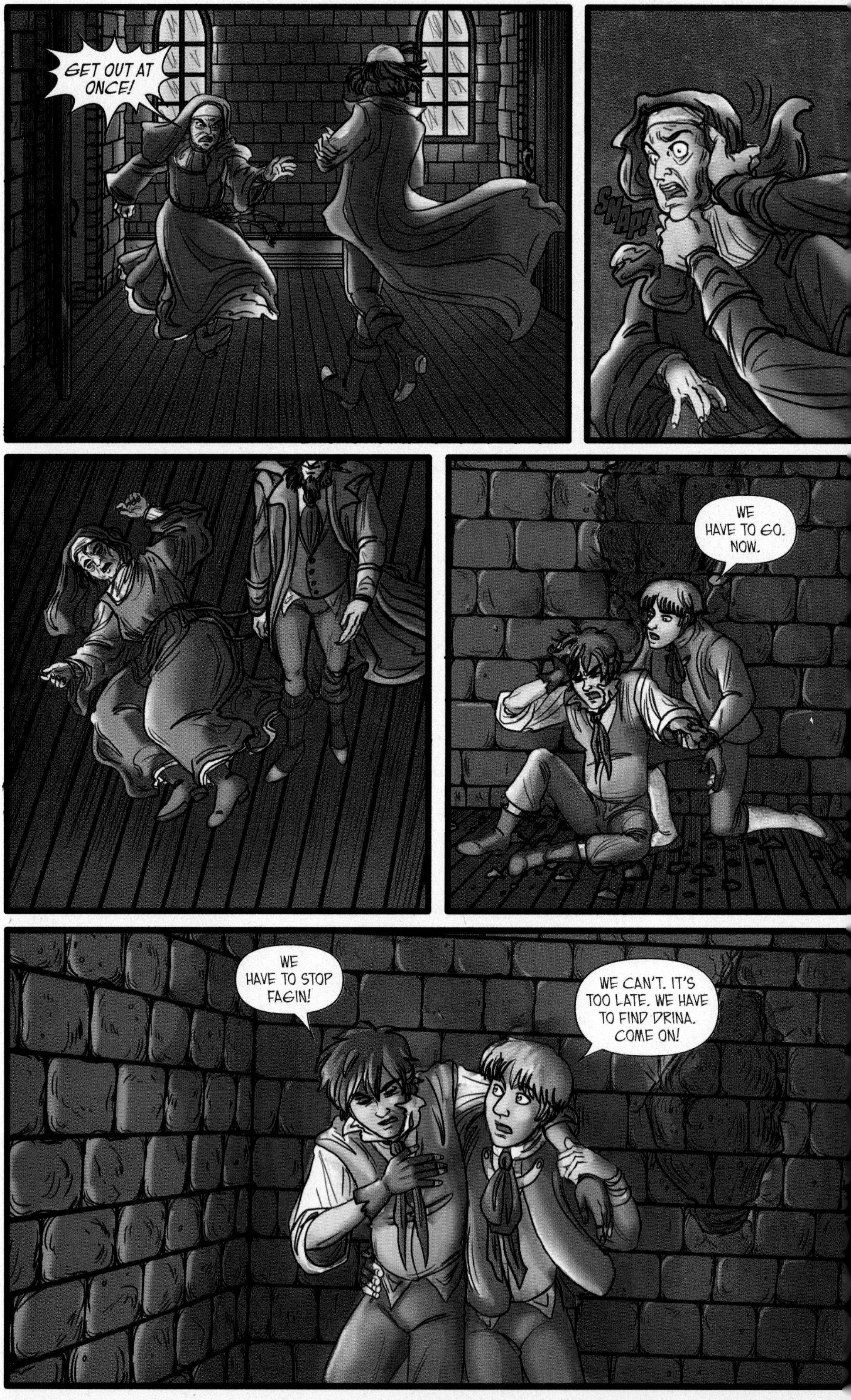
GET OUT AT ONCE!
SNAP!
WE HAVE TO GO. NOW.
WE HAVE TO STOP FAGIN!
WE CAN'T. IT'S TOO LATE. WE HAVE TO FIND DRINA. COME ON!

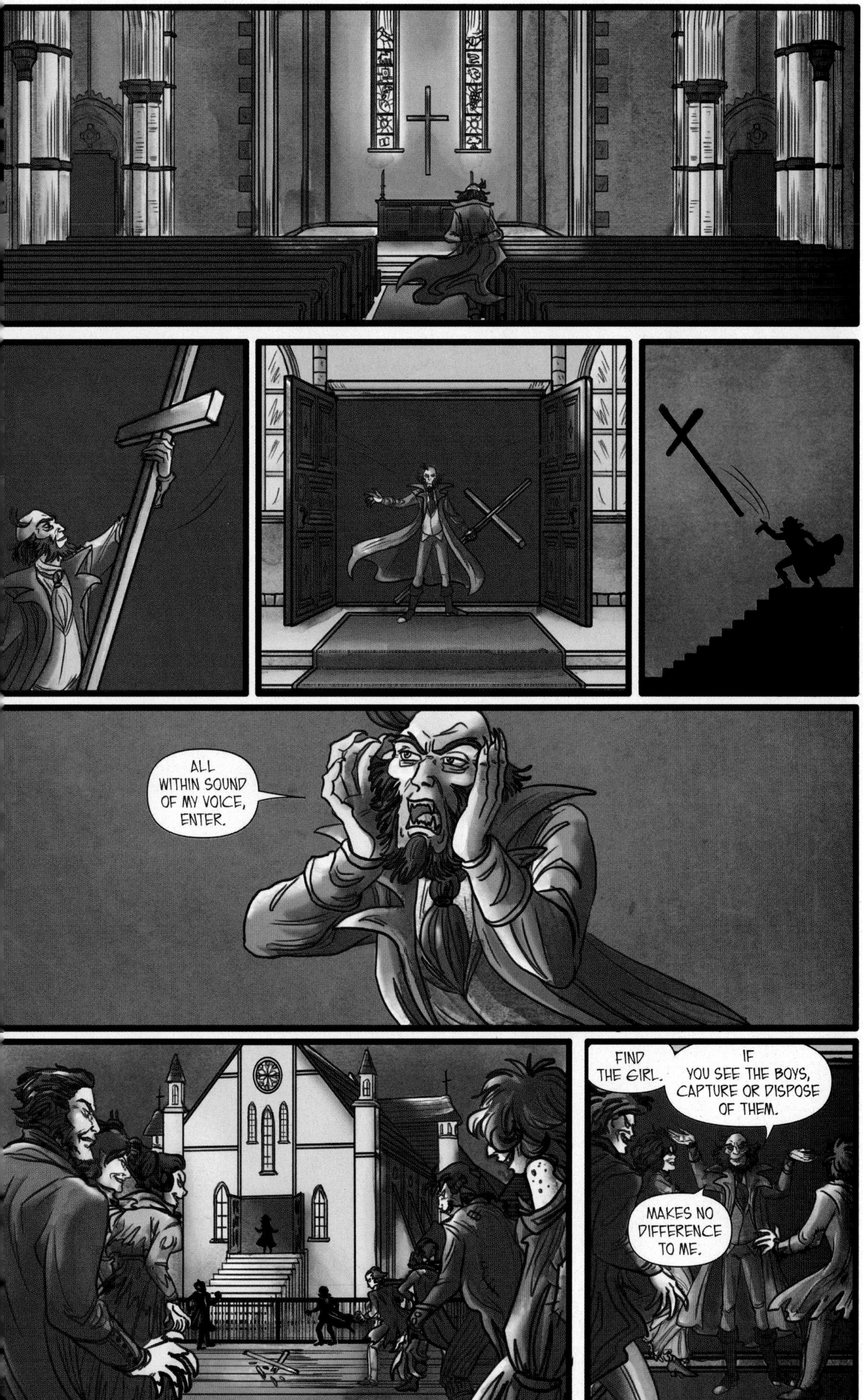
ALL WITHIN SOUND OF MY VOICE, ENTER.
FIND THE GIRL.
IF YOU SEE THE BOYS, CAPTURE OR DISPOSE OF THEM.
MAKES NO DIFFERENCE TO ME.

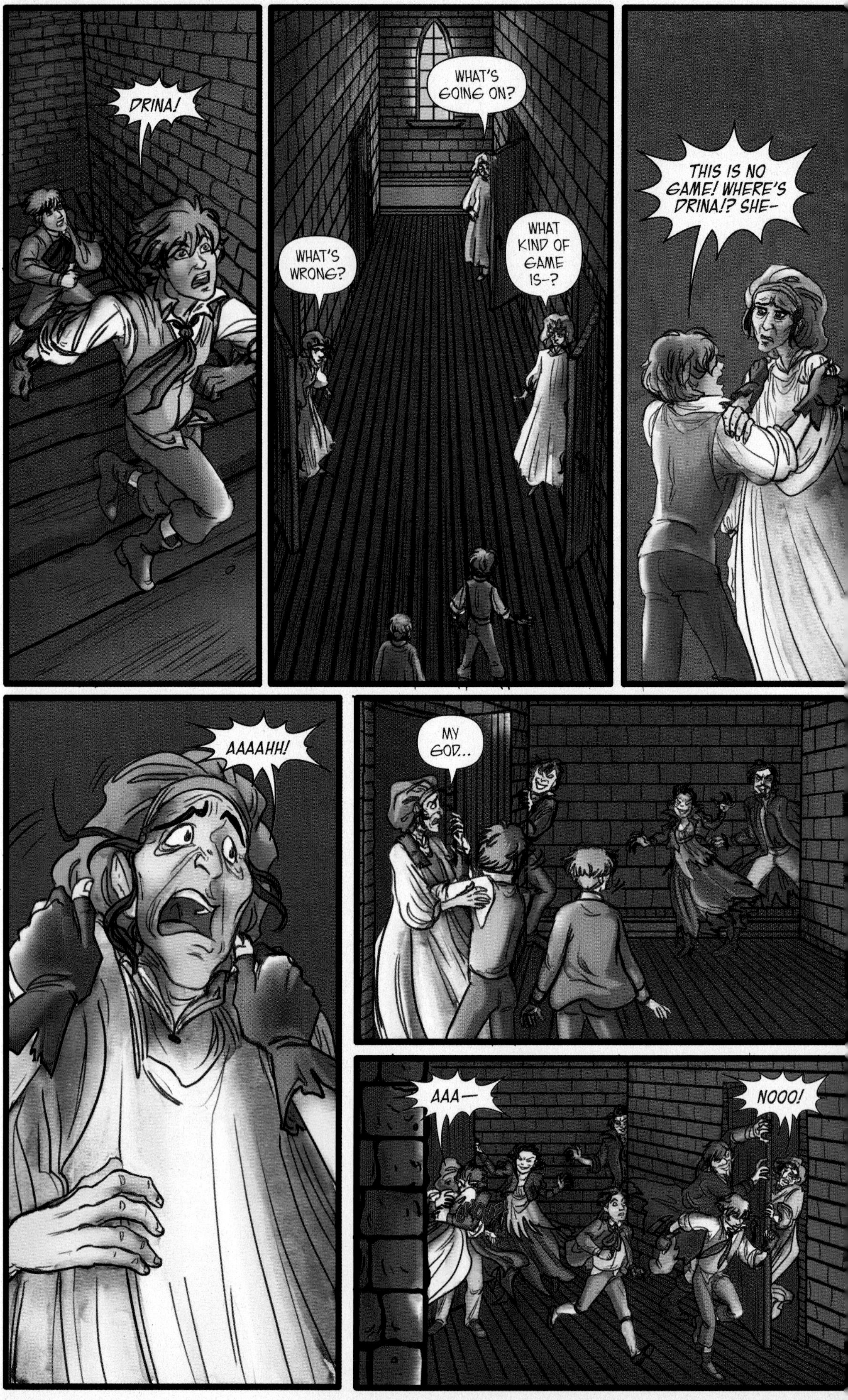
DRINA!
WHAT'S GOING ON?
WHAT'S WRONG?
WHAT KIND OF GAME IS-?
THIS IS NO GAME! WHERE'S DRINA!? SHE-
AAAAHH!
MY GOD...
AAA—
NOOO!

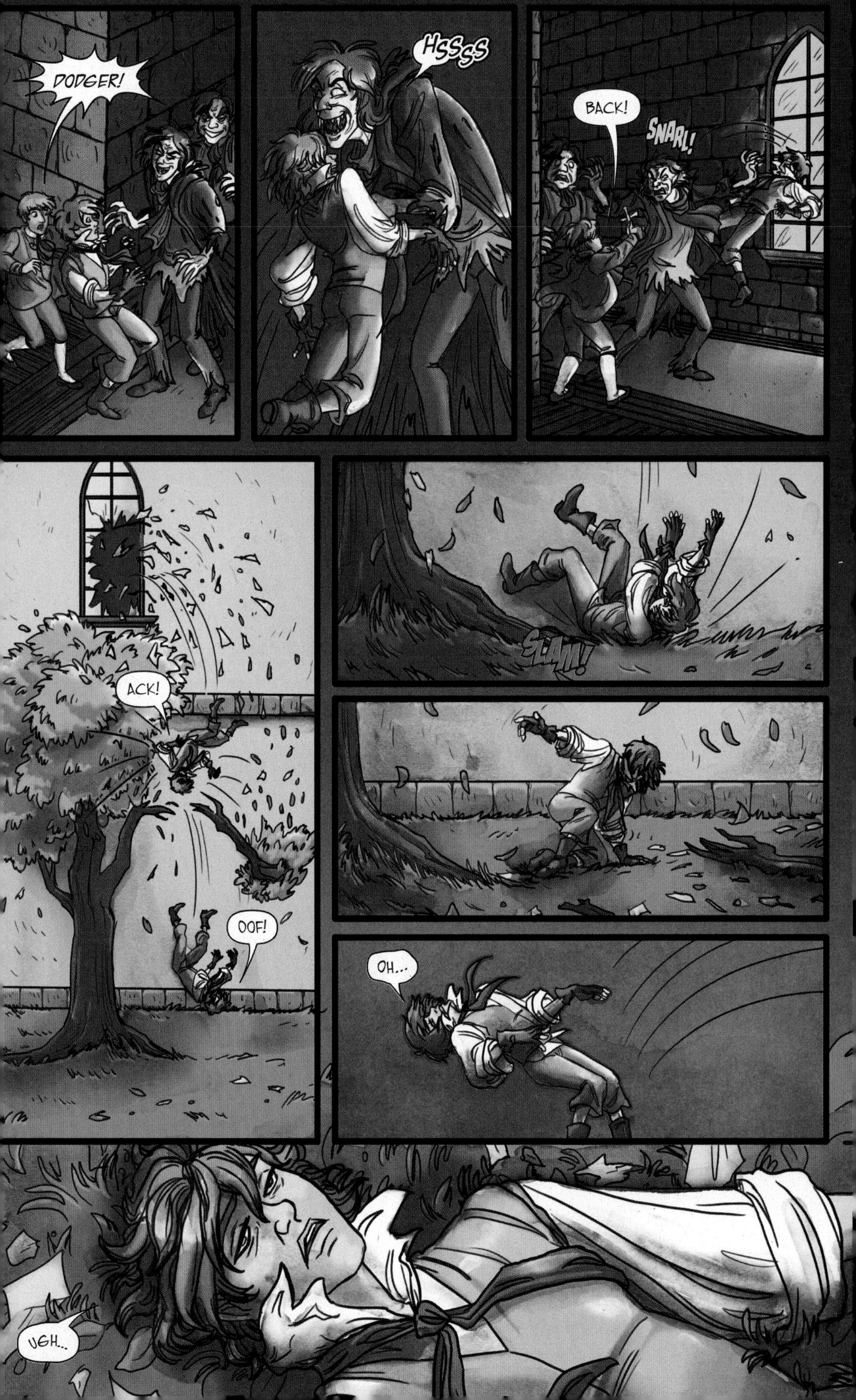
DODGER!
HSSSS
BACK!
SNARL!
ACK!
OOF!
SLAM!
OH...
UGH...

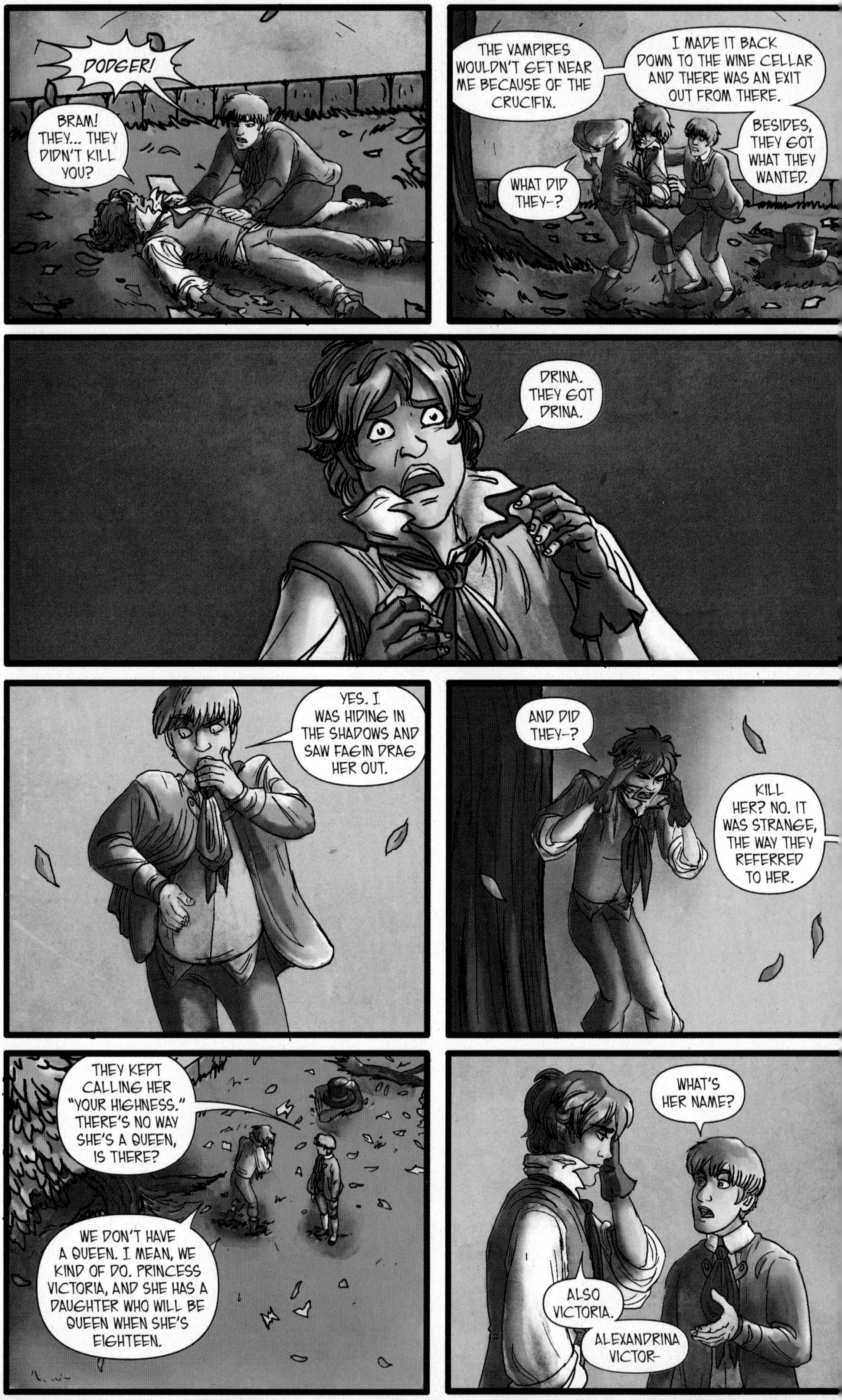
DODGER!
BRAM! THEY... THEY DIDN'T KILL YOU?
THE VAMPIRES WOULDN'T GET NEAR ME BECAUSE OF THE CRUCIFIX.
I MADE IT BACK DOWN TO THE WINE CELLAR AND THERE WAS AN EXIT OUT FROM THERE.
BESIDES, THEY GOT WHAT THEY WANTED.
WHAT DID THEY--?
DRINA. THEY GOT DRINA.
YES. I WAS HIDING IN THE SHADOWS AND SAW FAGIN DRAG HER OUT.
AND DID THEY--?
KILL HER? NO. IT WAS STRANGE, THE WAY THEY REFERRED TO HER.
THEY KEPT CALLING HER "YOUR HIGHNESS." THERE'S NO WAY SHE'S A QUEEN, IS THERE?
WE DON'T HAVE A QUEEN. I MEAN, WE KIND OF DO. PRINCESS VICTORIA, AND SHE HAS A DAUGHTER WHO WILL BE QUEEN WHEN SHE'S EIGHTEEN.
WHAT'S HER NAME?
ALSO VICTORIA.
ALEXANDRINA VICTOR-

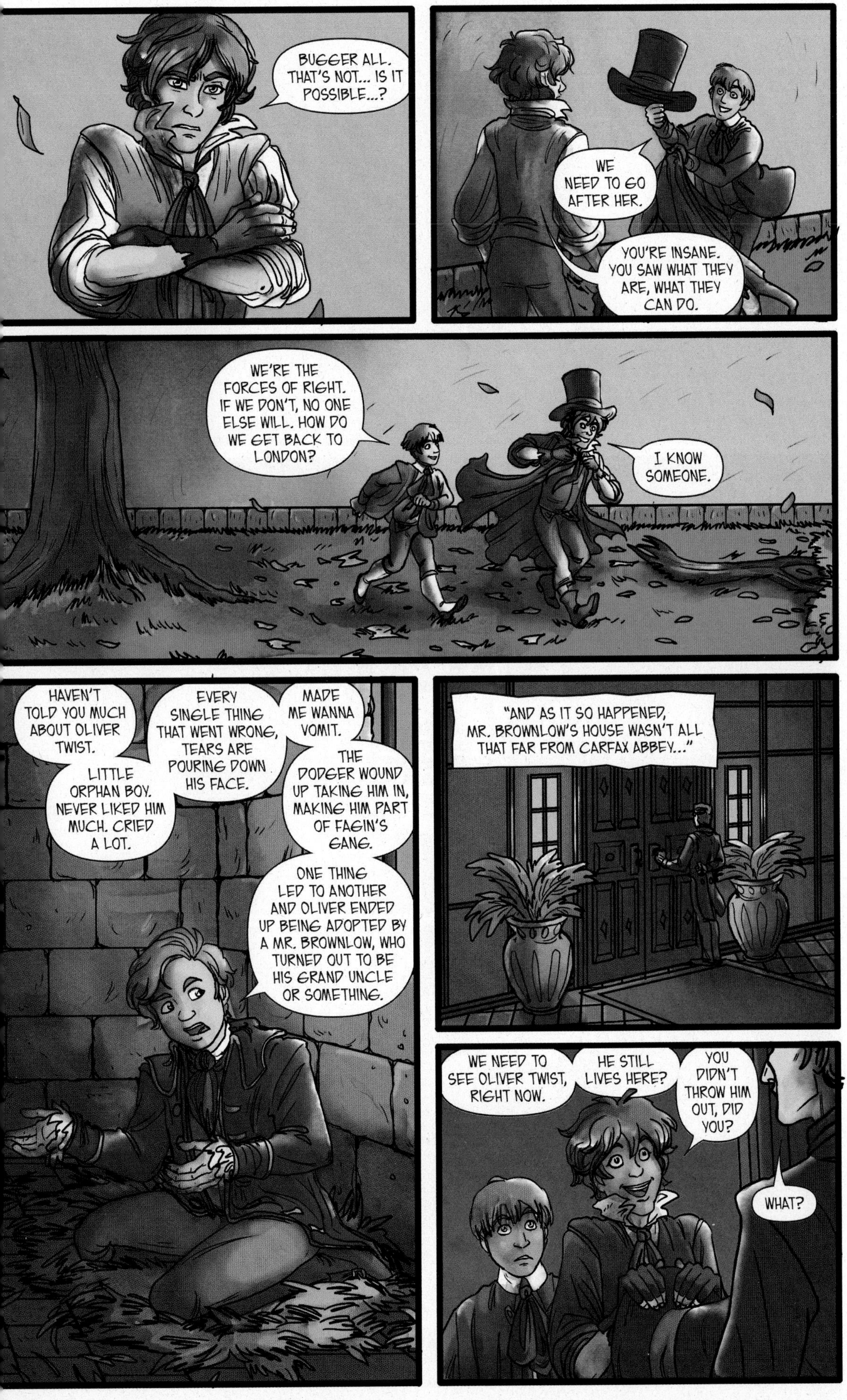
BUGGER ALL. THAT'S NOT... IS IT POSSIBLE...?
WE NEED TO GO AFTER HER.
YOU'RE INSANE. YOU SAW WHAT THEY ARE, WHAT THEY CAN DO.
WE'RE THE FORCES OF RIGHT. IF WE DON'T, NO ONE ELSE WILL. HOW DO WE GET BACK TO LONDON?
I KNOW SOMEONE.
HAVEN'T TOLD YOU MUCH ABOUT OLIVER TWIST.
LITTLE ORPHAN BOY. NEVER LIKED HIM MUCH. CRIED A LOT.
EVERY SINGLE THING THAT WENT WRONG, TEARS ARE POURING DOWN HIS FACE.
MADE ME WANNA VOMIT.
THE DODGER WOUND UP TAKING HIM IN, MAKING HIM PART OF FAGIN'S GANG.
ONE THING LED TO ANOTHER AND OLIVER ENDED UP BEING ADOPTED BY A MR. BROWNLOW, WHO TURNED OUT TO BE HIS GRAND UNCLE OR SOMETHING.
"AND AS IT SO HAPPENED, MR. BROWNLOW'S HOUSE WASN'T ALL THAT FAR FROM CARFAX ABBEY..."
WE NEED TO SEE OLIVER TWIST, RIGHT NOW.
HE STILL LIVES HERE?
YOU DIDN'T THROW HIM OUT, DID YOU?
WHAT?

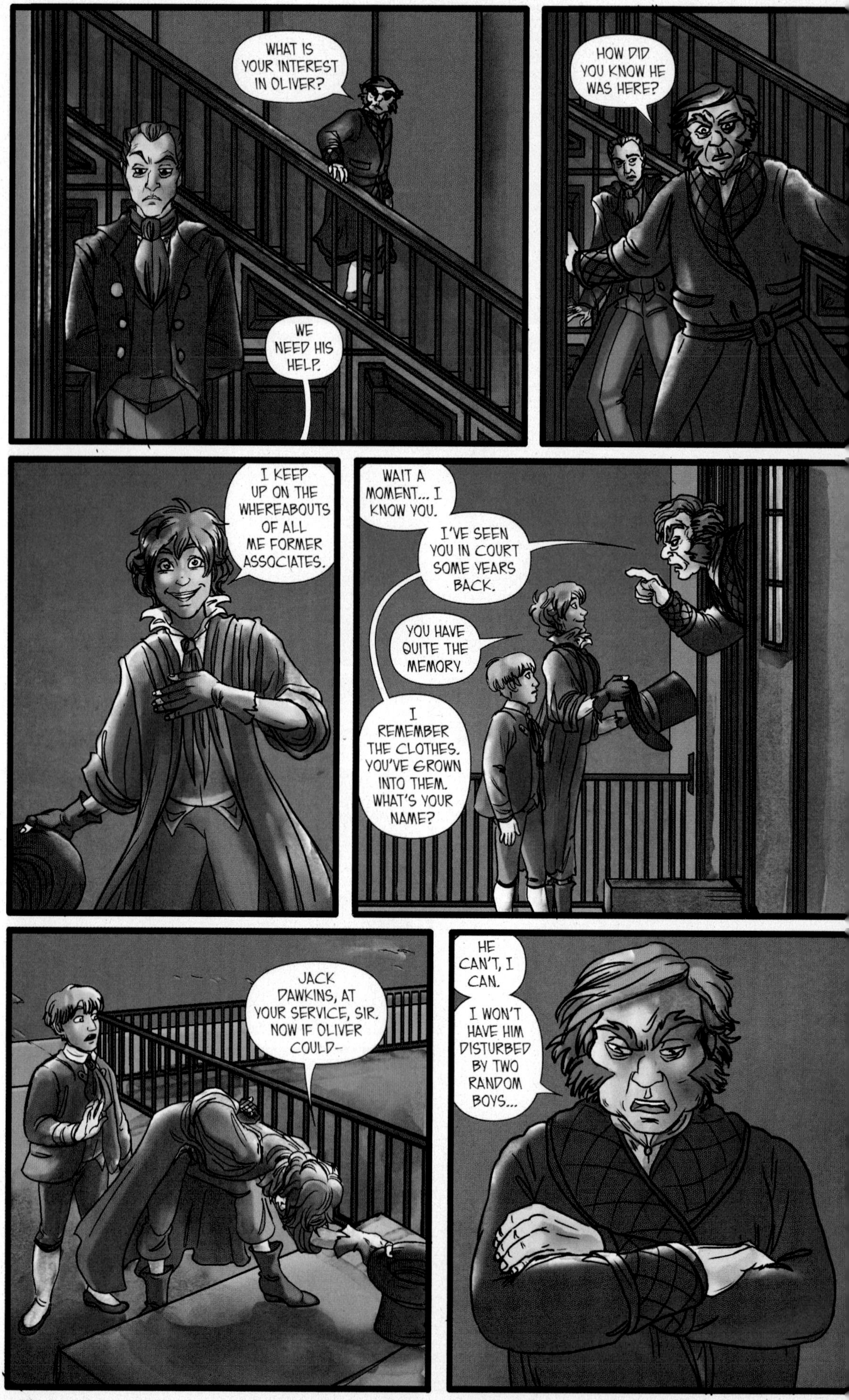
WHAT IS YOUR INTEREST IN OLIVER?
WE NEED HIS HELP.
HOW DID YOU KNOW HE WAS HERE?
I KEEP UP ON THE WHEREABOUTS OF ALL ME FORMER ASSOCIATES.
WAIT A MOMENT... I KNOW YOU.
I'VE SEEN YOU IN COURT SOME YEARS BACK.
YOU HAVE QUITE THE MEMORY.
I REMEMBER THE CLOTHES. YOU'VE GROWN INTO THEM. WHAT'S YOUR NAME?
JACK DAWKINS, AT YOUR SERVICE, SIR. NOW IF OLIVER COULD-
HE CAN'T, I CAN.
I WON'T HAVE HIM DISTURBED BY TWO RANDOM BOYS...

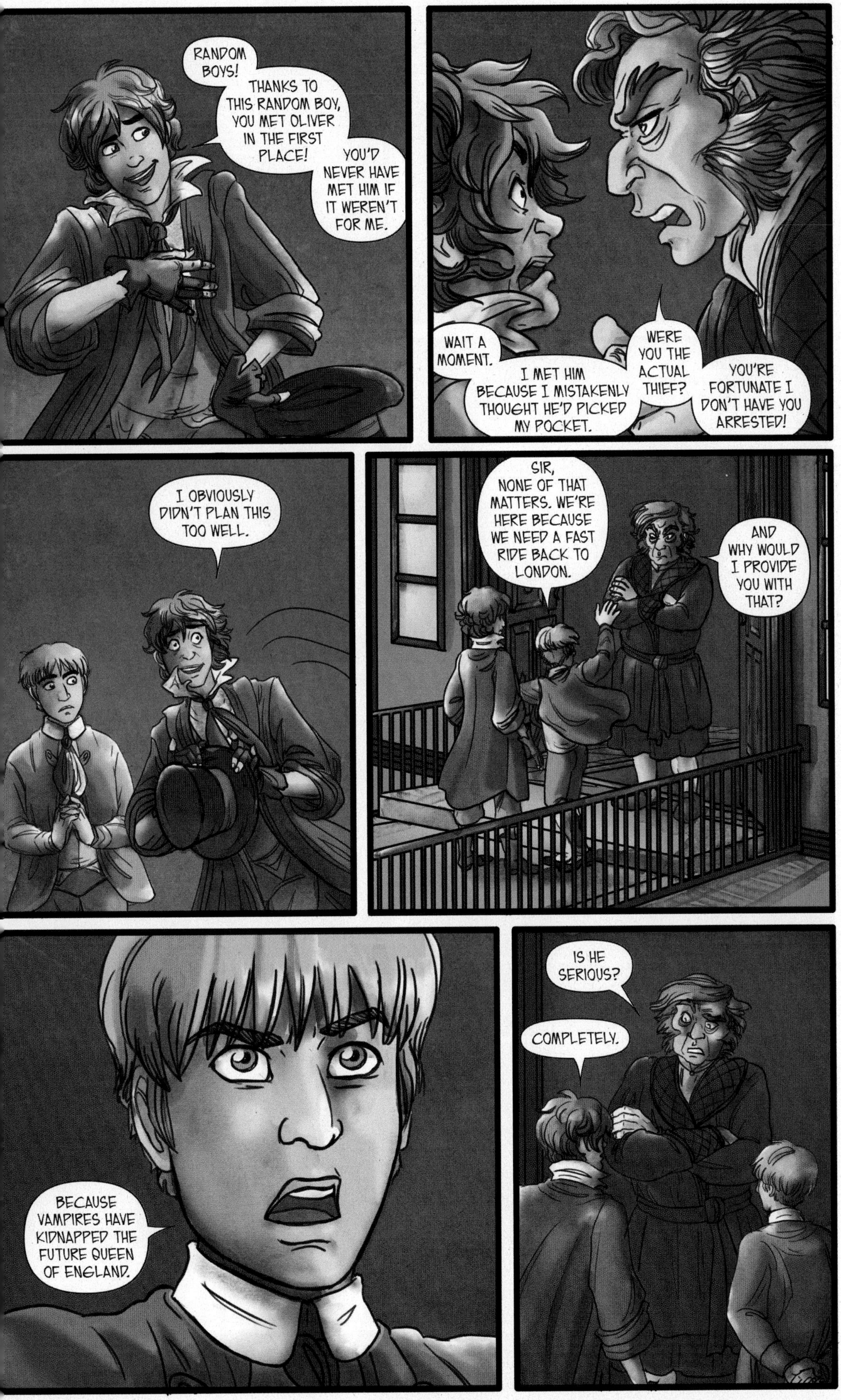

RANDOM BOYS!
THANKS TO THIS RANDOM BOY, YOU MET OLIVER IN THE FIRST PLACE!
YOU'D NEVER HAVE MET HIM IF IT WEREN'T FOR ME.
WAIT A MOMENT.
I MET HIM BECAUSE I MISTAKENLY THOUGHT HE'D PICKED MY POCKET.
WERE YOU THE ACTUAL THIEF?
YOU'RE FORTUNATE I DON'T HAVE YOU ARRESTED!
I OBVIOUSLY DIDN'T PLAN THIS TOO WELL.
SIR, NONE OF THAT MATTERS. WE'RE HERE BECAUSE WE NEED A FAST RIDE BACK TO LONDON.
AND WHY WOULD I PROVIDE YOU WITH THAT?
BECAUSE VAMPIRES HAVE KIDNAPPED THE FUTURE QUEEN OF ENGLAND.
IS HE SERIOUS?
COMPLETELY.

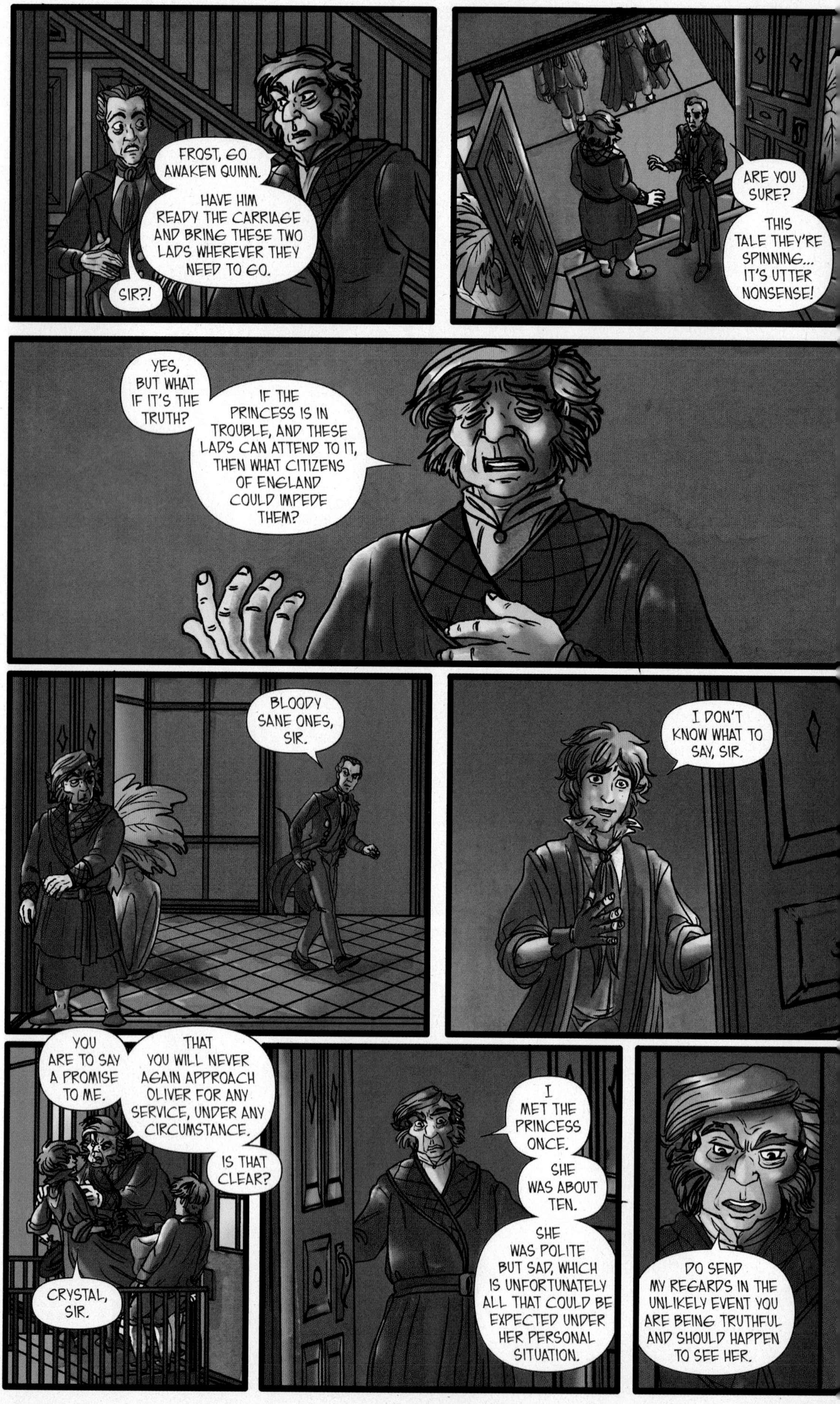
FROST, GO AWAKEN QUINN.
HAVE HIM READY THE CARRIAGE AND BRING THESE TWO LADS WHEREVER THEY NEED TO GO.
SIR?!
ARE YOU SURE?
THIS TALE THEY'RE SPINNING... IT'S UTTER NONSENSE!
YES, BUT WHAT IF IT'S THE TRUTH?
IF THE PRINCESS IS IN TROUBLE, AND THESE LADS CAN ATTEND TO IT, THEN WHAT CITIZENS OF ENGLAND COULD IMPEDE THEM?
BLOODY SANE ONES, SIR.
I DON'T KNOW WHAT TO SAY, SIR.
YOU ARE TO SAY A PROMISE TO ME.
THAT YOU WILL NEVER AGAIN APPROACH OLIVER FOR ANY SERVICE, UNDER ANY CIRCUMSTANCE.
IS THAT CLEAR?
CRYSTAL, SIR.
I MET THE PRINCESS ONCE.
SHE WAS ABOUT TEN.
SHE WAS POLITE BUT SAD, WHICH IS UNFORTUNATELY ALL THAT COULD BE EXPECTED UNDER HER PERSONAL SITUATION.
DO SEND MY REGARDS IN THE UNLIKELY EVENT YOU ARE BEING TRUTHFUL AND SHOULD HAPPEN TO SEE HER.

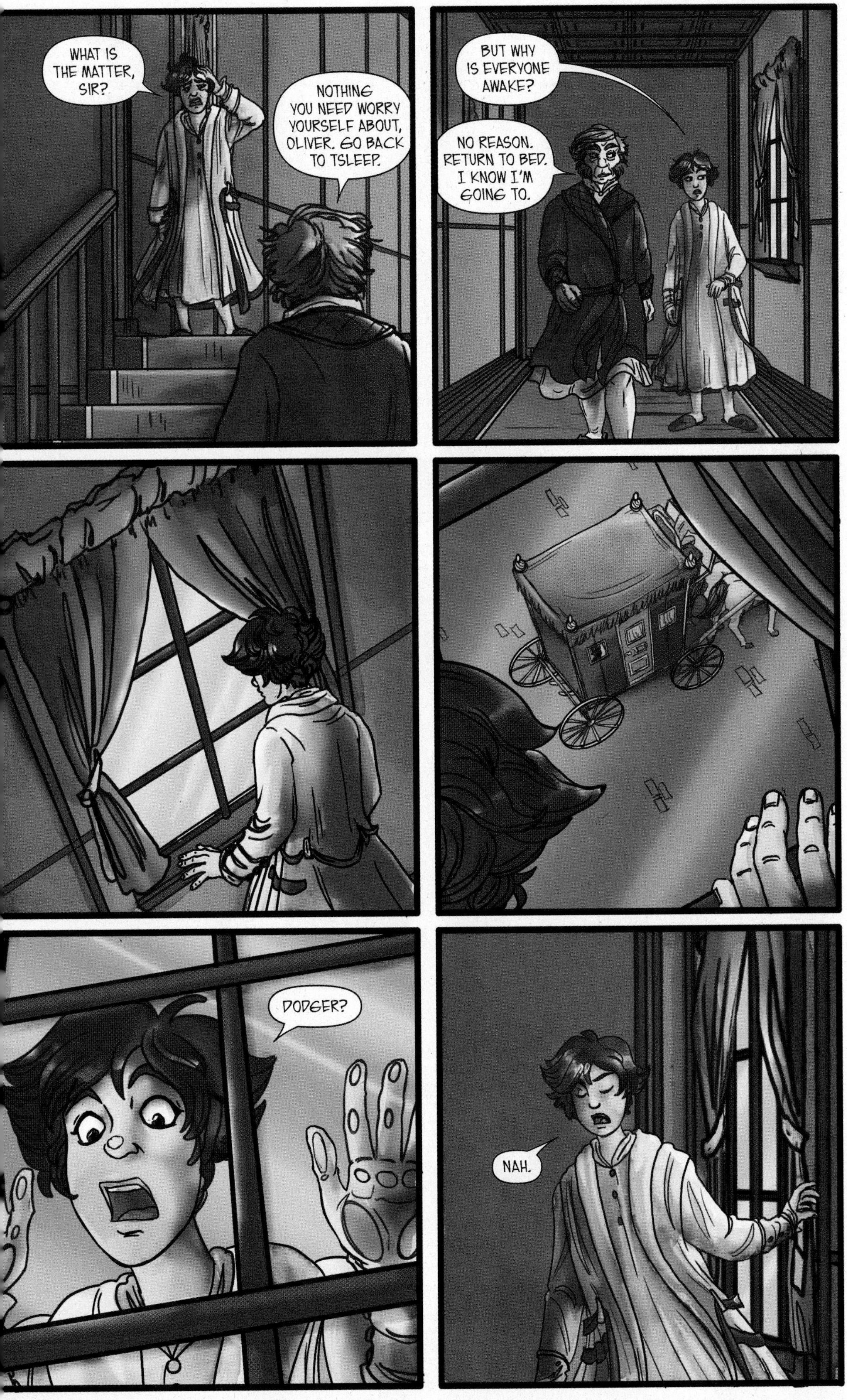
WHAT IS THE MATTER, SIR?
NOTHING YOU NEED WORRY YOURSELF ABOUT, OLIVER. GO BACK TO TSLEEP.
BUT WHY IS EVERYONE AWAKE?
NO REASON. RETURN TO BED. I KNOW I'M GOING TO.
DODGER?
NAH.

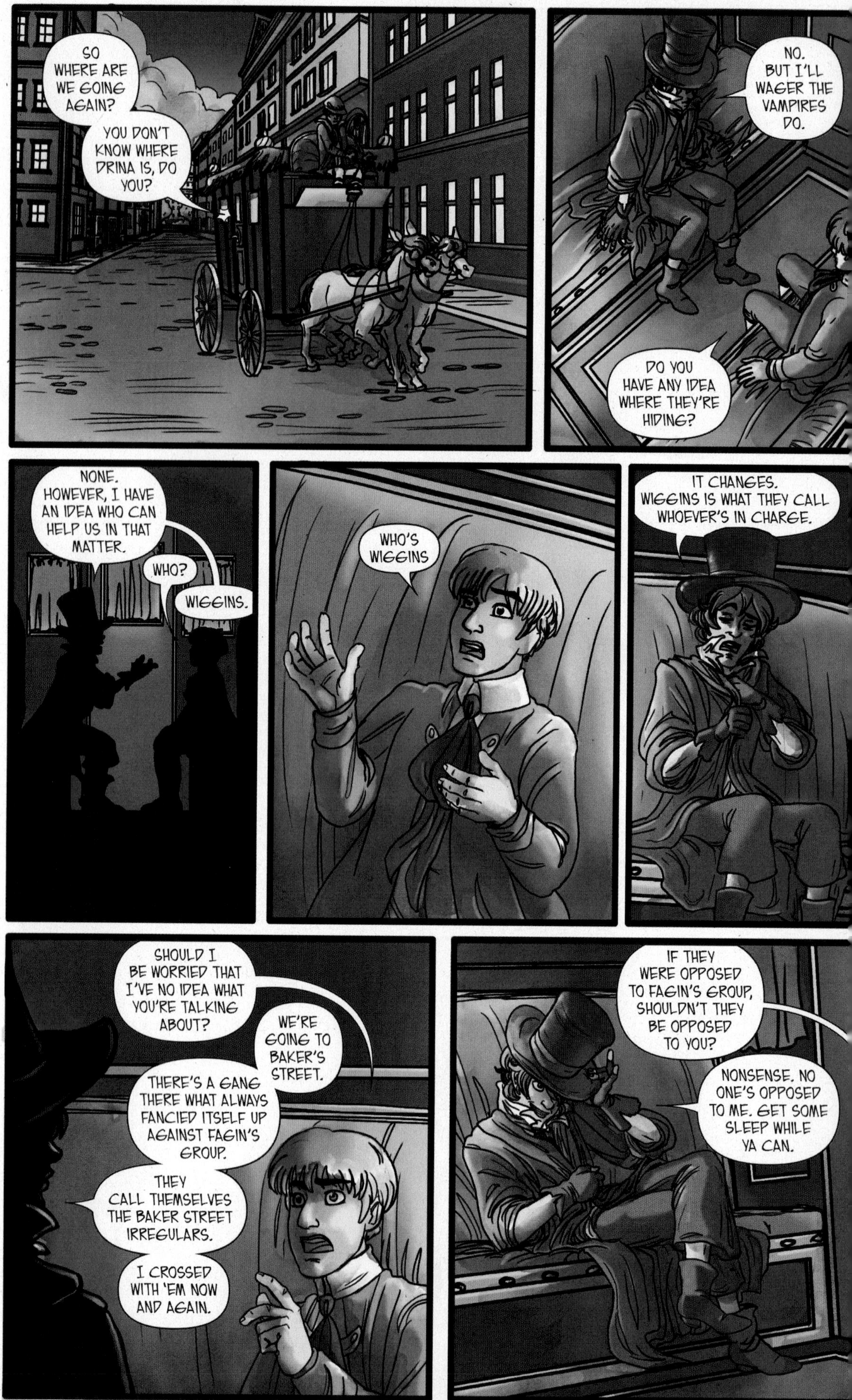

SO WHERE ARE WE GOING AGAIN?
YOU DON'T KNOW WHERE DRINA IS, DO YOU?
NO. BUT I'LL WAGER THE VAMPIRES DO.
DO YOU HAVE ANY IDEA WHERE THEY'RE HIDING?
NONE. HOWEVER, I HAVE AN IDEA WHO CAN HELP US IN THAT MATTER.
WHO?
WIGGINS.
WHO'S WIGGINS
IT CHANGES. WIGGINS IS WHAT THEY CALL WHOEVER'S IN CHARGE.
SHOULD I BE WORRIED THAT I'VE NO IDEA WHAT YOU'RE TALKING ABOUT?
WE'RE GOING TO BAKER'S STREET.
THERE'S A GANG THERE WHAT ALWAYS FANCIED ITSELF UP AGAINST FAGIN'S GROUP.
THEY CALL THEMSELVES THE BAKER STREET IRREGULARS.
I CROSSED WITH 'EM NOW AND AGAIN.
IF THEY WERE OPPOSED TO FAGIN'S GROUP, SHOULDN'T THEY BE OPPOSED TO YOU?
NONSENSE. NO ONE'S OPPOSED TO ME. GET SOME SLEEP WHILE YA CAN.

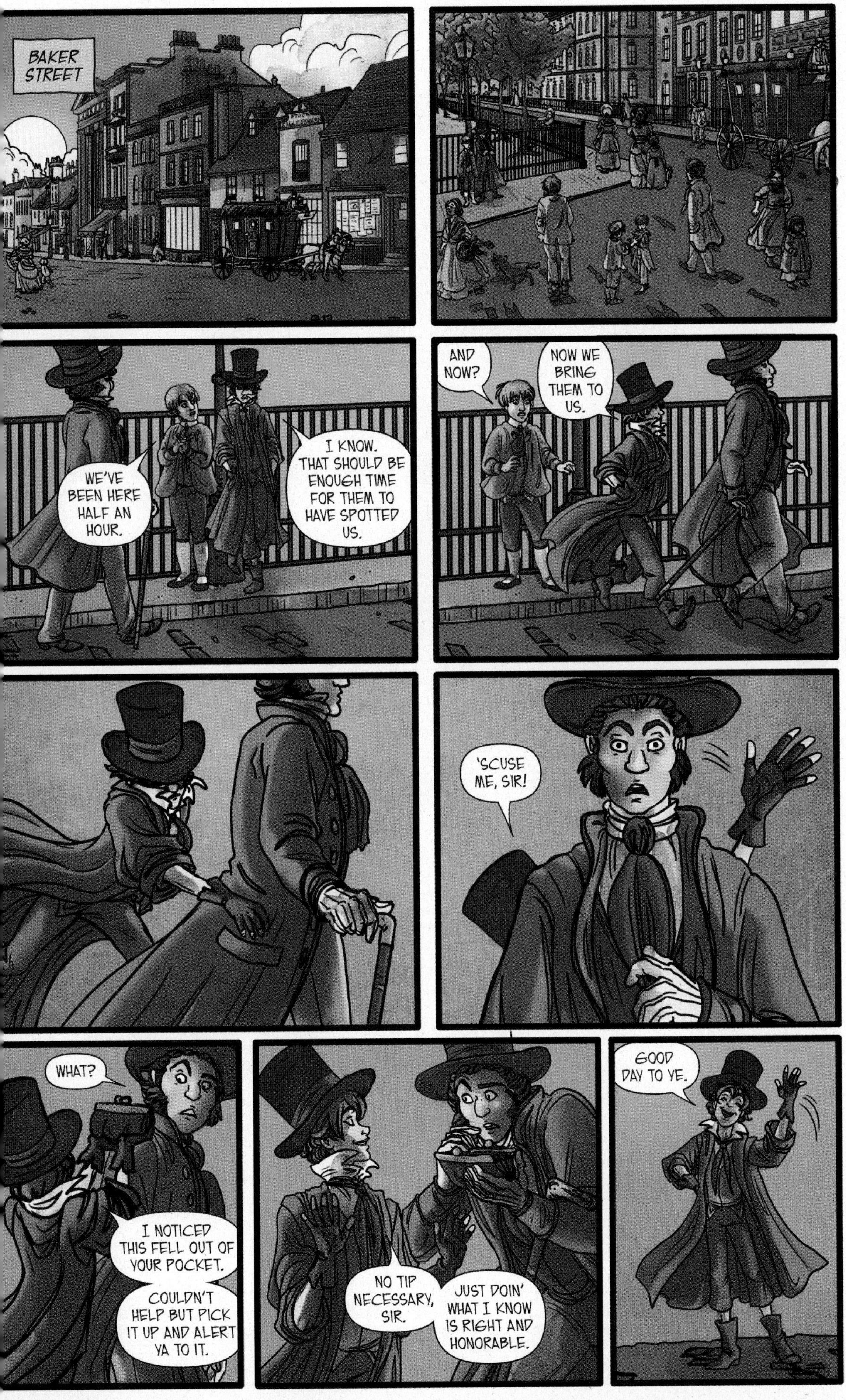
BAKER STREET
WE'VE BEEN HERE HALF AN HOUR.
I KNOW. THAT SHOULD BE ENOUGH TIME FOR THEM TO HAVE SPOTTED US.
AND NOW?
NOW WE BRING THEM TO US.
'SCUSE ME, SIR!
WHAT?
I NOTICED THIS FELL OUT OF YOUR POCKET.
COULDN'T HELP BUT PICK IT UP AND ALERT YA TO IT.
NO TIP NECESSARY, SIR.
JUST DOIN' WHAT I KNOW IS RIGHT AND HONORABLE.
GOOD DAY TO YE.

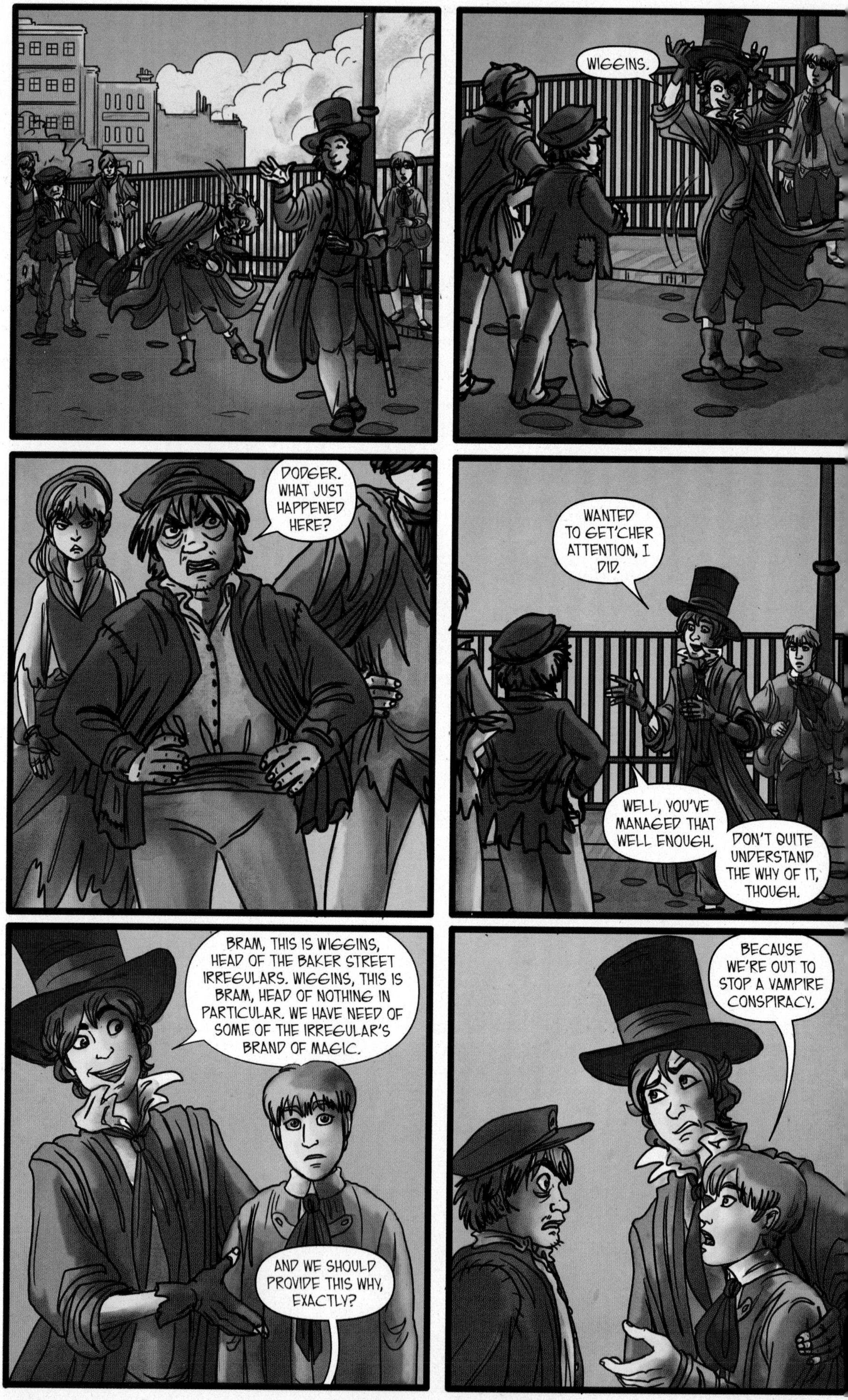
WIGGINS.
DODGER. WHAT JUST HAPPENED HERE?
WANTED TO GET'CHER ATTENTION, I DID.
WELL, YOU'VE MANAGED THAT WELL ENOUGH.
DON'T QUITE UNDERSTAND THE WHY OF IT, THOUGH.
BRAM, THIS IS WIGGINS, HEAD OF THE BAKER STREET IRREGULARS. WIGGINS, THIS IS BRAM, HEAD OF NOTHING IN PARTICULAR. WE HAVE NEED OF SOME OF THE IRREGULAR'S BRAND OF MAGIC.
AND WE SHOULD PROVIDE THIS WHY, EXACTLY?
BECAUSE WE'RE OUT TO STOP A VAMPIRE CONSPIRACY.

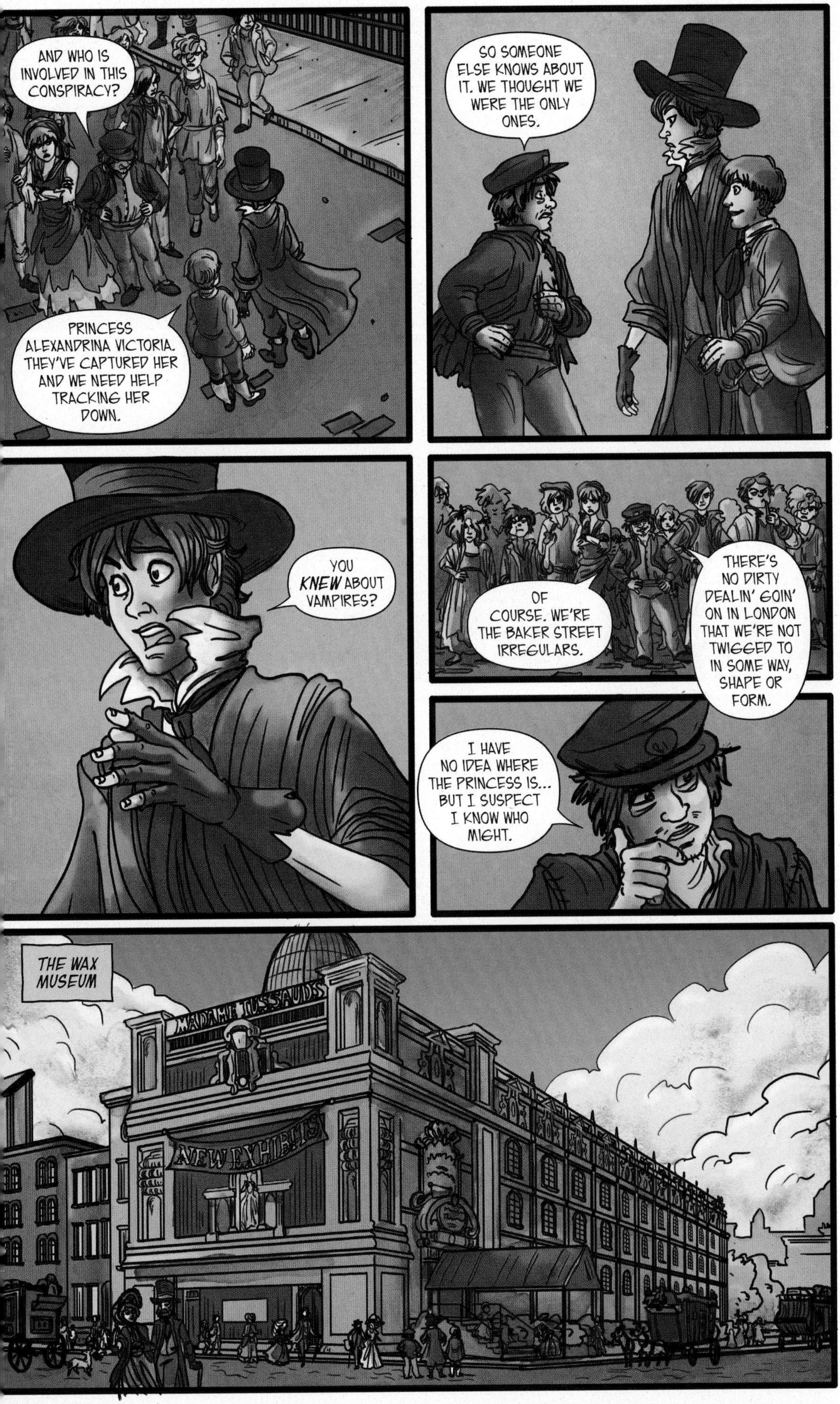
AND WHO IS INVOLVED IN THIS CONSPIRACY?
PRINCESS ALEXANDRINA VICTORIA. THEY'VE CAPTURED HER AND WE NEED HELP TRACKING HER DOWN.
SO SOMEONE ELSE KNOWS ABOUT IT. WE THOUGHT WE WERE THE ONLY ONES.
YOU KNEW ABOUT VAMPIRES?
OF COURSE. WE'RE THE BAKER STREET IRREGULARS.
THERE'S NO DIRTY DEALIN' GOIN' ON IN LONDON THAT WE'RE NOT TWIGGED TO IN SOME WAY, SHAPE OR FORM.
I HAVE NO IDEA WHERE THE PRINCESS IS... BUT I SUSPECT I KNOW WHO MIGHT.
THE WAX MUSEUM
MADAME TUSSAUDS
NEW EXHIBITS

ONE OF ME BOYS THINKS THERE MAY BE AN ACTUAL VAMPIRE IN THE CHAMBER OF HORRORS.

DOESN'T SOUND LIKELY TO ME.

YOU HAVE A BETTER IDEA?

ALL RIGHT. OFF YOU GO.

MONSTERS AND MYTHS

THE FRENCH REVOL

MONSTERS AND MYTHS

OVER THERE.

WHO'S DRACULA?

DRACULA

A FORMER ROMANIAN PRINCE.

WHEN HE WAS ALIVE, HE WAS KNOWN AS VLAD THE IMPALER FOR HIS HABIT OF BEHEADING HIS OPPONENTS AND PUTTING THEIR HEADS ON PIKES.

HOW LOVELY.

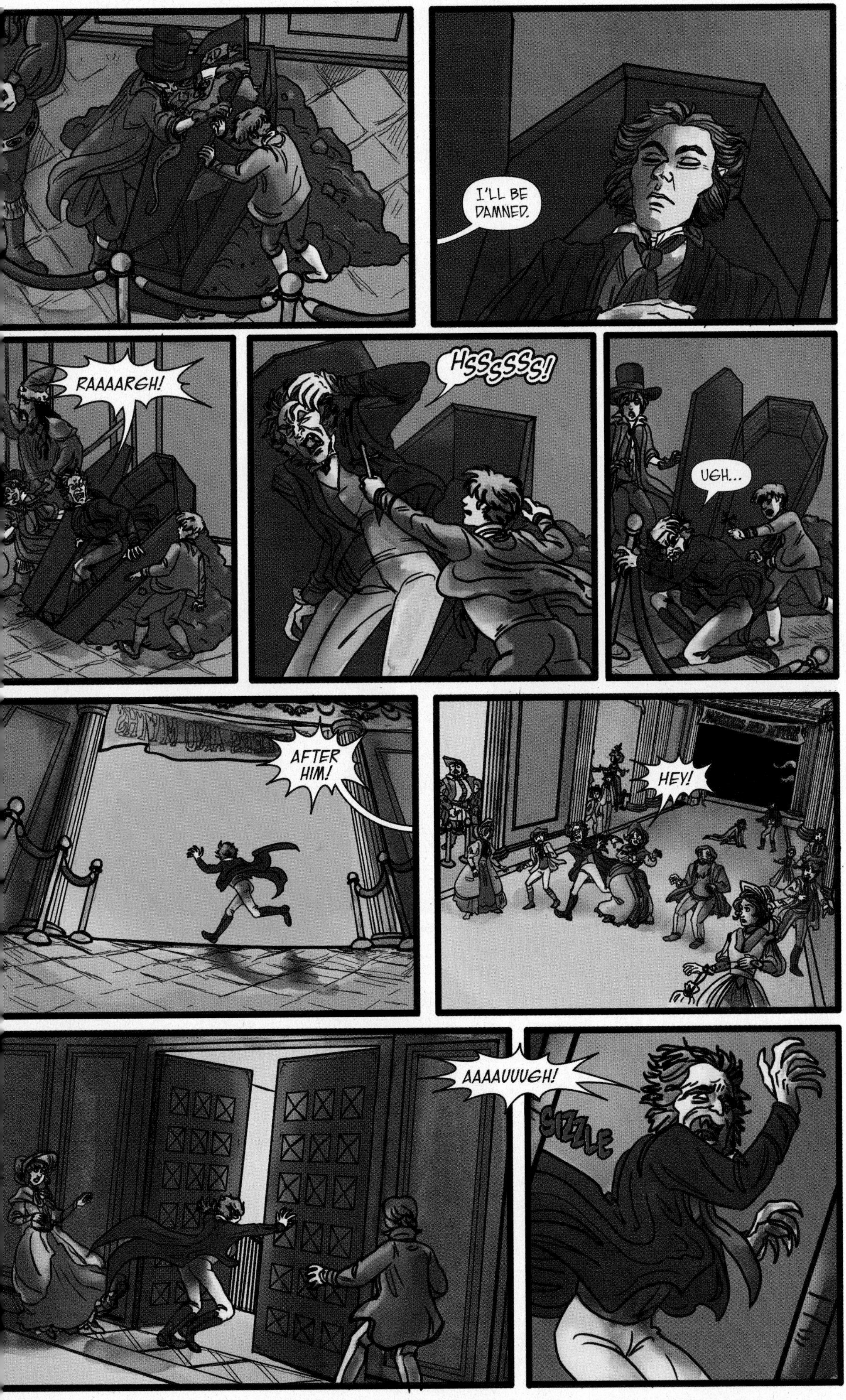
I'LL BE DAMNED.
RAAAARGH!
HSSSSSS!
UGH...
AFTER HIM!
HEY!
AAAAUUUGH!
SIZZLE

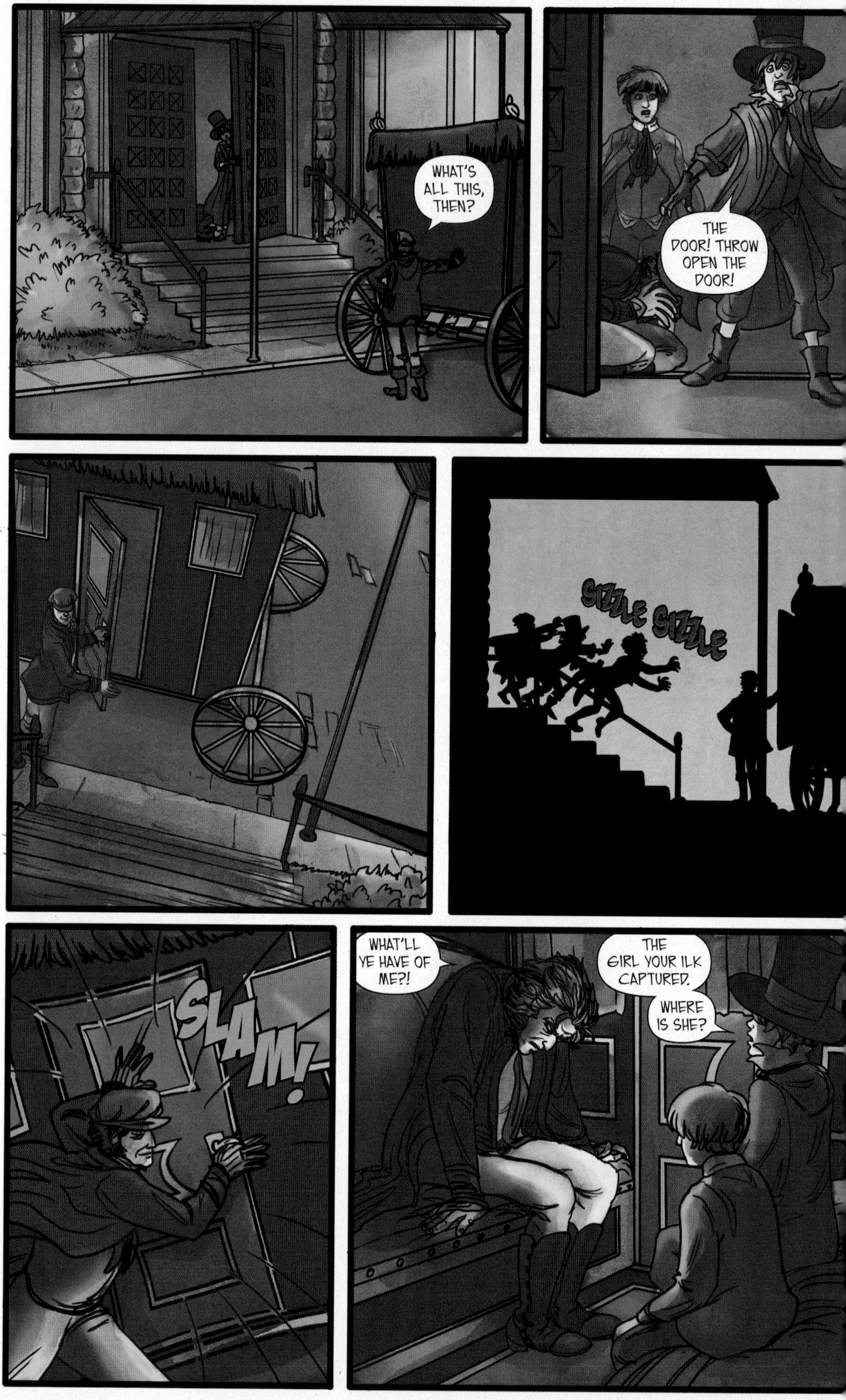
WHAT'S ALL THIS, THEN?
THE DOOR! THROW OPEN THE DOOR!
SIZZLE SIZZLE
SLAM!
WHAT'LL YE HAVE OF ME?!
THE GIRL YOUR ILK CAPTURED.
WHERE IS SHE?

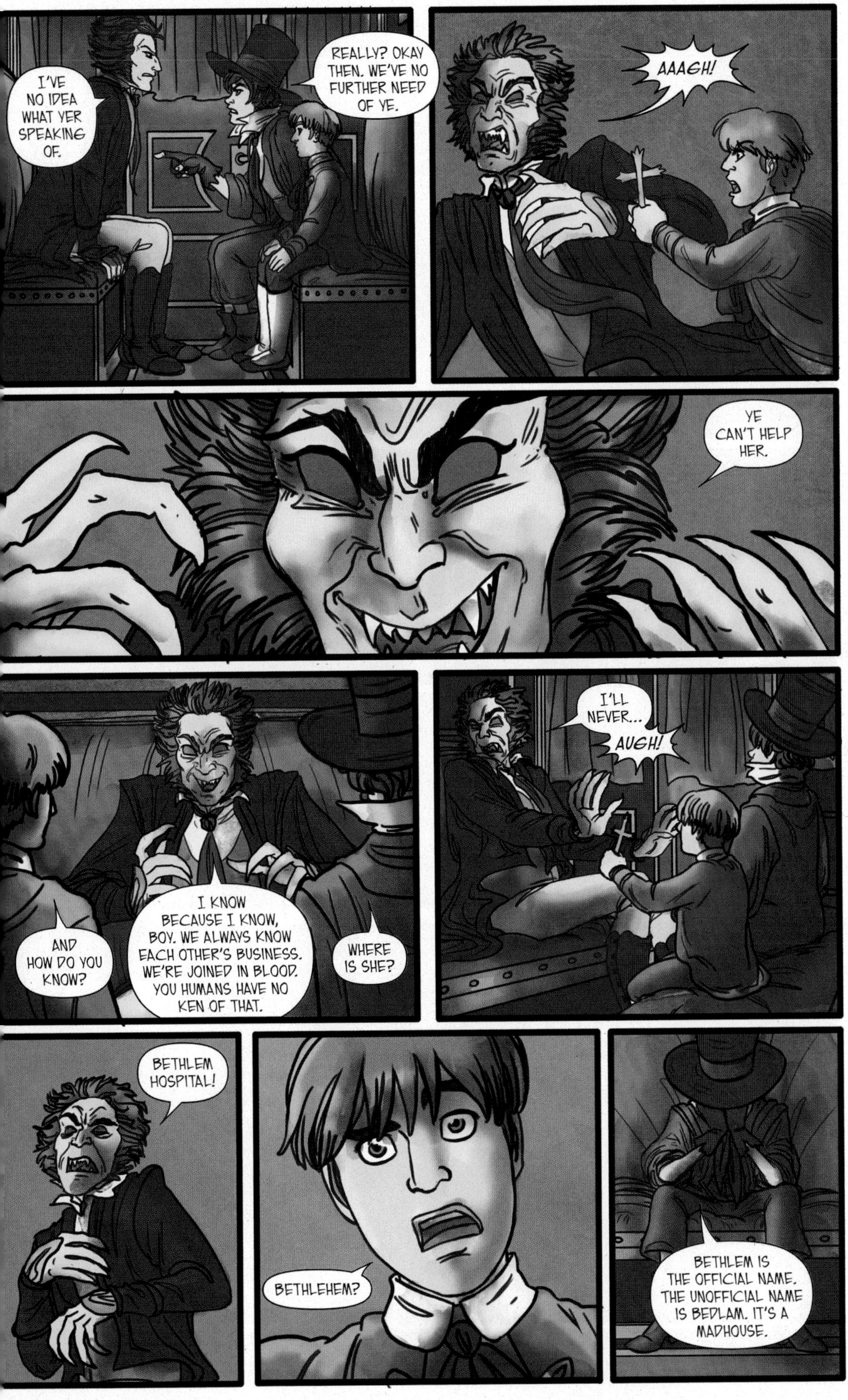
I'VE NO IDEA WHAT YER SPEAKING OF.
REALLY? OKAY THEN. WE'VE NO FURTHER NEED OF YE.
AAAGH!
YE CAN'T HELP HER.
AND HOW DO YOU KNOW?
I KNOW BECAUSE I KNOW, BOY. WE ALWAYS KNOW EACH OTHER'S BUSINESS. WE'RE JOINED IN BLOOD. YOU HUMANS HAVE NO KEN OF THAT.
WHERE IS SHE?
I'LL NEVER...
AUGH!
BETHLEM HOSPITAL!
BETHLEHEM?
BETHLEM IS THE OFFICIAL NAME. THE UNOFFICIAL NAME IS BEDLAM. IT'S A MADHOUSE.

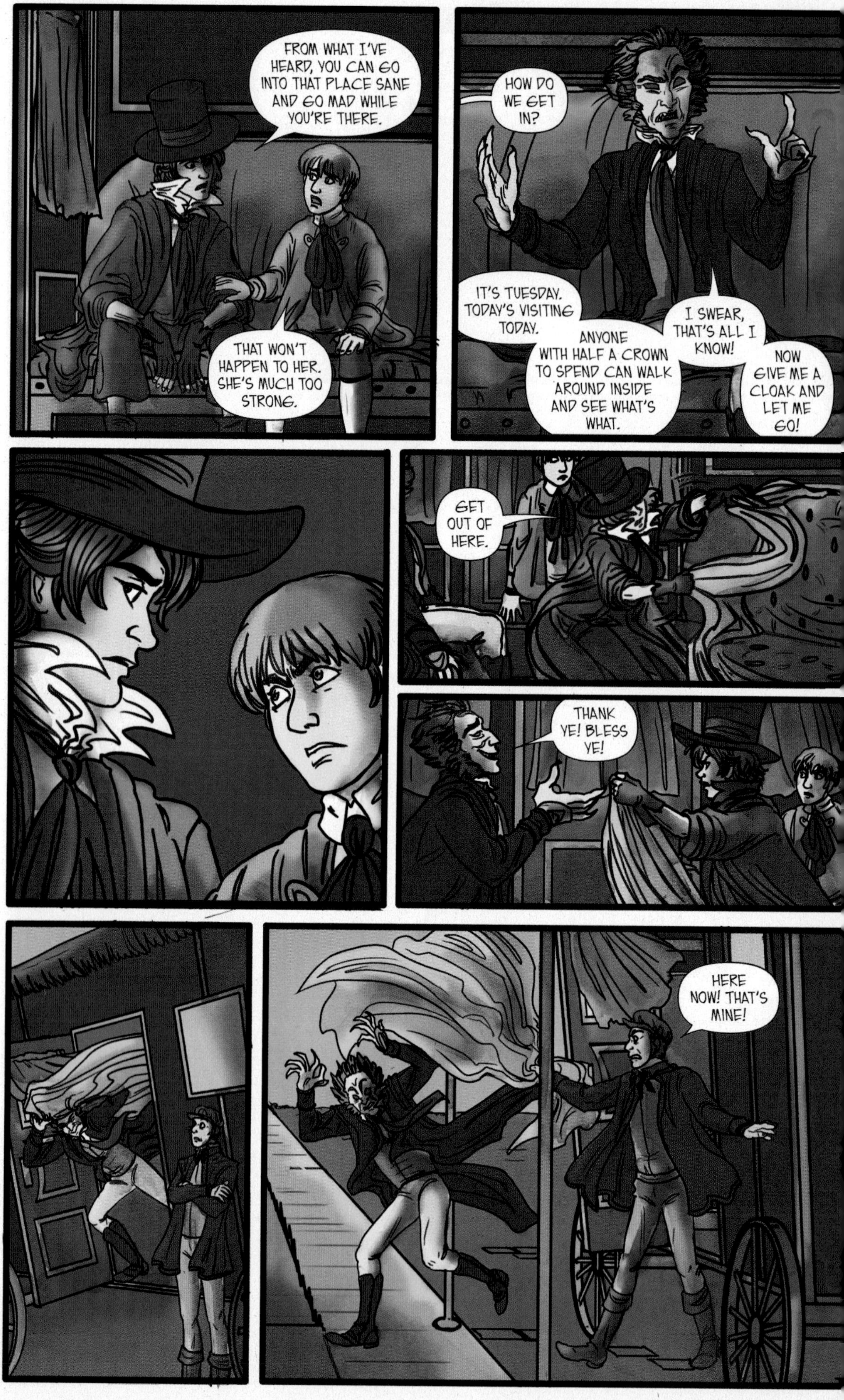
FROM WHAT I'VE HEARD, YOU CAN GO INTO THAT PLACE SANE AND GO MAD WHILE YOU'RE THERE.
THAT WON'T HAPPEN TO HER. SHE'S MUCH TOO STRONG.
HOW DO WE GET IN?
IT'S TUESDAY. TODAY'S VISITING TODAY.
ANYONE WITH HALF A CROWN TO SPEND CAN WALK AROUND INSIDE AND SEE WHAT'S WHAT.
I SWEAR, THAT'S ALL I KNOW!
NOW GIVE ME A CLOAK AND LET ME GO!
GET OUT OF HERE.
THANK YE! BLESS YE!
HERE NOW! THAT'S MINE!

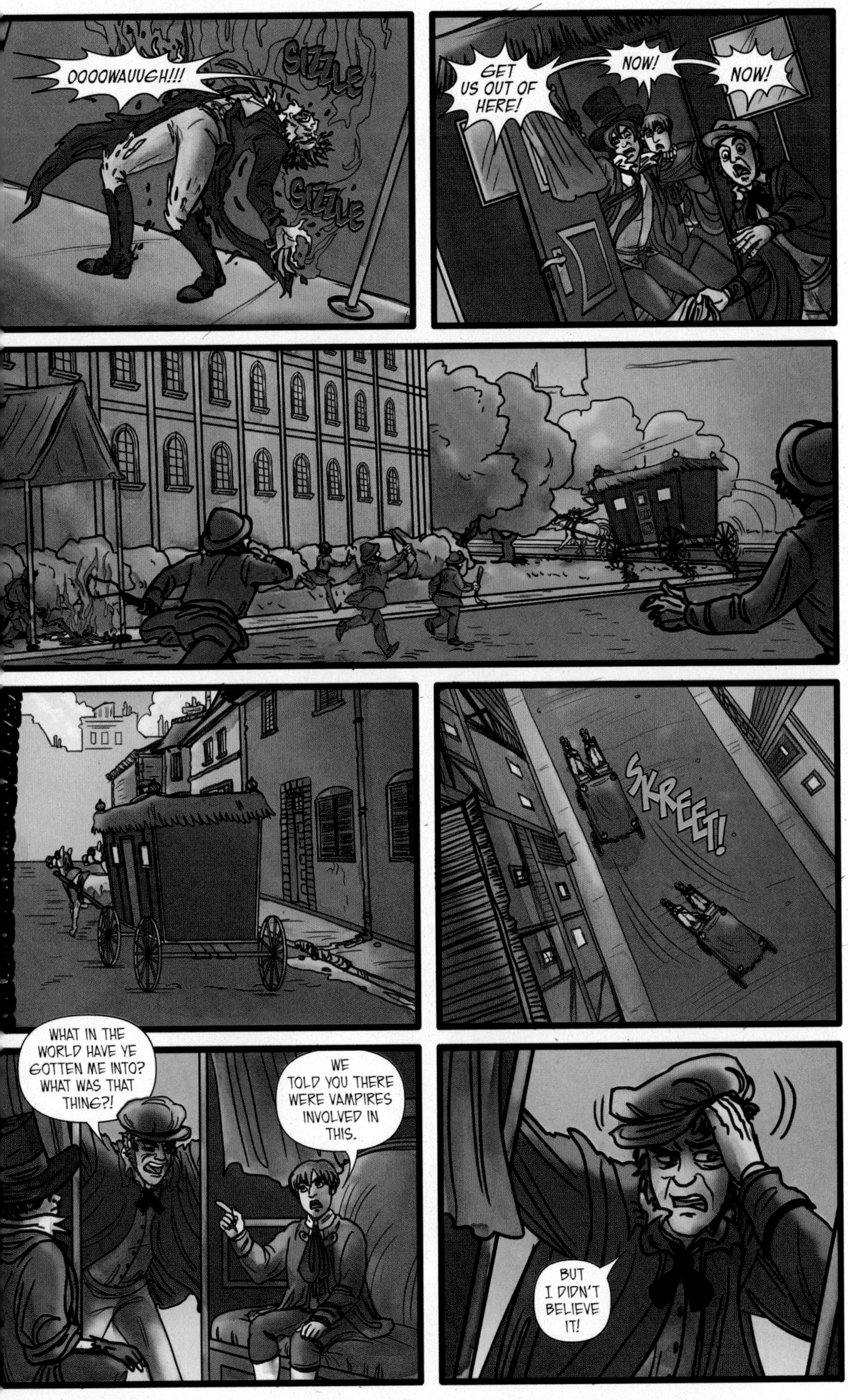
OOOOWAUUGH!!!
SIZZLE
SIZZLE
GET US OUT OF HERE!
NOW!
NOW!
SKREEET!
WHAT IN THE WORLD HAVE YE GOTTEN ME INTO? WHAT WAS THAT THING?!
WE TOLD YOU THERE WERE VAMPIRES INVOLVED IN THIS.
BUT I DIDN'T BELIEVE IT!

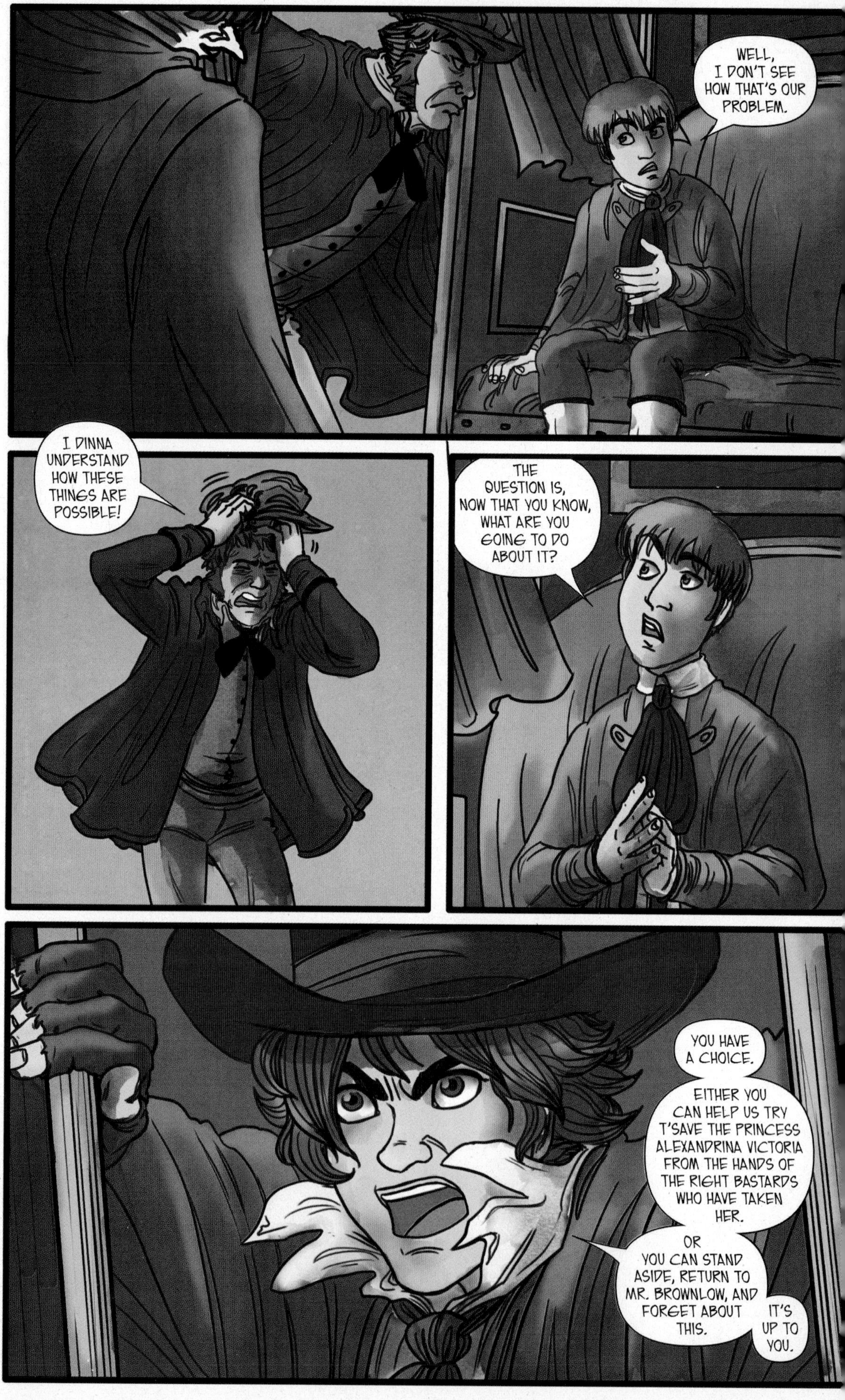
WELL, I DON'T SEE HOW THAT'S OUR PROBLEM.
I DINNA UNDERSTAND HOW THESE THINGS ARE POSSIBLE!
THE QUESTION IS, NOW THAT YOU KNOW, WHAT ARE YOU GOING TO DO ABOUT IT?
YOU HAVE A CHOICE.
EITHER YOU CAN HELP US TRY T'SAVE THE PRINCESS ALEXANDRINA VICTORIA FROM THE HANDS OF THE RIGHT BASTARDS WHO HAVE TAKEN HER.
OR YOU CAN STAND ASIDE, RETURN TO MR. BROWNLOW, AND FORGET ABOUT THIS.
IT'S UP TO YOU.

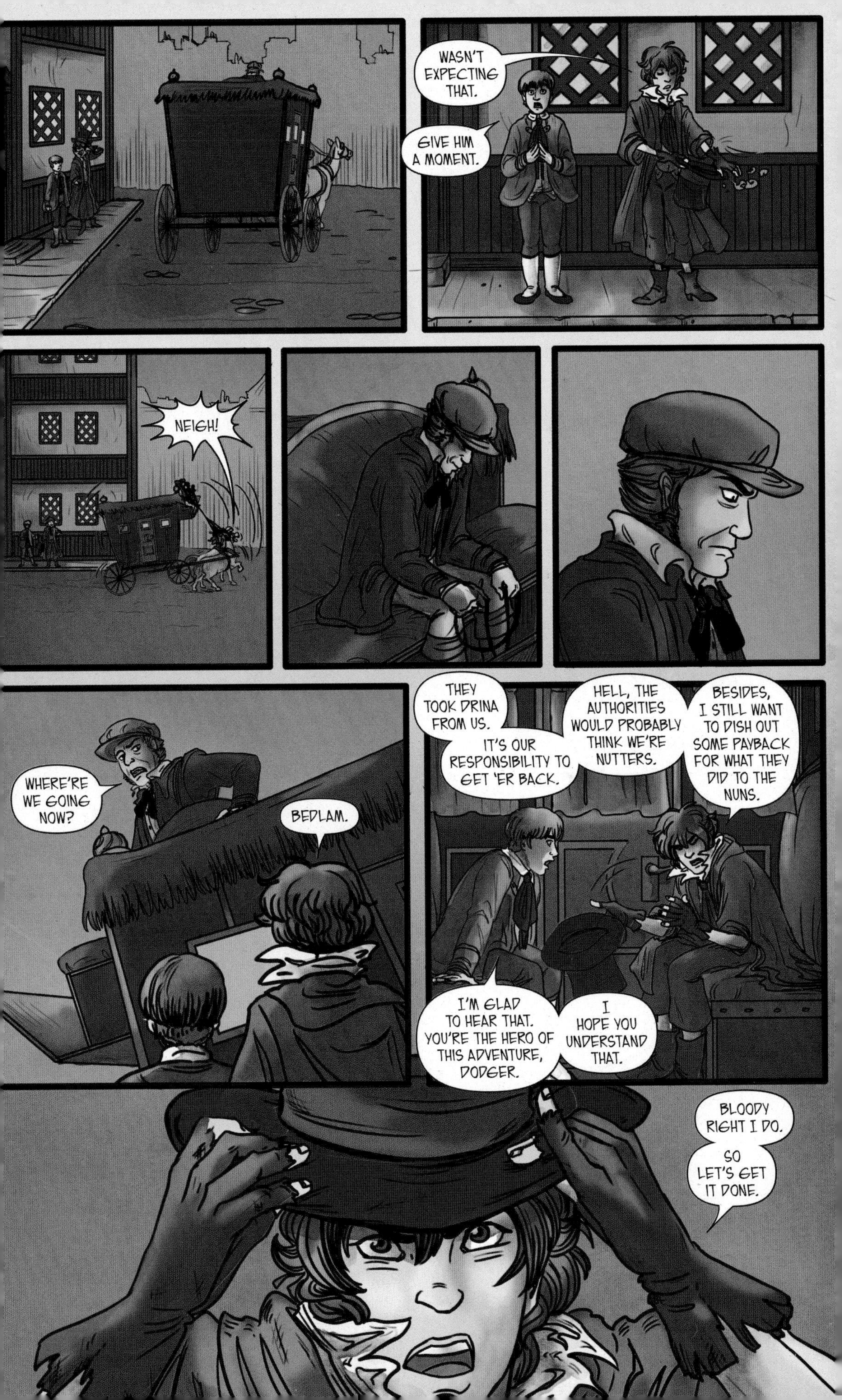
WASN'T EXPECTING THAT.
GIVE HIM A MOMENT.
NEIGH!
WHERE'RE WE GOING NOW?
BEDLAM.
THEY TOOK DRINA FROM US.
IT'S OUR RESPONSIBILITY TO GET 'ER BACK.
HELL, THE AUTHORITIES WOULD PROBABLY THINK WE'RE NUTTERS.
BESIDES, I STILL WANT TO DISH OUT SOME PAYBACK FOR WHAT THEY DID TO THE NUNS.
I'M GLAD TO HEAR THAT. YOU'RE THE HERO OF THIS ADVENTURE, DODGER.
I HOPE YOU UNDERSTAND THAT.
BLOODY RIGHT I DO.
SO LET'S GET IT DONE.

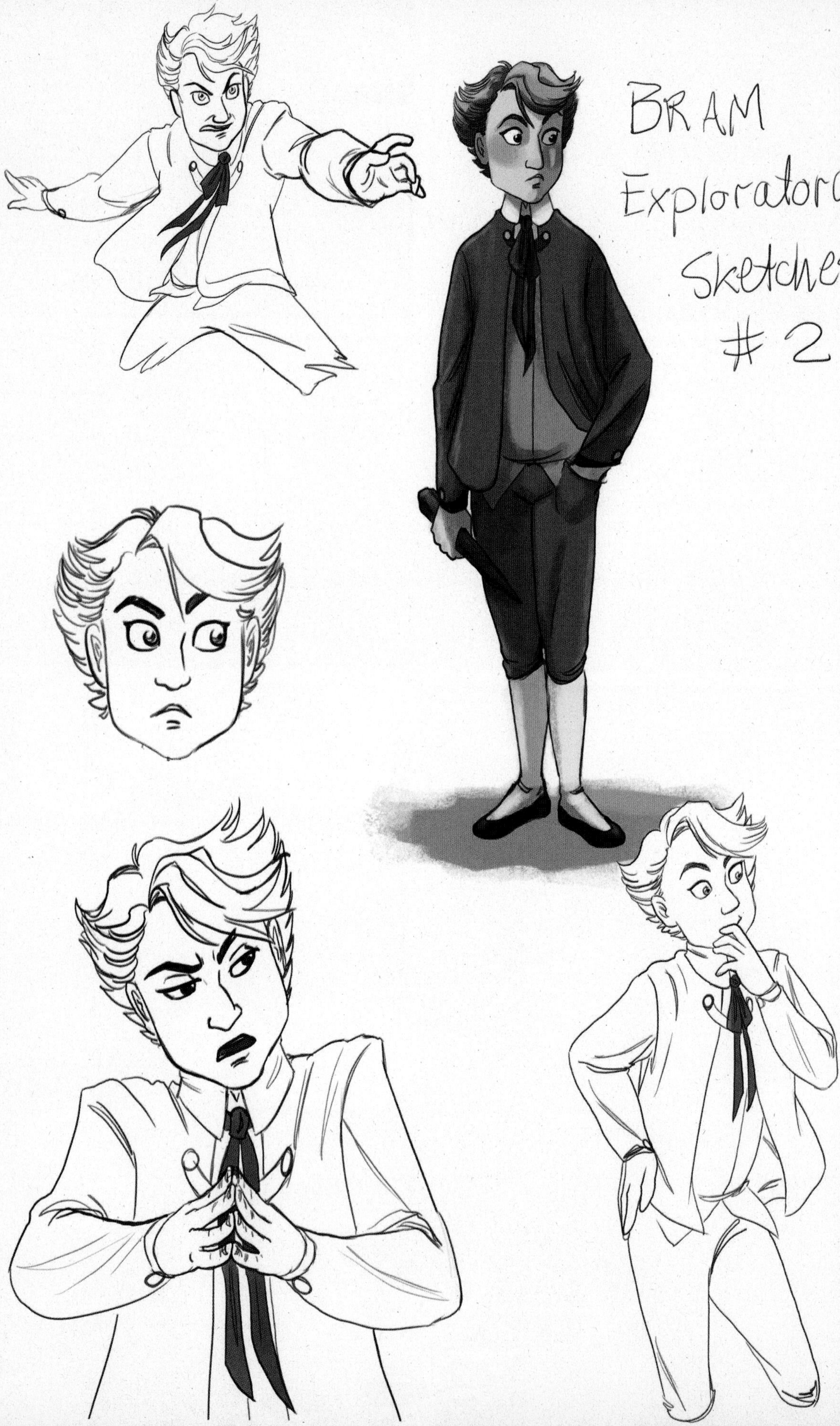
BRAM
Exploratory
Sketches
#2

CHAPTER FOUR

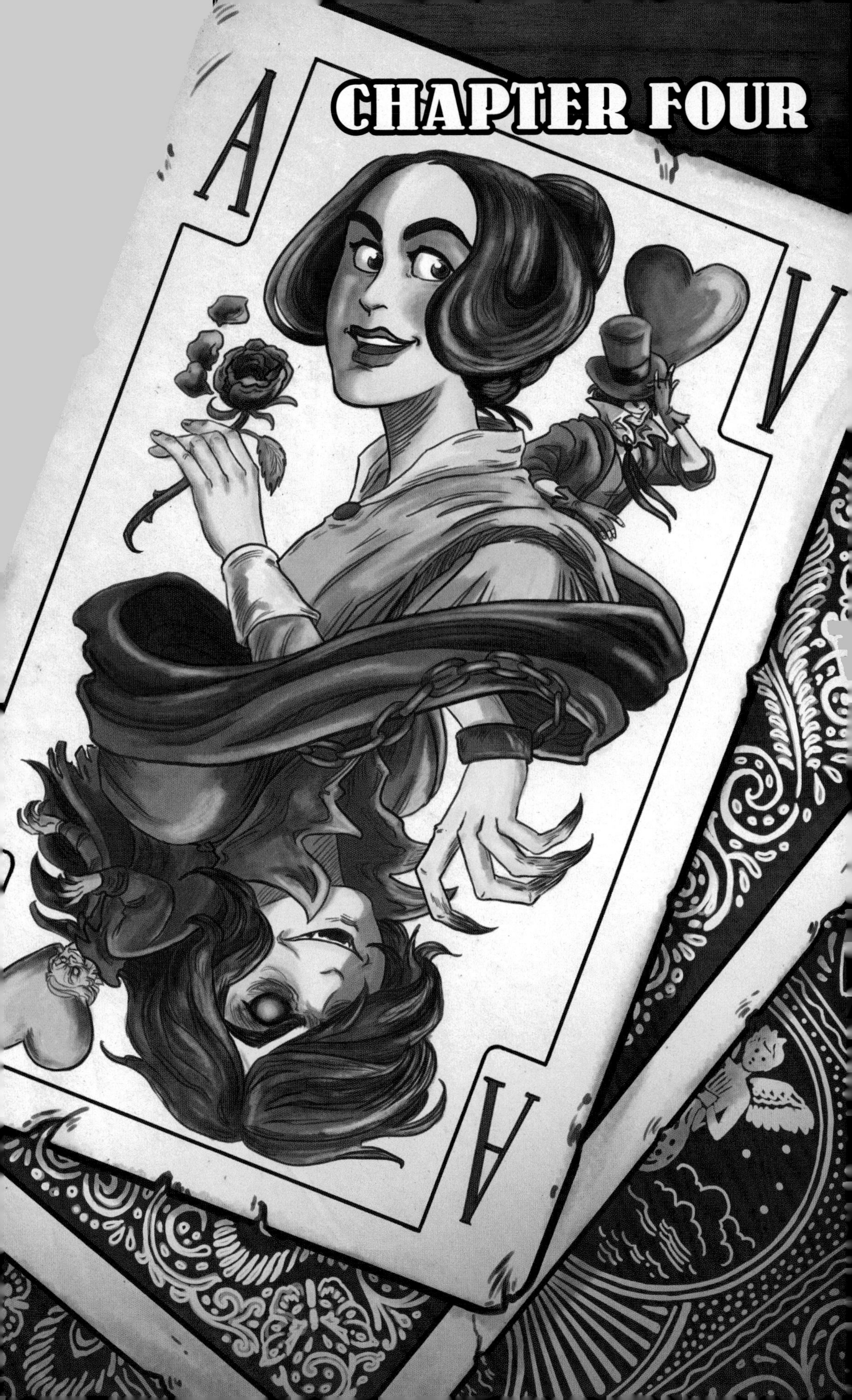

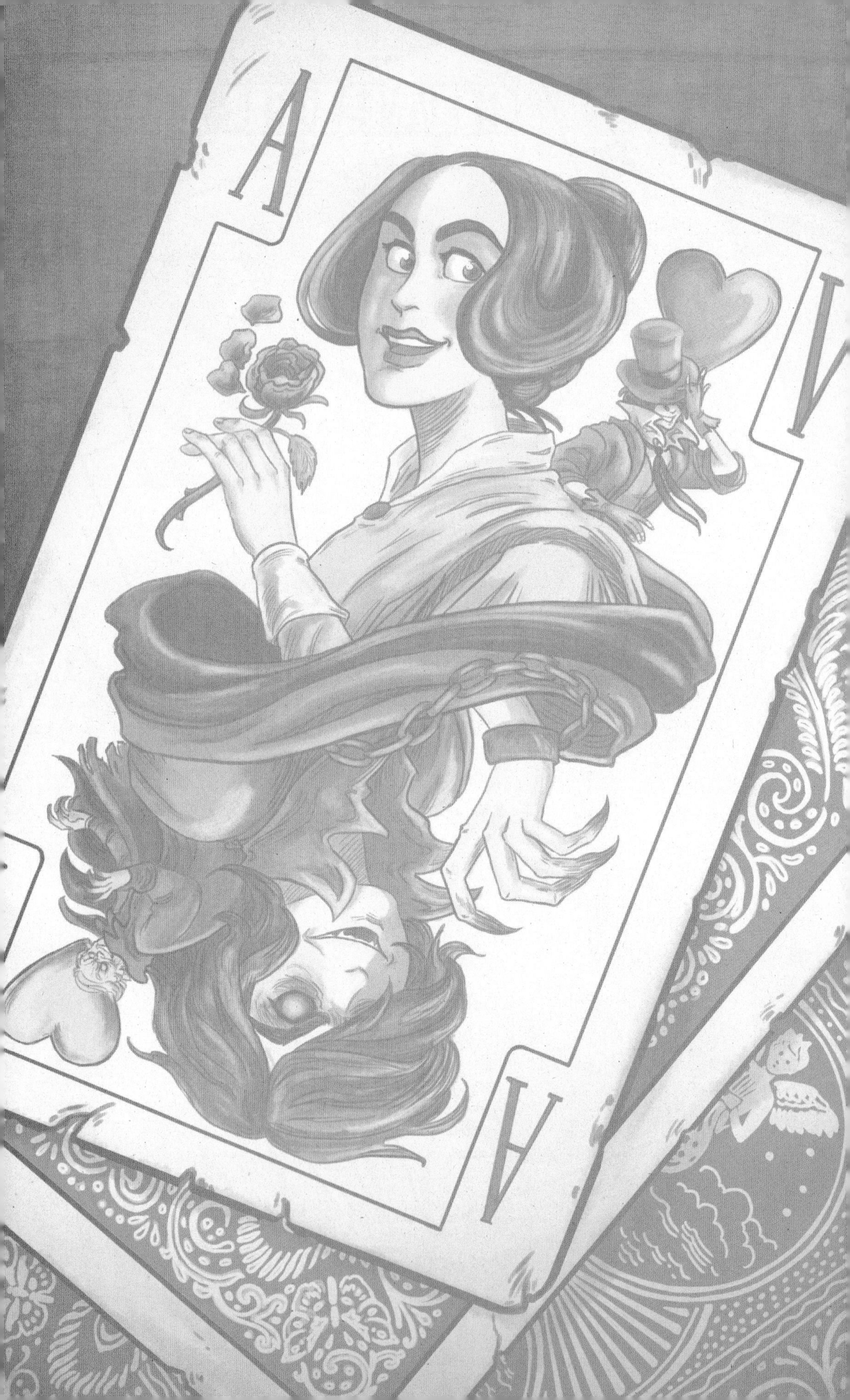
A
A

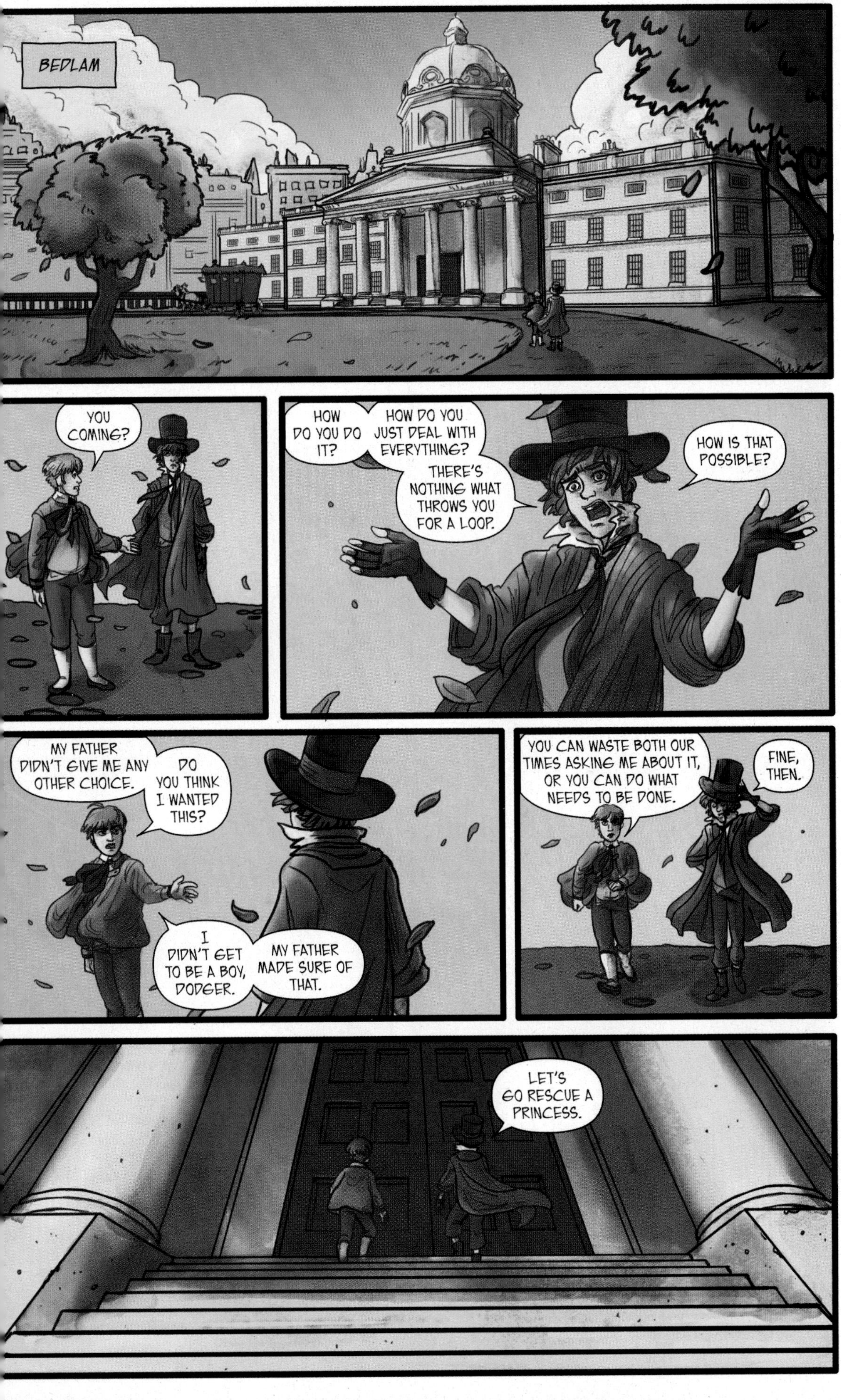
BEDLAM
YOU COMING?
HOW DO YOU DO IT?
HOW DO YOU JUST DEAL WITH EVERYTHING?
THERE'S NOTHING WHAT THROWS YOU FOR A LOOP.
HOW IS THAT POSSIBLE?
MY FATHER DIDN'T GIVE ME ANY OTHER CHOICE.
DO YOU THINK I WANTED THIS?
I DIDN'T GET TO BE A BOY, DODGER.
MY FATHER MADE SURE OF THAT.
YOU CAN WASTE BOTH OUR TIMES ASKING ME ABOUT IT, OR YOU CAN DO WHAT NEEDS TO BE DONE.
FINE, THEN.
LET'S GO RESCUE A PRINCESS.

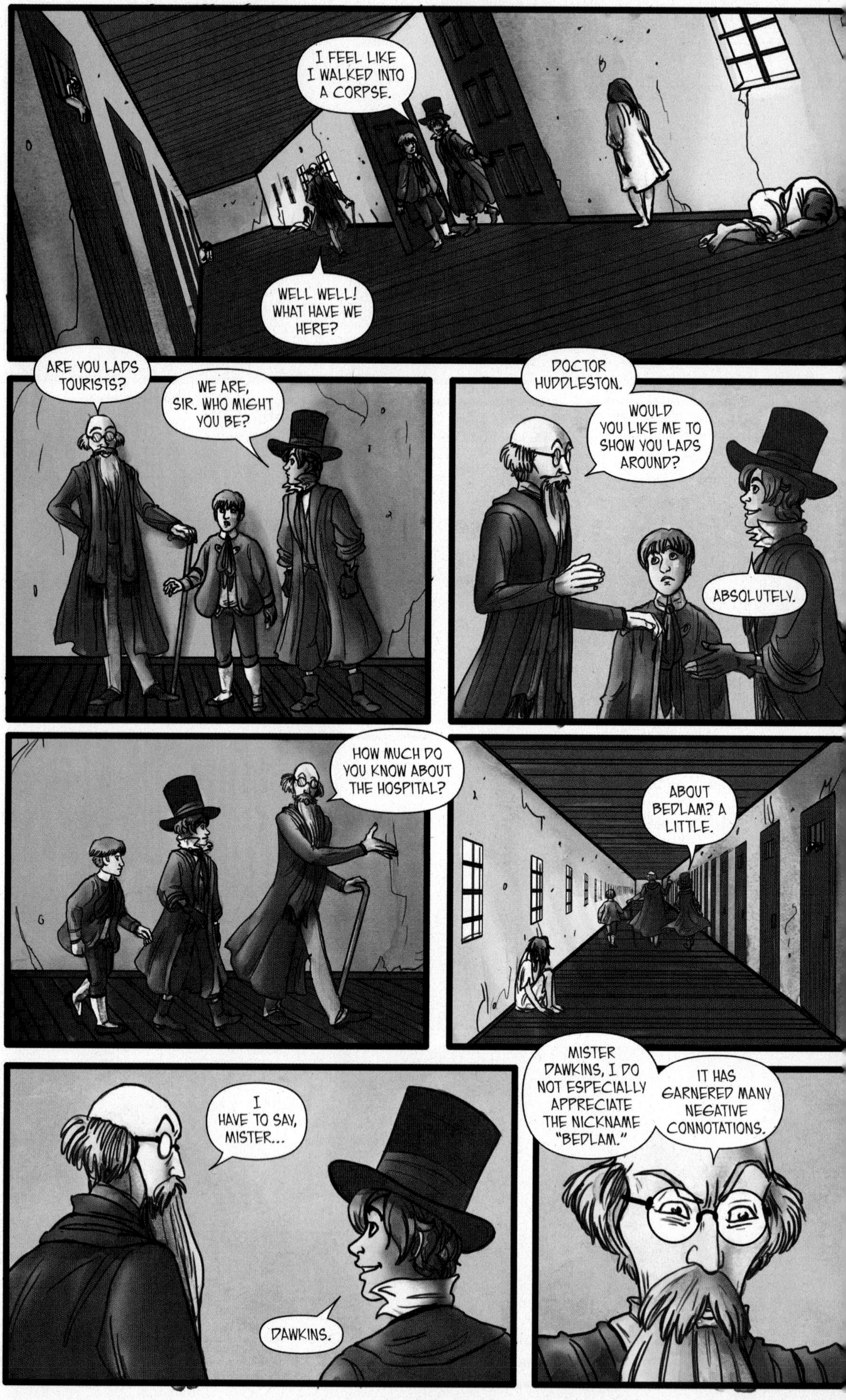
I FEEL LIKE I WALKED INTO A CORPSE.
WELL WELL! WHAT HAVE WE HERE?
ARE YOU LADS TOURISTS?
WE ARE, SIR. WHO MIGHT YOU BE?
DOCTOR HUDDLESTON.
WOULD YOU LIKE ME TO SHOW YOU LADS AROUND?
ABSOLUTELY.
HOW MUCH DO YOU KNOW ABOUT THE HOSPITAL?
ABOUT BEDLAM? A LITTLE.
I HAVE TO SAY, MISTER...
DAWKINS.
MISTER DAWKINS, I DO NOT ESPECIALLY APPRECIATE THE NICKNAME "BEDLAM."
IT HAS GARNERED MANY NEGATIVE CONNOTATIONS.

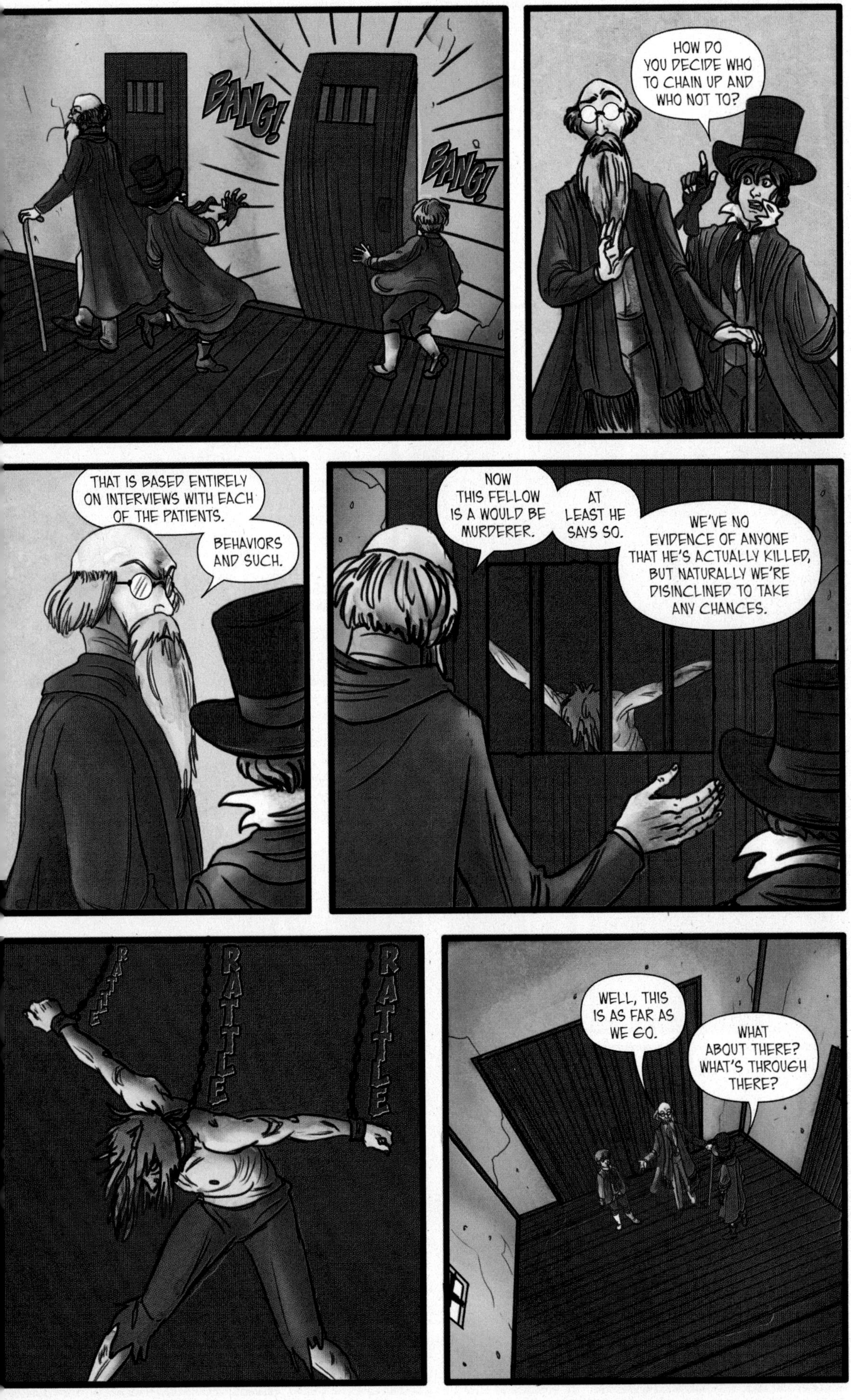
BANG!
BANG!
HOW DO YOU DECIDE WHO TO CHAIN UP AND WHO NOT TO?
THAT IS BASED ENTIRELY ON INTERVIEWS WITH EACH OF THE PATIENTS.
BEHAVIORS AND SUCH.
NOW THIS FELLOW IS A WOULD BE MURDERER.
AT LEAST HE SAYS SO.
WE'VE NO EVIDENCE OF ANYONE THAT HE'S ACTUALLY KILLED, BUT NATURALLY WE'RE DISINCLINED TO TAKE ANY CHANCES.
RATTLE
RATTLE
RATTLE
WELL, THIS IS AS FAR AS WE GO.
WHAT ABOUT THERE? WHAT'S THROUGH THERE?

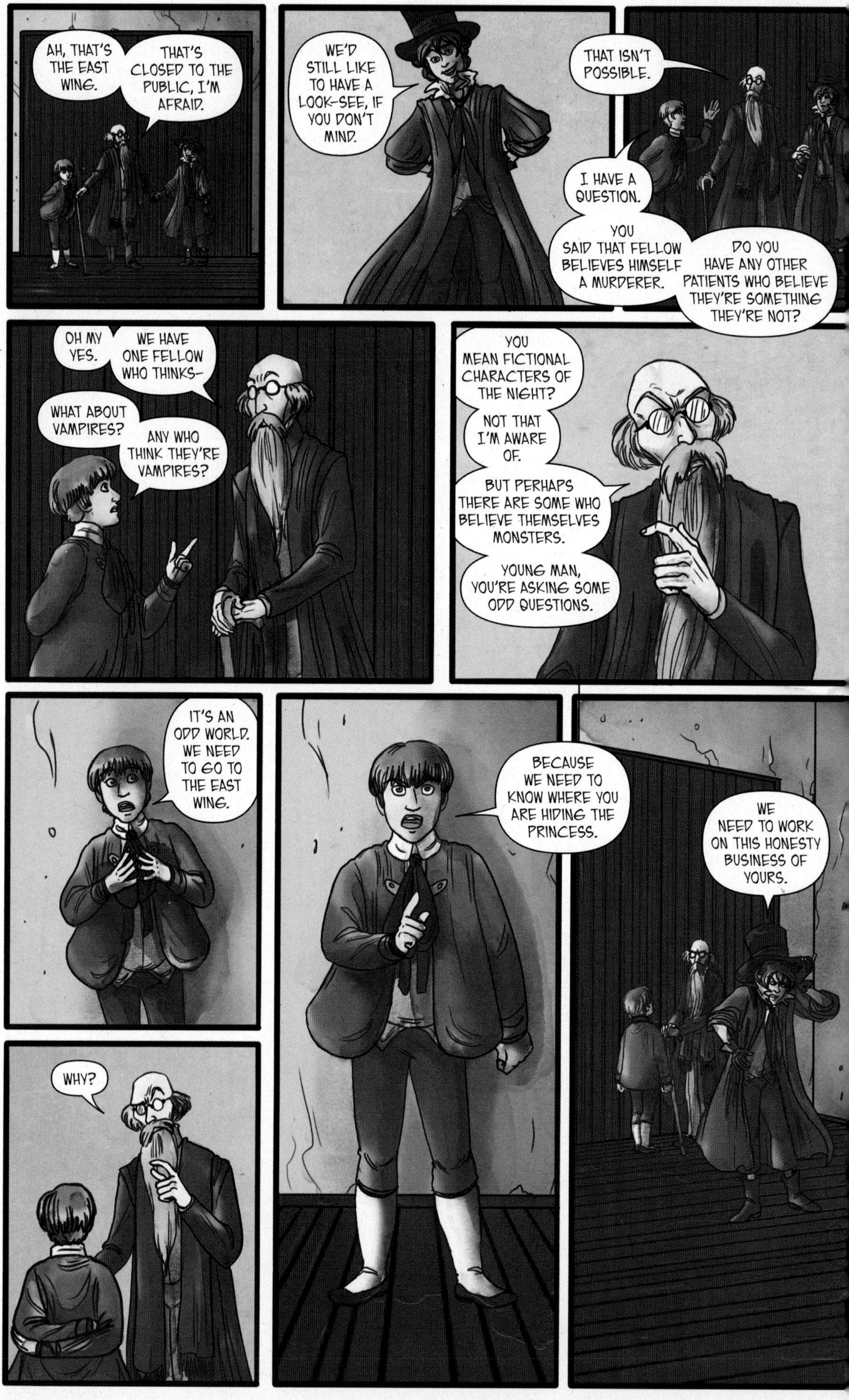
AH, THAT'S THE EAST WING.
THAT'S CLOSED TO THE PUBLIC, I'M AFRAID.
WE'D STILL LIKE TO HAVE A LOOK-SEE, IF YOU DON'T MIND.
THAT ISN'T POSSIBLE.
I HAVE A QUESTION.
YOU SAID THAT FELLOW BELIEVES HIMSELF A MURDERER.
DO YOU HAVE ANY OTHER PATIENTS WHO BELIEVE THEY'RE SOMETHING THEY'RE NOT?
OH MY YES.
WE HAVE ONE FELLOW WHO THINKS–
WHAT ABOUT VAMPIRES?
ANY WHO THINK THEY'RE VAMPIRES?
YOU MEAN FICTIONAL CHARACTERS OF THE NIGHT?
NOT THAT I'M AWARE OF.
BUT PERHAPS THERE ARE SOME WHO BELIEVE THEMSELVES MONSTERS.
YOUNG MAN, YOU'RE ASKING SOME ODD QUESTIONS.
IT'S AN ODD WORLD. WE NEED TO GO TO THE EAST WING.
WHY?
BECAUSE WE NEED TO KNOW WHERE YOU ARE HIDING THE PRINCESS.
WE NEED TO WORK ON THIS HONESTY BUSINESS OF YOURS.

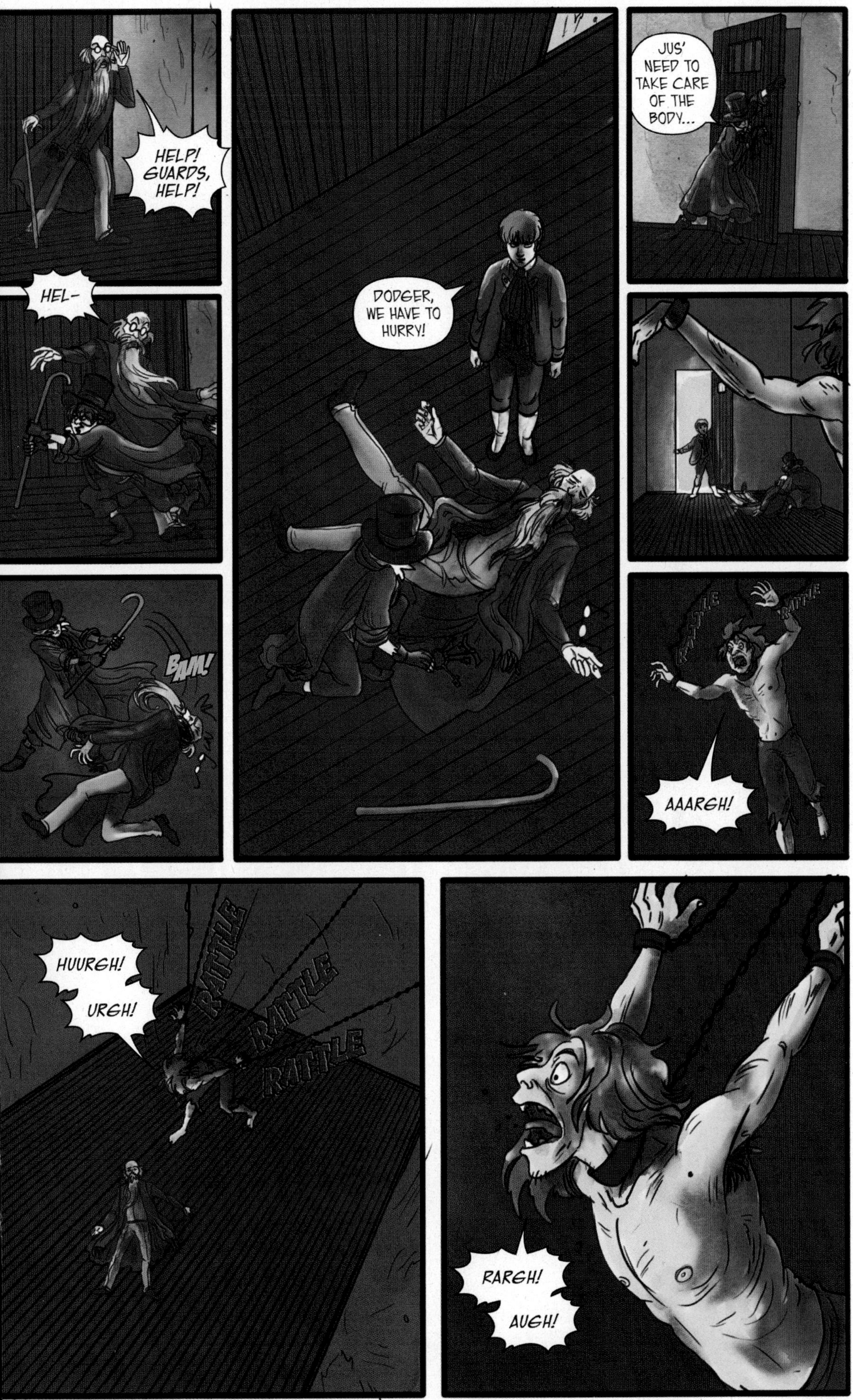
HELP! GUARDS, HELP!
JUS' NEED TO TAKE CARE OF THE BODY...
HEL-
DODGER, WE HAVE TO HURRY!
BAM!
RATTLE
RATTLE
AAARGH!
HUURGH!
URGH!
RATTLE
RATTLE
RATTLE
RARGH!
AUGH!

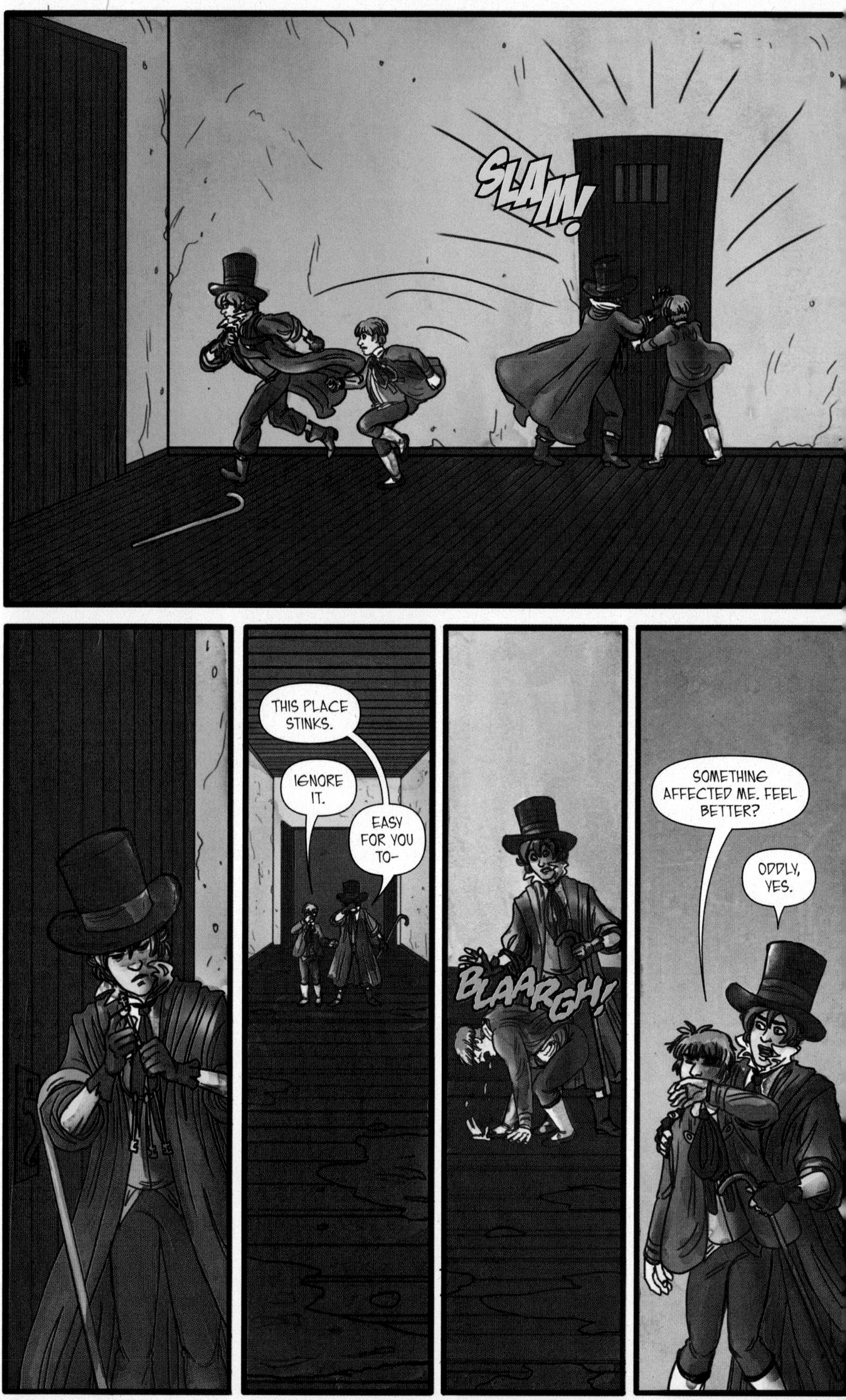
SLAM!
THIS PLACE STINKS.
IGNORE IT.
EASY FOR YOU TO-
BLAARGH!
SOMETHING AFFECTED ME. FEEL BETTER?
ODDLY, YES.

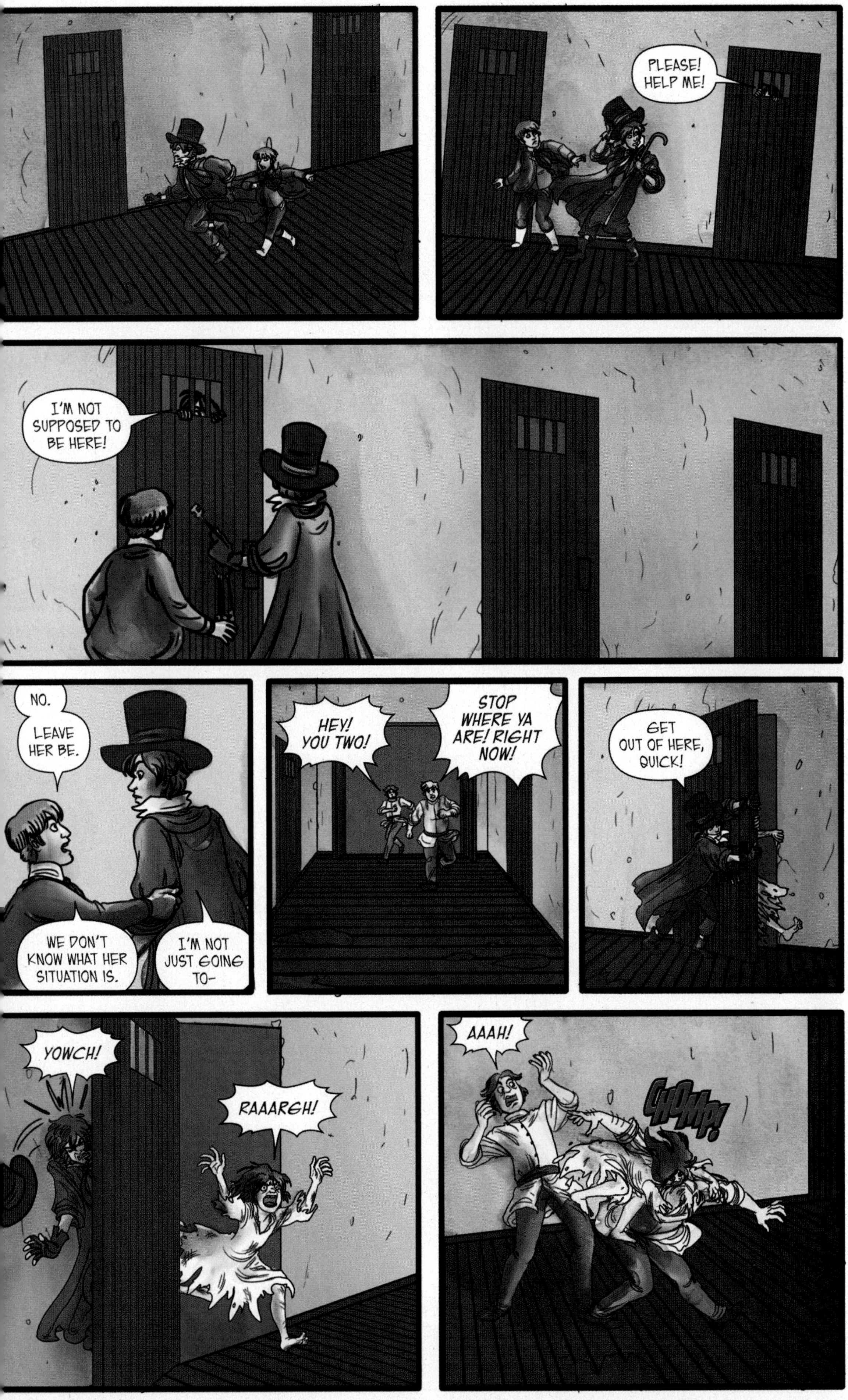
PLEASE! HELP ME!
I'M NOT SUPPOSED TO BE HERE!
NO.
LEAVE HER BE.
WE DON'T KNOW WHAT HER SITUATION IS.
I'M NOT JUST GOING TO-
HEY! YOU TWO!
STOP WHERE YA ARE! RIGHT NOW!
GET OUT OF HERE, QUICK!
YOWCH!
RAAARGH!
AAAH!
CHOMP!

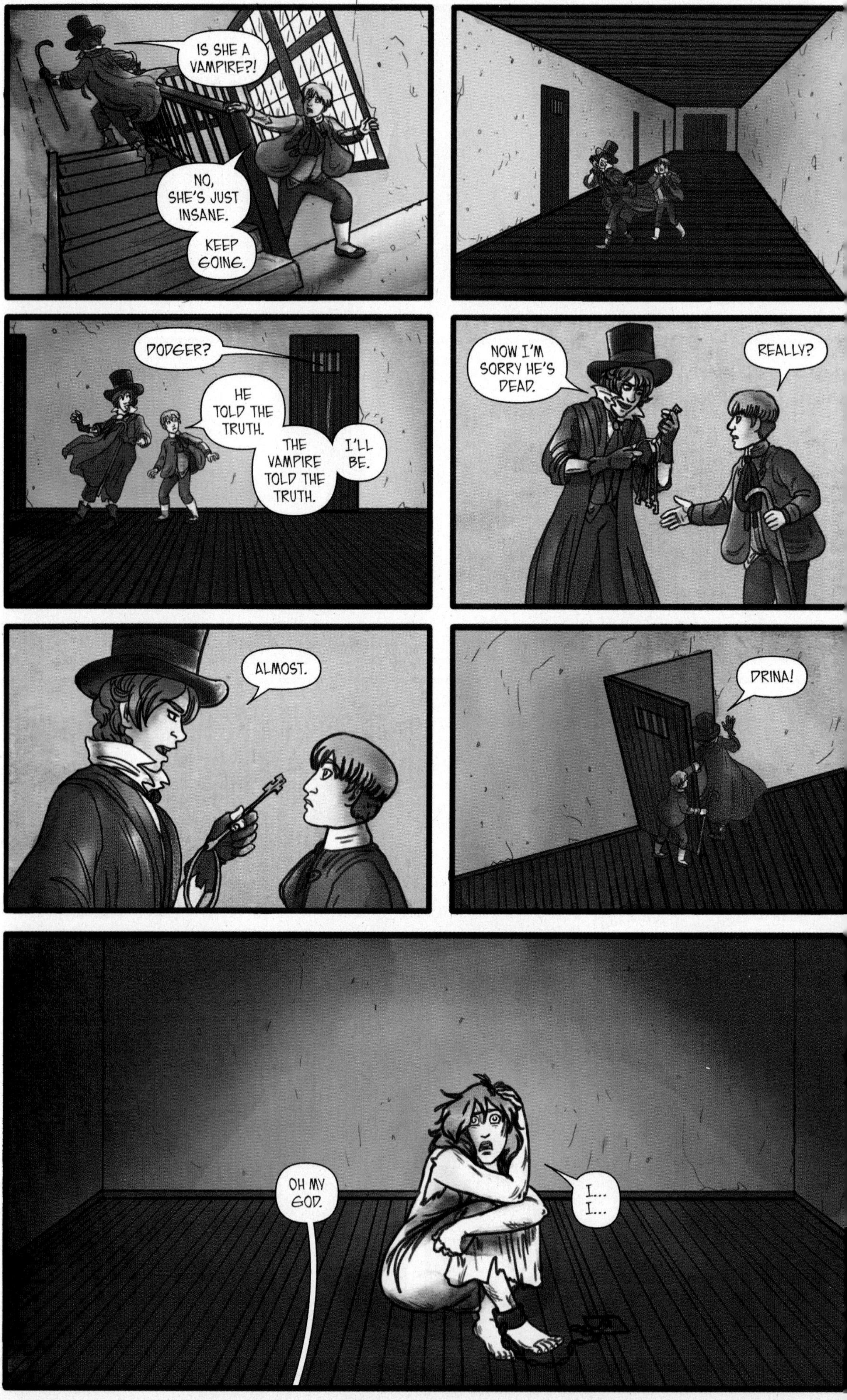
IS SHE A VAMPIRE?!
NO, SHE'S JUST INSANE.
KEEP GOING.
DODGER?
HE TOLD THE TRUTH.
THE VAMPIRE TOLD THE TRUTH.
I'LL BE.
NOW I'M SORRY HE'S DEAD.
REALLY?
ALMOST.
DRINA!
OH MY GOD.
I... I...

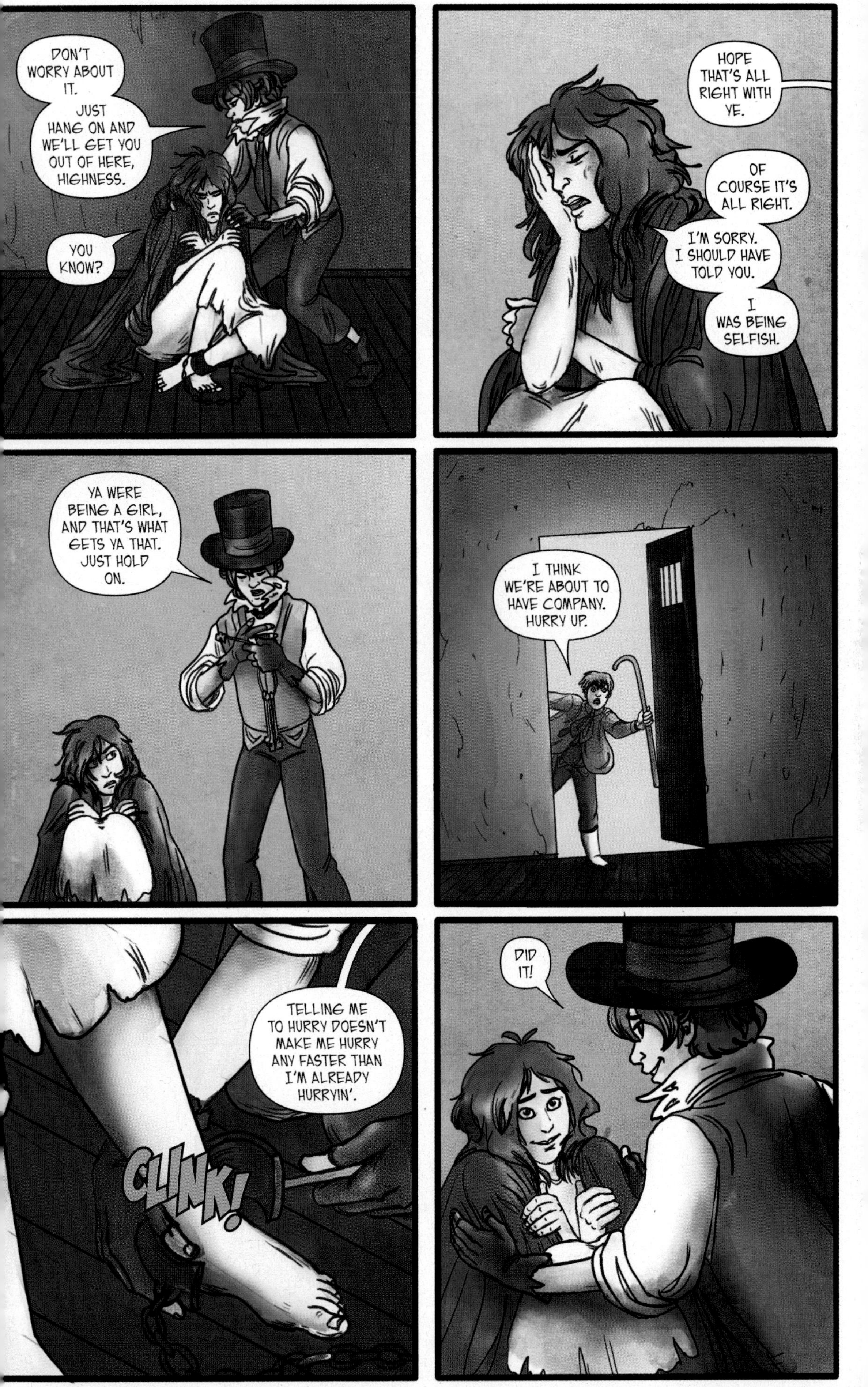
DON'T WORRY ABOUT IT.
JUST HANG ON AND WE'LL GET YOU OUT OF HERE, HIGHNESS.
YOU KNOW?
HOPE THAT'S ALL RIGHT WITH YE.
OF COURSE IT'S ALL RIGHT.
I'M SORRY. I SHOULD HAVE TOLD YOU.
I WAS BEING SELFISH.
YA WERE BEING A GIRL, AND THAT'S WHAT GETS YA THAT. JUST HOLD ON.
I THINK WE'RE ABOUT TO HAVE COMPANY. HURRY UP.
TELLING ME TO HURRY DOESN'T MAKE ME HURRY ANY FASTER THAN I'M ALREADY HURRYIN'.
CLINK!
DID IT!

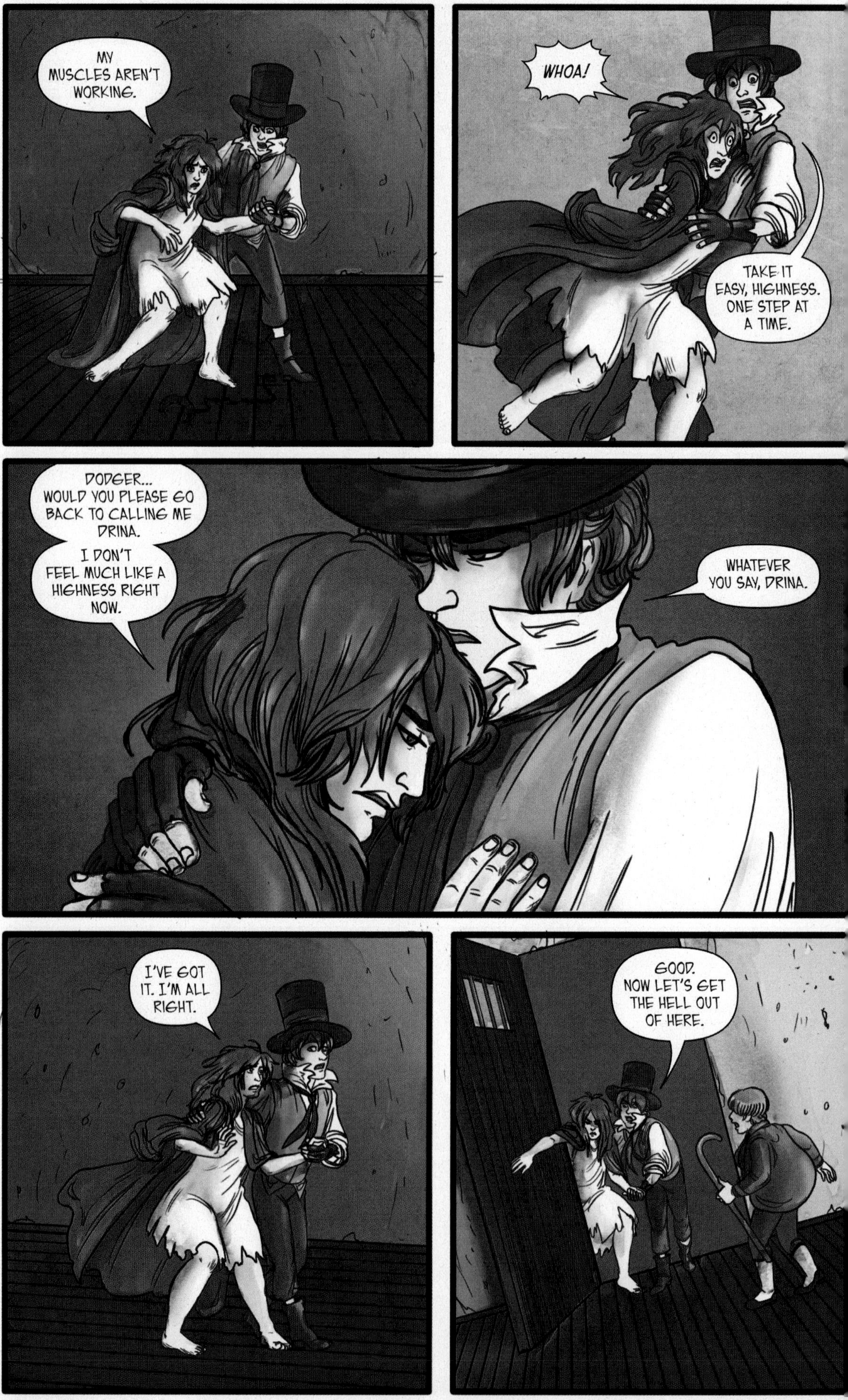
MY MUSCLES AREN'T WORKING.
WHOA!
TAKE IT EASY, HIGHNESS. ONE STEP AT A TIME.
DODGER... WOULD YOU PLEASE GO BACK TO CALLING ME DRINA.
I DON'T FEEL MUCH LIKE A HIGHNESS RIGHT NOW.
WHATEVER YOU SAY, DRINA.
I'VE GOT IT. I'M ALL RIGHT.
GOOD. NOW LET'S GET THE HELL OUT OF HERE.

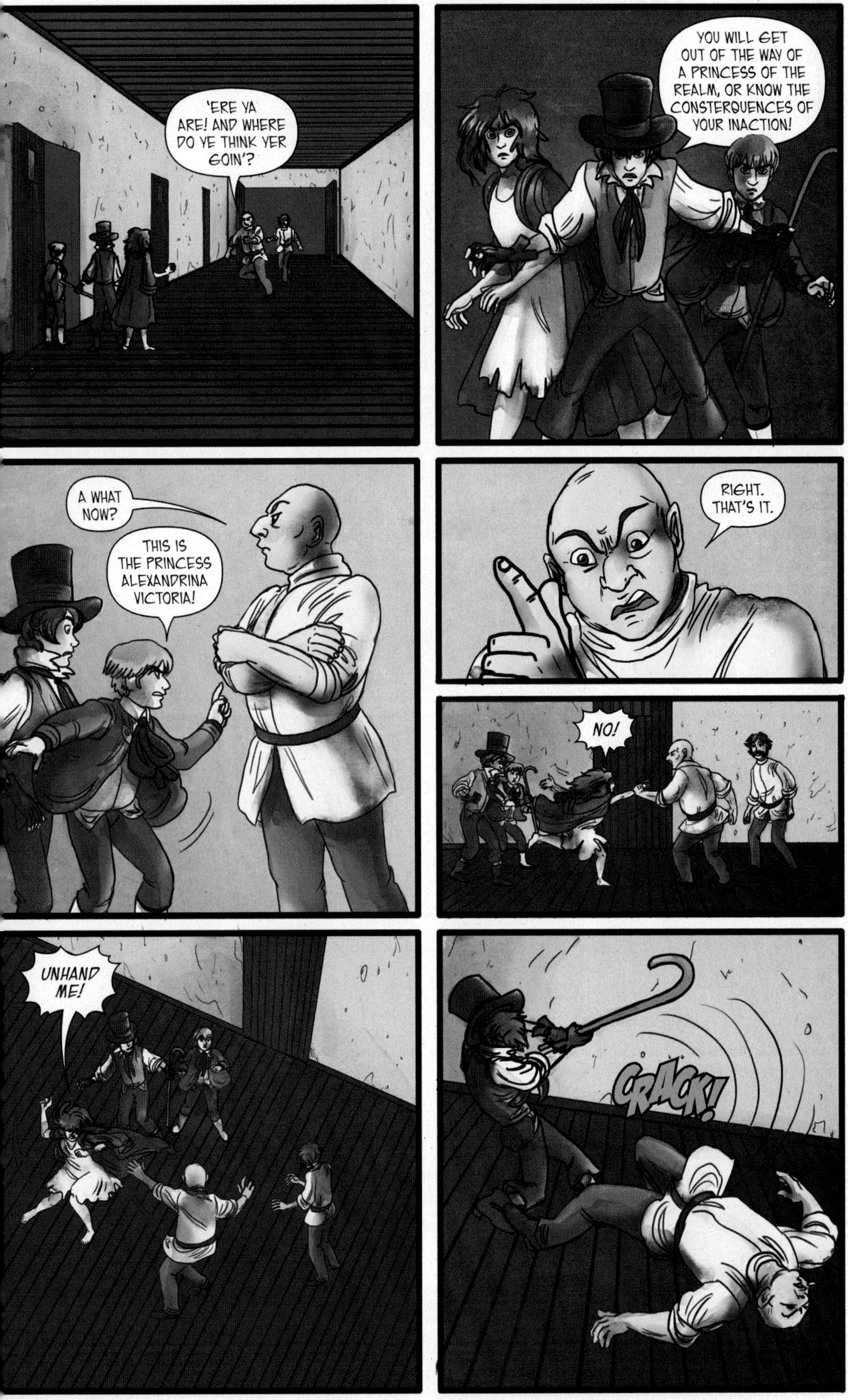
'ERE YA ARE! AND WHERE DO YE THINK YER GOIN'?
YOU WILL GET OUT OF THE WAY OF A PRINCESS OF THE REALM, OR KNOW THE CONSTERQUENCES OF YOUR INACTION!
A WHAT NOW?
THIS IS THE PRINCESS ALEXANDRINA VICTORIA!
RIGHT. THAT'S IT.
NO!
UNHAND ME!
CRACK!

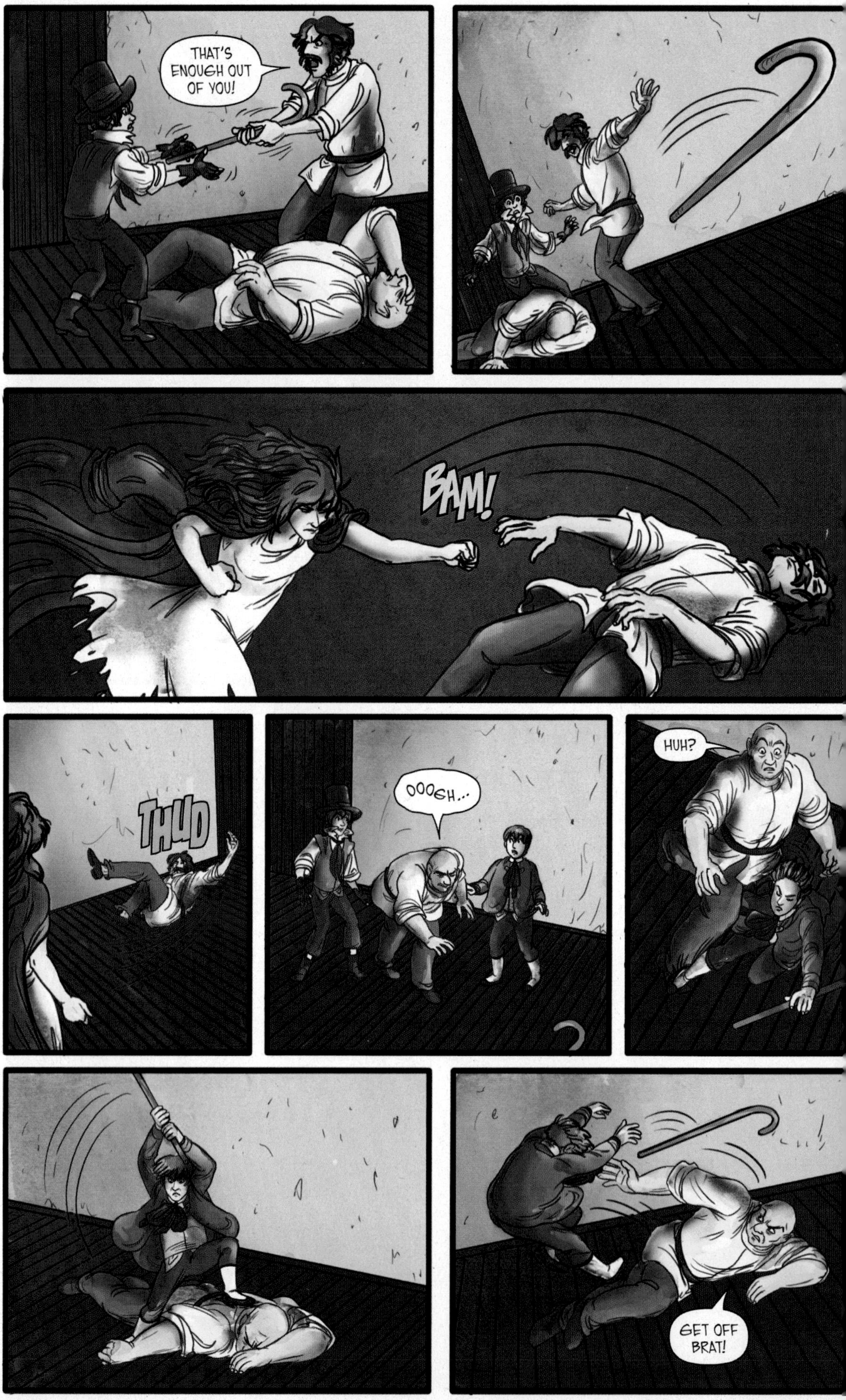
THAT'S ENOUGH OUT OF YOU!
BAM!
THUD
OOOGH...
HUH?
GET OFF BRAT!

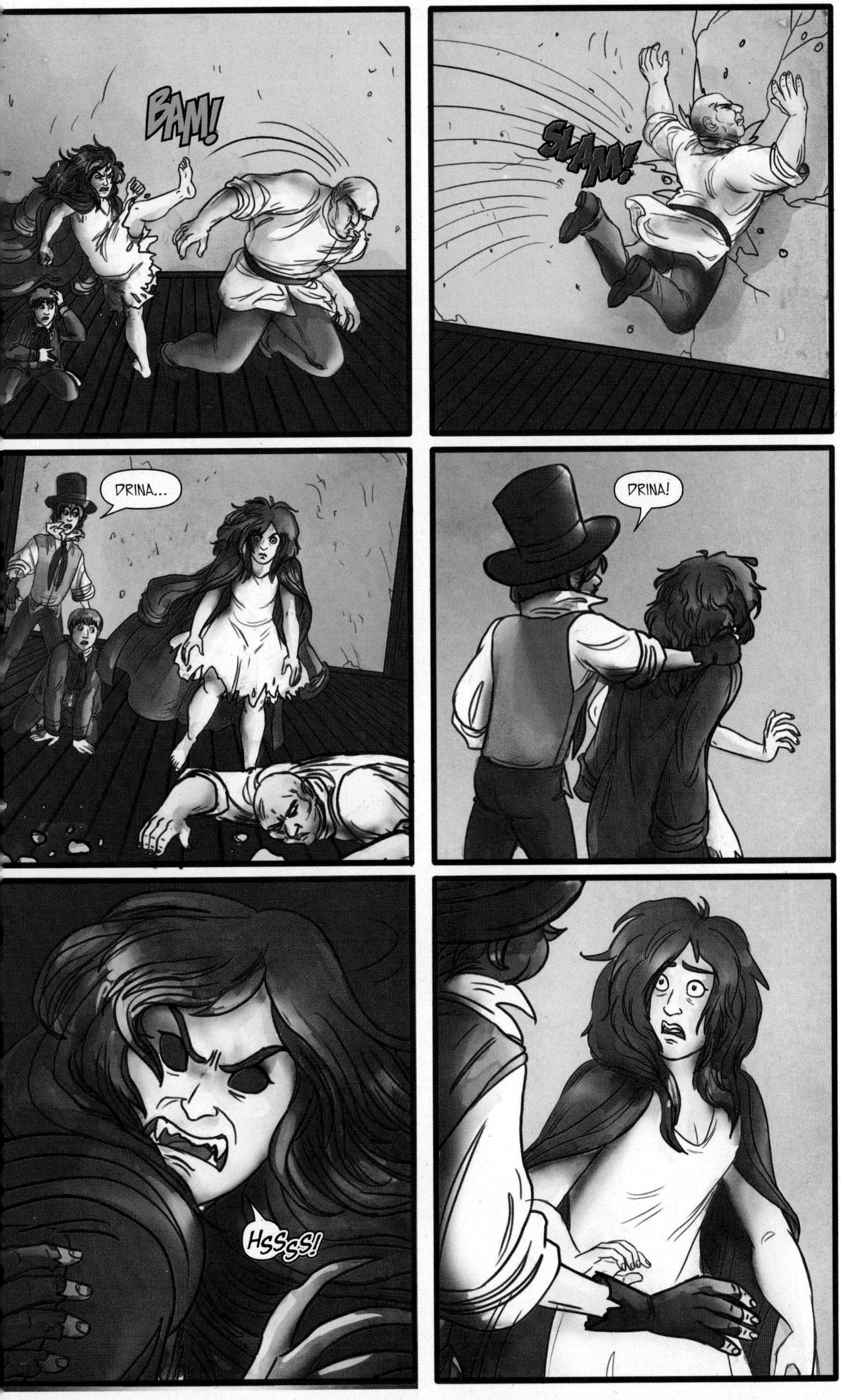
BAM!
SLAM!
DRINA...
DRINA!
HSSSS!

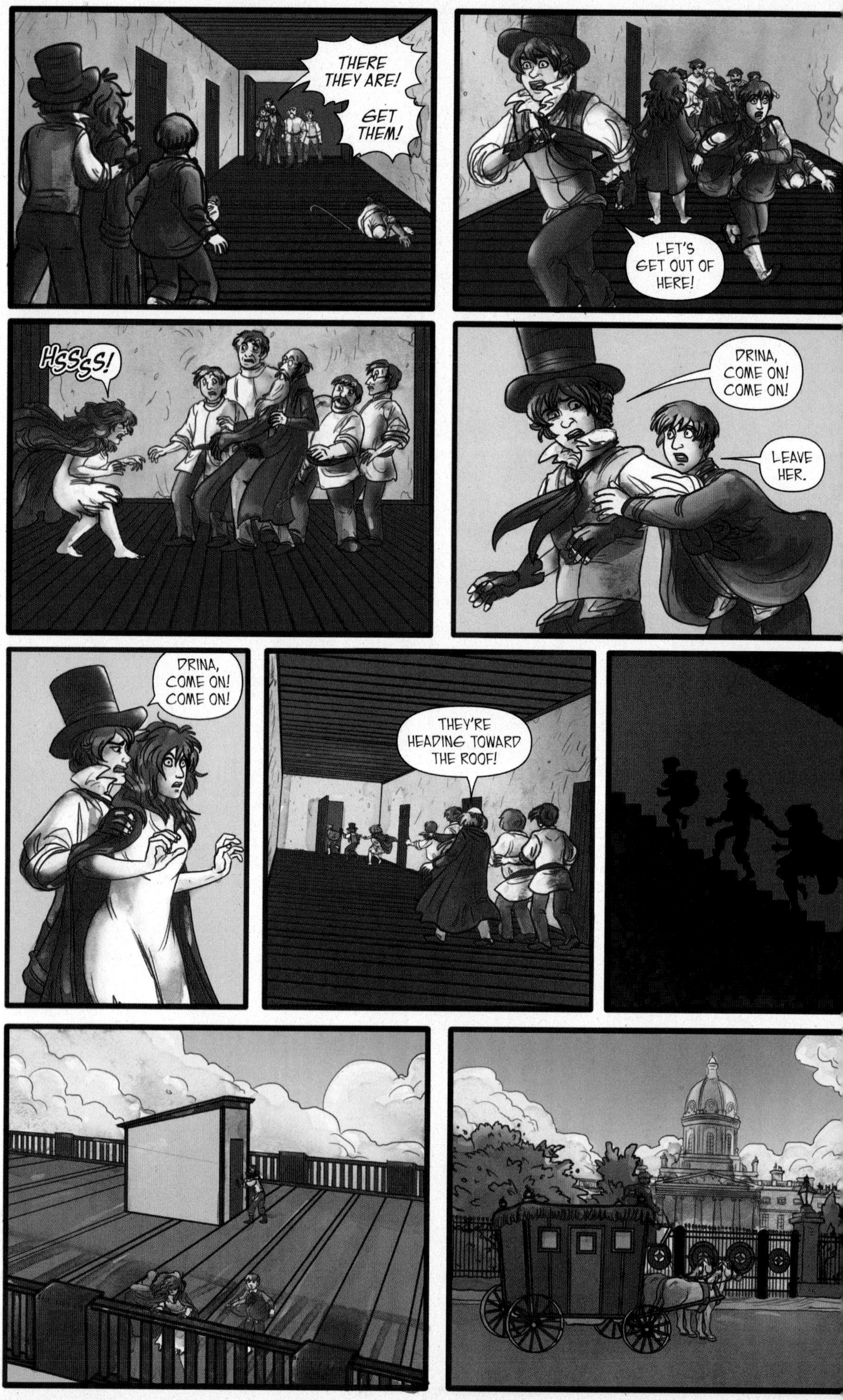
THERE THEY ARE!
GET THEM!
LET'S GET OUT OF HERE!
HSSSS!
DRINA, COME ON! COME ON!
LEAVE HER.
DRINA, COME ON! COME ON!
THEY'RE HEADING TOWARD THE ROOF!

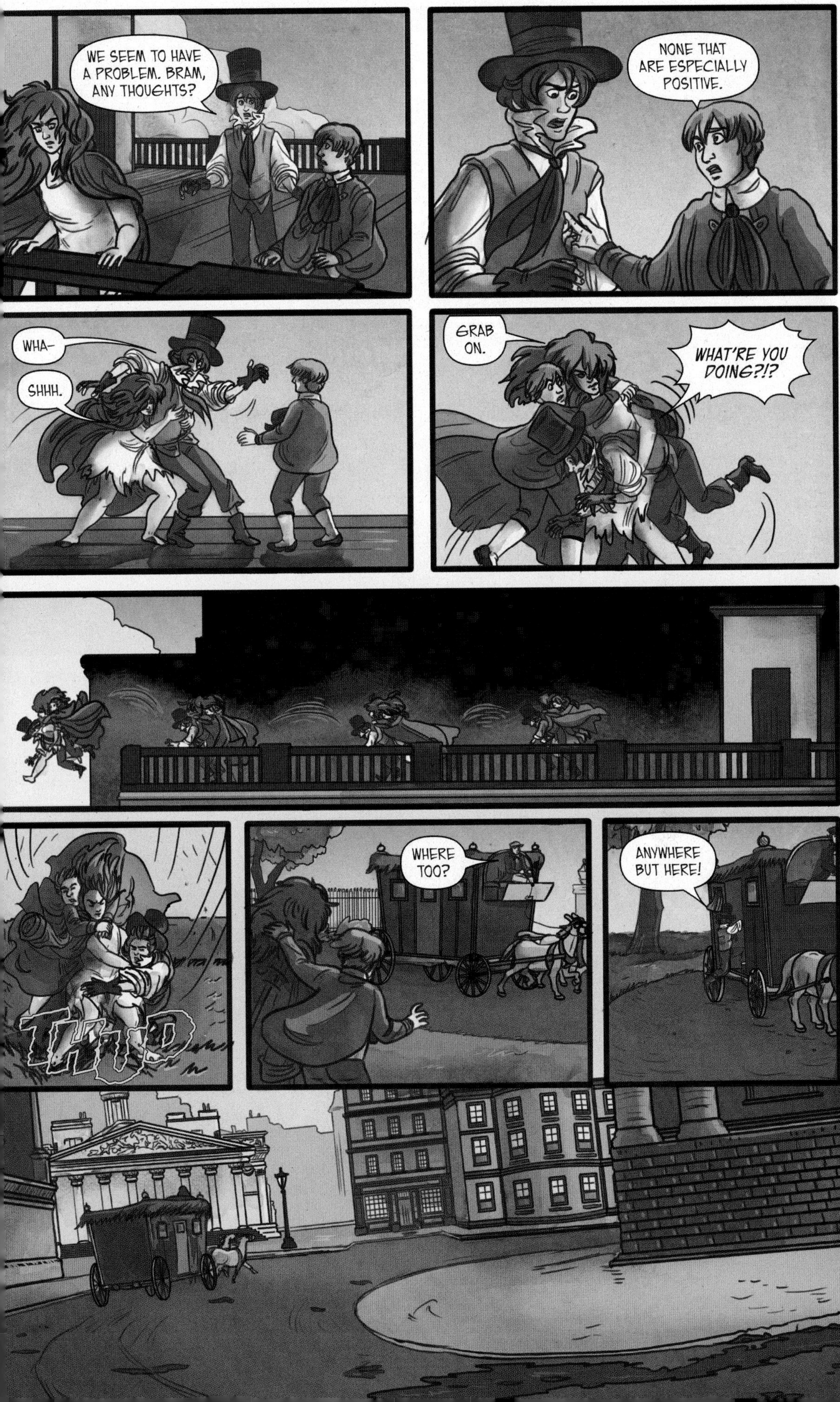
WE SEEM TO HAVE A PROBLEM. BRAM, ANY THOUGHTS?
NONE THAT ARE ESPECIALLY POSITIVE.
WHA-
SHHH.
GRAB ON.
WHAT'RE YOU DOING?!?
THUD
WHERE TOO?
ANYWHERE BUT HERE!

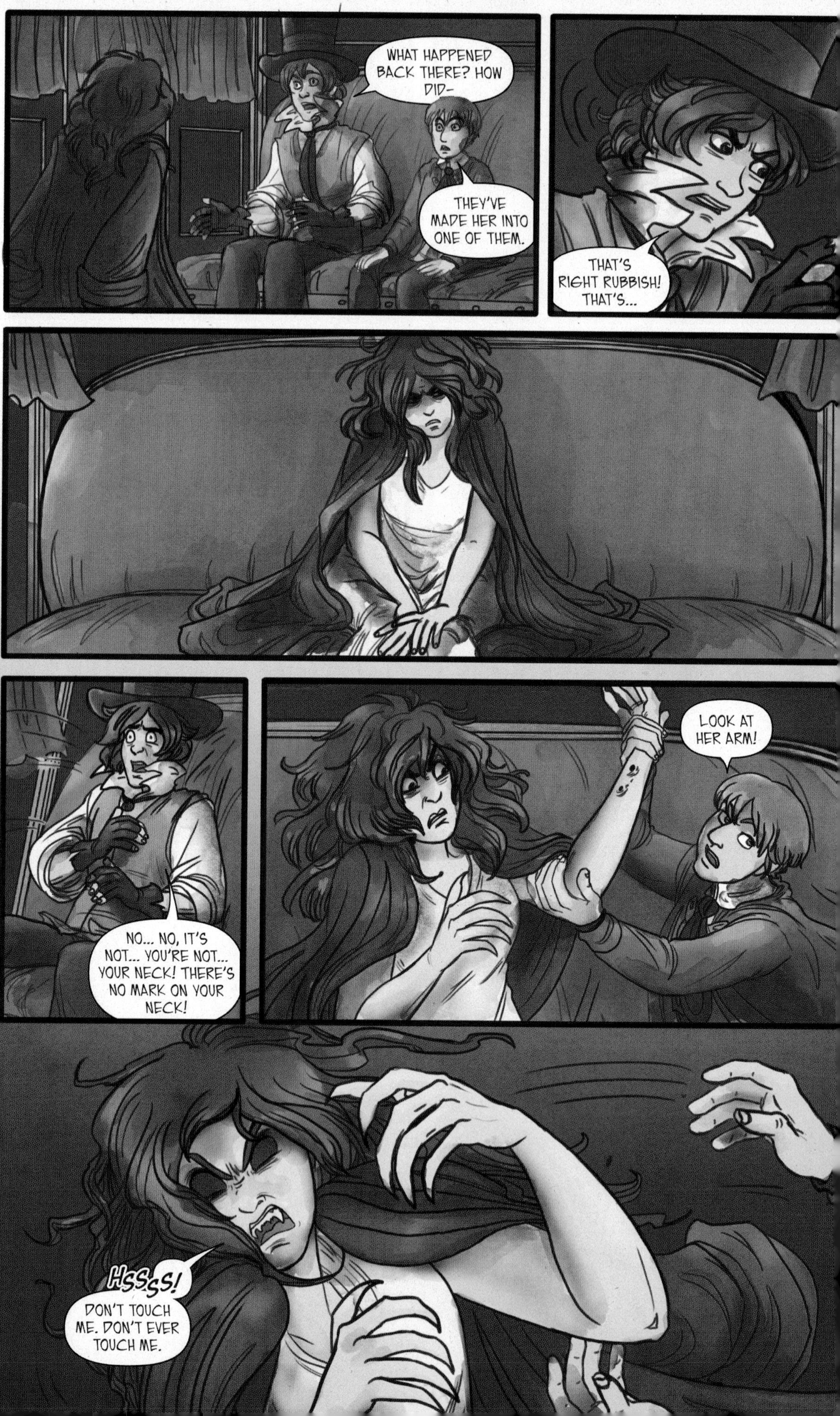
WHAT HAPPENED BACK THERE? HOW DID-
THEY'VE MADE HER INTO ONE OF THEM.
THAT'S RIGHT RUBBISH! THAT'S...
NO... NO, IT'S NOT... YOU'RE NOT... YOUR NECK! THERE'S NO MARK ON YOUR NECK!
LOOK AT HER ARM!
HSSSS!
DON'T TOUCH ME. DON'T EVER TOUCH ME.

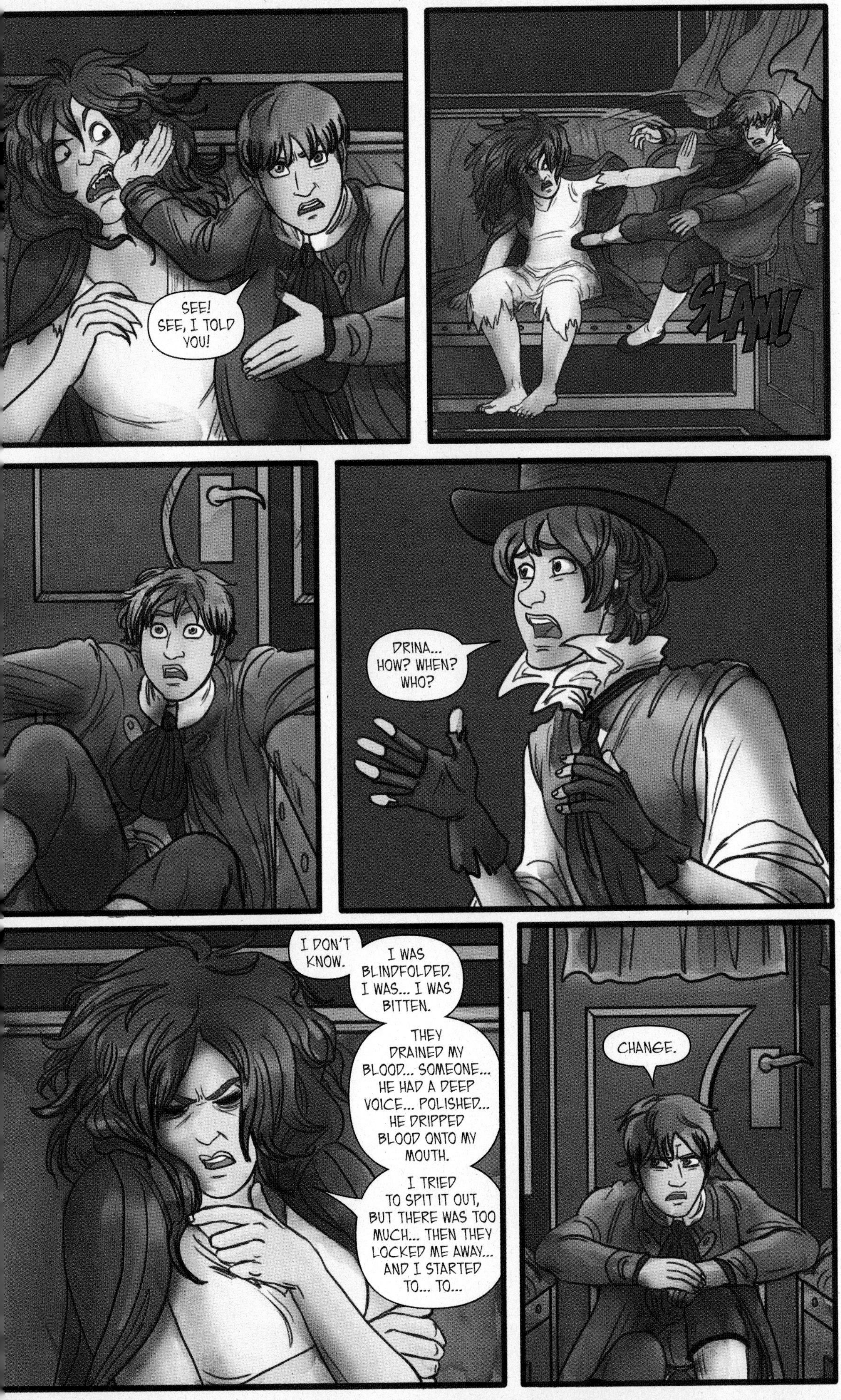
SEE! SEE, I TOLD YOU!
SLAM!
DRINA... HOW? WHEN? WHO?
I DON'T KNOW.
I WAS BLINDFOLDED. I WAS... I WAS BITTEN.
THEY DRAINED MY BLOOD... SOMEONE... HE HAD A DEEP VOICE... POLISHED... HE DRIPPED BLOOD ONTO MY MOUTH.
I TRIED TO SPIT IT OUT, BUT THERE WAS TOO MUCH... THEN THEY LOCKED ME AWAY... AND I STARTED TO... TO...
CHANGE.

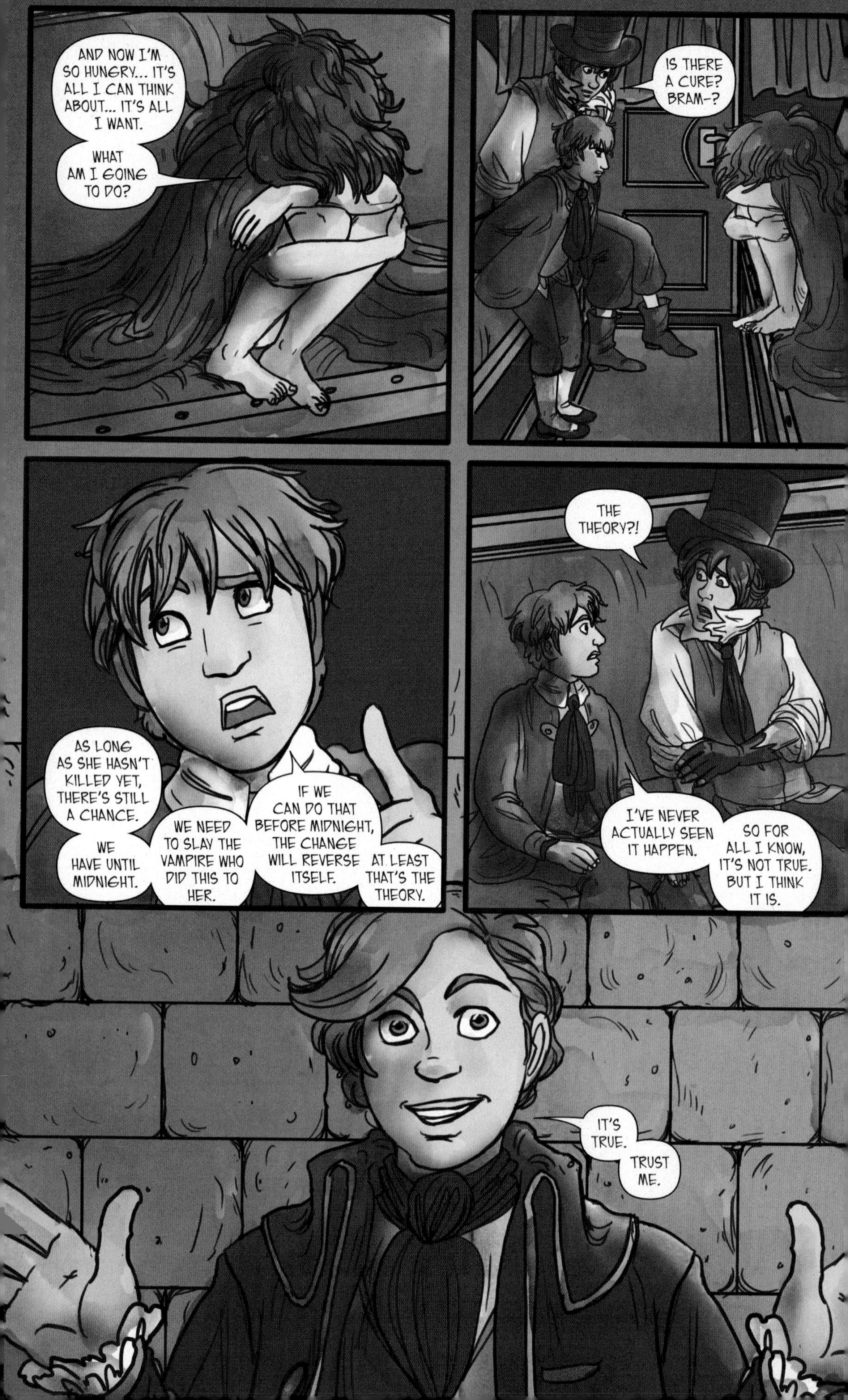
AND NOW I'M SO HUNGRY... IT'S ALL I CAN THINK ABOUT... IT'S ALL I WANT.
WHAT AM I GOING TO DO?
IS THERE A CURE? BRAM-?
AS LONG AS SHE HASN'T KILLED YET, THERE'S STILL A CHANCE.
WE HAVE UNTIL MIDNIGHT.
WE NEED TO SLAY THE VAMPIRE WHO DID THIS TO HER.
IF WE CAN DO THAT BEFORE MIDNIGHT, THE CHANGE WILL REVERSE ITSELF.
AT LEAST THAT'S THE THEORY.
THE THEORY?!
I'VE NEVER ACTUALLY SEEN IT HAPPEN.
SO FOR ALL I KNOW, IT'S NOT TRUE. BUT I THINK IT IS.
IT'S TRUE.
TRUST ME.

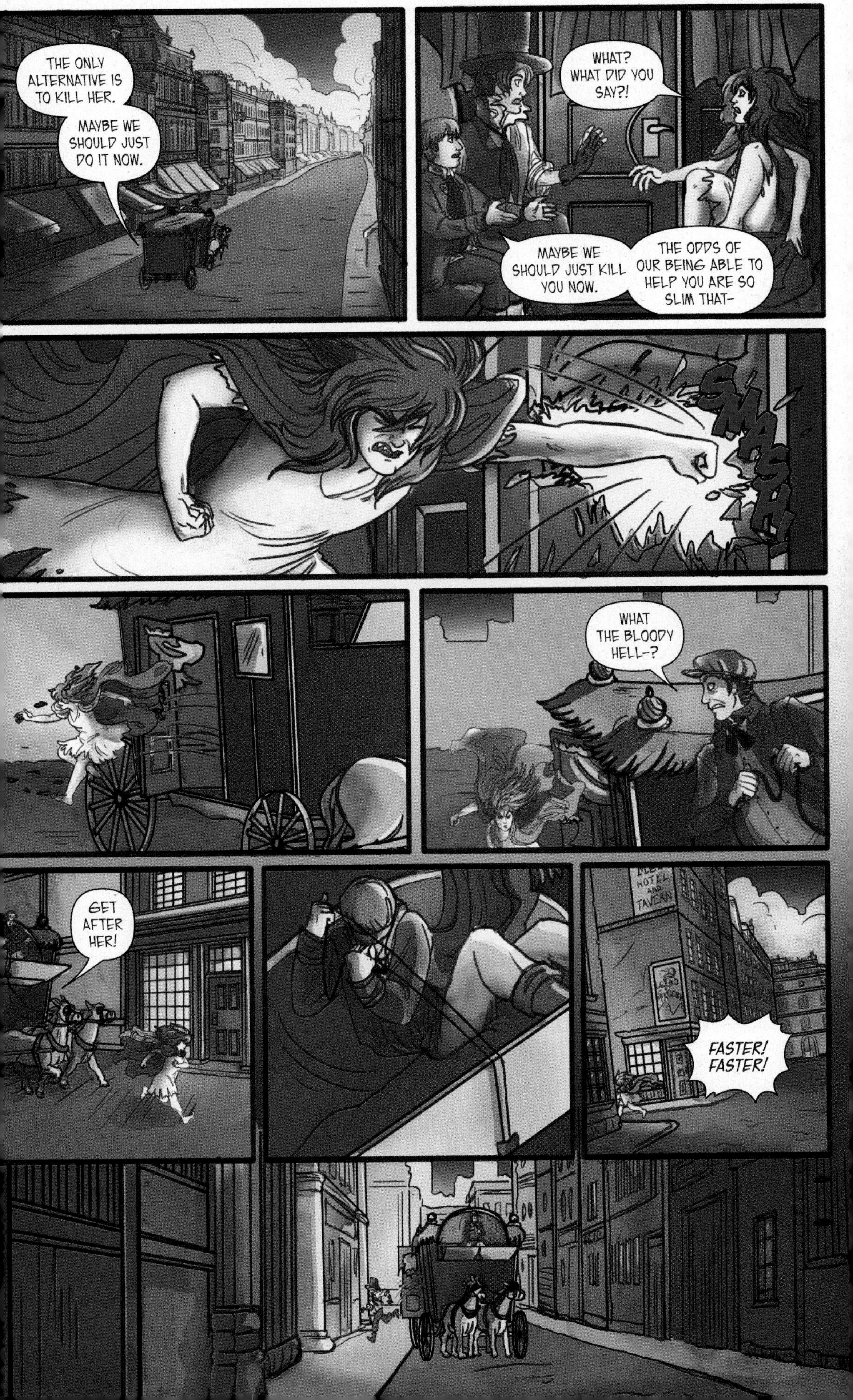
THE ONLY ALTERNATIVE IS TO KILL HER.
MAYBE WE SHOULD JUST DO IT NOW.
WHAT? WHAT DID YOU SAY?!
MAYBE WE SHOULD JUST KILL YOU NOW.
THE ODDS OF OUR BEING ABLE TO HELP YOU ARE SO SLIM THAT-
SMASH!
WHAT THE BLOODY HELL-?
GET AFTER HER!
HOTEL AND TAVERN
FASTER! FASTER!

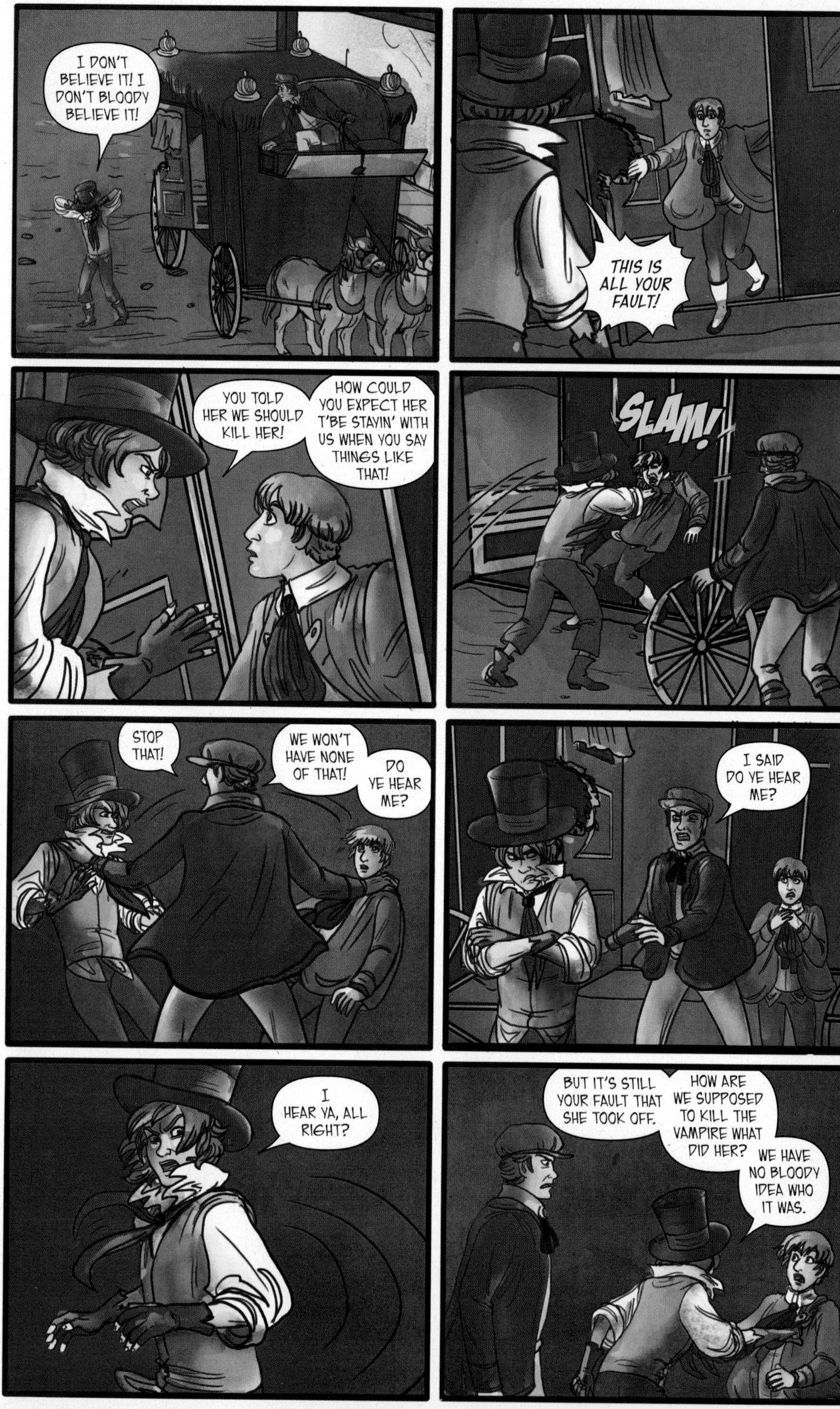
I DON'T BELIEVE IT! I DON'T BLOODY BELIEVE IT!
THIS IS ALL YOUR FAULT!
YOU TOLD HER WE SHOULD KILL HER!
HOW COULD YOU EXPECT HER T'BE STAYIN' WITH US WHEN YOU SAY THINGS LIKE THAT!
SLAM!
STOP THAT!
WE WON'T HAVE NONE OF THAT!
DO YE HEAR ME?
I SAID DO YE HEAR ME?
I HEAR YA, ALL RIGHT?
BUT IT'S STILL YOUR FAULT THAT SHE TOOK OFF.
HOW ARE WE SUPPOSED TO KILL THE VAMPIRE WHAT DID HER?
WE HAVE NO BLOODY IDEA WHO IT WAS.

IT WAS THE VAMPIRE IN CHARGE.

HOW THE HELL DO YOU KNOW THAT?

SHE'S WAY HIGH UP ON THE HUMAN FOOD CHAIN.

WHEN SOMEONE MAKES YOU INTO A VAMPIRE, THE NEWLY MADE VAMPIRE HAS TO ANSWER TO WHOEVER MADE HIM OR HER.

IF YOU'RE MAKING AN ENGLISH PRINCESS INTO A VAMPIRE, THAT'S GOING TO BE THE JOB OF WHOEVER'S IN CHARGE.

MY FATHER SPOKE TO SOME OTHER CHAPS ABOUT THIS TOP VAMPIRE. MR. FANG.

EVERYONE IN MY LINE OF WORK KNOWS MR. FANG. A MAGISTRATE, HE IS. HE'S A VAMPIRE, EH?

MY FATHER SEEMED PRETTY SURE AND HE'S RARELY WRONG IN SUCH MATTERS.

THEN WE GO AFTER HIM.

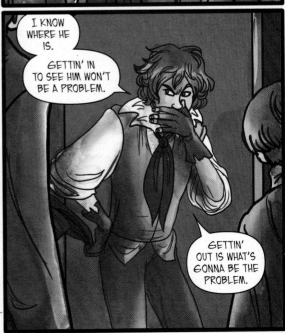

I KNOW WHERE HE IS.

GETTIN' IN TO SEE HIM WON'T BE A PROBLEM.

GETTIN' OUT IS WHAT'S GONNA BE THE PROBLEM.

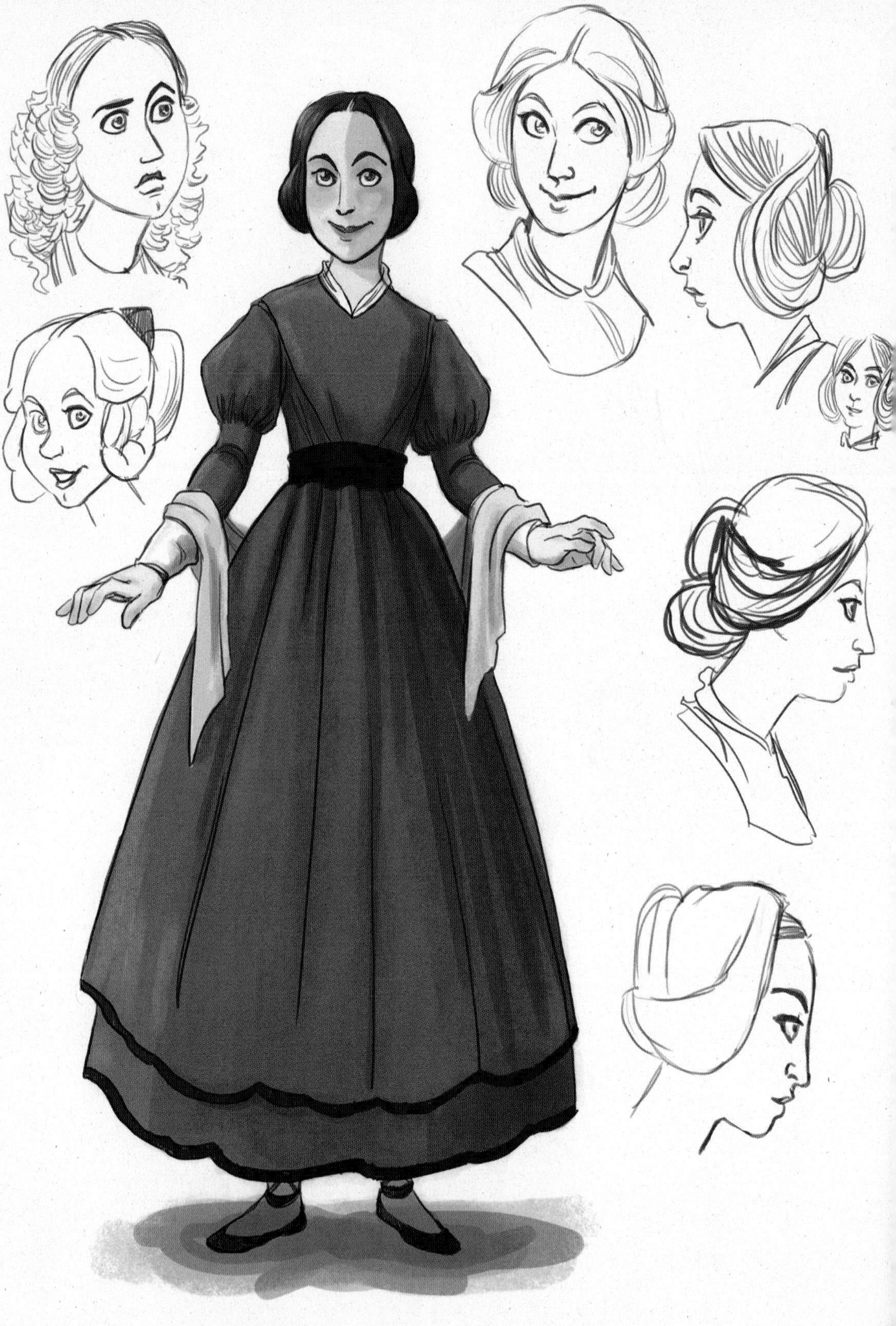

Exploratory Sketches For Drina

CHAPTER FIVE

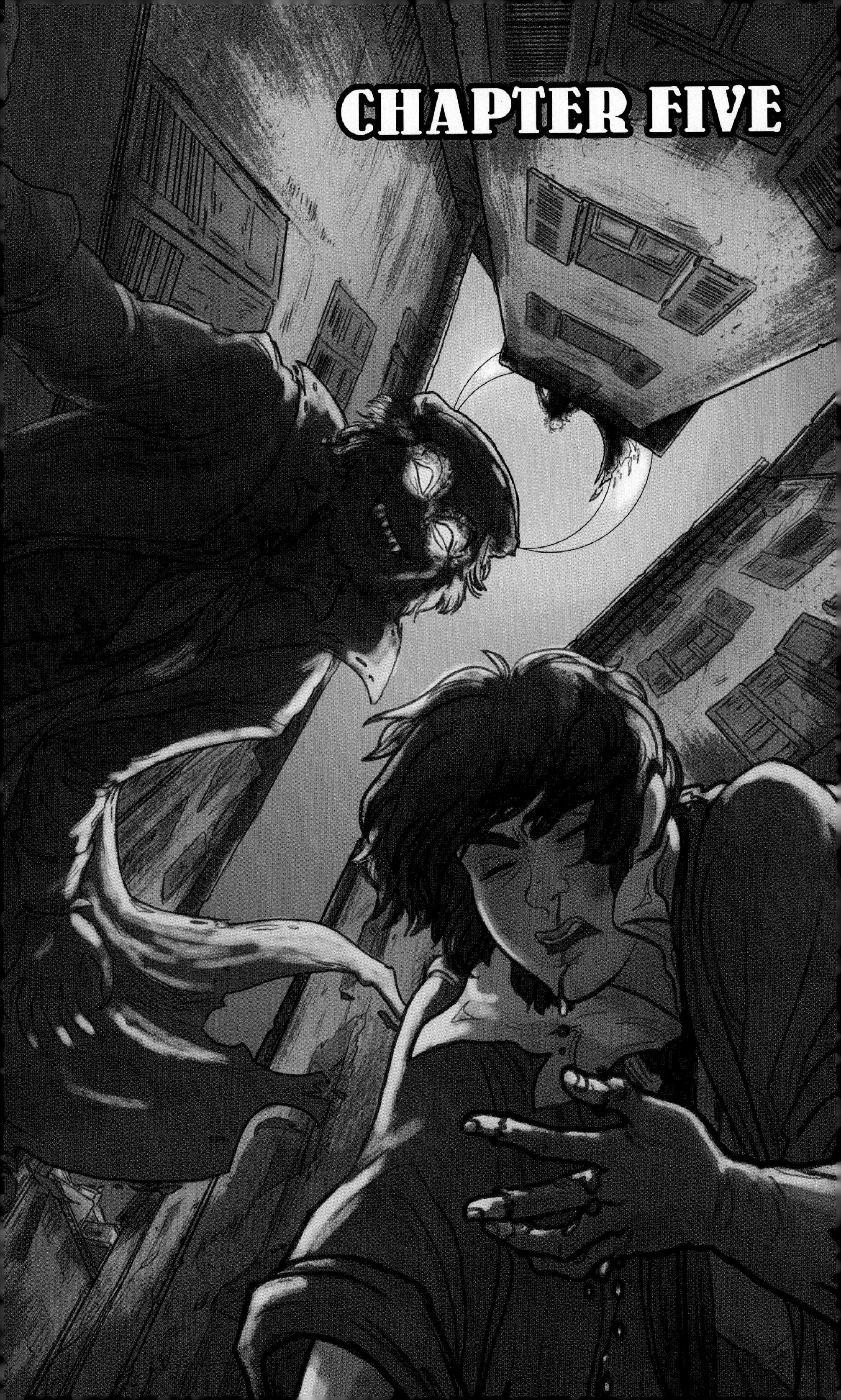

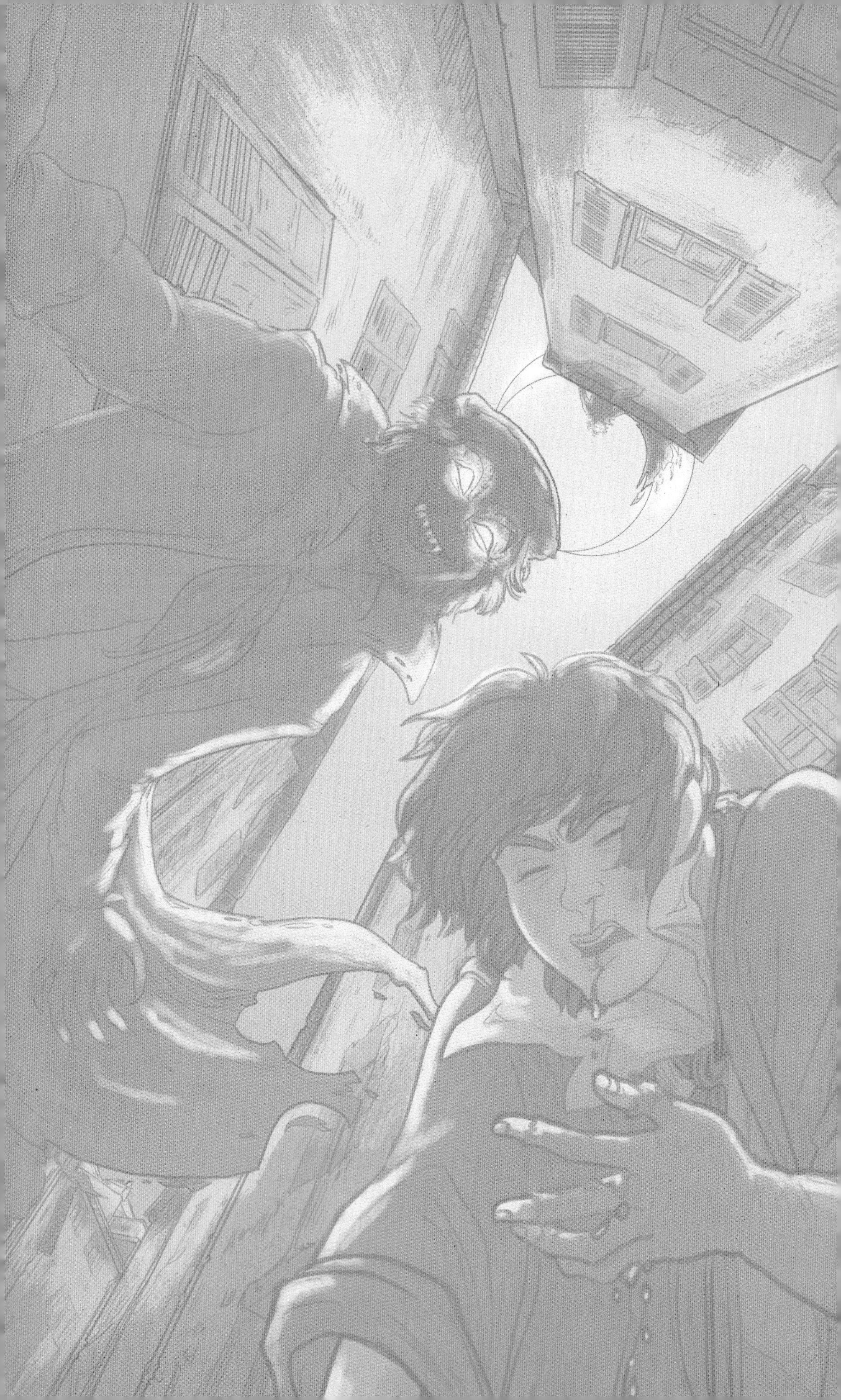

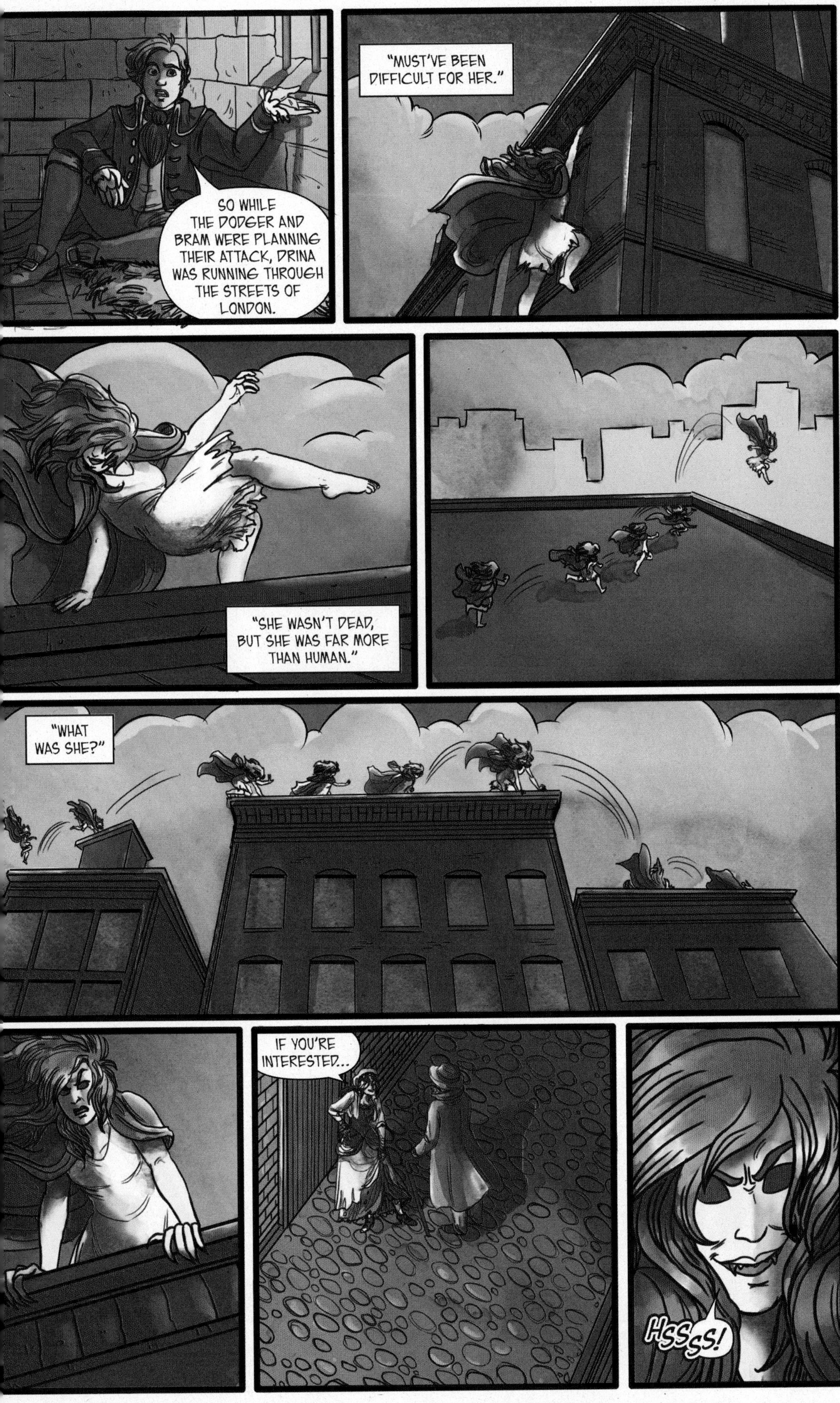
SO WHILE THE DODGER AND BRAM WERE PLANNING THEIR ATTACK, DRINA WAS RUNNING THROUGH THE STREETS OF LONDON.
"MUST'VE BEEN DIFFICULT FOR HER."
"SHE WASN'T DEAD, BUT SHE WAS FAR MORE THAN HUMAN."
"WHAT WAS SHE?"
IF YOU'RE INTERESTED...
HSSSS!

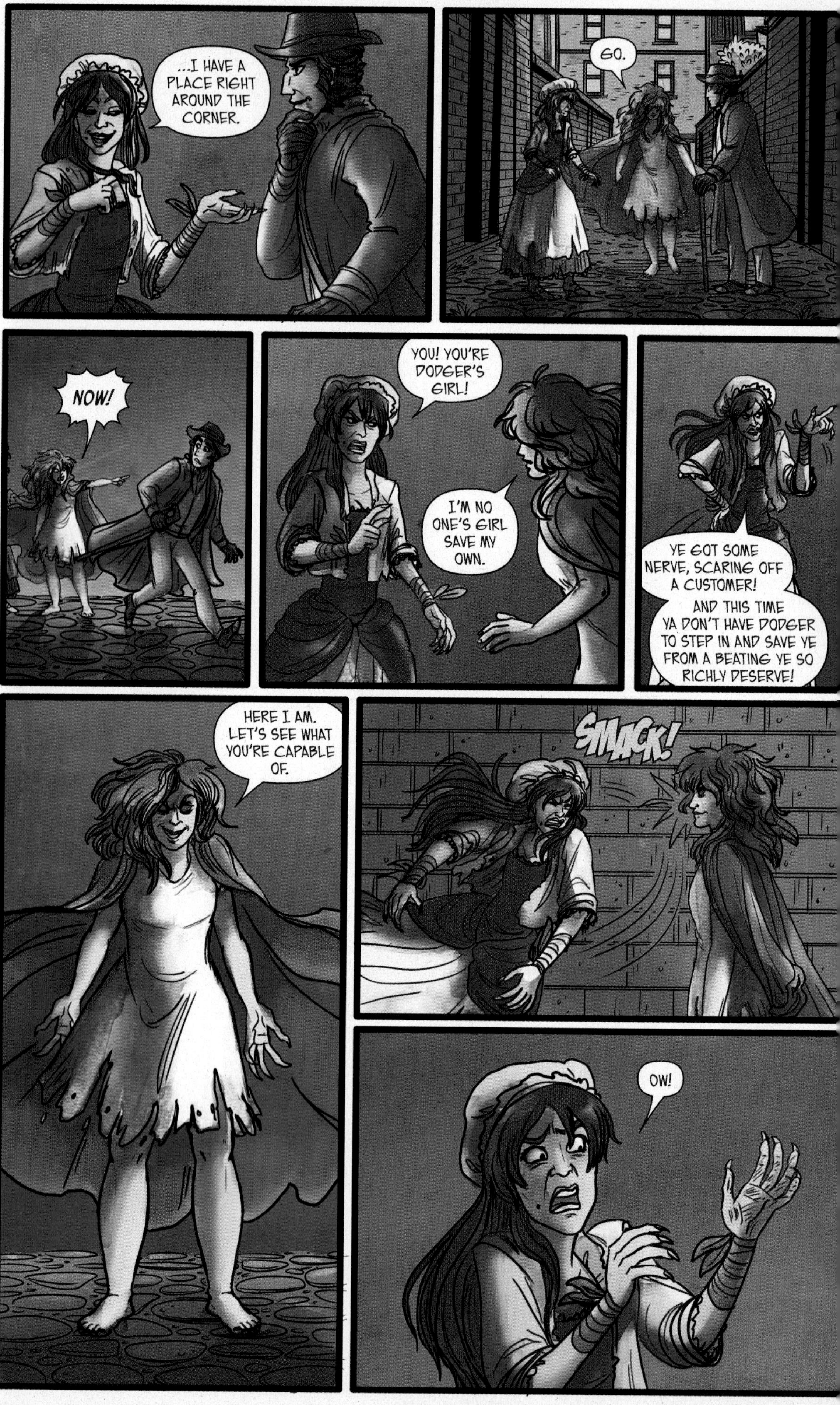
...I HAVE A PLACE RIGHT AROUND THE CORNER.
GO.
NOW!
YOU! YOU'RE DODGER'S GIRL!
I'M NO ONE'S GIRL SAVE MY OWN.
YE GOT SOME NERVE, SCARING OFF A CUSTOMER!
AND THIS TIME YA DON'T HAVE DODGER TO STEP IN AND SAVE YE FROM A BEATING YE SO RICHLY DESERVE!
HERE I AM. LET'S SEE WHAT YOU'RE CAPABLE OF.
SMACK!
OW!

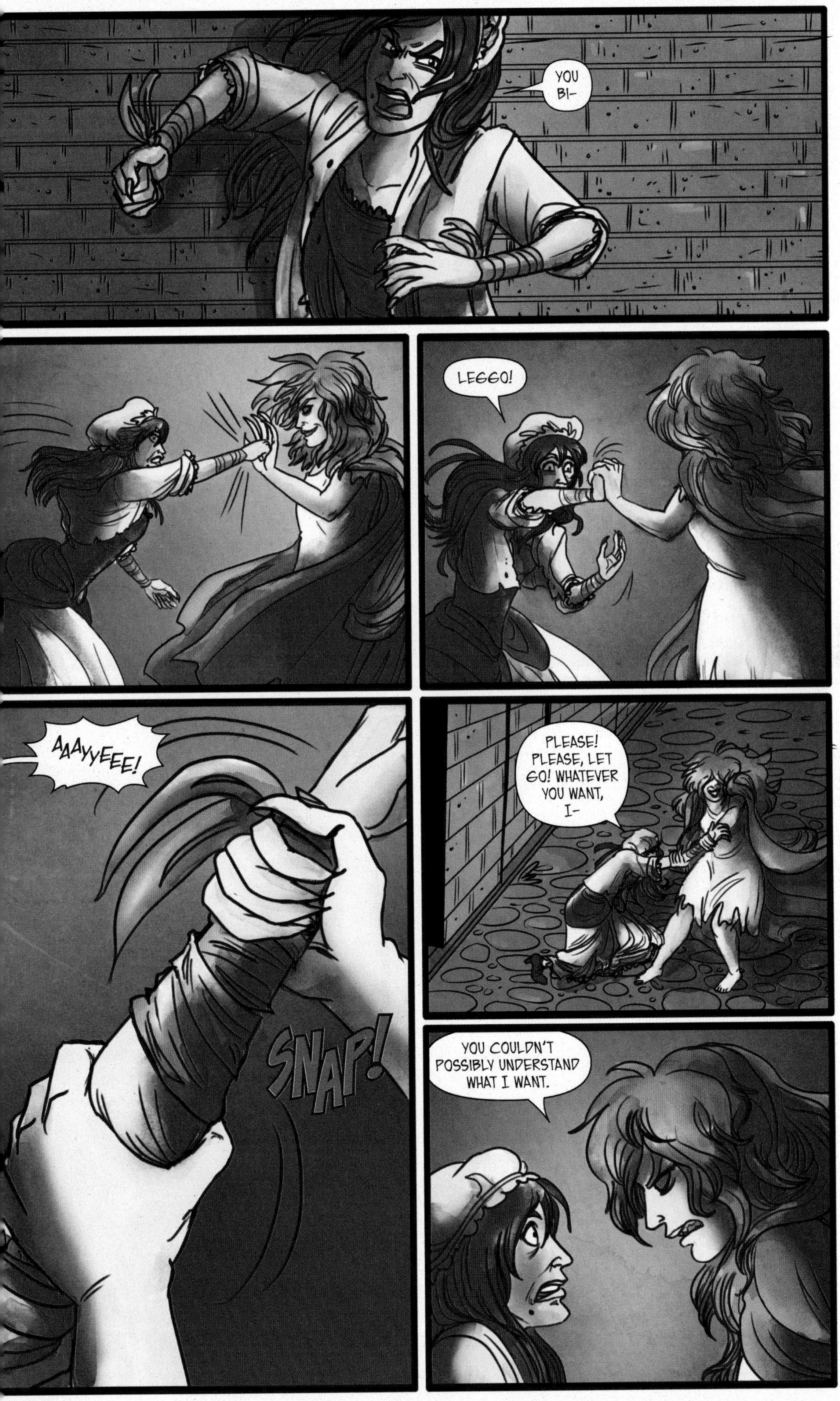

YOU BI-
LEGGO!
AAAyyEEE!
SNAP!
PLEASE! PLEASE, LET GO! WHATEVER YOU WANT, I-
YOU COULDN'T POSSIBLY UNDERSTAND WHAT I WANT.

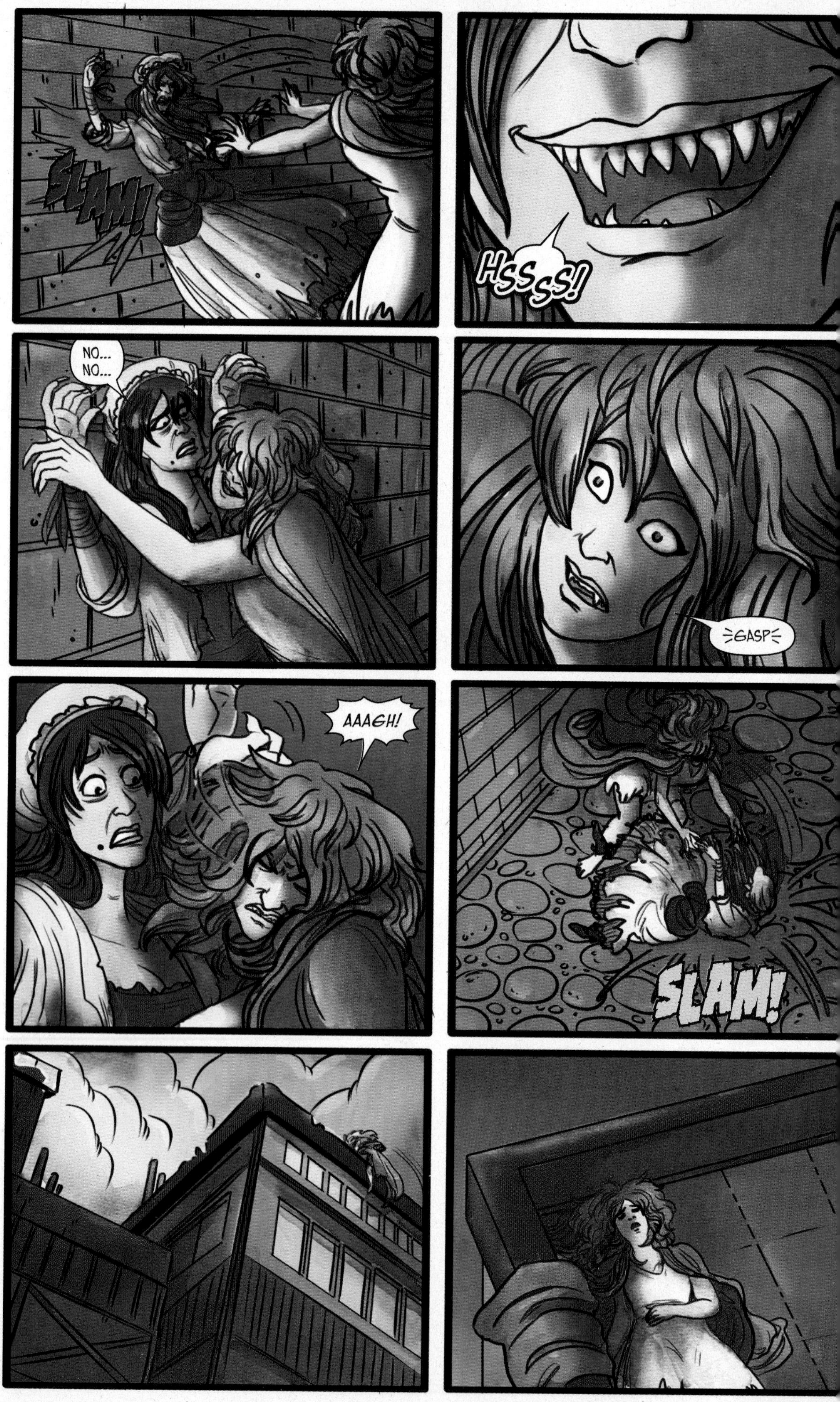
SLAM!
HSSSS!
NO...
NO...
GASP
AAAGH!
SLAM!

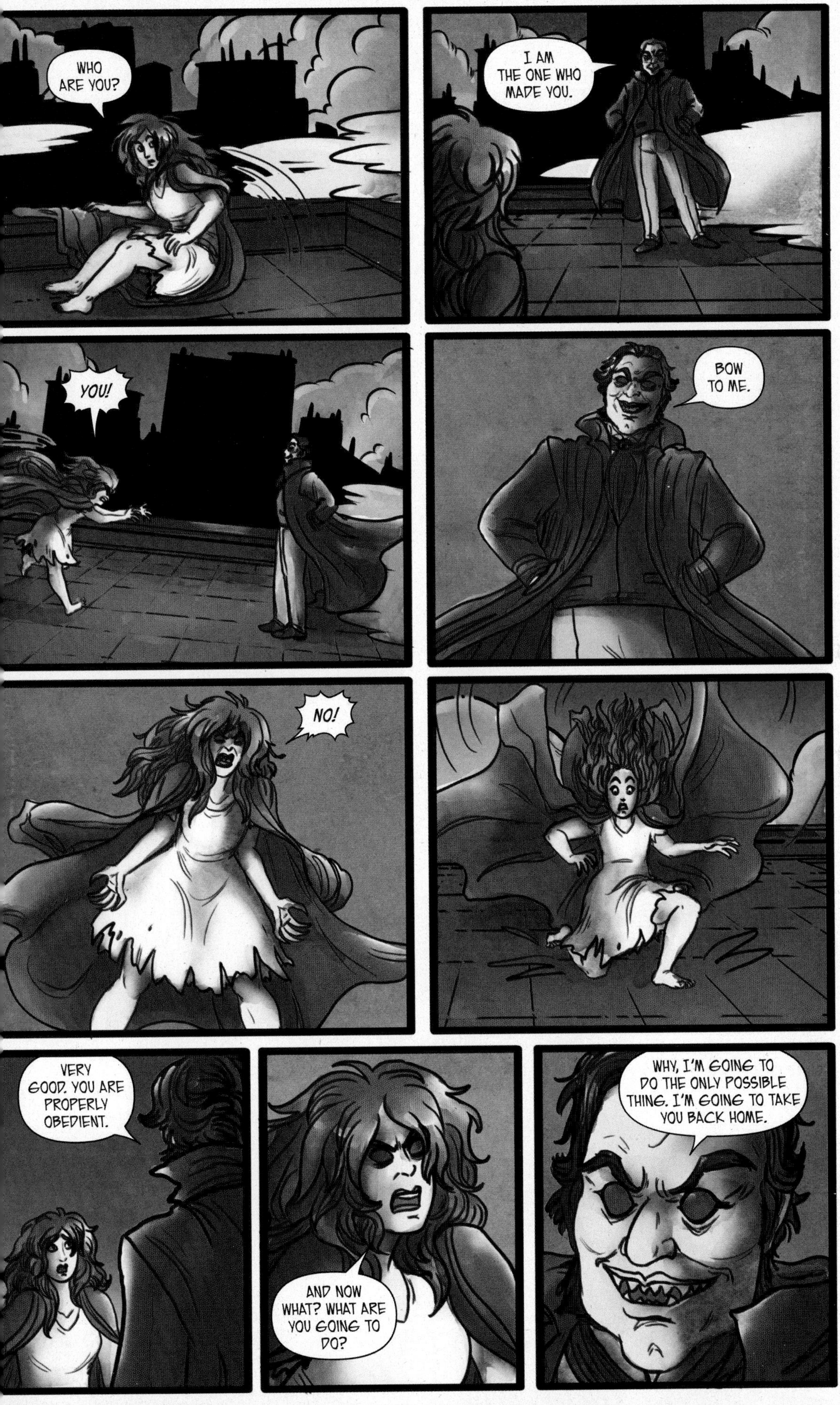
WHO ARE YOU?
I AM THE ONE WHO MADE YOU.
YOU!
BOW TO ME.
NO!
VERY GOOD. YOU ARE PROPERLY OBEDIENT.
AND NOW WHAT? WHAT ARE YOU GOING TO DO?
WHY, I'M GOING TO DO THE ONLY POSSIBLE THING. I'M GOING TO TAKE YOU BACK HOME.

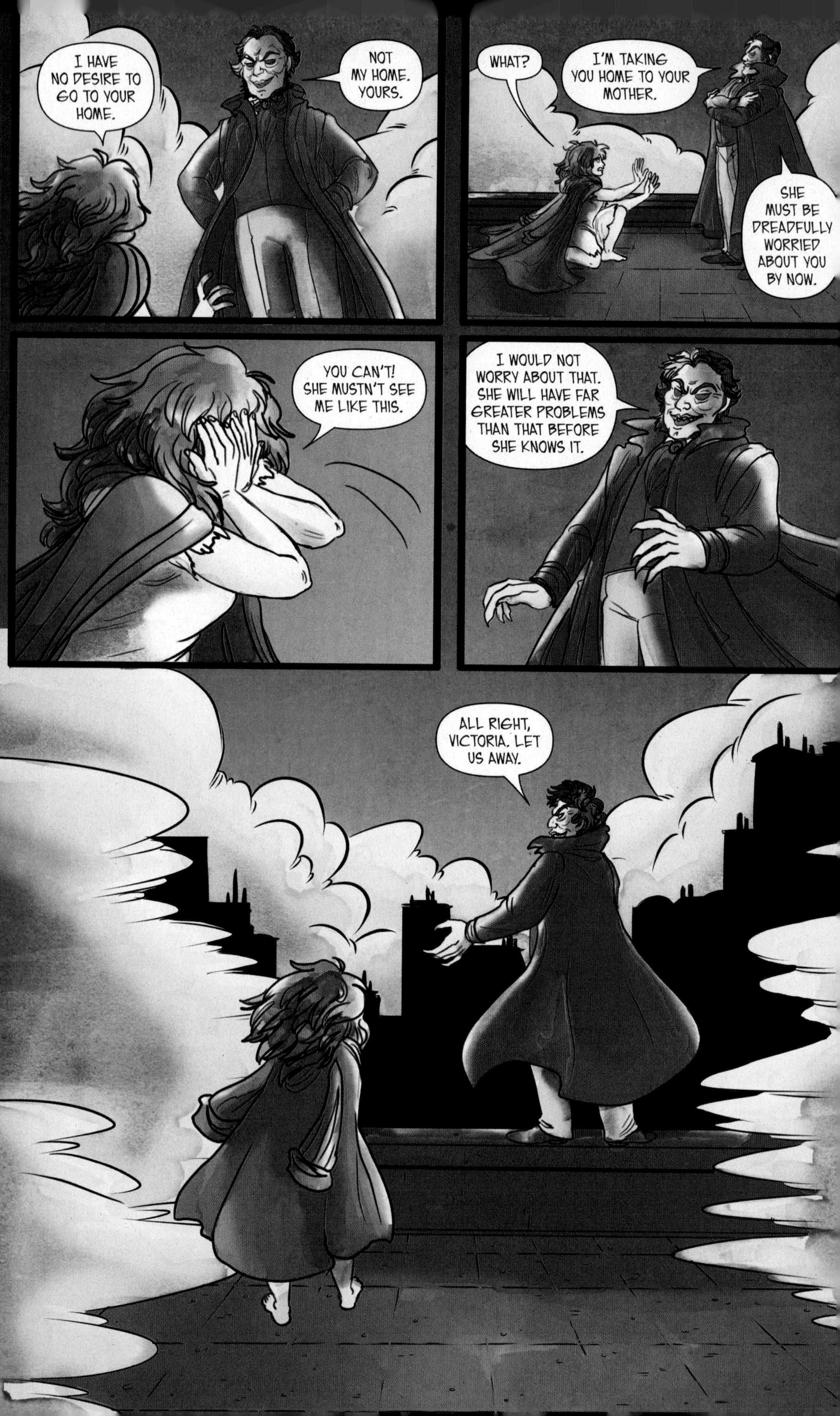
I HAVE NO DESIRE TO GO TO YOUR HOME.
NOT MY HOME. YOURS.
WHAT?
I'M TAKING YOU HOME TO YOUR MOTHER.
SHE MUST BE DREADFULLY WORRIED ABOUT YOU BY NOW.
YOU CAN'T! SHE MUSTN'T SEE ME LIKE THIS.
I WOULD NOT WORRY ABOUT THAT. SHE WILL HAVE FAR GREATER PROBLEMS THAN THAT BEFORE SHE KNOWS IT.
ALL RIGHT, VICTORIA. LET US AWAY.

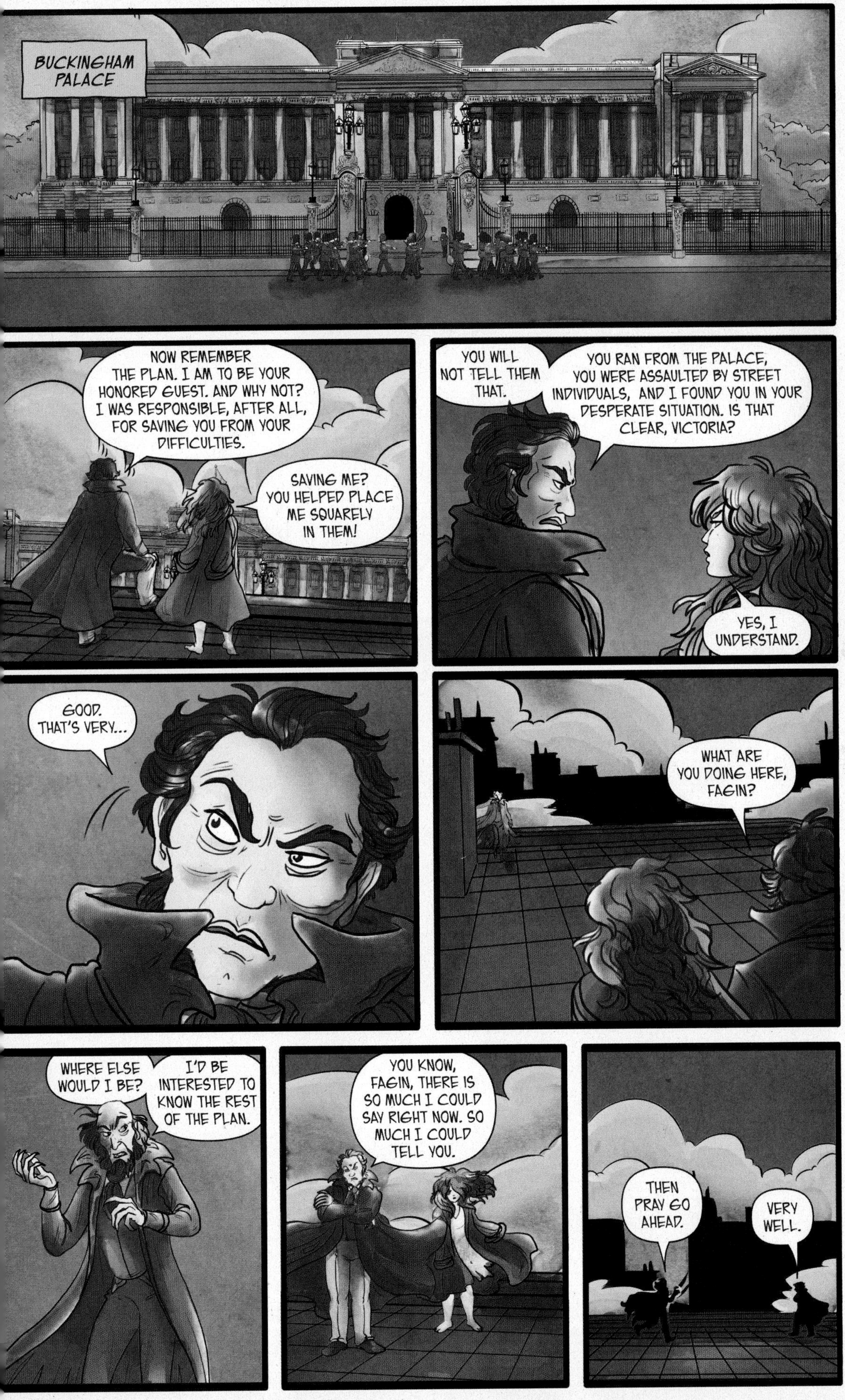
BUCKINGHAM PALACE
NOW REMEMBER THE PLAN. I AM TO BE YOUR HONORED GUEST. AND WHY NOT? I WAS RESPONSIBLE, AFTER ALL, FOR SAVING YOU FROM YOUR DIFFICULTIES.
SAVING ME? YOU HELPED PLACE ME SQUARELY IN THEM!
YOU WILL NOT TELL THEM THAT.
YOU RAN FROM THE PALACE, YOU WERE ASSAULTED BY STREET INDIVIDUALS, AND I FOUND YOU IN YOUR DESPERATE SITUATION. IS THAT CLEAR, VICTORIA?
YES, I UNDERSTAND.
GOOD. THAT'S VERY...
WHAT ARE YOU DOING HERE, FAGIN?
WHERE ELSE WOULD I BE?
I'D BE INTERESTED TO KNOW THE REST OF THE PLAN.
YOU KNOW, FAGIN, THERE IS SO MUCH I COULD SAY RIGHT NOW. SO MUCH I COULD TELL YOU.
THEN PRAY GO AHEAD.
VERY WELL.

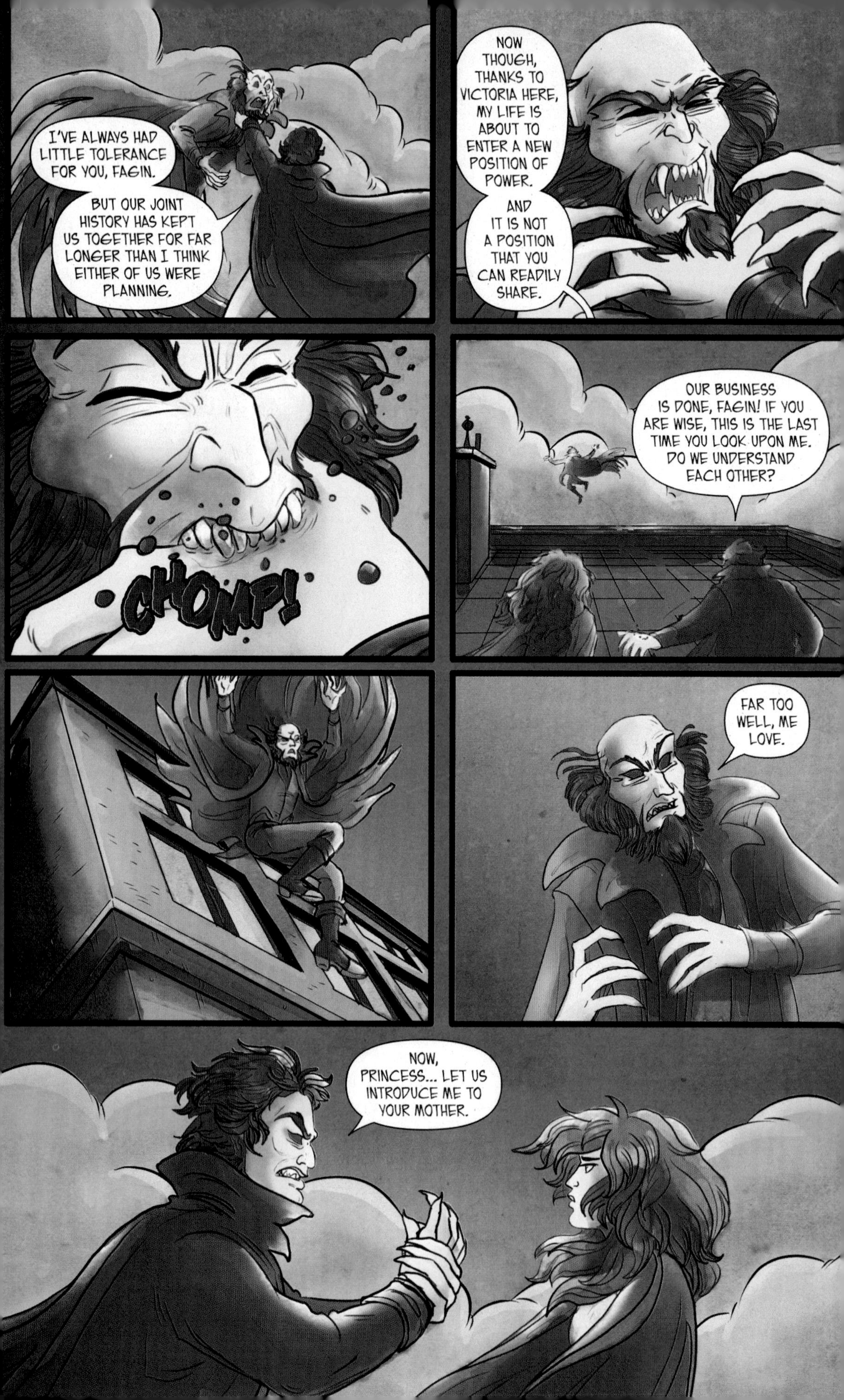
I'VE ALWAYS HAD LITTLE TOLERANCE FOR YOU, FAGIN.
BUT OUR JOINT HISTORY HAS KEPT US TOGETHER FOR FAR LONGER THAN I THINK EITHER OF US WERE PLANNING.
NOW THOUGH, THANKS TO VICTORIA HERE, MY LIFE IS ABOUT TO ENTER A NEW POSITION OF POWER.
AND IT IS NOT A POSITION THAT YOU CAN READILY SHARE.
CHOMP!
OUR BUSINESS IS DONE, FAGIN! IF YOU ARE WISE, THIS IS THE LAST TIME YOU LOOK UPON ME. DO WE UNDERSTAND EACH OTHER?
FAR TOO WELL, ME LOVE.
NOW, PRINCESS... LET US INTRODUCE ME TO YOUR MOTHER.

NOW THE ARTFUL DODGER KNEW EVERY SQUARE FOOT OF LONDON TOWN, WHICH IS TO SAY HE KNEW THE AREAS THAT WERE BOUNTIFUL WITH POLICE OFFICERS AND THE ONES THAT WEREN'T.

AND IF THERE WAS ONE THING HE'D LEARNED, IT WAS TO GIVE A WIDE BERTH TO MUTTON HILL.

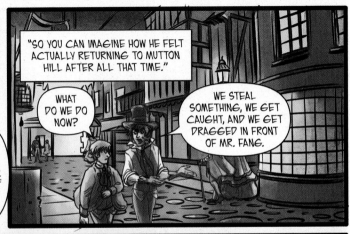

"SO YOU CAN IMAGINE HOW HE FELT ACTUALLY RETURNING TO MUTTON HILL AFTER ALL THAT TIME."

WHAT DO WE DO NOW?

WE STEAL SOMETHING, WE GET CAUGHT, AND WE GET DRAGGED IN FRONT OF MR. FANG.

WHEN WE'RE BROUGHT BEFORE MR. FANG, YOU BRING OUT THE CROSS. HE SHRINKS BACK FROM IT. WE USE HIS SCREAMING AND HATING THE CROSS TO GET THE OTHER POLICE OFFICERS TO REALIZE WHAT HE IS. THEY HELP US KILL HIM, AND THE PROBLEM IS SOLVED.

WE'RE COUNTING ON THE HELP OF THE POLICE? IS THAT WISE?

YOU HAVE A BETTER PLAN?

NO, BUT THAT DOESN'T MAKE YOURS A GOOD ONE.

WELL, IT'S WHAT WE'VE GOT. AH, THERE'S A LIKELY SUBJECT.

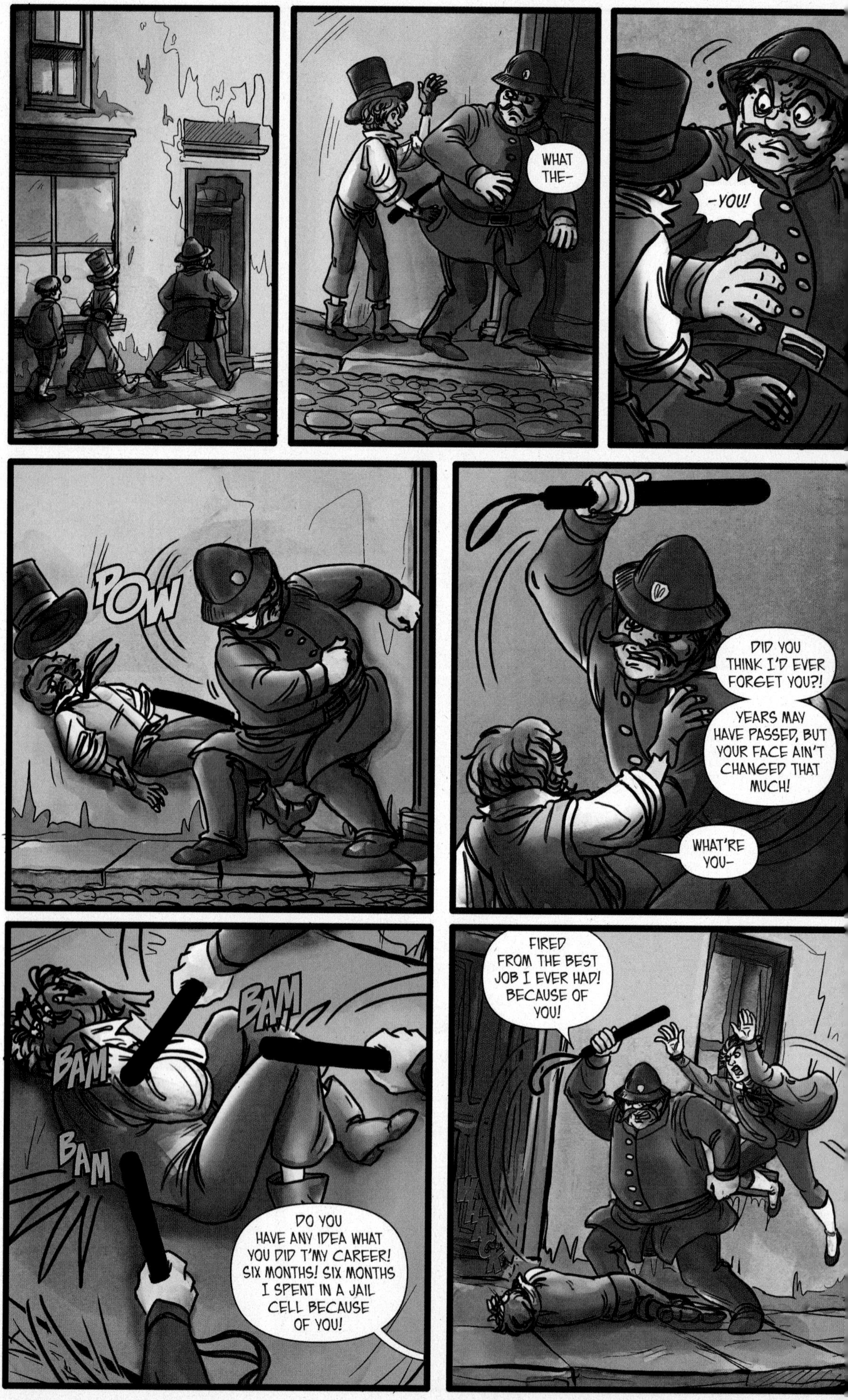
WHAT THE-
-YOU!
POW
DID YOU THINK I'D EVER FORGET YOU?!
YEARS MAY HAVE PASSED, BUT YOUR FACE AIN'T CHANGED THAT MUCH!
WHAT'RE YOU-
BAM
BAM
BAM
DO YOU HAVE ANY IDEA WHAT YOU DID T'MY CAREER! SIX MONTHS! SIX MONTHS I SPENT IN A JAIL CELL BECAUSE OF YOU!
FIRED FROM THE BEST JOB I EVER HAD! BECAUSE OF YOU!

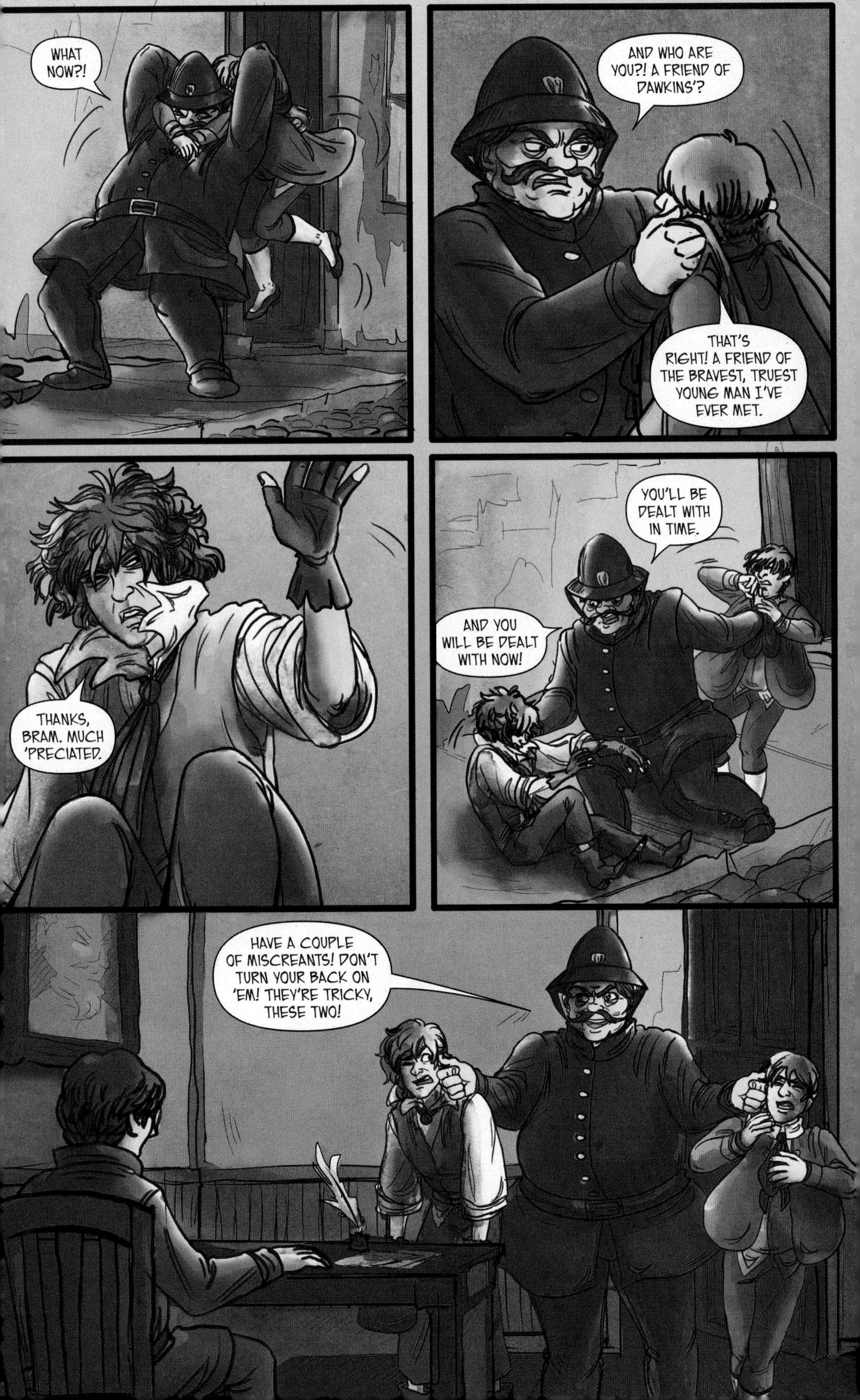
WHAT NOW?!
AND WHO ARE YOU?! A FRIEND OF DAWKINS'?
THAT'S RIGHT! A FRIEND OF THE BRAVEST, TRUEST YOUNG MAN I'VE EVER MET.
THANKS, BRAM. MUCH 'PRECIATED.
YOU'LL BE DEALT WITH IN TIME.
AND YOU WILL BE DEALT WITH NOW!
HAVE A COUPLE OF MISCREANTS! DON'T TURN YOUR BACK ON 'EM! THEY'RE TRICKY, THESE TWO!

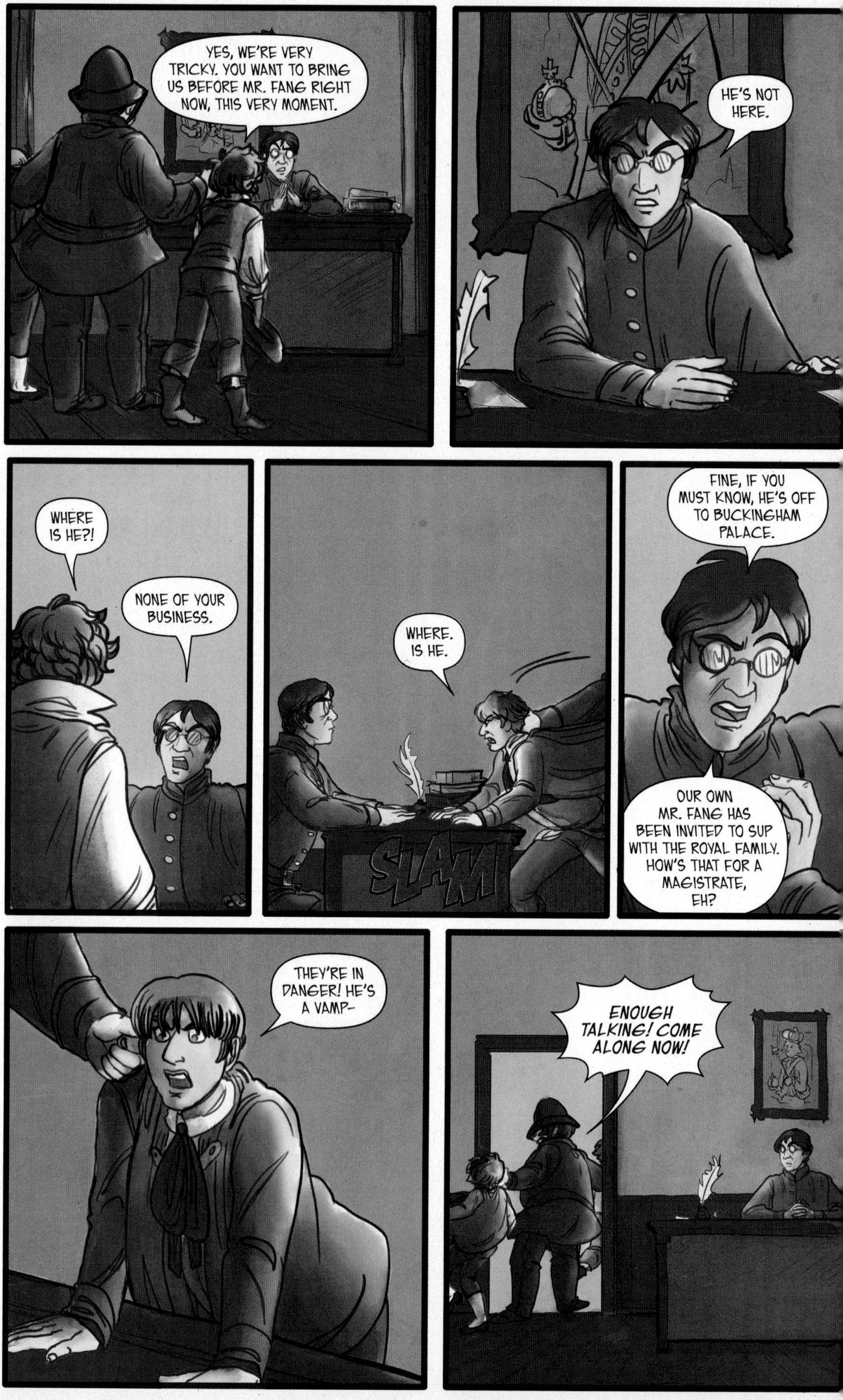
YES, WE'RE VERY TRICKY. YOU WANT TO BRING US BEFORE MR. FANG RIGHT NOW, THIS VERY MOMENT.
HE'S NOT HERE.
WHERE IS HE?!
NONE OF YOUR BUSINESS.
WHERE. IS HE.
SLAM
FINE, IF YOU MUST KNOW, HE'S OFF TO BUCKINGHAM PALACE.
OUR OWN MR. FANG HAS BEEN INVITED TO SUP WITH THE ROYAL FAMILY. HOW'S THAT FOR A MAGISTRATE, EH?
THEY'RE IN DANGER! HE'S A VAMP-
ENOUGH TALKING! COME ALONG NOW!

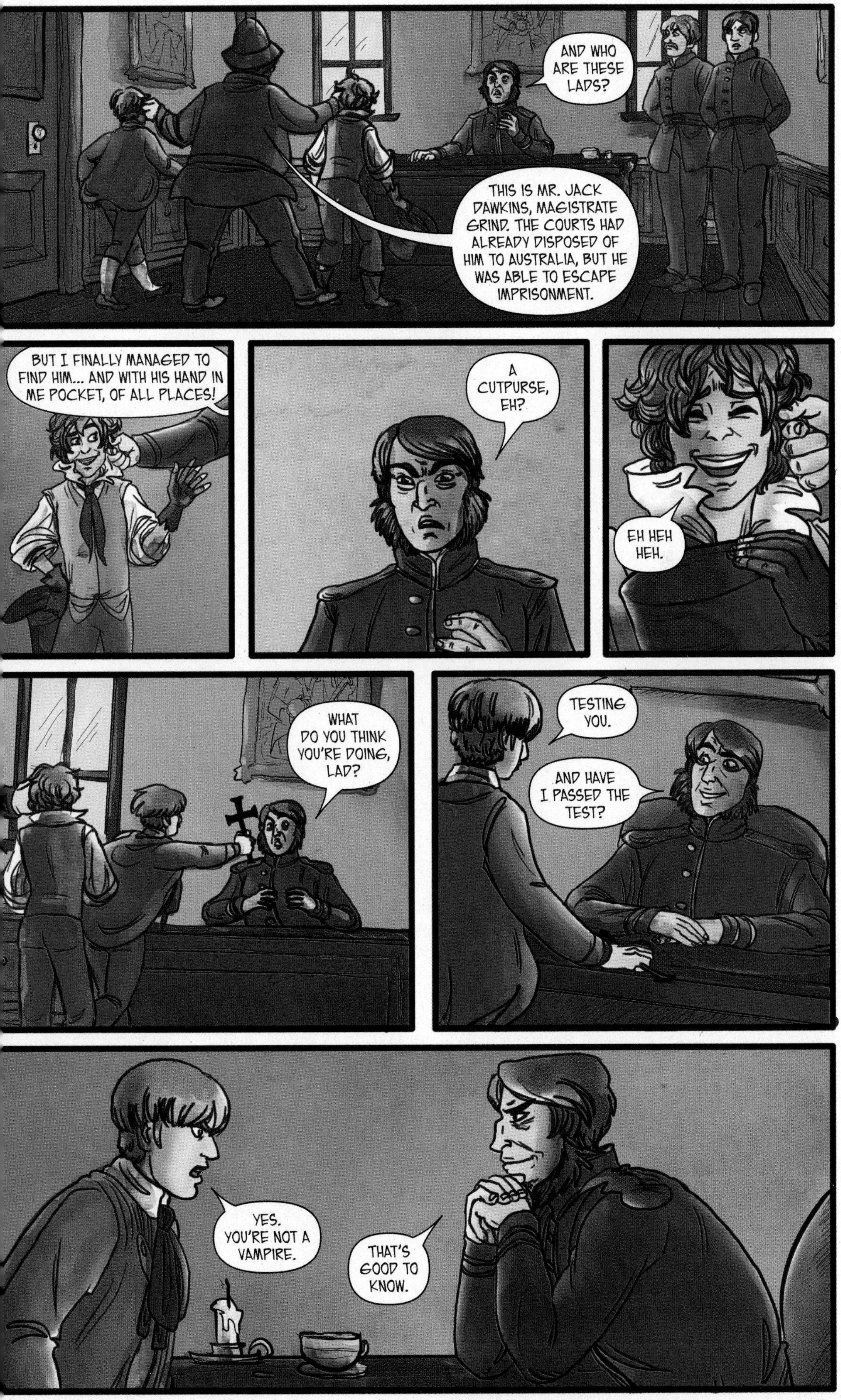
AND WHO ARE THESE LADS?
THIS IS MR. JACK DAWKINS, MAGISTRATE GRIND. THE COURTS HAD ALREADY DISPOSED OF HIM TO AUSTRALIA, BUT HE WAS ABLE TO ESCAPE IMPRISONMENT.
BUT I FINALLY MANAGED TO FIND HIM... AND WITH HIS HAND IN ME POCKET, OF ALL PLACES!
A CUTPURSE, EH?
EH HEH HEH.
WHAT DO YOU THINK YOU'RE DOING, LAD?
TESTING YOU.
AND HAVE I PASSED THE TEST?
YES. YOU'RE NOT A VAMPIRE.
THAT'S GOOD TO KNOW.

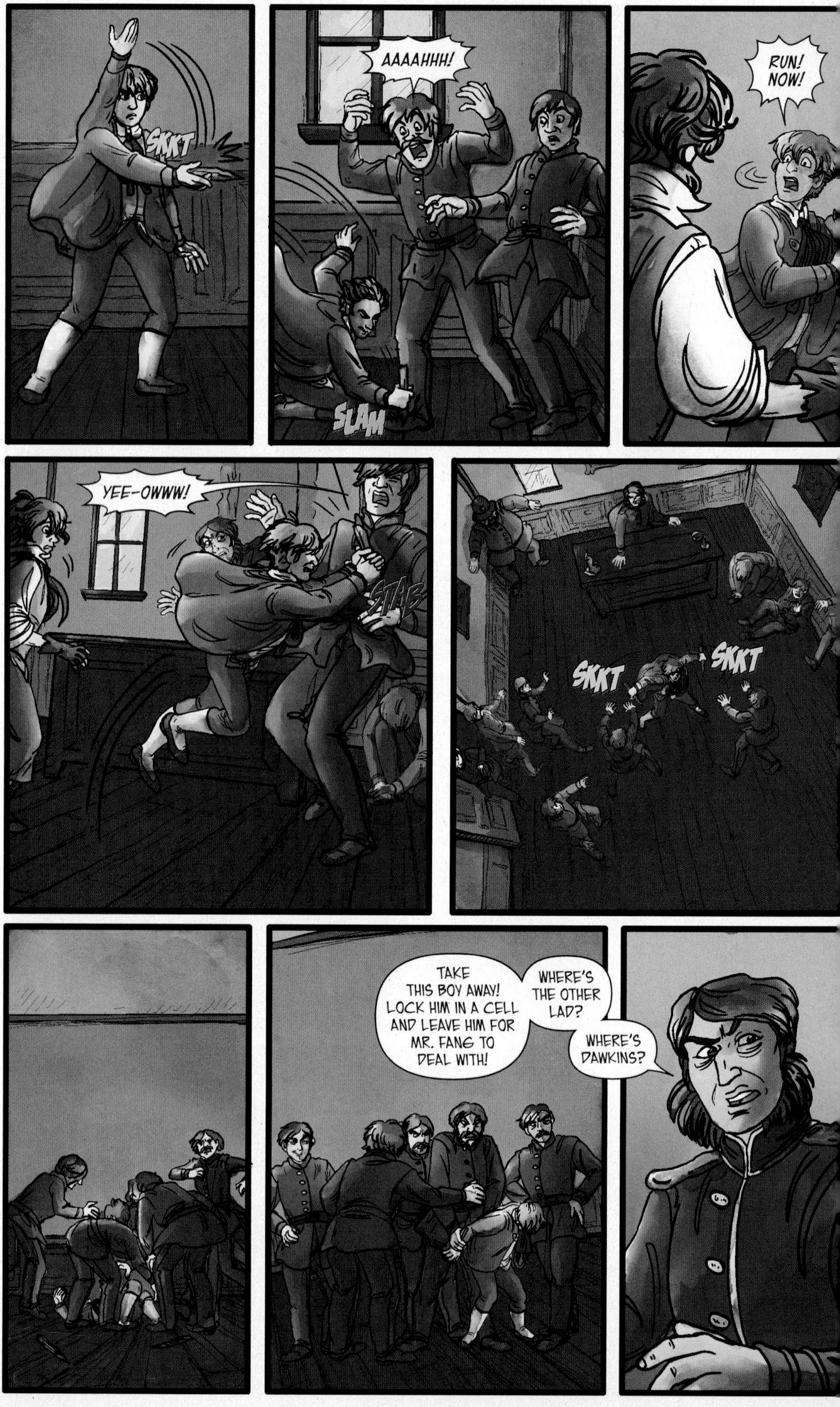
SKKT
AAAAHHH!
SLAM
RUN! NOW!
YEE-OWWW!
STAB
SKKT
SKKT
TAKE THIS BOY AWAY! LOCK HIM IN A CELL AND LEAVE HIM FOR MR. FANG TO DEAL WITH!
WHERE'S THE OTHER LAD?
WHERE'S DAWKINS?

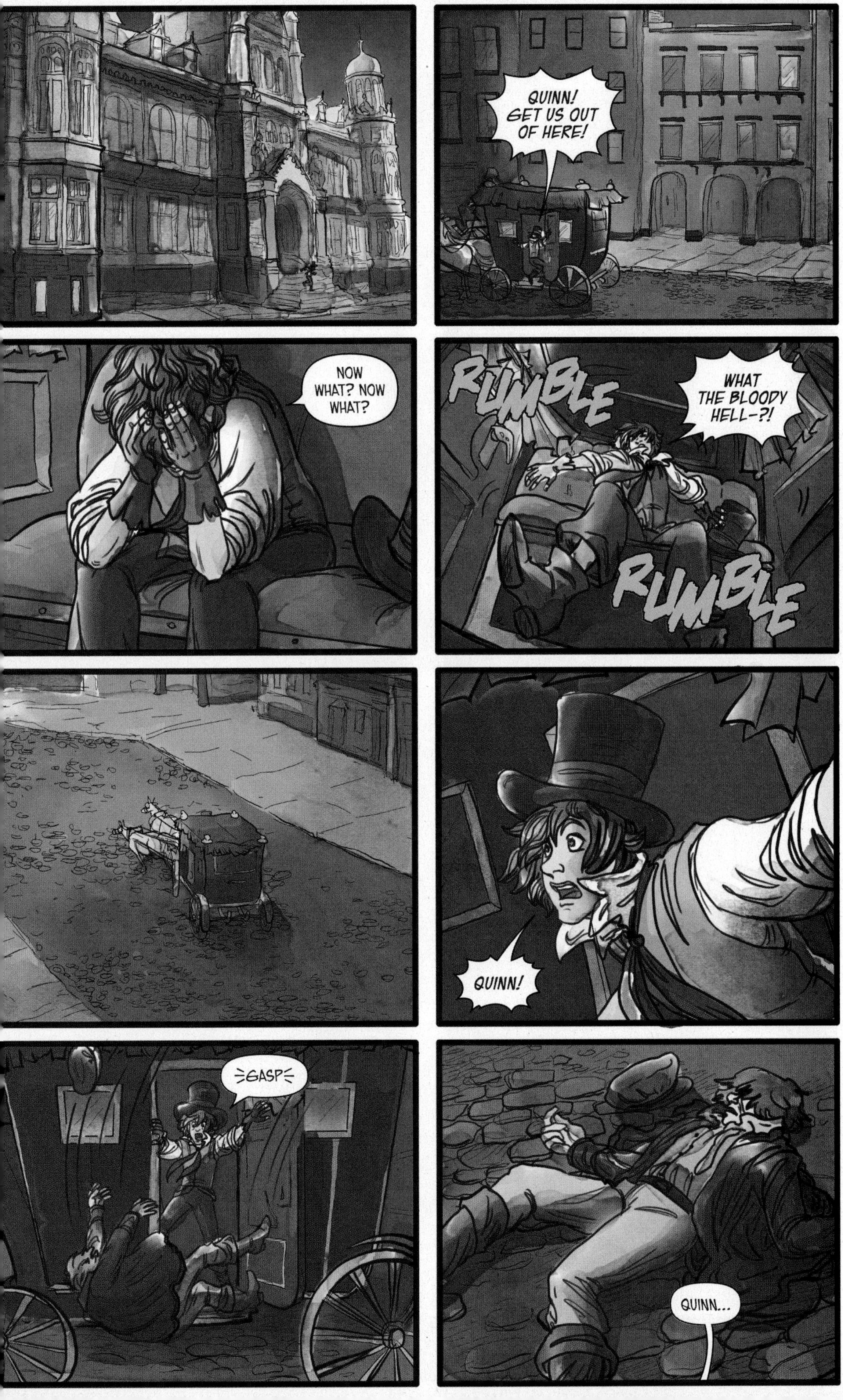
QUINN! GET US OUT OF HERE!
NOW WHAT? NOW WHAT?
RUMBLE
WHAT THE BLOODY HELL-?!
RUMBLE
QUINN!
GASP
QUINN...

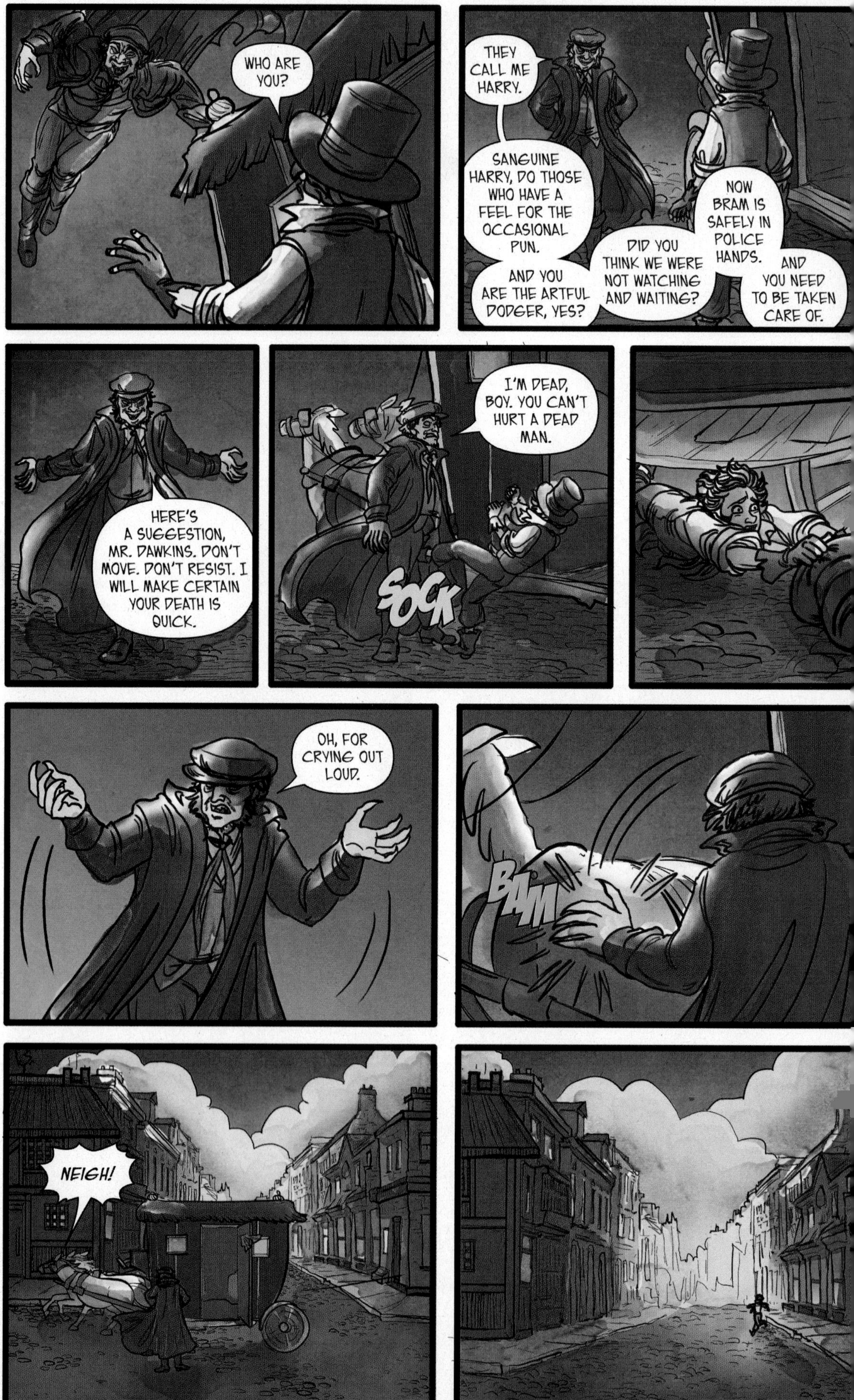
WHO ARE YOU?
THEY CALL ME HARRY.
SANGUINE HARRY, DO THOSE WHO HAVE A FEEL FOR THE OCCASIONAL PUN.
AND YOU ARE THE ARTFUL DODGER, YES?
DID YOU THINK WE WERE NOT WATCHING AND WAITING?
NOW BRAM IS SAFELY IN POLICE HANDS.
AND YOU NEED TO BE TAKEN CARE OF.
HERE'S A SUGGESTION, MR. DAWKINS. DON'T MOVE. DON'T RESIST. I WILL MAKE CERTAIN YOUR DEATH IS QUICK.
I'M DEAD, BOY. YOU CAN'T HURT A DEAD MAN.
SOCK
OH, FOR CRYING OUT LOUD.
BAM
NEIGH!

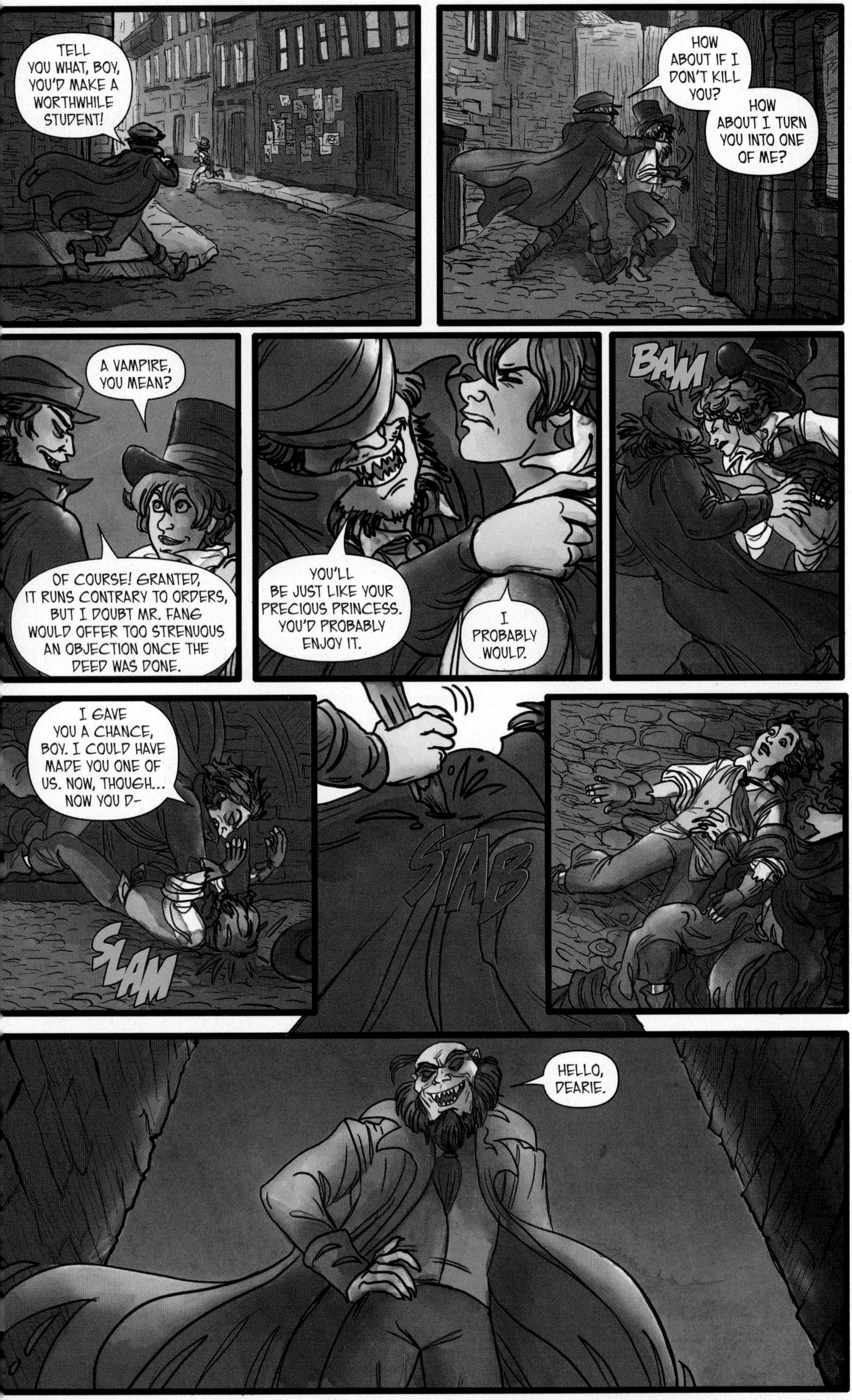
TELL YOU WHAT, BOY, YOU'D MAKE A WORTHWHILE STUDENT!
HOW ABOUT IF I DON'T KILL YOU?
HOW ABOUT I TURN YOU INTO ONE OF ME?
A VAMPIRE, YOU MEAN?
OF COURSE! GRANTED, IT RUNS CONTRARY TO ORDERS, BUT I DOUBT MR. FANG WOULD OFFER TOO STRENUOUS AN OBJECTION ONCE THE DEED WAS DONE.
YOU'LL BE JUST LIKE YOUR PRECIOUS PRINCESS. YOU'D PROBABLY ENJOY IT.
I PROBABLY WOULD.
BAM
I GAVE YOU A CHANCE, BOY. I COULD HAVE MADE YOU ONE OF US. NOW, THOUGH... NOW YOU D-
SLAM
STAB
HELLO, DEARIE.

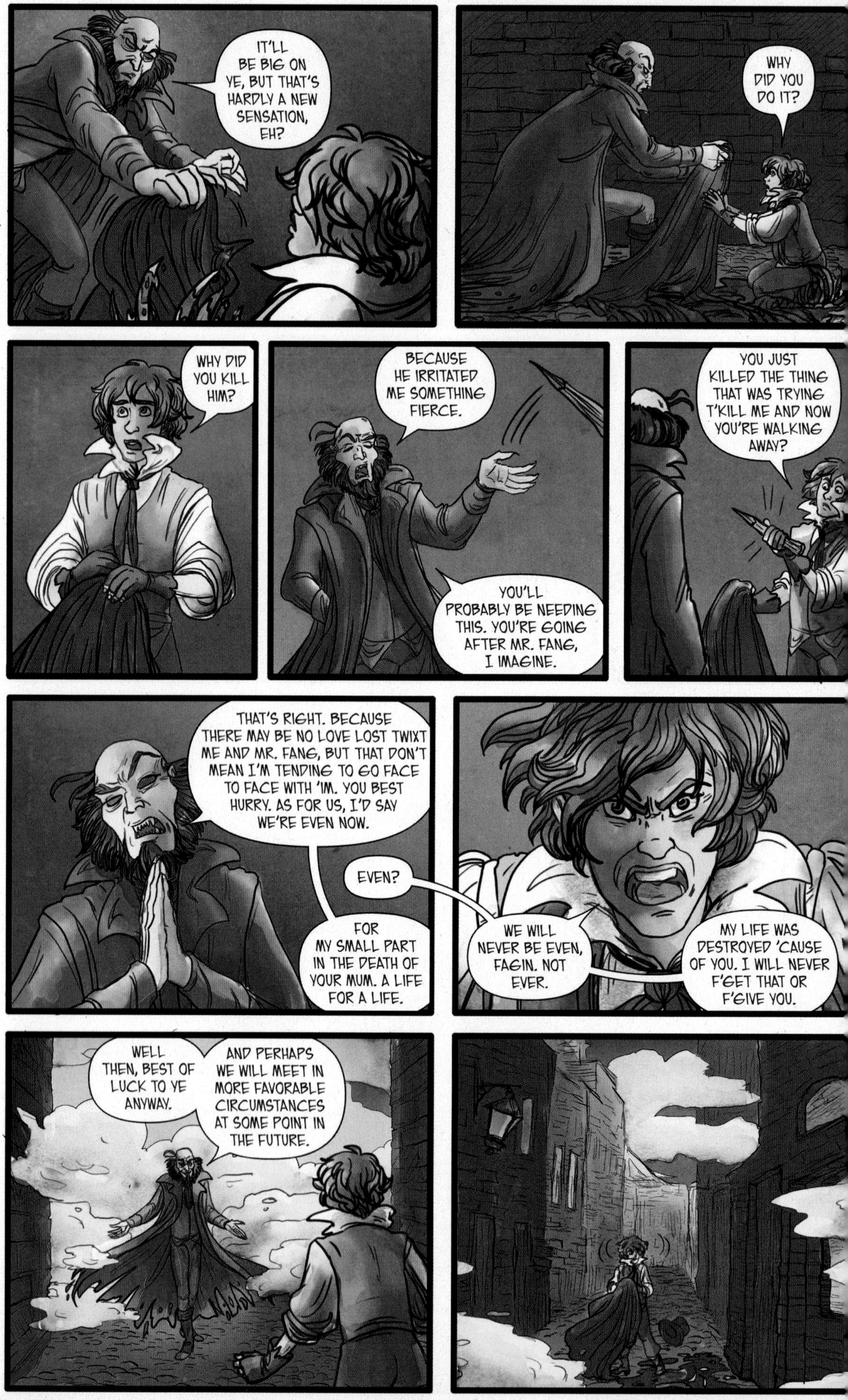
IT'LL BE BIG ON YE, BUT THAT'S HARDLY A NEW SENSATION, EH?
WHY DID YOU DO IT?
WHY DID YOU KILL HIM?
BECAUSE HE IRRITATED ME SOMETHING FIERCE.
YOU'LL PROBABLY BE NEEDING THIS. YOU'RE GOING AFTER MR. FANG, I IMAGINE.
YOU JUST KILLED THE THING THAT WAS TRYING T'KILL ME AND NOW YOU'RE WALKING AWAY?
THAT'S RIGHT. BECAUSE THERE MAY BE NO LOVE LOST TWIXT ME AND MR. FANG, BUT THAT DON'T MEAN I'M TENDING TO GO FACE TO FACE WITH 'IM. YOU BEST HURRY. AS FOR US, I'D SAY WE'RE EVEN NOW.
EVEN?
FOR MY SMALL PART IN THE DEATH OF YOUR MUM. A LIFE FOR A LIFE.
WE WILL NEVER BE EVEN, FAGIN. NOT EVER.
MY LIFE WAS DESTROYED 'CAUSE OF YOU. I WILL NEVER F'GET THAT OR F'GIVE YOU.
WELL THEN, BEST OF LUCK TO YE ANYWAY.
AND PERHAPS WE WILL MEET IN MORE FAVORABLE CIRCUMSTANCES AT SOME POINT IN THE FUTURE.

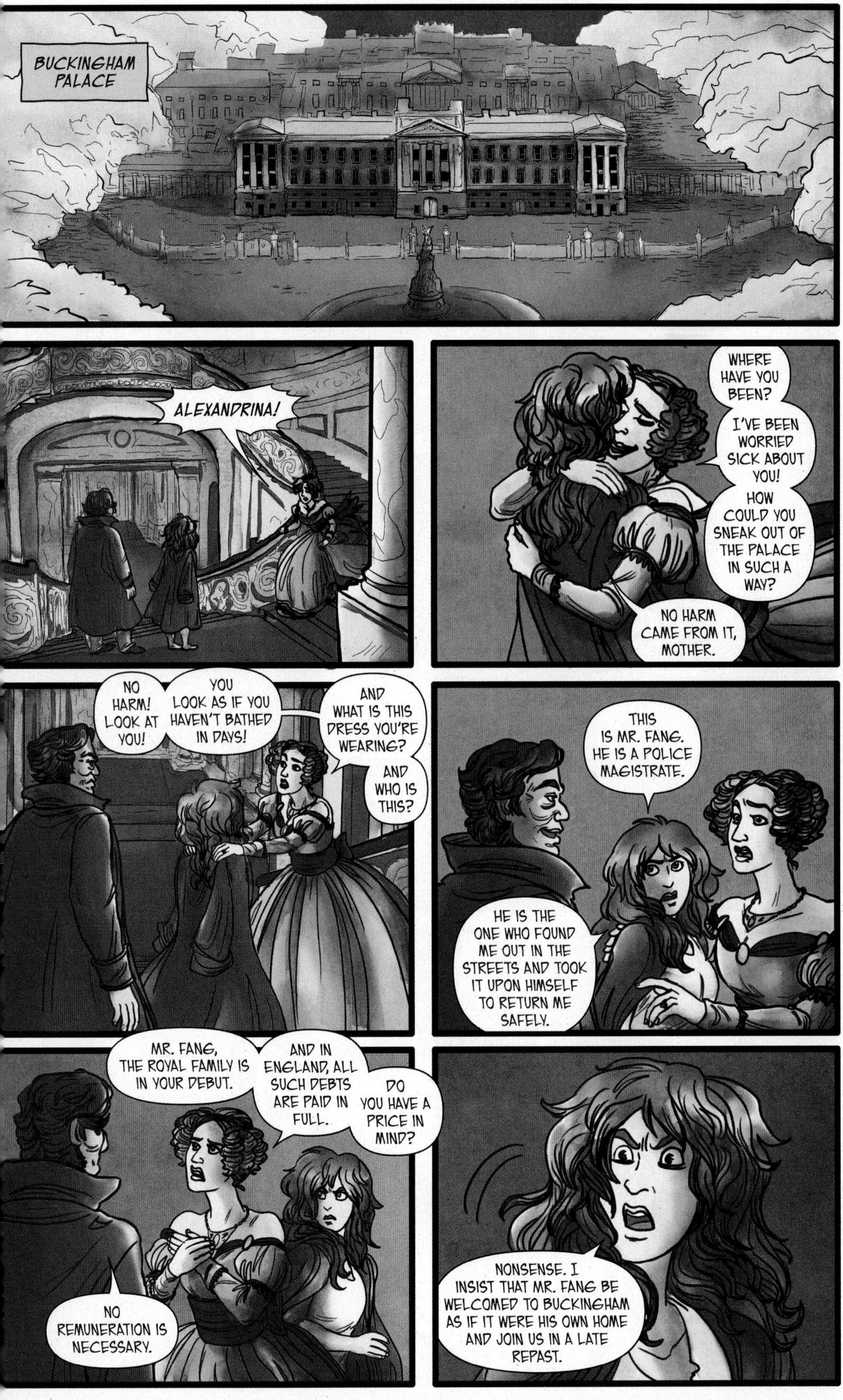
BUCKINGHAM PALACE
ALEXANDRINA!
WHERE HAVE YOU BEEN?
I'VE BEEN WORRIED SICK ABOUT YOU!
HOW COULD YOU SNEAK OUT OF THE PALACE IN SUCH A WAY?
NO HARM CAME FROM IT, MOTHER.
NO HARM! LOOK AT YOU!
YOU LOOK AS IF YOU HAVEN'T BATHED IN DAYS!
AND WHAT IS THIS DRESS YOU'RE WEARING?
AND WHO IS THIS?
THIS IS MR. FANG. HE IS A POLICE MAGISTRATE.
HE IS THE ONE WHO FOUND ME OUT IN THE STREETS AND TOOK IT UPON HIMSELF TO RETURN ME SAFELY.
MR. FANG, THE ROYAL FAMILY IS IN YOUR DEBUT.
AND IN ENGLAND, ALL SUCH DEBTS ARE PAID IN FULL.
DO YOU HAVE A PRICE IN MIND?
NO REMUNERATION IS NECESSARY.
NONSENSE. I INSIST THAT MR. FANG BE WELCOMED TO BUCKINGHAM AS IF IT WERE HIS OWN HOME AND JOIN US IN A LATE REPAST.

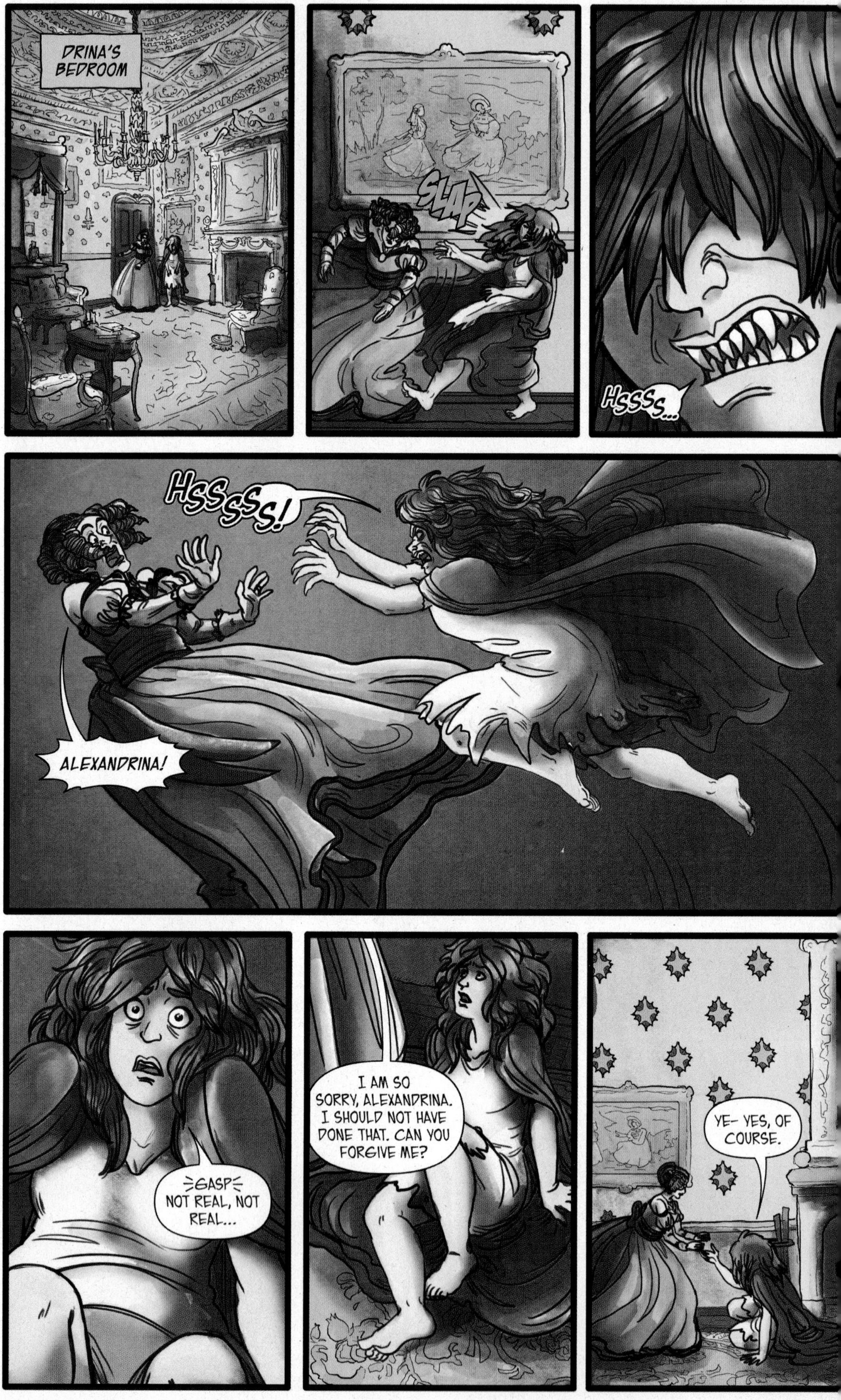
DRINA'S BEDROOM
SLAP
HSSSS...
HSSSSS!
ALEXANDRINA!
GASP
NOT REAL, NOT REAL...
I AM SO SORRY, ALEXANDRINA. I SHOULD NOT HAVE DONE THAT. CAN YOU FORGIVE ME?
YE- YES, OF COURSE.

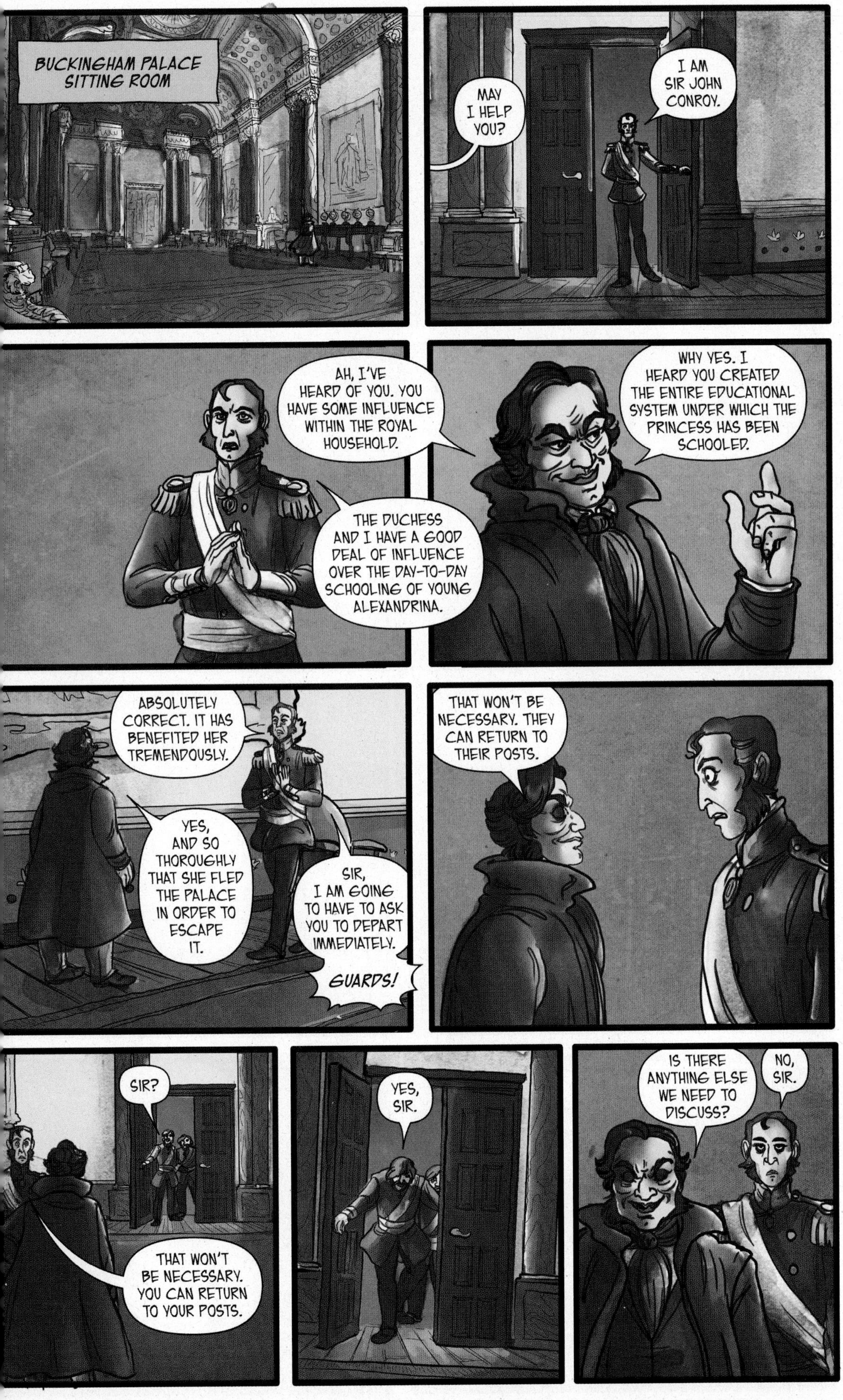
BUCKINGHAM PALACE
SITTING ROOM
MAY I HELP YOU?
I AM SIR JOHN CONROY.
AH, I'VE HEARD OF YOU. YOU HAVE SOME INFLUENCE WITHIN THE ROYAL HOUSEHOLD.
THE DUCHESS AND I HAVE A GOOD DEAL OF INFLUENCE OVER THE DAY-TO-DAY SCHOOLING OF YOUNG ALEXANDRINA.
WHY YES. I HEARD YOU CREATED THE ENTIRE EDUCATIONAL SYSTEM UNDER WHICH THE PRINCESS HAS BEEN SCHOOLED.
ABSOLUTELY CORRECT. IT HAS BENEFITED HER TREMENDOUSLY.
YES, AND SO THOROUGHLY THAT SHE FLED THE PALACE IN ORDER TO ESCAPE IT.
SIR, I AM GOING TO HAVE TO ASK YOU TO DEPART IMMEDIATELY.
GUARDS!
THAT WON'T BE NECESSARY. THEY CAN RETURN TO THEIR POSTS.
SIR?
THAT WON'T BE NECESSARY. YOU CAN RETURN TO YOUR POSTS.
YES, SIR.
IS THERE ANYTHING ELSE WE NEED TO DISCUSS?
NO, SIR.

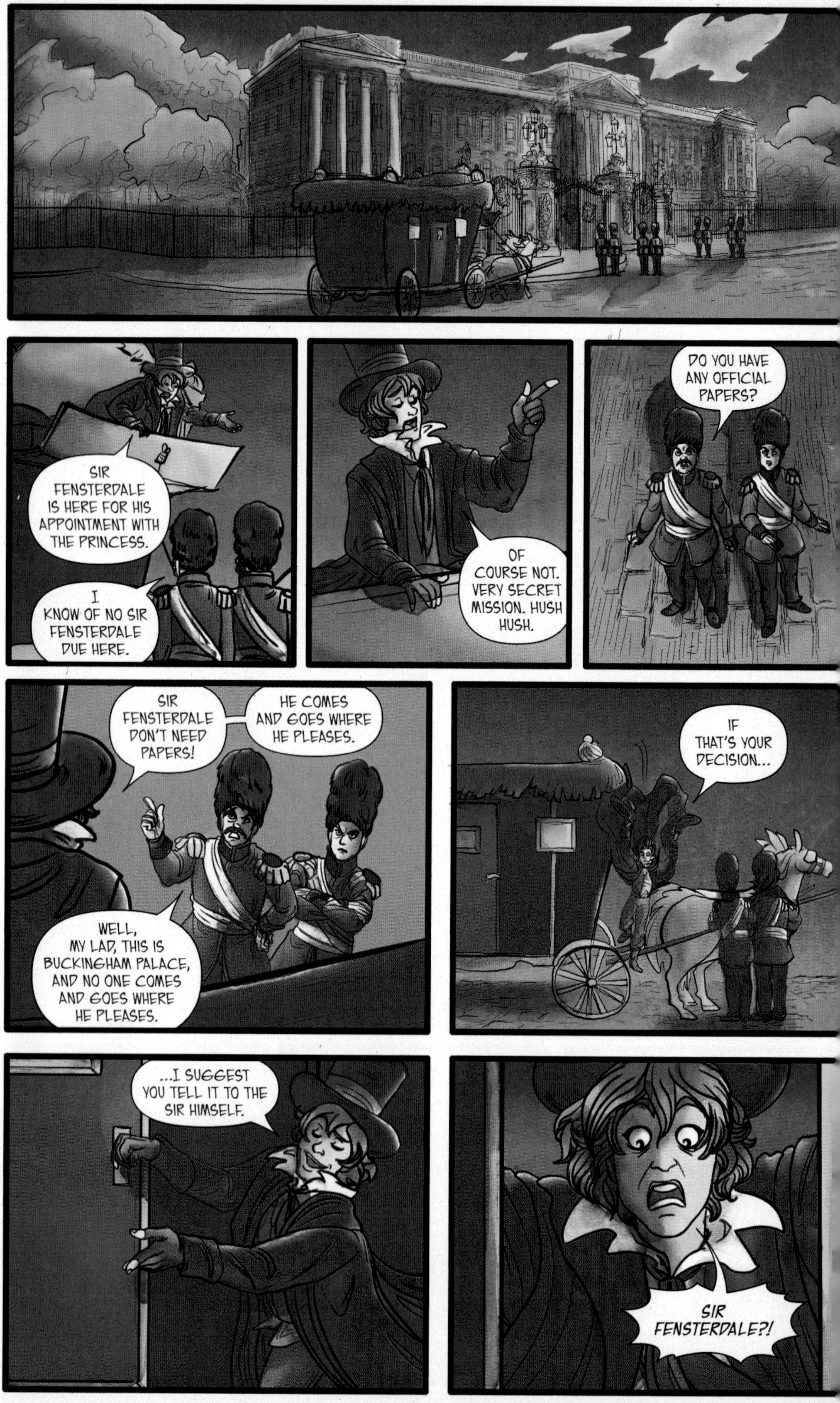
SIR FENSTERDALE IS HERE FOR HIS APPOINTMENT WITH THE PRINCESS.
I KNOW OF NO SIR FENSTERDALE DUE HERE.
OF COURSE NOT. VERY SECRET MISSION. HUSH HUSH.
DO YOU HAVE ANY OFFICIAL PAPERS?
SIR FENSTERDALE DON'T NEED PAPERS!
HE COMES AND GOES WHERE HE PLEASES.
WELL, MY LAD, THIS IS BUCKINGHAM PALACE, AND NO ONE COMES AND GOES WHERE HE PLEASES.
IF THAT'S YOUR DECISION...
...I SUGGEST YOU TELL IT TO THE SIR HIMSELF.
SIR FENSTERDALE?!

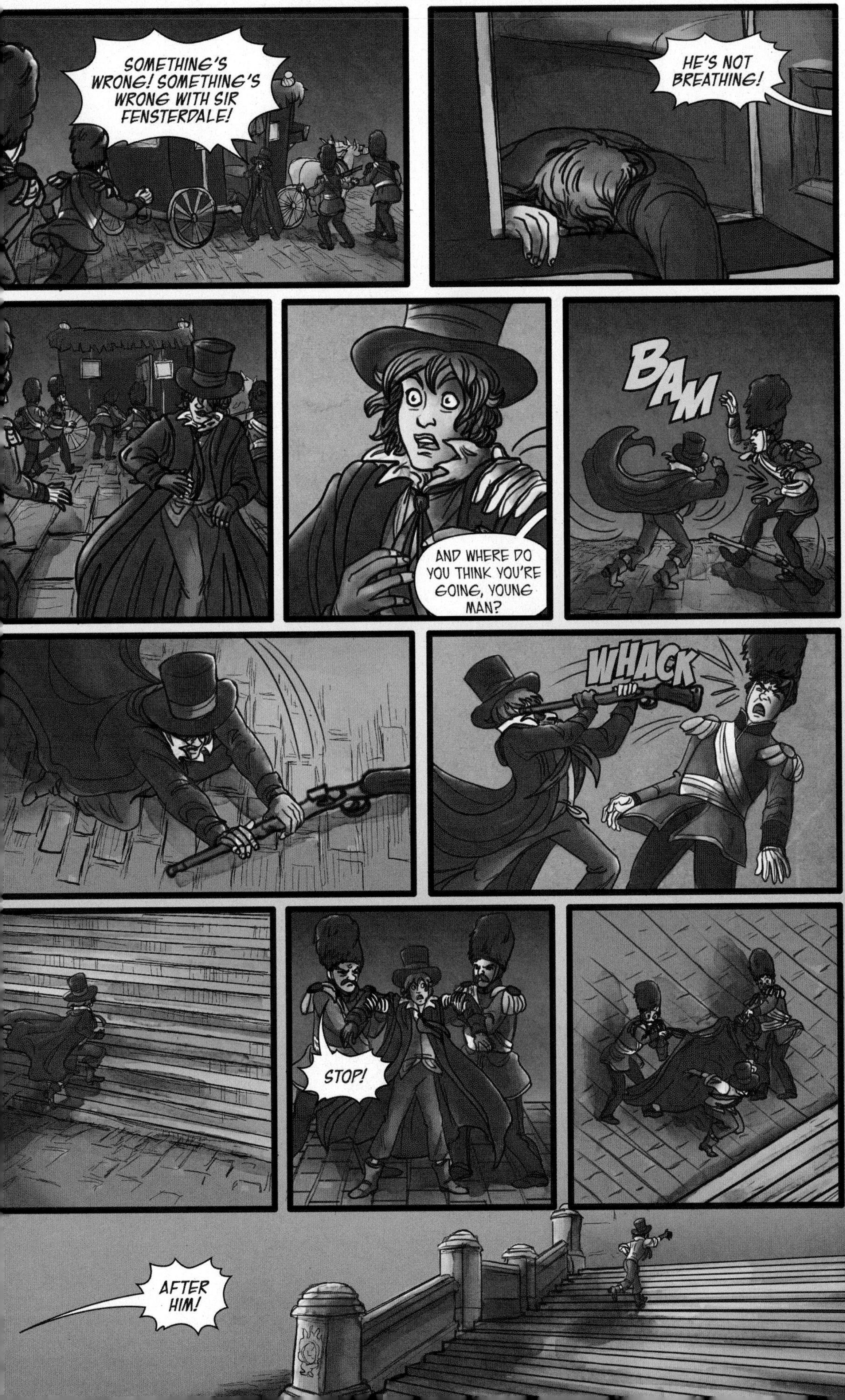
SOMETHING'S WRONG! SOMETHING'S WRONG WITH SIR FENSTERDALE!
HE'S NOT BREATHING!
AND WHERE DO YOU THINK YOU'RE GOING, YOUNG MAN?
BAM
WHACK
STOP!
AFTER HIM!

FAGIN

EXPLORATORY SKETCHES

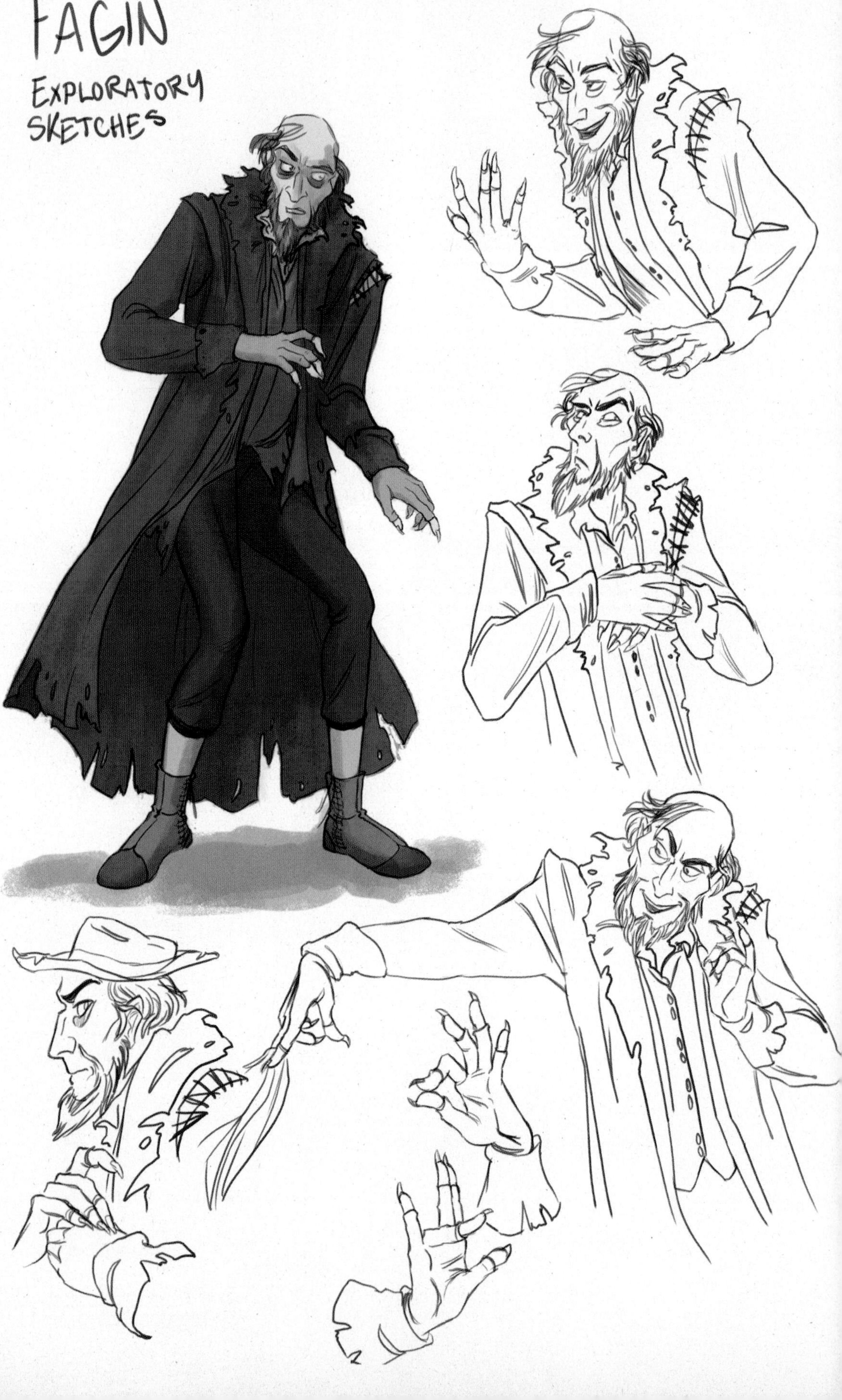

CHAPTER SIX

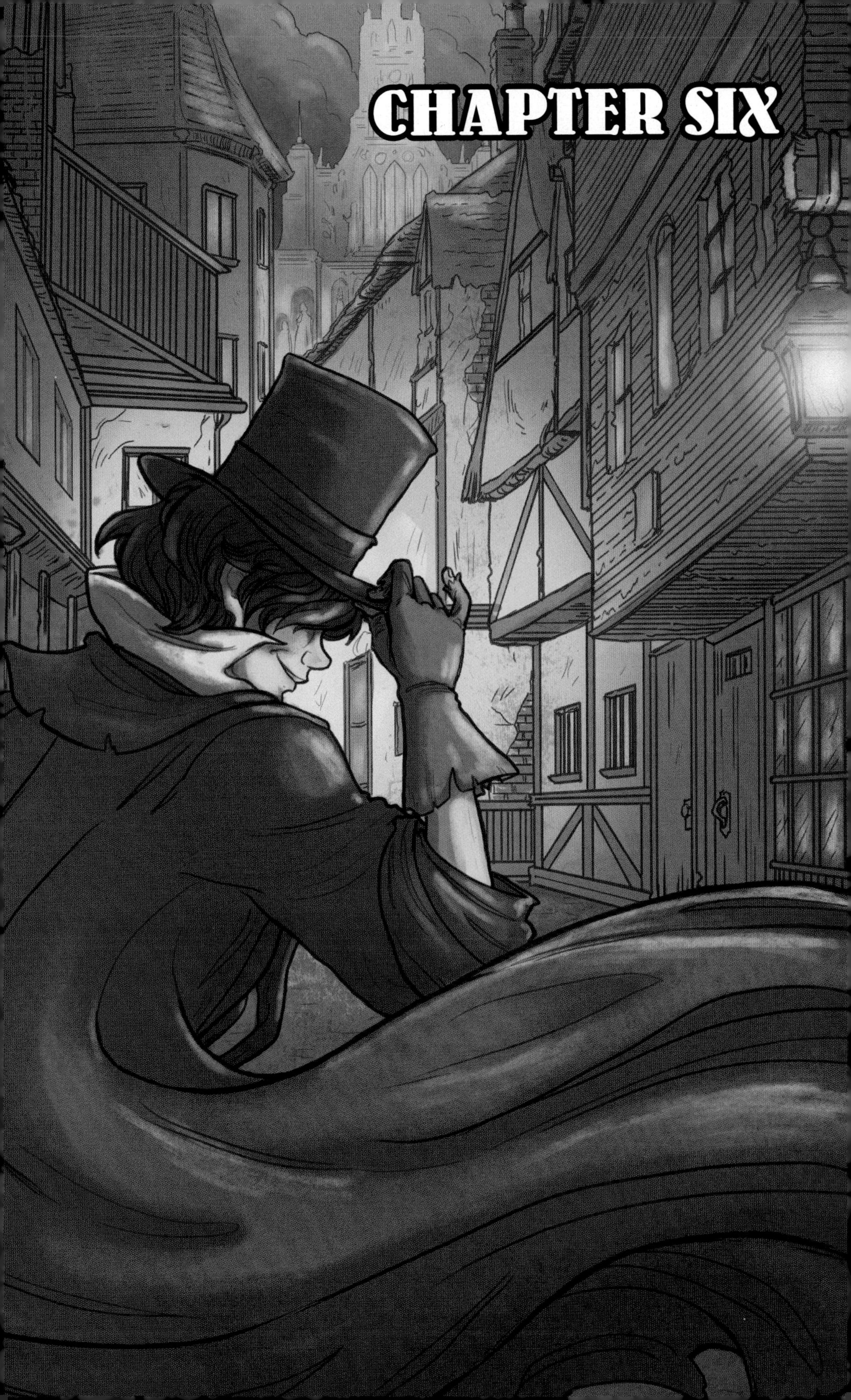

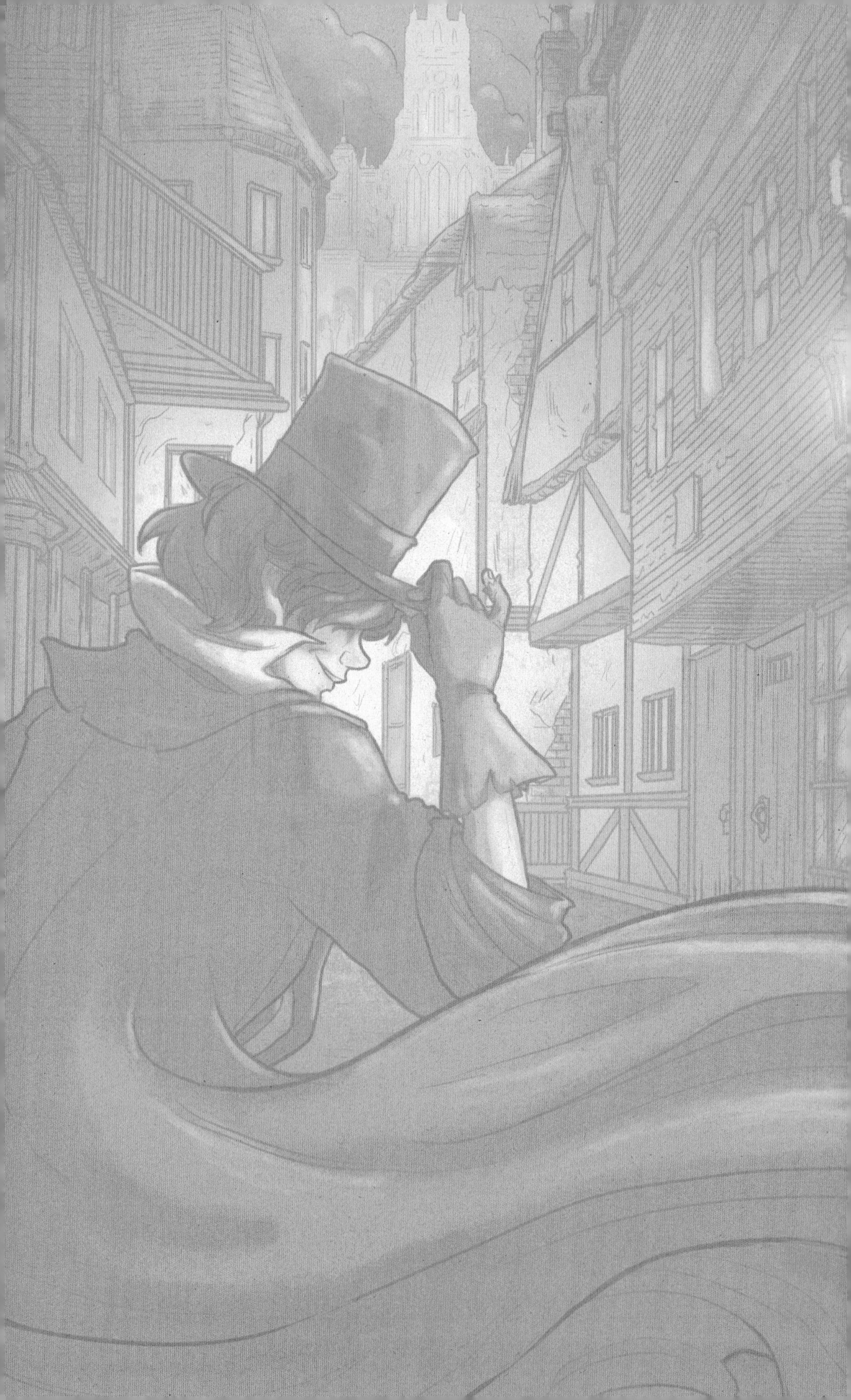

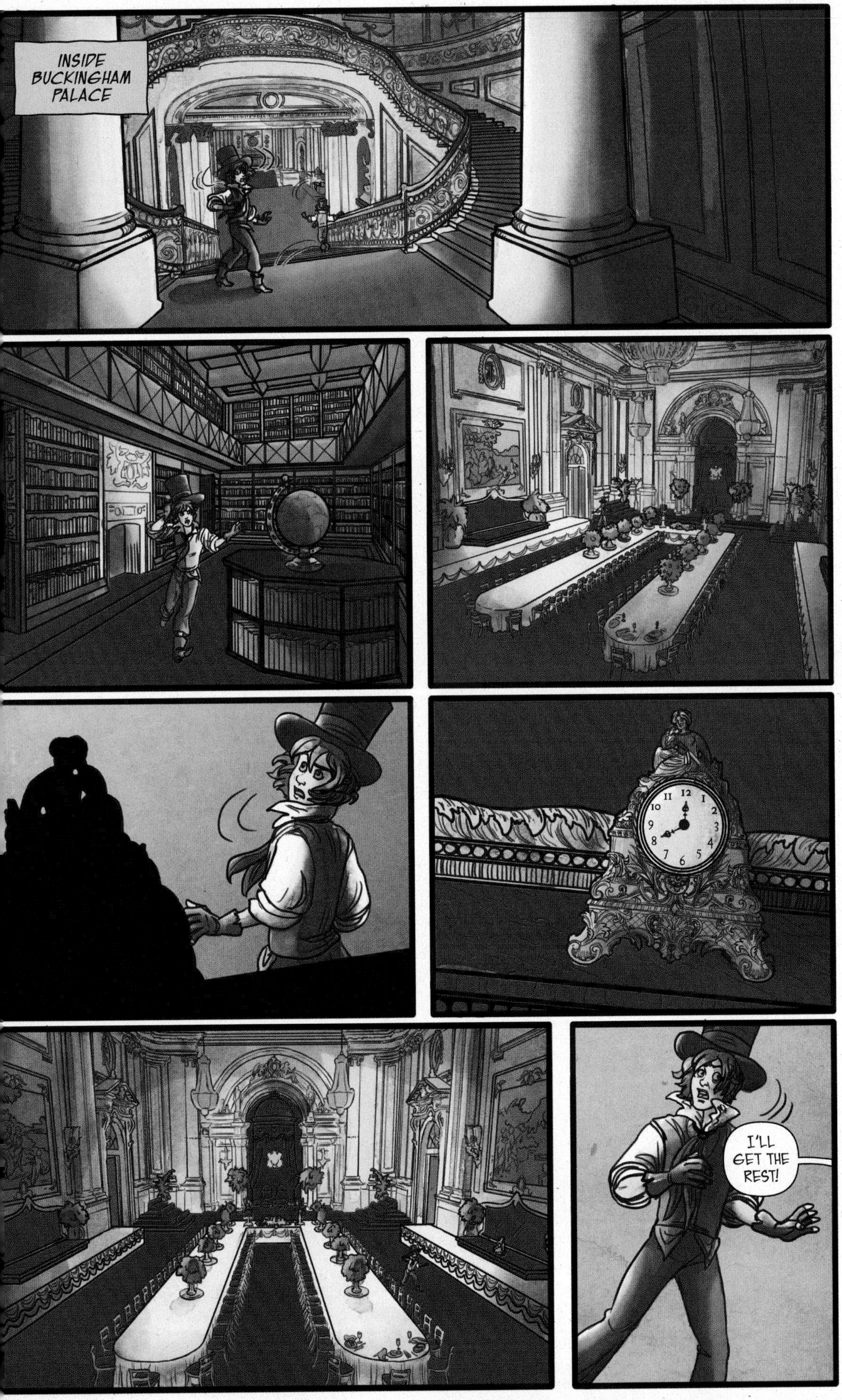
INSIDE BUCKINGHAM PALACE
I'LL GET THE REST!

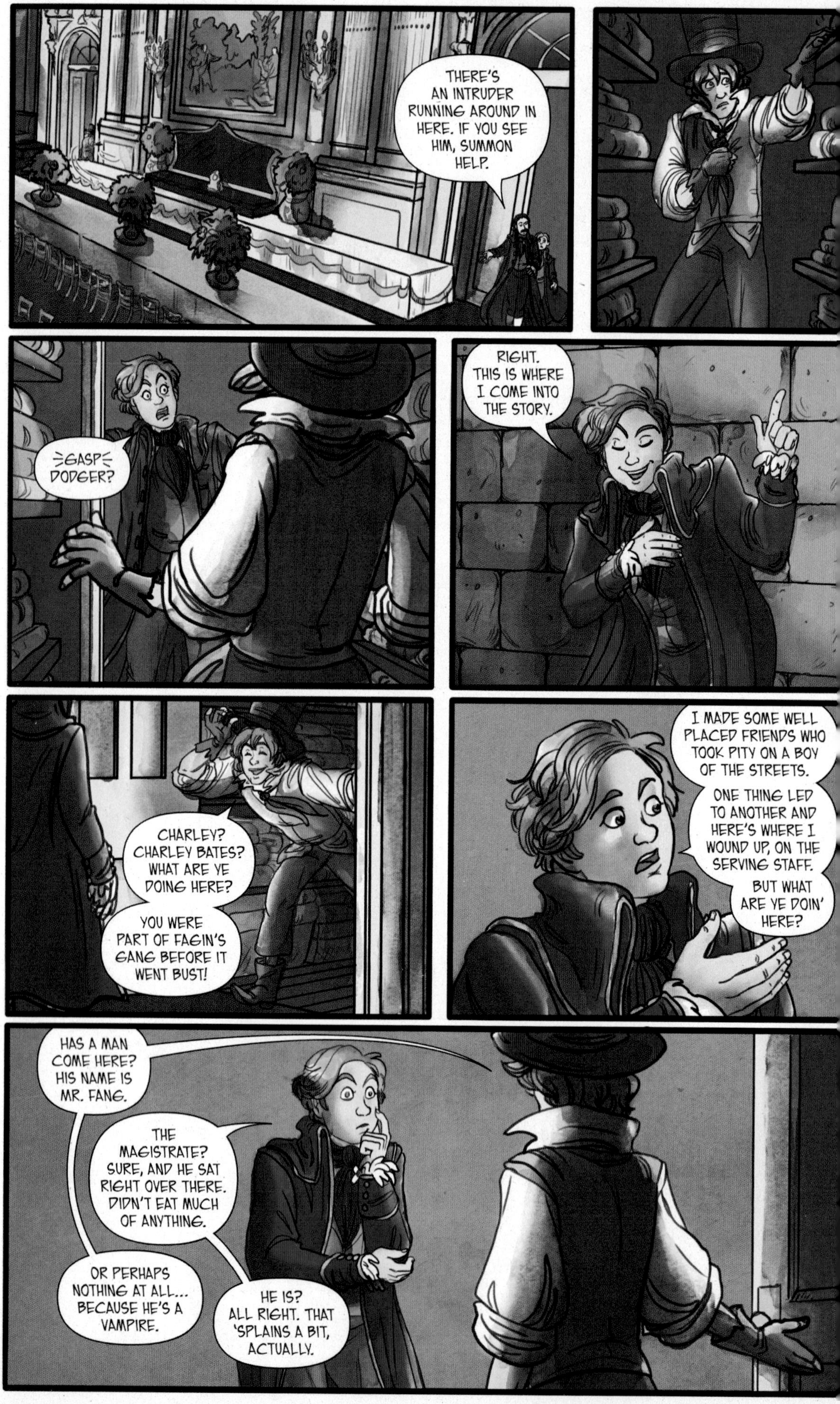

THERE'S AN INTRUDER RUNNING AROUND IN HERE. IF YOU SEE HIM, SUMMON HELP.
GASP DODGER?
RIGHT. THIS IS WHERE I COME INTO THE STORY.
CHARLEY? CHARLEY BATES? WHAT ARE YE DOING HERE?
YOU WERE PART OF FAGIN'S GANG BEFORE IT WENT BUST!
I MADE SOME WELL PLACED FRIENDS WHO TOOK PITY ON A BOY OF THE STREETS.
ONE THING LED TO ANOTHER AND HERE'S WHERE I WOUND UP, ON THE SERVING STAFF.
BUT WHAT ARE YE DOIN' HERE?
HAS A MAN COME HERE? HIS NAME IS MR. FANG.
THE MAGISTRATE? SURE, AND HE SAT RIGHT OVER THERE. DIDN'T EAT MUCH OF ANYTHING.
OR PERHAPS NOTHING AT ALL... BECAUSE HE'S A VAMPIRE.
HE IS? ALL RIGHT. THAT 'SPLAINS A BIT, ACTUALLY.

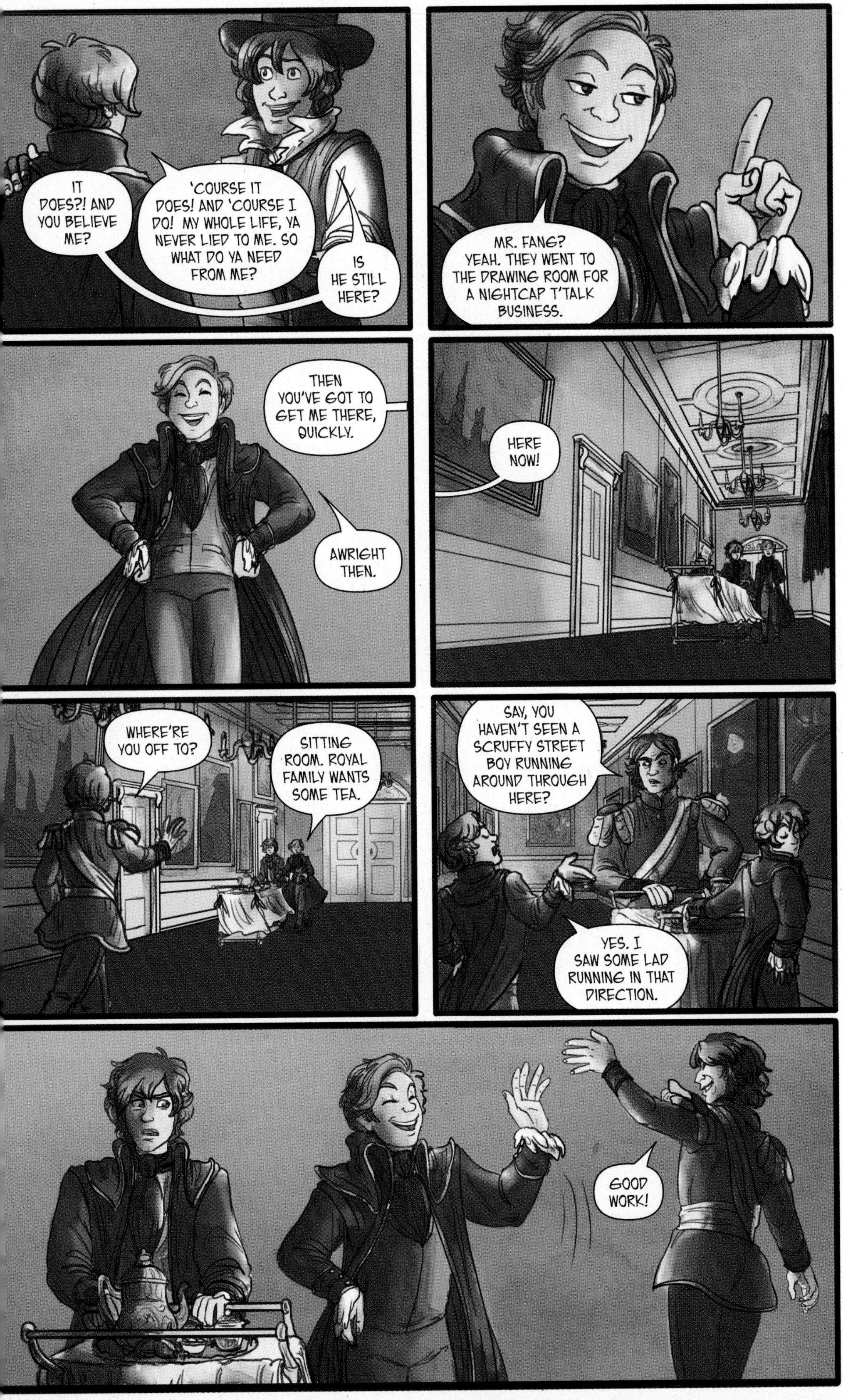

IT DOES?! AND YOU BELIEVE ME?
'COURSE IT DOES! AND 'COURSE I DO! MY WHOLE LIFE, YA NEVER LIED TO ME. SO WHAT DO YA NEED FROM ME?
IS HE STILL HERE?
MR. FANG? YEAH. THEY WENT TO THE DRAWING ROOM FOR A NIGHTCAP T'TALK BUSINESS.
THEN YOU'VE GOT TO GET ME THERE, QUICKLY.
AWRIGHT THEN.
HERE NOW!
WHERE'RE YOU OFF TO?
SITTING ROOM. ROYAL FAMILY WANTS SOME TEA.
SAY, YOU HAVEN'T SEEN A SCRUFFY STREET BOY RUNNING AROUND THROUGH HERE?
YES. I SAW SOME LAD RUNNING IN THAT DIRECTION.
GOOD WORK!

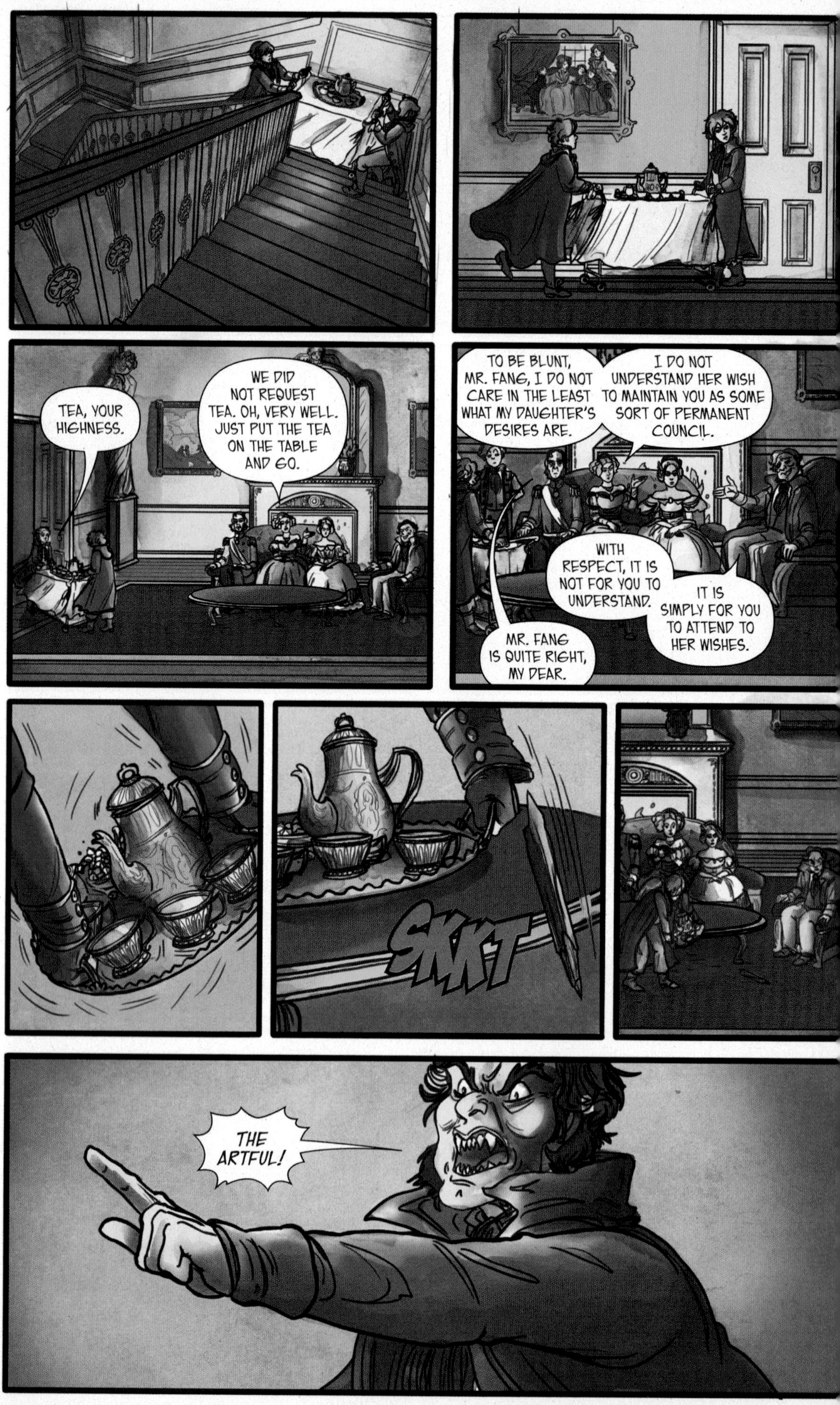

TEA, YOUR HIGHNESS.
WE DID NOT REQUEST TEA. OH, VERY WELL. JUST PUT THE TEA ON THE TABLE AND GO.
TO BE BLUNT, MR. FANG, I DO NOT CARE IN THE LEAST WHAT MY DAUGHTER'S DESIRES ARE.
I DO NOT UNDERSTAND HER WISH TO MAINTAIN YOU AS SOME SORT OF PERMANENT COUNCIL.
WITH RESPECT, IT IS NOT FOR YOU TO UNDERSTAND.
IT IS SIMPLY FOR YOU TO ATTEND TO HER WISHES.
MR. FANG IS QUITE RIGHT, MY DEAR.
SKKT
THE ARTFUL!

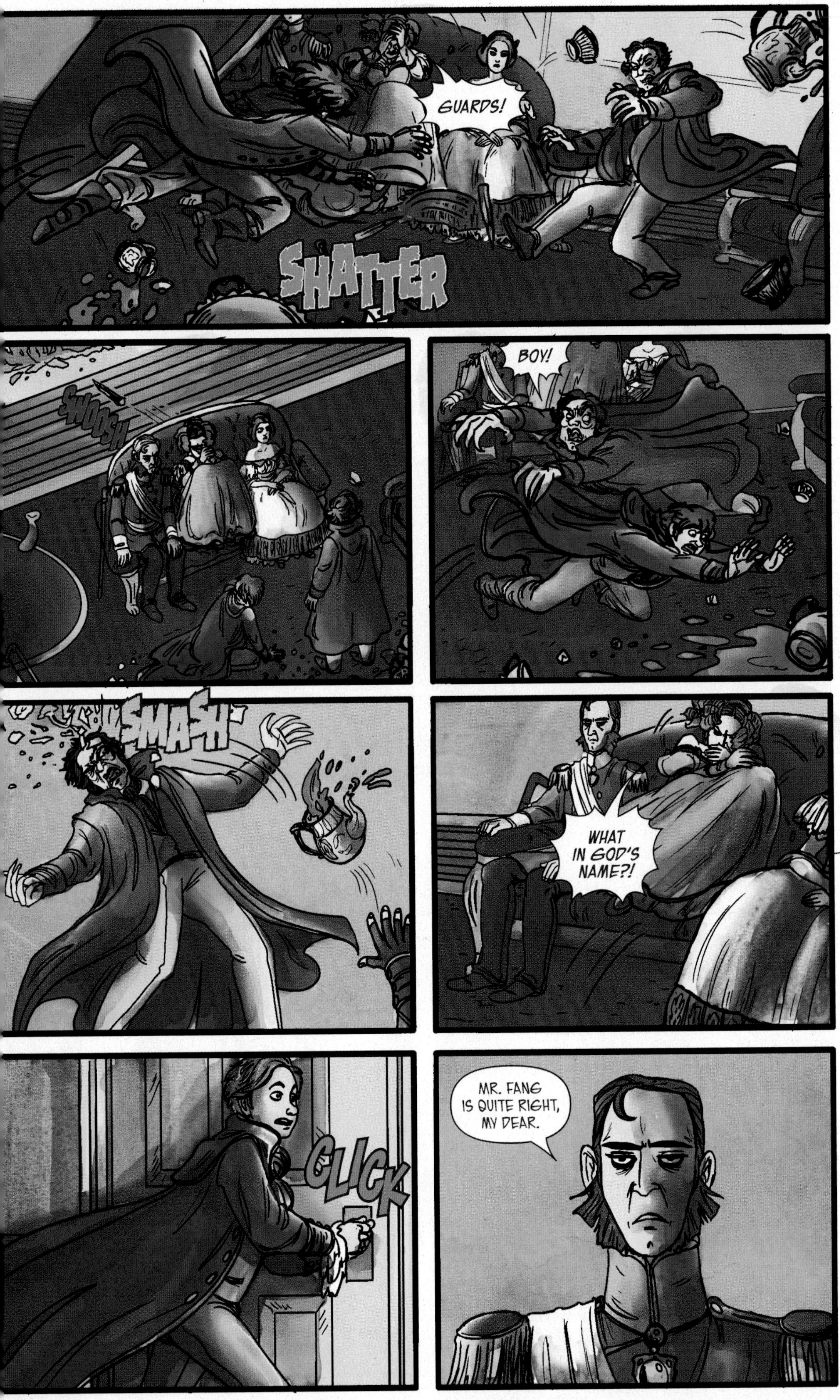
GUARDS!
SHATTER
SWOOSH
BOY!
SMASH
WHAT IN GOD'S NAME?!
CLICK
MR. FANG IS QUITE RIGHT, MY DEAR.

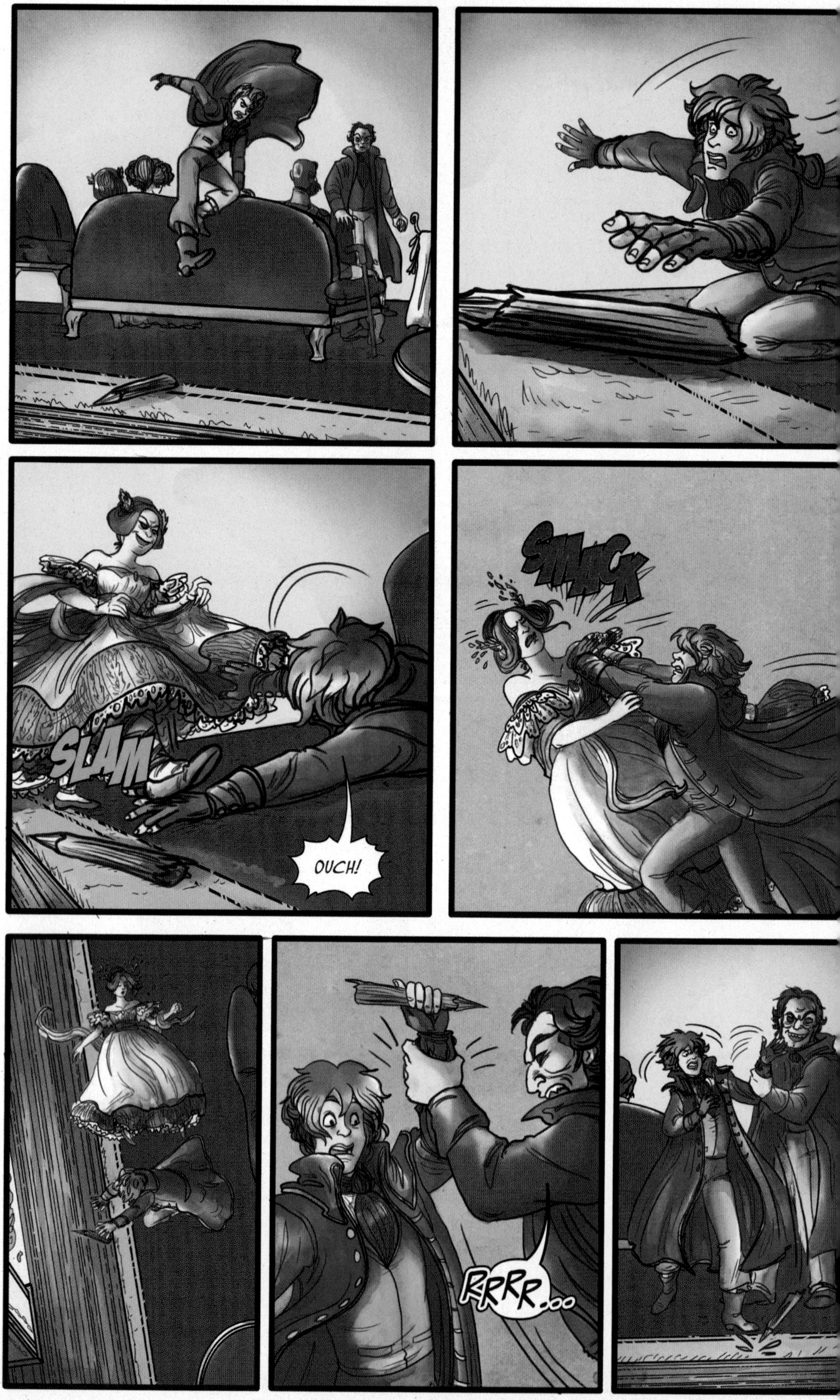
SLAM
OUCH!
SMACK
RRRR...

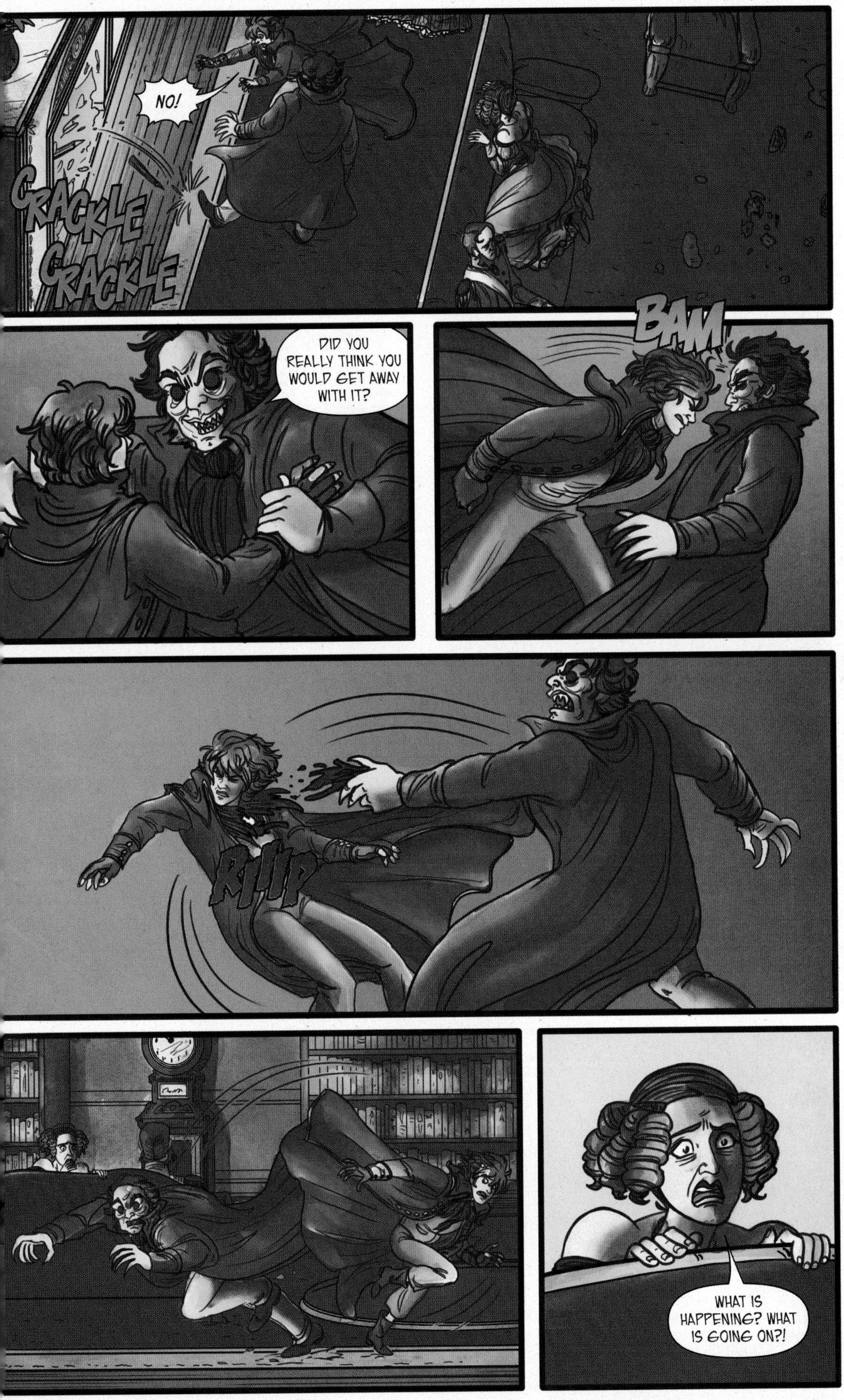
NO!
CRACKLE
CRACKLE
DID YOU REALLY THINK YOU WOULD GET AWAY WITH IT?
BAM
RIIIP
WHAT IS HAPPENING? WHAT IS GOING ON?!

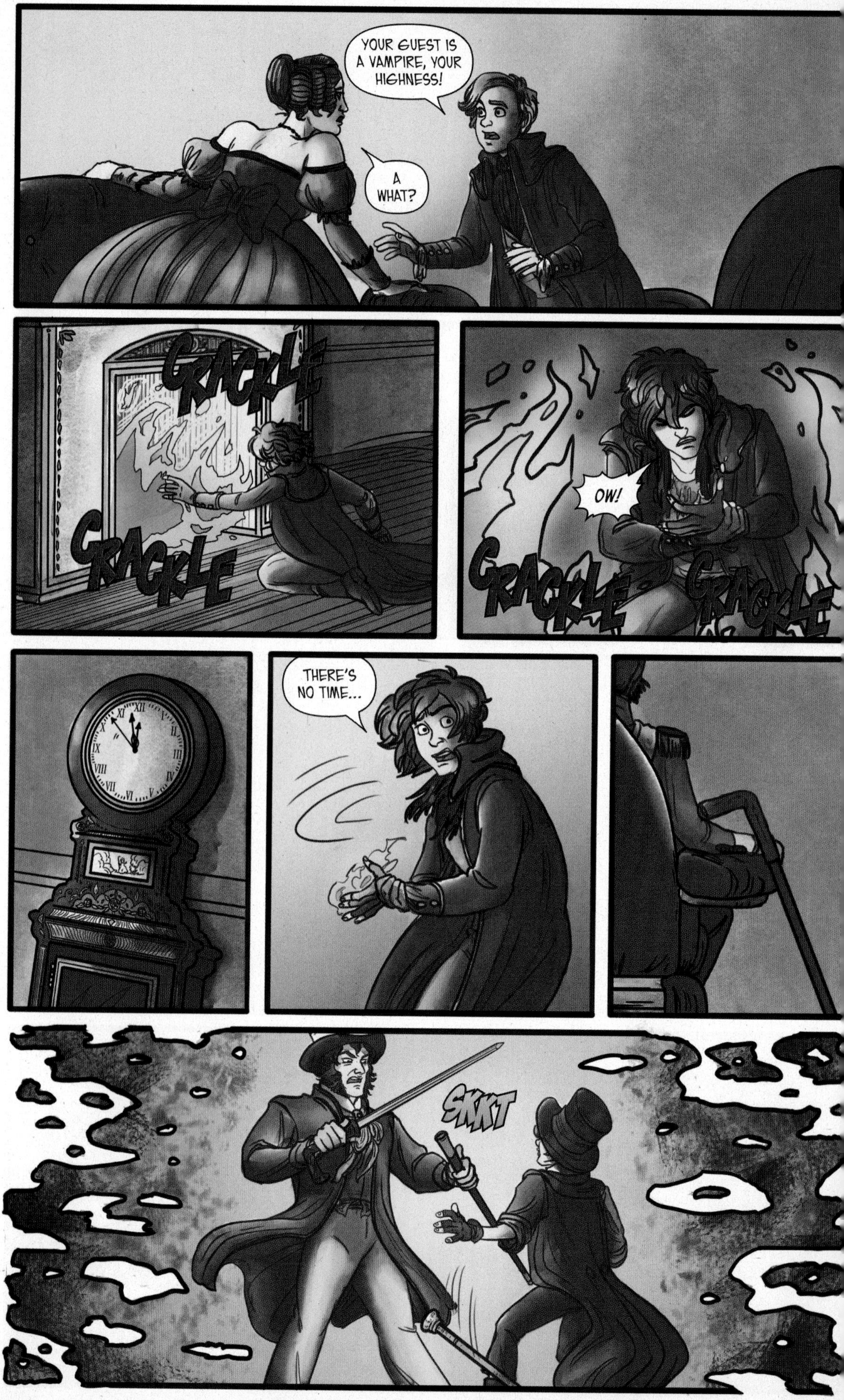
YOUR GUEST IS A VAMPIRE, YOUR HIGHNESS!
A WHAT?
CRACKLE
CRACKLE
OW!
CRACKLE
CRACKLE
THERE'S NO TIME...
SKKT

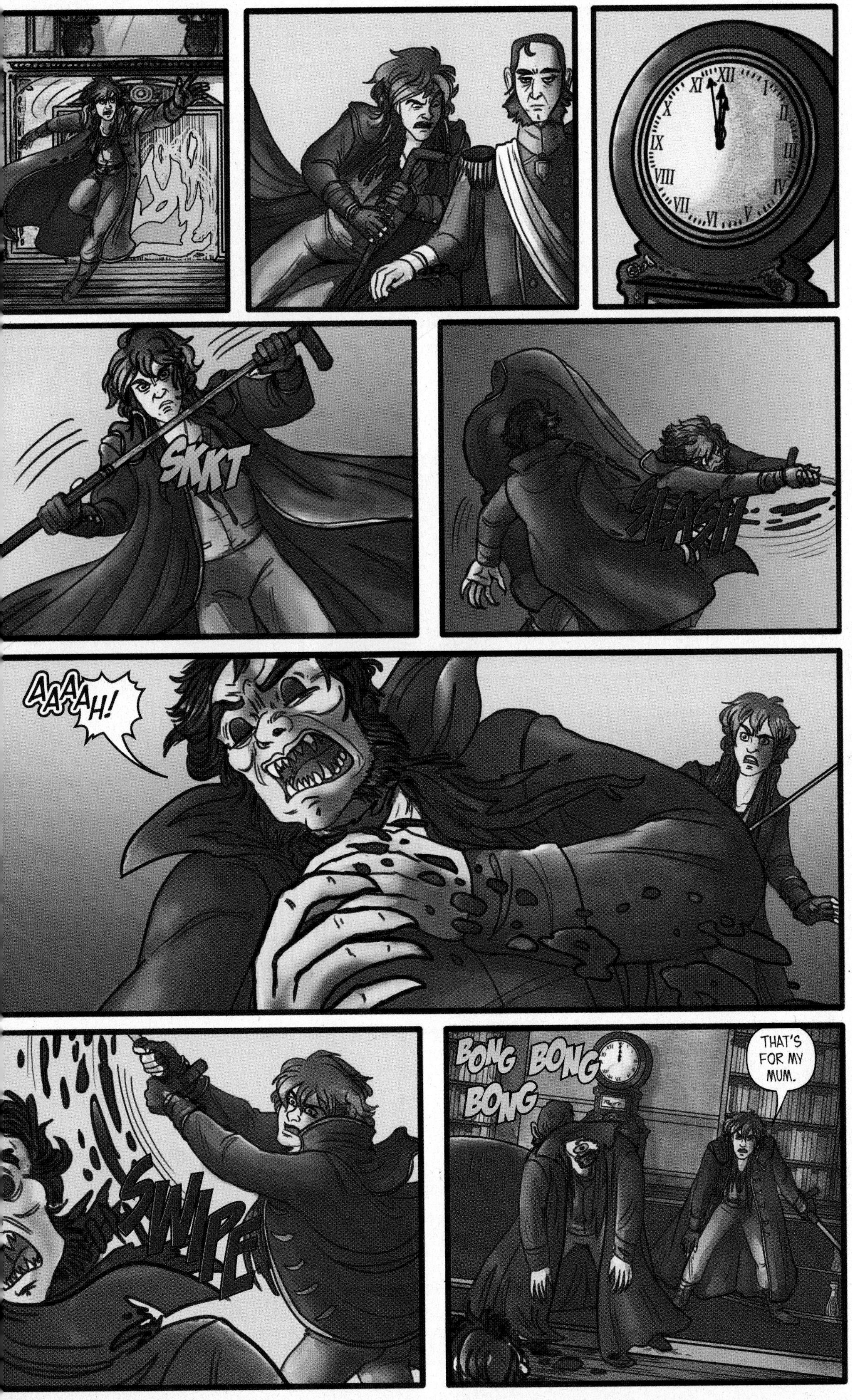
SKKT
SLASH
AAAAH!
SWIPE
BONG BONG
BONG
THAT'S FOR MY MUM.

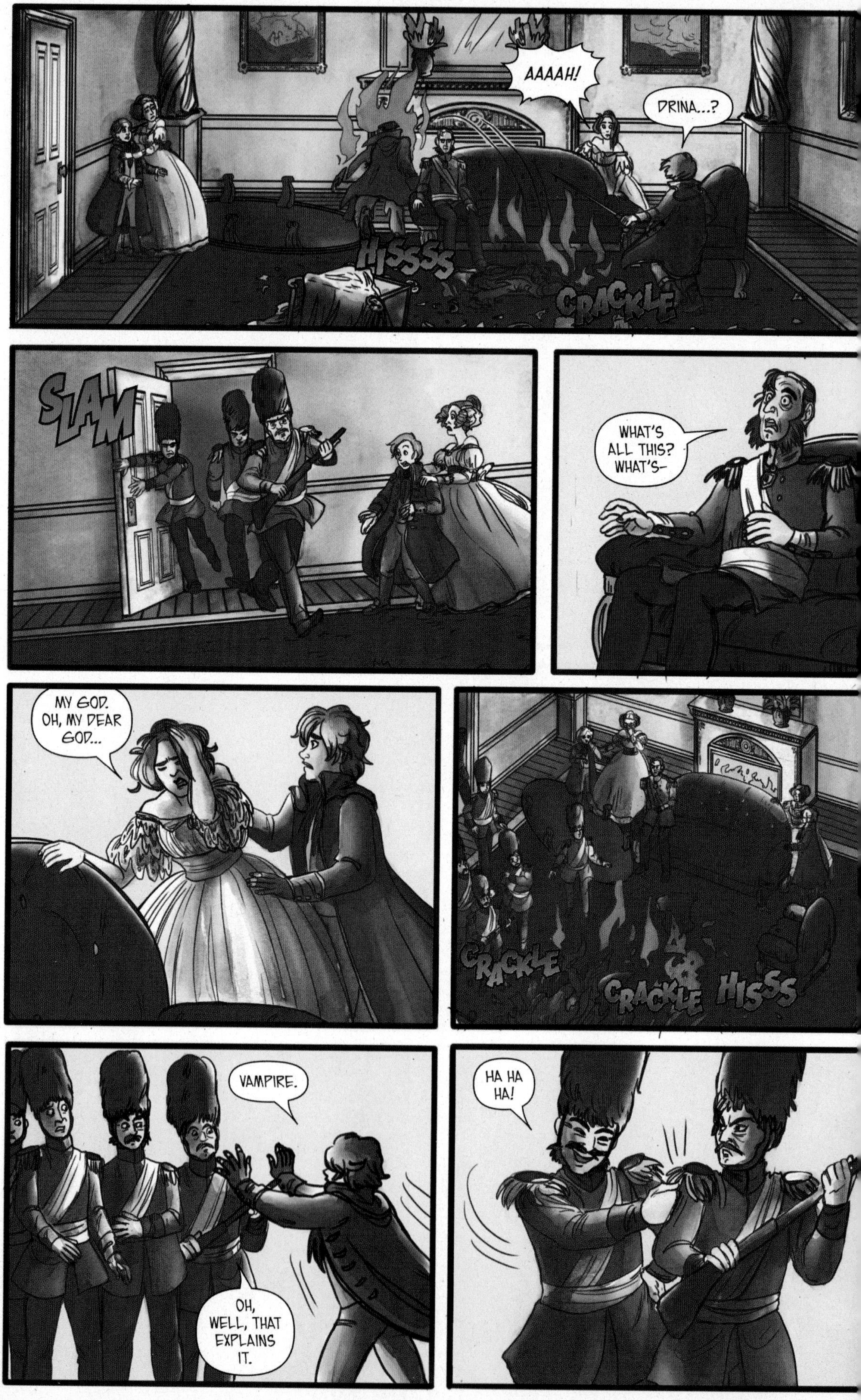
AAAAH!
DRINA...?
HISSSS
CRACKLE
SLAM
WHAT'S ALL THIS? WHAT'S-
MY GOD. OH, MY DEAR GOD...
CRACKLE
CRACKLE
HISSS
VAMPIRE.
OH, WELL, THAT EXPLAINS IT.
HA HA HA!

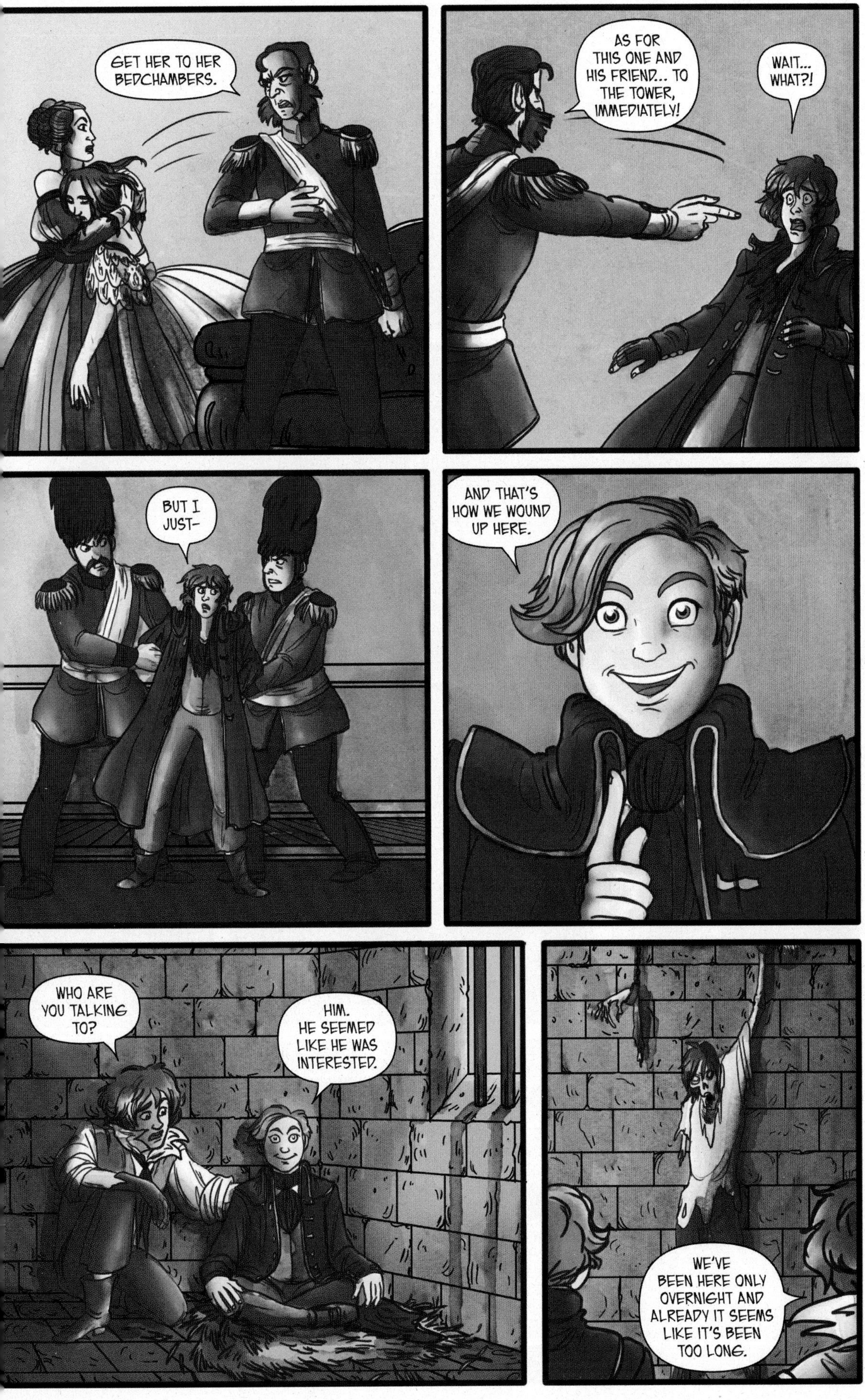
GET HER TO HER BEDCHAMBERS.
AS FOR THIS ONE AND HIS FRIEND... TO THE TOWER, IMMEDIATELY!
WAIT... WHAT?!
BUT I JUST-
AND THAT'S HOW WE WOUND UP HERE.
WHO ARE YOU TALKING TO?
HIM. HE SEEMED LIKE HE WAS INTERESTED.
WE'VE BEEN HERE ONLY OVERNIGHT AND ALREADY IT SEEMS LIKE IT'S BEEN TOO LONG.

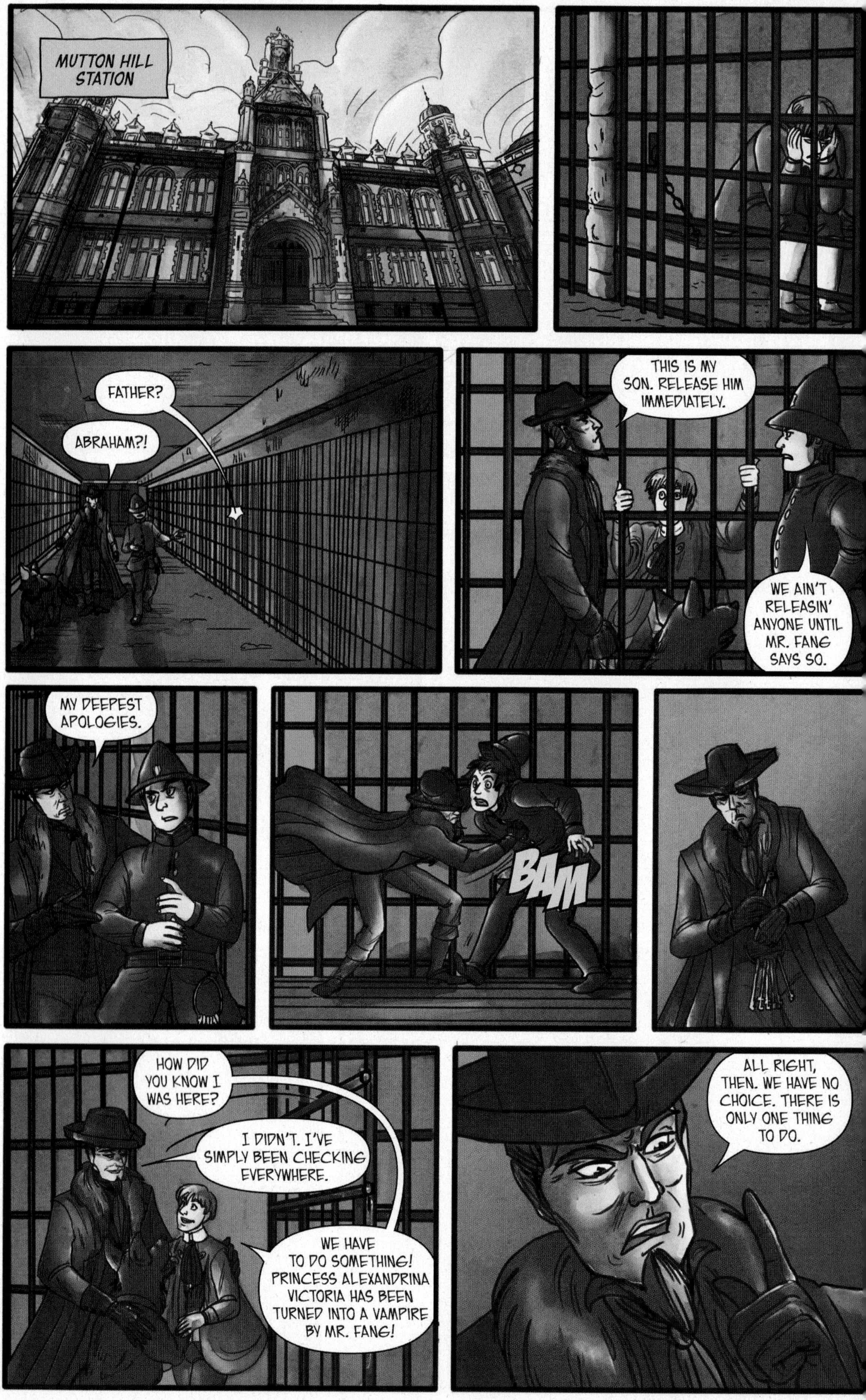
MUTTON HILL STATION
FATHER?
ABRAHAM?!
THIS IS MY SON. RELEASE HIM IMMEDIATELY.
WE AIN'T RELEASIN' ANYONE UNTIL MR. FANG SAYS SO.
MY DEEPEST APOLOGIES.
BAM
HOW DID YOU KNOW I WAS HERE?
I DIDN'T. I'VE SIMPLY BEEN CHECKING EVERYWHERE.
WE HAVE TO DO SOMETHING! PRINCESS ALEXANDRINA VICTORIA HAS BEEN TURNED INTO A VAMPIRE BY MR. FANG!
ALL RIGHT, THEN. WE HAVE NO CHOICE. THERE IS ONLY ONE THING TO DO.

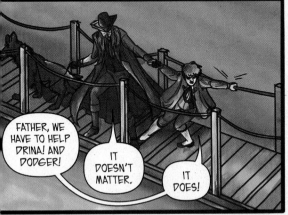

FATHER, WE HAVE TO HELP DRINA! AND DODGER!

IT DOESN'T MATTER.

IT DOES!

NO, IT DOES NOT.

YOU ARE TELLING ME THAT MR. FANG HAS TAKEN OVER THE ROYAL FAMILY.

IF THAT IS THE CASE, WE'VE NO CHOICE SAVE TO FLEE THE COUNTRY AS QUICKLY AS POSSIBLE.

WE HAVE ALREADY LOST.

YOUR MAJOR CRIME WAS HOLDING THE DOOR CLOSED.

SO YOU MIGHT SEE DAYLIGHT IN TEN, MAYBE TWENTY YEARS.
ME... THEY'RE PROB'LY BUILDIN' A NOOSE TO DANGLE ME FROM RIGHT NOW.

OH, I DOUBT THAT.
THEY ALREADY HAVE PLENTY OF NOOSES, SO THEY DON'T HAVE TO BUILD NO...

OH, SORRY! WEREN'T THINKIN' NONE.

TAP TAP TAP

ON YOUR FEET, CHARLEY. THINK WE'RE ABOUT T'HAVE COMPANY.

COME WITH US.

WHERE TO? A COURT? AUSTRALIA? OR STRAIGHT TO THE HANGMAN?

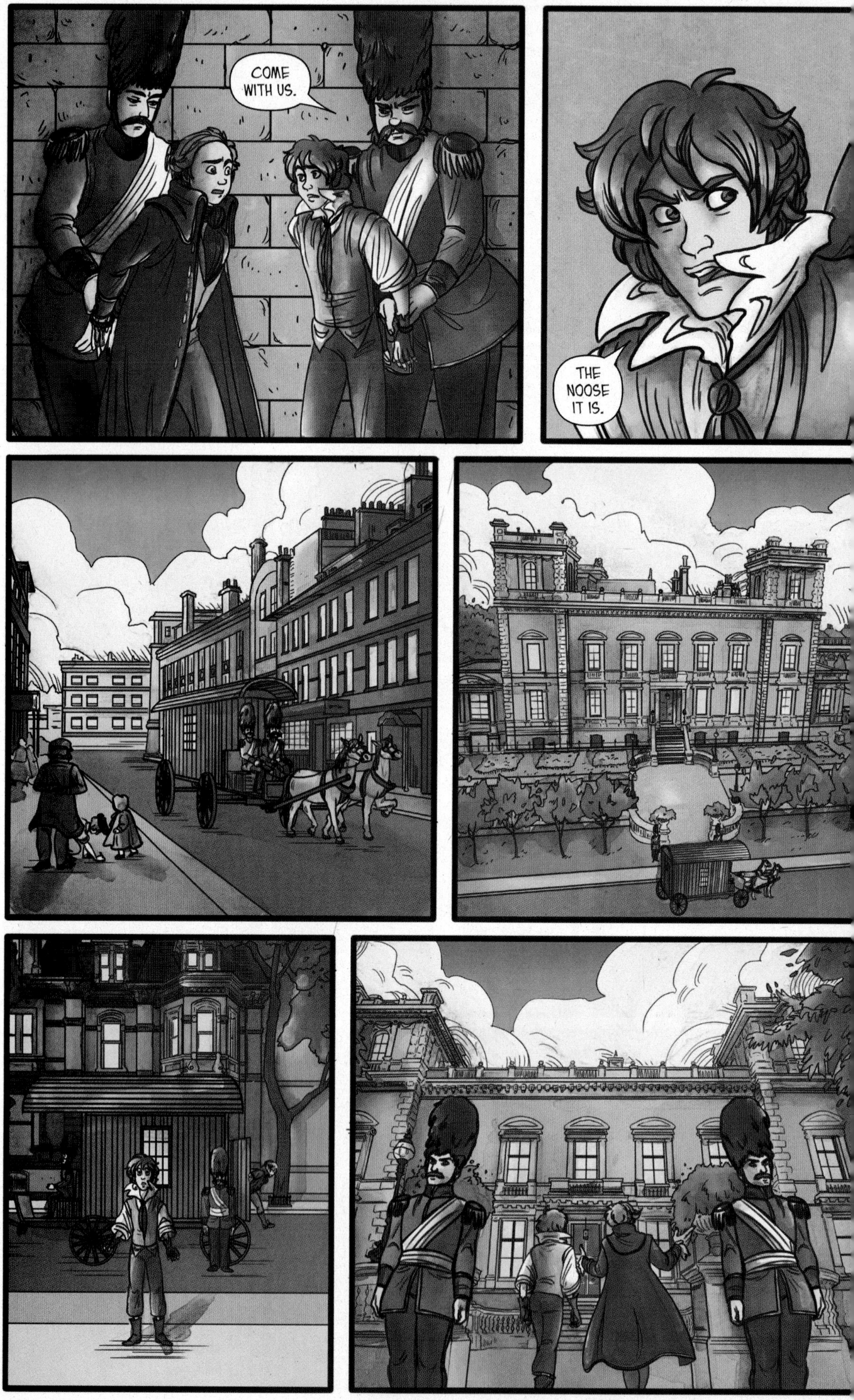
COME WITH US.
THE NOOSE IT IS.

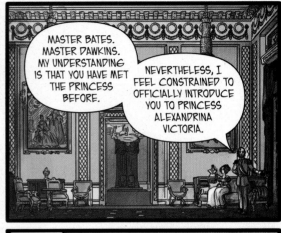

MASTER BATES. MASTER DAWKINS. MY UNDERSTANDING IS THAT YOU HAVE MET THE PRINCESS BEFORE.

NEVERTHELESS, I FEEL CONSTRAINED TO OFFICIALLY INTRODUCE YOU TO PRINCESS ALEXANDRINA VICTORIA.

THESE ARE YOURS.

THE PRINCESS' MOTHER WOULD BE HERE, BUT SHE IS... NOT WELL AT THE MOMENT.

RECENT EVENTS WERE RATHER STRESSFUL FOR HER.

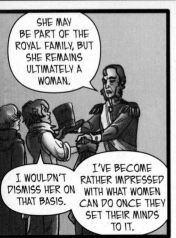

SHE MAY BE PART OF THE ROYAL FAMILY, BUT SHE REMAINS ULTIMATELY A WOMAN.

I WOULDN'T DISMISS HER ON THAT BASIS.

I'VE BECOME RATHER IMPRESSED WITH WHAT WOMEN CAN DO ONCE THEY SET THEIR MINDS TO IT.

SO, MASTER BATES... DO YOU WISH TO RETURN TO YOUR EMPLOY AT THE PALACE?

YES, SIR. I LOVE IT THERE.

VERY WELL.

THIS OFFICER WILL ESCORT YOU THERE IMMEDIATELY.

GOOD DAY TO YOU.

I'LL SEE YOU AGAIN, I'M SURE.

NOW, SIR, AS FOR YOU...

SIR CONROY, I WOULD LIKE TO HANDLE THIS. YOU MAY LEAVE.

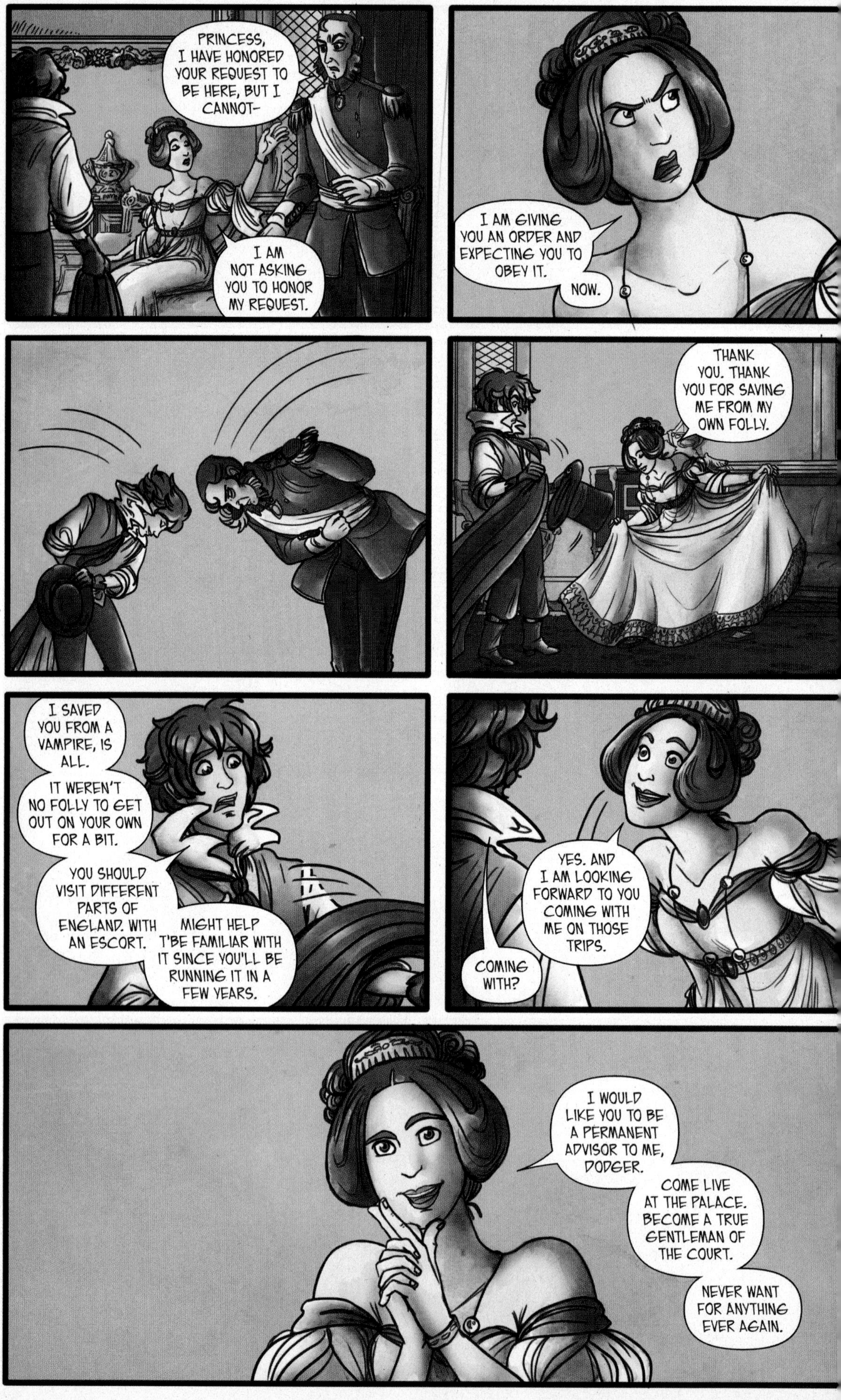
PRINCESS, I HAVE HONORED YOUR REQUEST TO BE HERE, BUT I CANNOT-
I AM NOT ASKING YOU TO HONOR MY REQUEST.
I AM GIVING YOU AN ORDER AND EXPECTING YOU TO OBEY IT.
NOW.
THANK YOU. THANK YOU FOR SAVING ME FROM MY OWN FOLLY.
I SAVED YOU FROM A VAMPIRE, IS ALL.
IT WEREN'T NO FOLLY TO GET OUT ON YOUR OWN FOR A BIT.
YOU SHOULD VISIT DIFFERENT PARTS OF ENGLAND. WITH AN ESCORT.
MIGHT HELP T'BE FAMILIAR WITH IT SINCE YOU'LL BE RUNNING IT IN A FEW YEARS.
YES. AND I AM LOOKING FORWARD TO YOU COMING WITH ME ON THOSE TRIPS.
COMING WITH?
I WOULD LIKE YOU TO BE A PERMANENT ADVISOR TO ME, DODGER.
COME LIVE AT THE PALACE. BECOME A TRUE GENTLEMAN OF THE COURT.
NEVER WANT FOR ANYTHING EVER AGAIN.

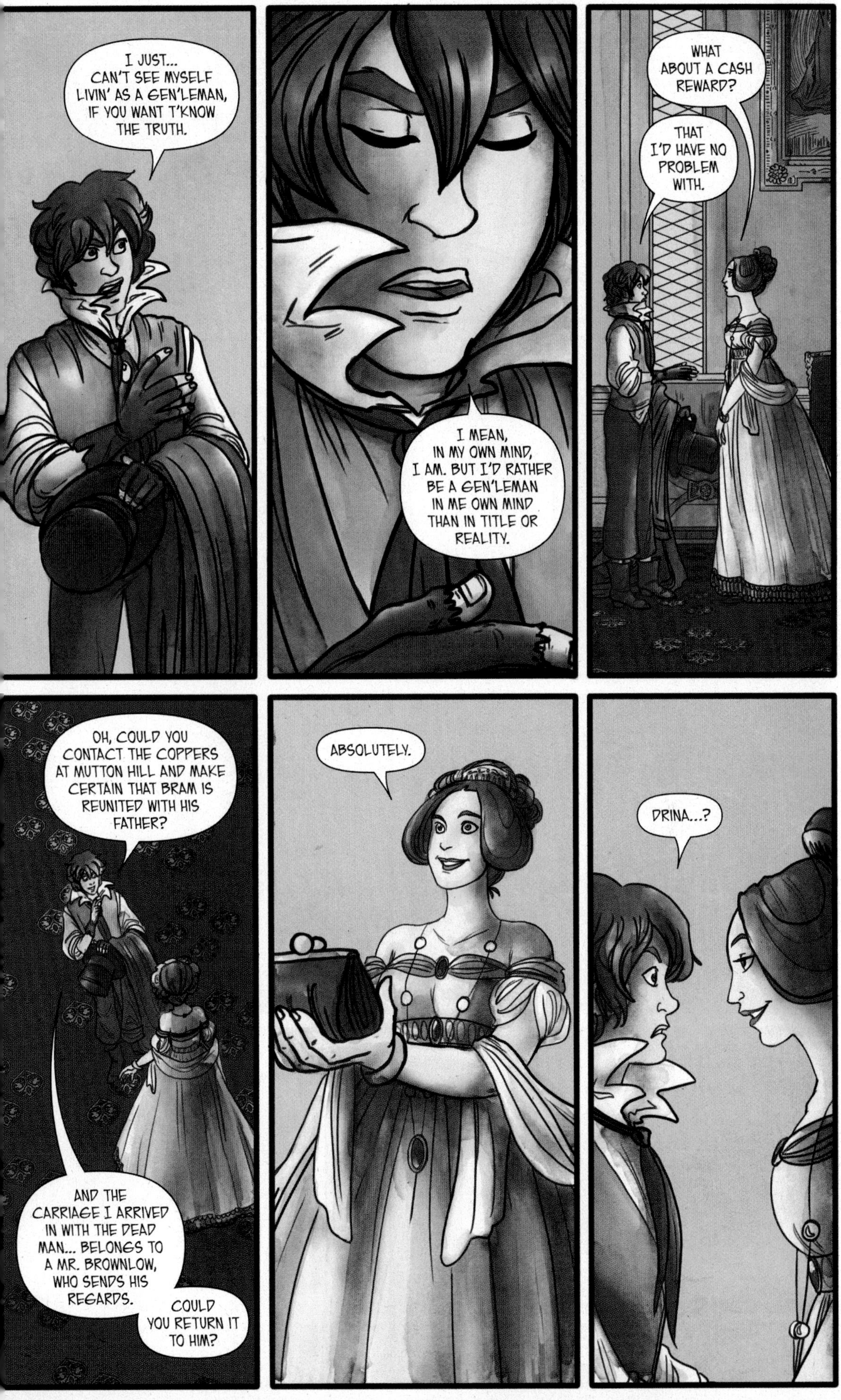
I JUST... CAN'T SEE MYSELF LIVIN' AS A GEN'LEMAN, IF YOU WANT T'KNOW THE TRUTH.
I MEAN, IN MY OWN MIND, I AM. BUT I'D RATHER BE A GEN'LEMAN IN ME OWN MIND THAN IN TITLE OR REALITY.
WHAT ABOUT A CASH REWARD?
THAT I'D HAVE NO PROBLEM WITH.
OH, COULD YOU CONTACT THE COPPERS AT MUTTON HILL AND MAKE CERTAIN THAT BRAM IS REUNITED WITH HIS FATHER?
AND THE CARRIAGE I ARRIVED IN WITH THE DEAD MAN... BELONGS TO A MR. BROWNLOW, WHO SENDS HIS REGARDS.
COULD YOU RETURN IT TO HIM?
ABSOLUTELY.
DRINA...?

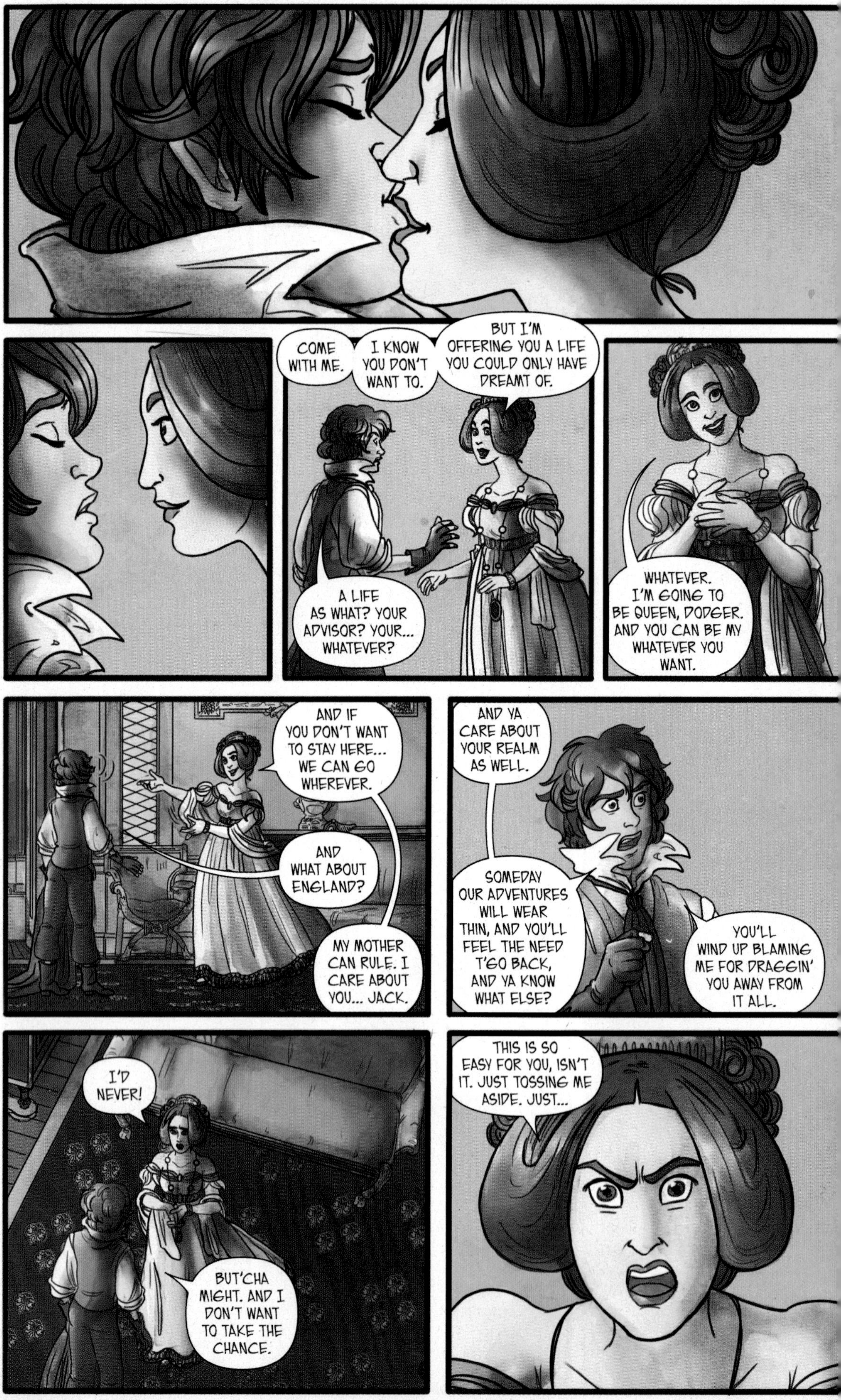
COME WITH ME.
I KNOW YOU DON'T WANT TO.
BUT I'M OFFERING YOU A LIFE YOU COULD ONLY HAVE DREAMT OF.
A LIFE AS WHAT? YOUR ADVISOR? YOUR... WHATEVER?
WHATEVER. I'M GOING TO BE QUEEN, DODGER. AND YOU CAN BE MY WHATEVER YOU WANT.
AND IF YOU DON'T WANT TO STAY HERE... WE CAN GO WHEREVER.
AND WHAT ABOUT ENGLAND?
MY MOTHER CAN RULE. I CARE ABOUT YOU... JACK.
AND YA CARE ABOUT YOUR REALM AS WELL.
SOMEDAY OUR ADVENTURES WILL WEAR THIN, AND YOU'LL FEEL THE NEED T'GO BACK, AND YA KNOW WHAT ELSE?
YOU'LL WIND UP BLAMING ME FOR DRAGGIN' YOU AWAY FROM IT ALL.
I'D NEVER!
BUT'CHA MIGHT. AND I DON'T WANT TO TAKE THE CHANCE.
THIS IS SO EASY FOR YOU, ISN'T IT. JUST TOSSING ME ASIDE. JUST...

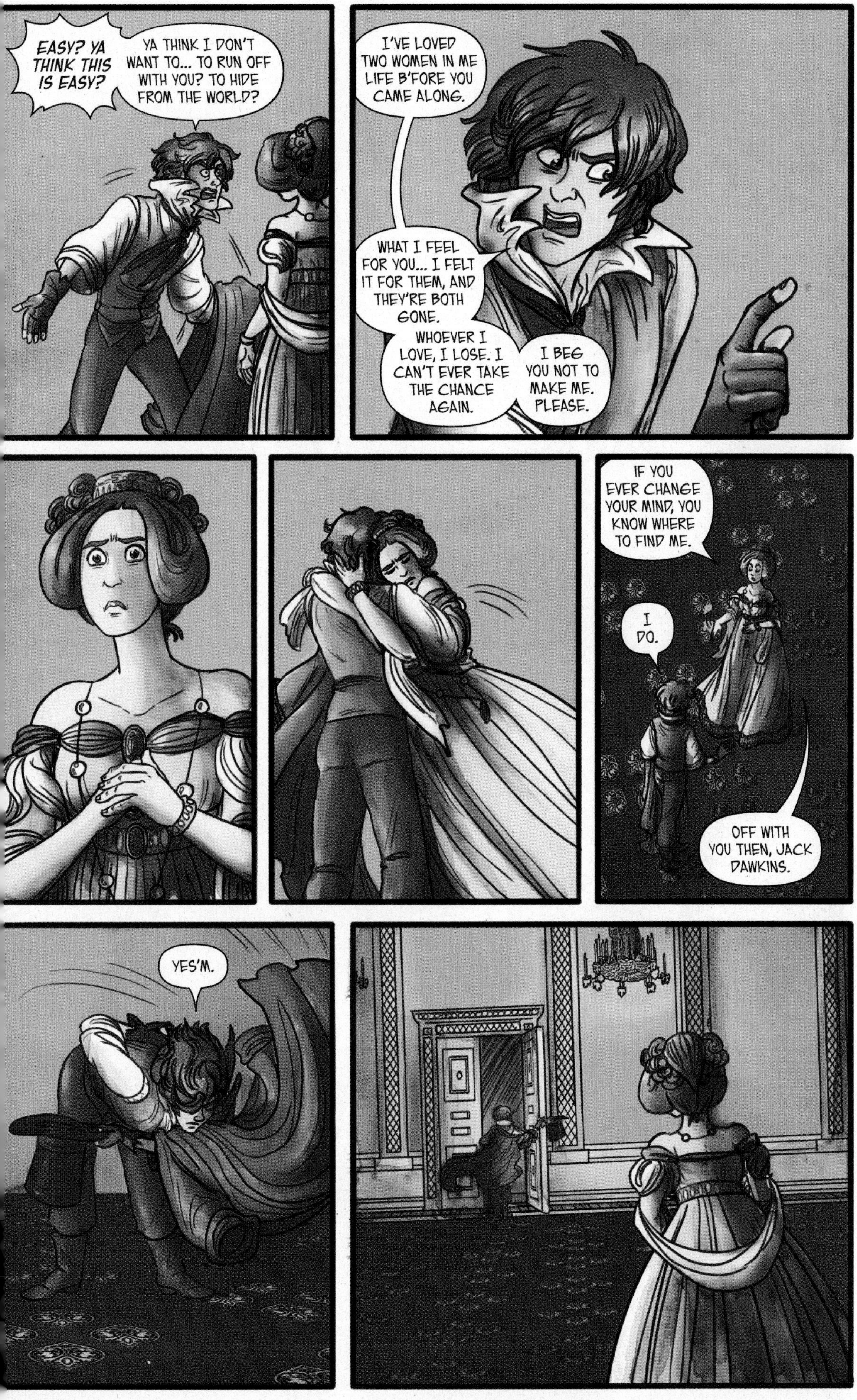
EASY? YA THINK THIS IS EASY?
YA THINK I DON'T WANT TO... TO RUN OFF WITH YOU? TO HIDE FROM THE WORLD?
I'VE LOVED TWO WOMEN IN ME LIFE B'FORE YOU CAME ALONG.
WHAT I FEEL FOR YOU... I FELT IT FOR THEM, AND THEY'RE BOTH GONE.
WHOEVER I LOVE, I LOSE. I CAN'T EVER TAKE THE CHANCE AGAIN.
I BEG YOU NOT TO MAKE ME. PLEASE.
IF YOU EVER CHANGE YOUR MIND, YOU KNOW WHERE TO FIND ME.
I DO.
OFF WITH YOU THEN, JACK DAWKINS.
YES'M.

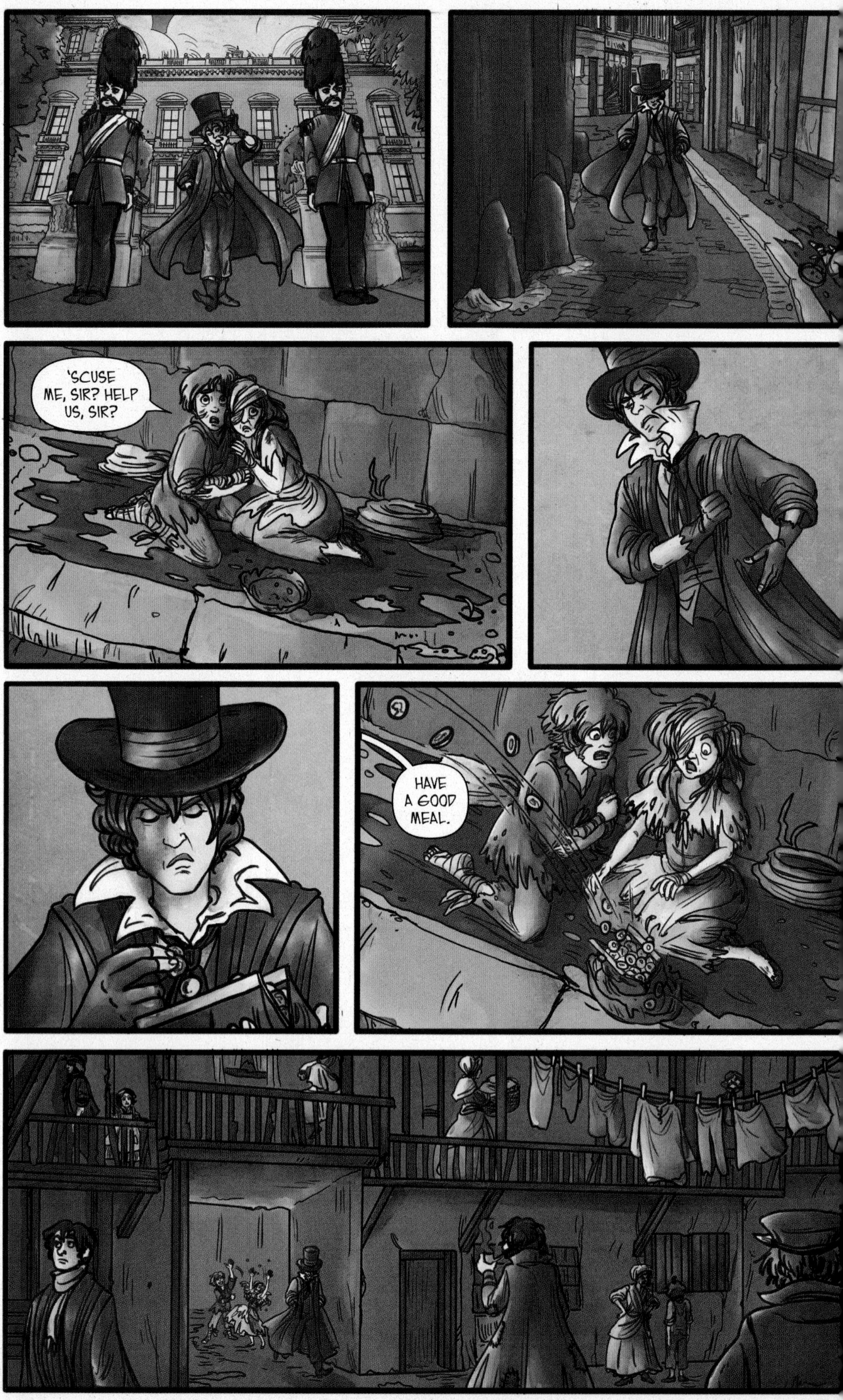
'SCUSE ME, SIR? HELP US, SIR?
HAVE A GOOD MEAL.

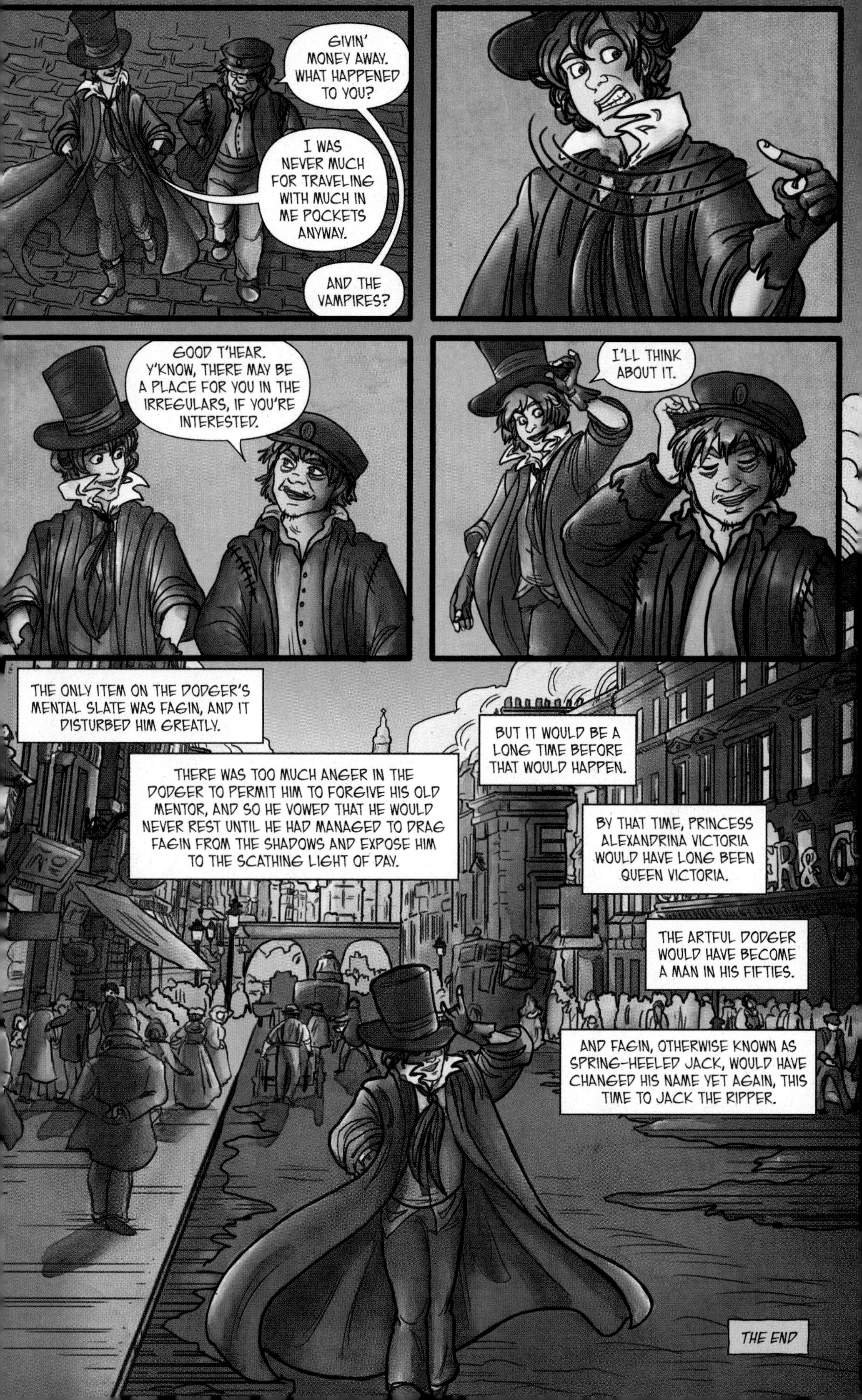
GIVIN' MONEY AWAY. WHAT HAPPENED TO YOU?
I WAS NEVER MUCH FOR TRAVELING WITH MUCH IN ME POCKETS ANYWAY.
AND THE VAMPIRES?
GOOD T'HEAR. Y'KNOW, THERE MAY BE A PLACE FOR YOU IN THE IRREGULARS, IF YOU'RE INTERESTED.
I'LL THINK ABOUT IT.
THE ONLY ITEM ON THE DODGER'S MENTAL SLATE WAS FAGIN, AND IT DISTURBED HIM GREATLY.
THERE WAS TOO MUCH ANGER IN THE DODGER TO PERMIT HIM TO FORGIVE HIS OLD MENTOR, AND SO HE VOWED THAT HE WOULD NEVER REST UNTIL HE HAD MANAGED TO DRAG FAGIN FROM THE SHADOWS AND EXPOSE HIM TO THE SCATHING LIGHT OF DAY.
BUT IT WOULD BE A LONG TIME BEFORE THAT WOULD HAPPEN.
BY THAT TIME, PRINCESS ALEXANDRINA VICTORIA WOULD HAVE LONG BEEN QUEEN VICTORIA.
THE ARTFUL DODGER WOULD HAVE BECOME A MAN IN HIS FIFTIES.
AND FAGIN, OTHERWISE KNOWN AS SPRING-HEELED JACK, WOULD HAVE CHANGED HIS NAME YET AGAIN, THIS TIME TO JACK THE RIPPER.
THE END

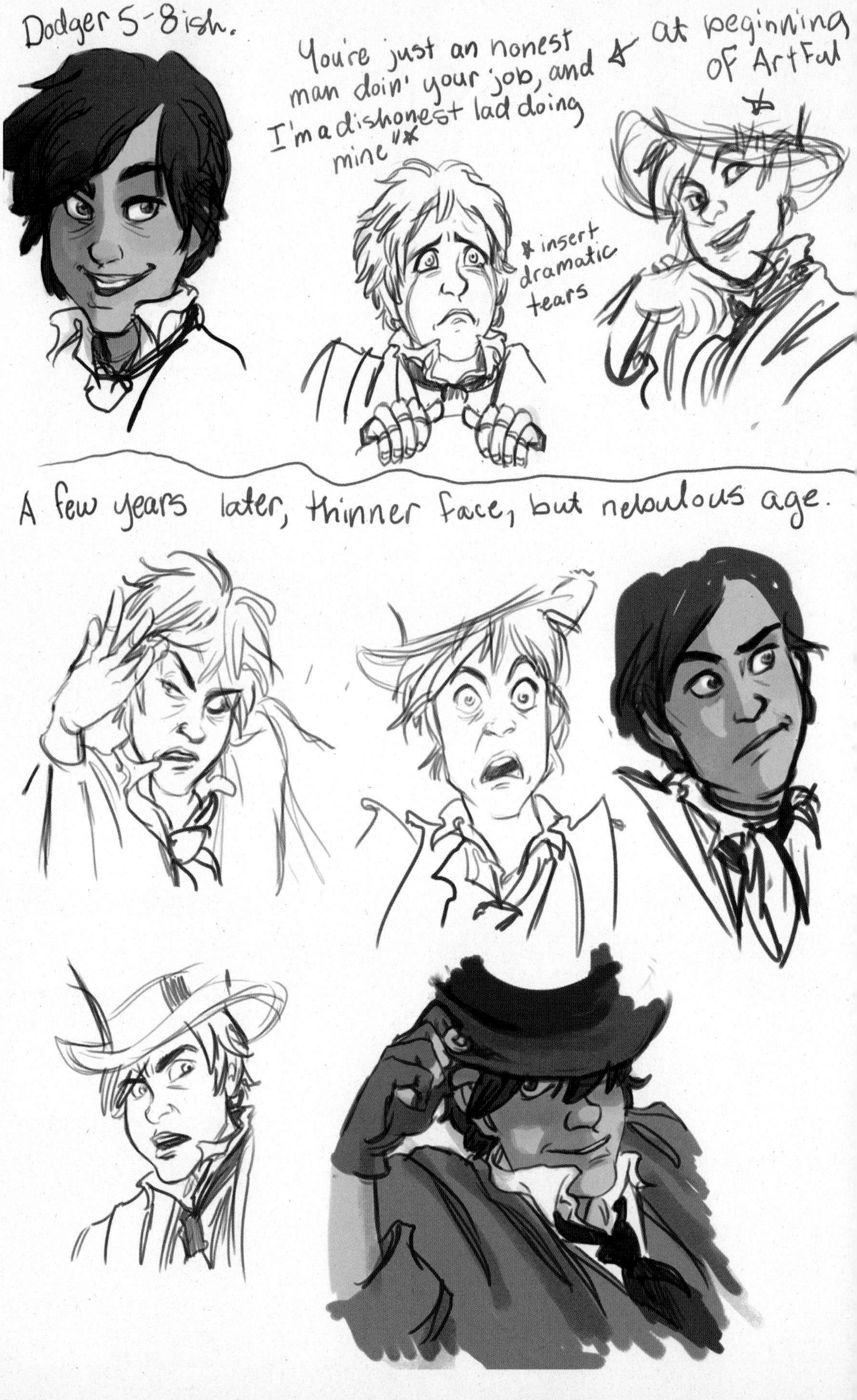
Dodger 5-8ish.
You're just an honest man doin' your job, and I'm a dishonest lad doing mine"*
☆ at beginning of ArtFul
*insert dramatic tears
A few years later, thinner face, but nebulous age.

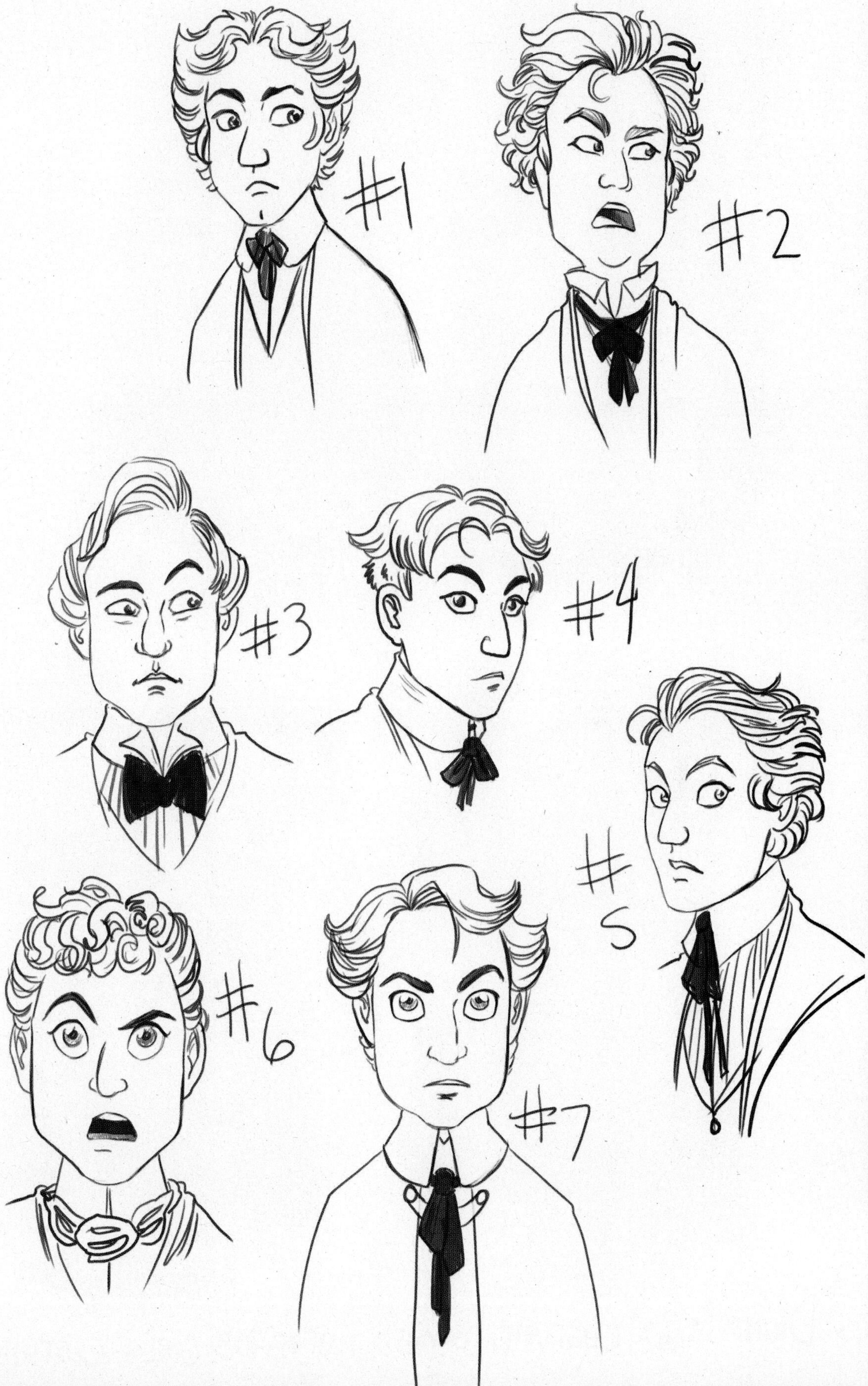
#1
#2
#3
#4
#5
#6
#7

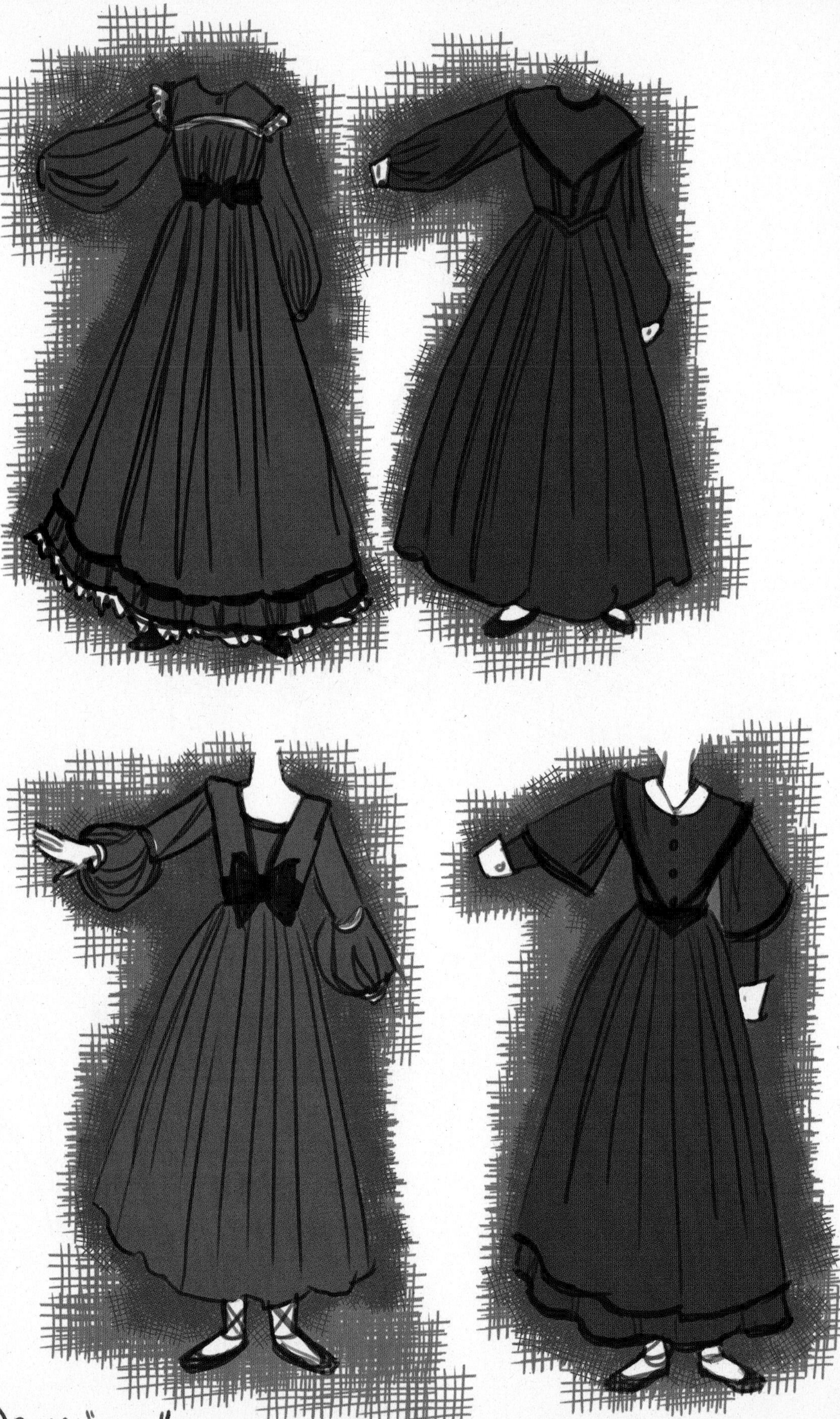

DRINA "MAID" COSTUME BASED ON 1840'S GIRLS CLOTHING

PENCILS & COLOR PROGRESSION

PENCILS OF ARTFUL #1, PAGE 1

COLORS OF ARTFUL #1, PAGE 1

PENCILS & COLOR PROGRESSION

PENCILS OF ARTFUL #6, PAGE 21

COLORS OF ARTFUL #6, PAGE 21